THE POST-FO

CRITICAL EDUCATION PRACTICE
VOLUME 20
GARLAND REFERENCE LIBRARY OF SOCIAL SCIENCE
VOLUME 912

CRITICAL EDUCATION PRACTICE

SHIRLEY R. STEINBERG AND JOE L. KINCHELOE, *SERIES EDITORS*

The Post-formal Reader
Cognition and Education

Edited by
Shirley R. Steinberg, Joe L. Kincheloe,
and Patricia H. Hinchey

Falmer Press
a member of the Taylor & Francis Group
New York and London
1999

Library of Congress Cataloging-in-Publication Data

The Post-formal Reader : cognition and education / edited by Shirley R.
Steinberg, Joe L. Kincheloe, and Patricia H. Hinchey.
        p.   cm. — (Garland reference library of social science ; v.
912. Critical education practice ; v. 20)
    Includes bibliographical references and index.
    ISBN 0-8153-1415-9 (hardcover : alk. paper). — ISBN 0-8153-3399-4
(paperback : alk. paper)
    1. Educational psychology. 2. Critical pedagogy. 3. Postmodernism
and education.   I. Steinberg, Shirley R., 1952– .   II. Kincheloe, Joe L.
III. Hinchey, Patricia H., 1951– .   IV. Series: Garland reference library of
social science ; v. 912.   V. Series: Garland reference library of social
science. Critical education practice ; vol. 20.
LB1051.P5677   1999   98–52828
370.15—dc21   CIP

Printed on acid-free, 250-year-life paper
Manufactured in the United States of America

Table of Contents

PART THREE—INFORMED PRACTICE

Introduction

I suppose one has a greater sense of intellectual degradation after an
interview with a doctor than from any human experience.
Alice James (1848-1892)

I don't really trust a sane person.
Pro football lineman Lyle Alzado

This text takes as its topic psychology in general, and educational psychology more specifically. Pretty weighty topics and ones whose
assumptions about what's *normal* permeate everyday discussions even
if they often go unnoticed. For example, the Unibomber, and before him
those anti-government folks holed up at Waco, and after him those folks
who declared themselves to be the Republic of Texas and unaffiliated
with the United States—they're obviously crazy, newspaper readers and
TV viewers readily agreed. Taxpayers and other casual conversational-
ists nod in agreement that SAT scores are still disappointing—and those
teachers better get back to teaching basics and doing things the way
they're supposed to, the way it was for all those decades before the
insane sixties, so that our kids learn more things that are *worth* learning.
And depression has come a long way, according to today's official version—it's an unsurprising, physiological condition, amenable to Prozac,
Paxil, and other modern wonder drugs. Everywhere, everyone seems
comfortable making pronouncements about the *normalness*, the *sanity*,
of what everyone else is doing.

This comfort level of others-at-large makes me personally decidedly *un*comfortable when I think about what a psychological researcher
might say if she—or more likely, he—looked closely at the individuals
who people the landscape of my personal life. My friend Pat, for example, nearly got herself fired for stubbornly refusing to comply with her
union contract by appearing in her classroom some eight minutes before

students arrived. She would be there four or five minutes before, yes, and sometimes even thirty (depending on circumstances), but because she always arrived comfortably before the students, she would *not* routinely comply with the eight-minute rule—until she accepted the reality that yes, the school *would* fire a teacher they openly described as one of their best and most cherished if she persisted in irrationally disobeying its rule. But then, that's Pat . . . who also fainted dead away at the first sight of the questions on the certification exam for her doctorate.

Then there's Dan, who earned his masters from an Ivy League school of education and took, as his first teaching job, a position in rural Hawaii. Within months, the environment took its toll and I got a letter in which he openly wondered—to me, one of his former professors, no less—whether someone should rethink the wisdom of a campaign to eradicate centuries-old oral traditions and replace them with print. And whether surfing might indeed qualify as a legitimate art form . . . and even whether every human being with a passing acquaintance with the English language *ought* to study Keats. Absurd thoughts, any number of people would readily tell him.

Meanwhile, Iz abandoned her effort to register for a graduate course she really wanted to take, because (though she has a doctorate she *showed* to officials) the school insisted she pay to have her undergraduate transcripts submitted. And Lynn abandoned her plan to do a masters at my university because it insisted that she take a standardized test before formally applying—even though she has racked up any number of A's in several graduate courses she has taken, including some *at* the university.

Then, there are the assorted lots of classroom teachers I associate with in classes, book clubs, and other social activities. Most of them are terribly insecure, believing they need expert approval for every classroom plan they design. And/or, they live in a state of constant fear of not getting or of losing their administrators' or their colleagues' approval. They suspect they're not *really* terribly bright people, and they generally keep their ideas to themselves so that their ineptness isn't discovered. Some are even so out of touch with reality, an expert might note, that instead of being *grateful* that a doctor takes a room at a local motel periodically for the express purpose of examining children and dispensing prescriptions for Ritalin to alleviate their sure-to-be-diagnosed ADD symptoms, my friends are actually *worried* by the convenience of this arrangement.

In schools, such folk are often most kindly labeled "troublemakers." Psychologists tend to be less kind: maladjusted, neurotic, self-destructive—there is probably no end to the labels that can be assigned, each indicating the specific area (or, more likely, areas) in which each person is deficit. I shudder to think of what they'd say about someone like me, who apparently has some sort of weird need to surround herself with obviously broken and dysfunctional people.

This is not, however, how I see things. I find these people terribly interesting and thoughtful human beings, and I vote with Emily Dickinson on the issue of their sanity: "Much madness is divinest sense," said Em. In her wisdom, she also noted that such people are "straightway labeled dangerous" and "handled with a chain." Dangerous? You bet. What would happen if one troublemaking teacher led others to think *they* could pick and choose rules to obey? Chains? Again: you bet. "We'll fire you if you don't comply with our senseless regulation, even if you are an incredibly gifted teacher and doing important work for us," threatens the school superintendent. "We won't let you in if you don't provide the meaningless numbers we demand," threatens the university official. "Do you want a *second* year's contract?" the department chair blusters to the new teacher. "How would you like to be in a new building, teaching a new subject or grade?" the principal snarls at a tenured teacher.

This text looks again at the territory that psychology has demarcated *"normal, productive, desirable"* and *"abnormal, nonproductive, undesirable"* and at what kind of people have been assigned to which area, based on what criteria. *The Post-formal Reader: Cognition and Education* explores such questions as why the mapping was ever entrusted to psychologists, what they did with their power, who ended up in chains as a result, what the nature of those chains are for a wide range of populations, what damage has resulted, and, most importantly, how things might be otherwise. Joe L. Kincheloe and Shirley R. Steinberg have done invaluable pioneering by formulating preliminary answers to these crucial questions in the opening chapters, and the many other authors in this text explore nooks and crannies all over the educational landscape, advancing their own thoughts on relevant topics.

The educator who has ever doubted his or her own sanity, the educator who has ever been pained by the damage schooling imposes on individual human beings, adults as well as students, will find the following pages interesting, provocative—and also reassuring. With a certain irony, I follow earlier references to Emily Dickinson's perspective on what constitutes madness with a quote from C. G. Jung:

> Show me a sane man and I will cure him for you.

For readers who have been behaving *sanely* while harboring *insane* private doubts, I trust the following articles will at least initiate a similar healing process.

Patricia H. Hinchey
Penn State University

The Post-formal Reader

PART ONE
INTRODUCTION

Trouble Ahead, Trouble Behind: Grounding the Post-formal Critique of Educational Psychology

Joe L. Kincheloe

There is something deeply amiss in human lives, in the human psyche, at the end of the second millennium. People who live in the (post) modern world too often live socially isolated, despiritualized lives, made anxious by overwhelming commitments. Phenomenal numbers of people find themselves aimless and without purpose, feeling that the life they lead is not what their body, mind, and spirit were designed to negotiate. Such a diagnosis is not all that difficult to make when one suffers or watches others suffer from debilitating depression and perpetual anxiety—the fashionable diseases of (post) modernity. When anthropologists study so-called "primitive" tribes people of Samoa, New Guinea, or the rain forests of South America, they often don't find mental or physical evidence of depression or anxiety. In contrast to such peoples, the inhabitants of contemporary Western societies have in their electronic isolation lost trust in one another, found social relations empty, and been stripped of the affiliative aspects of our cultural heritage— love, generosity, empathy, remorse, affection, etc. . . . Contemporary Western human beings live in (as the Unibomber argues) "conditions radically different from those under which (we) evolved" (Wright, 1995, p. 50). Evolutionary psychologists label the Unibomber's thesis "mismatch theory"—a social psychological approach that analyzes the maladies emanating from the differences between the contemporary environment and the ancestral environment—the one, proponents argue, for which human beings were designed.

No one has to search for psychological pathologies in Western societies. The numbers of individuals suffering from depression have been doubling every decade. Among young people in North America suicide is the third most common cause of death—automobile accidents and murder are numbers one and two. Three out of twenty Americans have been diagnosed with clinical anxiety disorder and homicidal alienation continues to grow. Proponents of mismatch theory maintain that humans in the Stone Age were psychologically healthier than people today and certainly more creative. Since life was not routinized, men and women could move freely, establish relationships without hierarchy, and play without rigid organizational inhibitions. In such conditions creativity could be expressed in ordinary, everyday experiences. My point here is not to romanticize or advocate a return to Stone Age lifestyles. Creativity had its costs, as tribespeople were confronted with occasional starvation, plagues, and the chance of becoming a snack for a beast of prey. While most of us don't want to live in such a cosmos, we can learn from it. Compared to the twentieth century, for example, the Stone Age world was relatively peaceful, illustrating, contrary to conventional wisdom, that the primordial dynamics of the human psyche are not predisposed to aggression and conflict (Bohm and Edwards, 1991; Wright, 1995; Alford, 1993).

Even conservative analysts have come to understand the negative psychological impact of market-driven capitalism with its commodification of desire and its destruction of community. The quest for economic opportunity drew farm children from their extended families to the isolation of the city and has been shattering communal ties ever since. Business relationships have undermined friendships for decades, and industrial/post-industrial workers have had to repress significant portions of their psychic energy in order to perform boring and miserable jobs, submit to authority, and live with low-status, subordinate positions. Even among the affluent, who are released from the emotional indignities of the lower socio-economic classes, an emotional/spiritual emptiness often undermines emotional health—a vacuum that consumption of sex, drugs, or rock n' roll can't fill. It has become a cliché by now to assert that psychological progress has not matched technological progress. How do we deal with the meaninglessness and socio-psychological pathology that to some degree affect all of us individually and institutionally? I believe that critical theory, feminist theory, critical multiculturalism, cultural studies, ecological theory, postmodernist epistemologies, indigenous knowledges, situated cognition, and poststructuralist psychoanalysis all can provide insight into this question. Using ideas taken from this variety of discourses, my purpose here involves the tentative formulation of a democratic educational psychology that is ethically and culturally grounded and that supports a critical pedagogy. Such a psychology I will refer to as post-formal thinking in its cognitive manifestation and as post-formal educational psychology in a more holistic sciences-of-the-psyche expression. Such an holistic discipline would include the domains typically addressed by cognitive studies, psychoanalysis, and social psychology.

Socio-Psychological Schizophrenia

Our post-formal educational psychology addresses this psychic crisis of the late twentieth century and its relationship to the pedagogical/educational domain. I use the term pedagogy to broaden the definition of education in order to include education at the cultural level as well as the formal school level. Pedagogical issues as defined here include the production/transmission of knowledge, the construction of consciousness/subjectivity, and the inculcation of values. A key aspect of the contemporary psychic crisis involves a division of human intellect and emotion—a bifurcation that results in a socio-psychological schizophrenia. Such a metaphorical schizophrenia manifests itself in our personal relationships, international affairs, human relationships with nature, and our ability to create meaning. It is exacerbated by a postmodern condition (a hyperreality) characterized by a proliferation of images and information that bombard us from every angle. In this hypercontext meaning and emotional affect are rent asunder, as signifier and signified are separated as in a Diesel jeans advertisement or a Benneton billboard. No matter what, we must consume; no matter how boring our jobs may be, we must make more money to get the products available to us (McLaren et al., 1995; Bohm and Edwards, 1991).

In the human brain the emotions and the intellect are in a constant relationship with one another in a way not fully understood. While we must be careful of grandiose pronouncements, it is safe to say that together they harmonize with and synergize one another. Both modernist and postmodernist social impulses, however, have disturbed this bi-modal coherence. The effects of this disturbance are profound and multidimensional. In the modernist context a logocentrism (reason-centeredness) began to develop with the scientific revolution (the Age of Reason) in the seventeenth and eighteenth centuries that considered intuition and emotion incompatible with male-centered logic. This logocentric masculinization of thinking negated the potential insight derived from the body, feeling, and subjective personal experience. Western logocentrism has viewed higher-order thinking as a facility with abstract principles, thus denigrating emotional investments and the wisdom gained through feeling (Carlson, 1991). Thus, Western education over the last three centuries has tended to upset the balance between emotion and intellect. As the postmodern condition has developed in late modernist era with its technology-driven bombardment of images and information, a very different cognitive impulse has emerged. As noted previously, this hyperreal condition has torn apart meaning and affect. As advertisers and politicians have by-passed reason on their way to the seduction of human desire, they have undermined the role of reason in the public conversation. Such socio-psychological dynamics have created a dualistic phenomenon that manifests itself in a Western schooling that devalues feeling and emotion and a Western public culture that subverts rationality. Neither sphere provides a space where the relationship between logic and emotion can be studied and cultivated in a psychologically, cognitively, and socially productive manner.

What can schools do to effect this synthesis? To begin with educational psychologists can approach emotion as a mode of perception, a sense similar to sight, touch, or hearing. In this context emotion is viewed actively, like the other senses, as a human function, something people do. Indeed, the manner in which we deal with situations is not approached in isolation from feelings but is constituted by them. Emotion plays an extraordinary role in life situations, providing the self with instantaneous feedback on what is happening in relation to what we anticipated. Having provided such data, emotion then prepares us to take appropriate action. In a research context, for example, such information is invaluable in making sense of a cultural/educational phenom- *emotion* enon. But according to the dictates of Western modernist positivism such data are disallowed—they constitute a corruption of objective research methodology. From a critical perspective emotion is one of many ways we know the world; thus, it is not the antithesis of reason. The relationship is one of partnerships, not antagonism. Emotion can connect us to the world in ways that reason cannot—and vice versa. The Western modernist positivist connection of emotion with irrationality reflects a masculine fear of connection more than a well-considered theory of cognition. No doubt unfiltered feeling may deform sensibility and subvert analysis, but the dismissal of emotion promises the same effect (Ferguson, 1984).

Individuals who have lost touch with their emotions have no cognitive radar to warn them of the importance of an encounter, a recollection, or a precipice; a person out of touch with his or her emotions has few clues to figuring out how to deal with the world. The point is commonsensical: everyone understands that when a person is emotionally upset, he or she doesn't think clearly, that when logic and emotion are separated, anxiety results. Emotions are the disc drive to thinking, that is, they create the need to think. Without an integration of reason and emotion, creativity is impossible. With such notions in mind it becomes essential that a new educational psychology provide for the education of emotions and the integration between feeling and reason. Without a recognition of modernist schooling/science's and hyperreality's bifurcation of human understanding, the cognitive disability, the emotional pathology, and social alienation of the late twentieth century will only intensify—socio-psychological schizophrenia will become a way of life (Beck, 1992; Bohm and Edwards, 1991).

Socio-Psychological Schizophrenia at School and Work: The Wounded Spirit, the Cognitive Illness

In a culture beset by the bifurcation of intellect and emotion, young people no longer look to school or to work as venues in which the creative spirit can be developed. Instead, they endure school, and they find slots in the workplace where they can insert their labor. Once in place in the economic machine, they confront boredom, the requirements of technological devices, and faceless supervisors (Borgmann, 1992). The concept of rewarding work becomes a source of ironic humor, nothing more. Jobs are not big enough for the human spirit, so workers emotionally withdraw from their labor. Students learn this behavior early in their school lives, moving through the day without affect, staring straight ahead at nothing in particular (Terkel, 1972). They see no larger purpose to school. No one has provided a convincing account of the meaning of education—they discern no direction in their everyday activities. They quickly learn that school has nothing to do with their passions—indeed, their emotional health is irrelevant.

A crisis of motivation accompanies the loss of meaning in the postmodern condition. Both work and schools are characterized by evidence of a malaise—low quality work, absenteeism, sullen hostility, waste, alcohol and drug abuse. Americans don't like to talk about malaise. Jimmy Carter became an object of ridicule for broaching the subject. Ronald Reagan built a political career by denying its existence. There is no concerted effort to address this postmodern crisis of motivation in the public conversation; it doesn't even have a name. It doesn't take much, however, to evoke an understanding that the problem exists. When I discuss the situation with my students, they quickly grasp the concept and within minutes are providing examples of the crisis in their personal lives, their lives as students and workers. They can all empathize with my description of the classroom of students with their heads on their desks as the teacher drones on. We want to be good workers and good students, they tell me, but they are so unmotivated by the nature of their jobs and their classes (Kellner, 1989; Wirth, 1983; Zunker, 1986).

Often, those who decry this crisis of motivation are the very same individuals who exacerbate it with "just-say-no" types of solutions. These types of solutions, this type of thinking emerges from the rationalistic tendencies of modernist science to fragment the world in the attempt to understand it. Such decontextualization separates the study of schools from society. Finding their roots in this modernist fragmentation, recent educational reform movements have produced a "factoid syndrome" where students learn isolated bits and pieces of information for tests. The relationship between the facts or their applications to the problems of the world is irrelevant. As such, meaning is undermined, and purpose is lost. The effect on motivation is devastating. I call this condition the cognitive illness. The complex condition of postmodernity magnifies the effects of the cognitive illness. Indeed, in hyperreality this pathology of thinking threatens the very survival of the human species.

The tendency of modernist positivism to reduce psychological, social, and educational issues to technical questions is an important aspect of the cognitive illness. This dynamic is referred to by critical theorists as instrumental rationality. Critical researchers in the new postmodern paradigm argue that the larger socio-cultural purpose of pedagogical activity must be central to any curriculum development or instructional strategy. When modernist positivists break learning into discrete pieces of data to be viewed in isolation, the cognitive illness is perpetuated. In the context of instrumental rationality the cognitive illness of modernism assumes the whole is never greater than the sum of the parts. Houses from this perspective are no more than the nails and lumber that go into them, and education is no more than the average number of objectives mastered. We are all familiar with classrooms consumed with the cognitive disease. Students copy information from chalkboards and overhead projectors and skim textbooks to find information fragments that would answer both the questions in the study guides and the multiple-choice tests. Children listen (when they're not talking); they respond when called upon; they read fragments of the textbook; they write short responses to questions provided on work-sheets. They rarely plan or initiate anything of length or conceptualize their own projects. They rarely even write essays. They are learning to be deskilled, to be passive, to be citizens who are governed, not citizens who govern. They are being taught not to seek deep structures which move events but to examine only the surface level of appearance. They will not understand the concept of consciousness construction or the subtlety of the process of hegemony. Ideology will remain a foreign abstraction in their eyes. Those students who will transcend such blind-nesses will make their emancipatory journey in spite of their classroom experiences, finding analytic inspiration outside the school context.

Shaped by the cognitive illness, education in the postmodern world becomes a pawn of powerful groups who attempt to use it as a means of solving social and economic problems in a way that serves their own interests. Pushed and pulled by such groups, schools are not moved by educational and political visions that value the human spirit but by self-serving and often cynical impulses that seek to control that very spirit. Thus, schools are caught in a meaning-destroying quicksand, trapped in the crisis of motivation. Stripped of a meaningful justification for the pursuit of learning, teachers and students wander aimlessly within a maze of fragmented information. Classrooms become spiritless places where rule-following teachers face a group of wounded students who have no conception of the value of the lessons being taught.

We don't have to be educational experts to realize that socio-psy-chological schizophrenia and the cognitive illness and the crisis of moti-vation that accompanies them can be cured only by redefining human purpose and suturing the rift between reason and emotion. The purpose of education in a democratic society is more than raising test scores and fitting students to corporate needs. As we envision them, schools in a democratic society should exist to help students locate themselves in history, obtain the ability to direct their own lives, understand the ways power influences the production of knowledge, appreciate the nature of good work, become smart workers, and connect with a cognitive revo-lution that leads to a deeper understanding of themselves and the world. In these ways, meaning is salvaged and spirit is protected—thus, motiva-tion emerges naturally as teachers and students share a sense of purpose.

The crisis of motivation is not difficult to understand. Students of the contemporary era just like students in other eras, are bored with school but fascinated with certain aspects of the world about them—

fashion, friends, cars, TV, rap music, skateboarding, etc. . . . As these students become increasingly uninvolved in classes that make little sense to them, discourage them, or even insult them, the schools begin to implement sophisticated psychological modification procedures. Such procedures establish rigid school objectives, then monitor and test the disenfranchised student's mastery of prearranged objectives. The deficiencies of the alienated student become the focus of her or his school life, thus further accelerating a vicious cycle of student hostility to education. Obsessed with details, with bits and pieces of knowledge, schools in the contemporary era miss what should be the first step of schooling—the search for personal meaning and its connection to one's passion for life and learning.

In this grim, depersonalized system of schools, teachers suffer from the loss of meaning and crisis of motivation just as much as students. More and more, the conservative reforms of the last fifteen years have turned teachers into semi-skilled functionaries. Activities such as setting purpose and conducting research are not the domain of teachers in the contemporary workplace. Experts will take care of such concerns; teachers should stick to the execution of their prescribed tasks (Altrichter and Posch, 1989). Indeed, teachers are supervised and evaluated not on the basis of notions of competence and creativity but on their adherence to format, that is, their compliance. Teachers become executors of managerial plans (Garman and Hazi, 1988). In light of such realities it is not surprising that teachers lose a sense of meaning. In their personal crisis of motivation, some of the best and brightest teachers leave the field after only a few years.

Rethinking Thinking: Developing a New Type of Intelligence

As a society we have had little public conversation about human thinking about the nature of intelligence. Only in such a society could Herrnstein and Murray's (1994) decontextualized treatise on white intellectual supremacy be taken seriously. In a world created by abstractions of thought we need a new form of intelligence, a way of thinking that can deal with hyperreality's explosion of visual images and printed data. School, of course, is little help with its decontextualized memory exercises that kill the adventurous spirit of young people. Too often the cognitive purpose of school involves the narrow attempt to raise I.Q. scores—an effort that takes place without an analysis of what exactly it is that I.Q. measures. Drawing on the research of students of situated cognition, an educational psychology that transcends the cognitive illness promotes a pedagogy that promotes thinking skills we would want democratic citizens and self-directed learners to possess. Thus, if we want to produce a new form of intelligence, incite a cognitive revolution, then we must rethink educational psychology and reshape schools accordingly. Such a reconceptualization will involve an exploration of the ways society-at-large undermines creativity. In this context the effects of bureaucratization and standardization must be examined, and the rules of scientific exploration must be reconceived. We must focus our energies on the attempt to increase the number of creative people.

Any development of a new view of intelligence needs to illustrate its connection or lack of such to what has previously been accepted in the field. Thus, a post-formal theory of educational psychology delineates its relationship to, in this particular case, Piagetian notions of thinking that have dominated cognitive psychology and thus educational psychology over the past few decades. Moving in this post-formal direction with one eye looking straight ahead and one eye on the etymology of present understandings, post-formal analysts collect new manifestations of intelligence, new ways of seeing. Also, they critique established definitions, using cognitive innovations to uncover flaws in accepted wisdom. In this context, for example, post-formal analysts expose the class-biased ramifications of mainstream psychology, pointing out the use of the terms, intelligence and genius, in academic/professional contexts but not in working-class venues. Such analysts point out the limitations of mathematical models and statistical formulas in the description of human consciousness and intelligence. In predicting and controlling the path of missiles or mapping the path of planets, such models are useful. Indeed, they are valuable when dealing with entities that change regularly and slowly. When dealing with the mind and intelligence, however, change is anything but regular and slow. Better described as nuanced, ambiguous, and transient, cognitive questions do not lend themselves to mathematical/psychometric analysis. As a result, modernist positivist methods often distort our picture of cognitive processes (Gardner, 1995; Ferguson, 1980; Bohm and Edwards, 1991; Beardsley, 1995).

The nature of the higher-order intelligence that we're looking for is subtle in its manifestation. The subtle nature of this form of intelligence involves its ability to move beyond mere memory or recall. The Latin root of the word intelligence is intelligere, which means "to gather and choose apart." The point of intelligence, therefore, is not to just to gather thoughts from memory but to find patterns in those ideas one has collected—i.e., to gather and choose apart. The process of pattern detection is not simple, however, as it involves the detection of multiple patterns depending on the context in which particular concepts are viewed. Thus, the pattern that memory imposed on thoughts must be transcended, as the thinker gains the imaginative ability to see events in ways not necessarily his or her own. Focusing on this multiple pattern recognition process, a post-formal pedagogy works to develop such abilities in students, to generate higher forms of cognition among diverse students in multiple contexts. Drawing upon the work of Lev Vygosky, such a cognitive perspective assumes no end point in relation to which the developmental process is aimed. This generative model is not very interested in comparing developmental levels of students against one another. It is more concerned with generating increased understandings and cognitive abilities in all students regardless of some "empirically objective" determination of potential. A generative model of cognition induces us to focus our attention on the development of what an individual already knows rather than designing instruments to discern what he or she doesn't know. Regardless of class or ethnic background, a generative notion of intelligence respects the abilities individuals bring to a learning situation (Andersen, 1994).

Anticipatory Accommodation: Applied Hermeneutics

In particular a critical generative cognition makes new meanings, uncovers new patterns of interrelationship, seeks new "takes" on the world. In this sense a higher-order thinking that unites intellect and emotion is hermeneutical. In this hermeneutical or interpretive sense post-formal thinking takes Piaget's notions of assimilation and accommodation and revivifies them in a critical new paradigmatic direction. To Piaget, intellectual adaptation was an equilibration between assimilation and accommodation. Assimilation involves the shaping of an event to fit into one's cognitive structure. No event, even if a student has never encountered it before, constitutes a new beginning. In other words, as assimilation fits an experience to the demands of one's logical structures, it is grafted on to previously developed schemes. Accommodation, on the other hand, refers to the restructuring of one's cognitive maps to take care of an event. In order to accommodate, an individual must actively change his or her existing intellectual structure to understand the dissonance produced by the novel demand. Piaget described accommodation as a reflective, integrative behavior that forces the realization that our present cognitive structure is insufficient to deal with the changing pressures of the environment (Kaufman, 1978; Fosnot, 1988).

Piaget argued that at the beginning assimilation and accommodation tend to move in different directions: assimilation as the conservative protector of existing cognitive structure, subordinating the environment to the existing organism; accommodation as the subversive agent of change leading the organism to adjust to the imperatives of the environment. In the long run, however, Piaget contends that the ostensibly divergent tasks are inseparable in the larger process of equilibration—the dynamic process of self-monitored behavior that balances assimilation and accommodation's polar behaviors. Over the last twenty years, however, critics have asserted that as Piaget described higher orders of thought, he privileged assimilation over accommodation. The effect of this assimilation-centeredness has been the progressive removal of the individual from her or his environment. The emphasis, thus, becomes not so much what an individual can do in the world of objects, what actions she or he can undertake, but how quickly the individual can learn to think outside of reality. The more an individual engages in disembedded thought, the higher level of cognition Piaget will ascribe to him or her. In a Cartesian-Newtonian framework, the higher-order thinker is detached from personal experience. The Piagetian image of the active learner in charge of his or her own fate is subverted by the lack of exchange between the thinker and the world of objects. Because of this removal of women and men from experience, Piaget's theory abstracts individuals from the cosmos in the process reducing the possibility of emancipatory personal and social change.

To Piaget, knowing involves the transformation of contradictory experience into stable structures. When subjected to the new paradigm's challenge to the stability of meaning, Piaget's confidence in the viability of structures is undermined. Meaning is far too ephemeral for a critical student of cognition to claim the existence of a stable structure, a balance between assimilation and accommodation—in Piaget's words, equilibration. The concept of negation, central to critical theory and to accommodation, involves the continuous criticism and reconstruction of what one thinks she knows. For example, critical theorist Max Horkheimer argued that through negation we develop a critical consciousness that allows us to transcend old codified world views and incorporate our new understandings into a new reflective attitude. Let us delve deeper into these connections between critical theory and Piagetian cognition.

Critical equilibration denies the possibility of any stable balance between assimilation and accommodation. Aware of the tendency of Piagetian formalism to de-emphasize accommodation, critical equilibration recognizes the radical potential of accommodation. As accommodation changes consciousness in order to understand new aspects of the environment, subjects gain awareness of their own limitations. Horkheimer maintained that through the awareness gained by way of critical negation—the philosophical analog to the cognitive act of accommodation—an individual develops and becomes open to radical change (Held, 1980). Thus, a key cognitive dimension of any critical pedagogy will involve accommodation—critical accommodation. Critical teachers in the new paradigm understand the value of difference with its power to initiate the process of critical accommodation. Such teachers see cultural difference within a classroom as an opportunity for cognitive growth.

A critical teacher, for example, exploring the meaning of intelligence and its relationship to his or her students would assimilate an understanding of the concept based on his or her own experience. The teacher would accommodate the concept as he or she began to examine students who were labeled unintelligent but upon a second look exhibited characteristics that in an unconventional way seemed sophisticated. The teacher would then integrate this recognition of exception (accommodation) into a broader definition of intelligence. The old definition of intelligence would have been negated; through exposure to diverse expressions of intelligence, new ways of seeing it would have been accommodated. They would be critically accommodated in the sense that the new ways of seeing would emancipate us from the privileged, racially and class-biased definitions of intelligence that were used to exclude cognitive styles that transcended the official codes. In this and many other cases accommodation becomes the emancipatory aspect of the thinking process in question. Critical teachers recognize this and use it in the struggle for democratic social and educational change, the effort to keep students who fall outside the boundaries of middle-class whiteness from getting hurt by the culture of schooling.

Critical accommodation in the classroom is the key to the creation of new student attitudes. Dialogical encounters between critical teachers and their students often involve the presentation of information that disrupts assimilated world views. It is at this point of disruption—a point at which cognitive dissonance reaches its zenith—that students realize that something in their consciousness is out of order and adjustment is required. This moment of accommodation is not to be subvert-ed by the unethical teacher who takes advantage of it to indoctrinate, to provide a facile resolution to the dissonance. Such resolutions are ethi-cally tantamount to behaviorist manipulation or the indoctrination of religious or political zealots. The critical teacher prolongs the accom-modation moment for days or weeks at a time, using it to stimulate searching, research-based student activities (Hultgren, 1987).

Critical teaching proceeds in no prearranged, standardized manner, but it does seem to embody a few common characteristics. At some point teachers and students are encouraged to examine the cognitive structures that impede transformative action, whether on the self or the environment. For example, an individual's growth may be undermined by a pedagogy grounded on a Piagetian formalism that emphasizes a procedural form of abstract logical thought—a form of thinking that removes the relationship among thinking and consciousness construc-tion and praxis (informed action) from consideration. Such forms of thinking tend to delegate teaching and learning to a cognitive realm sep-arate from commitment, emotion, and ethical action.

At the same time transformative action may be impeded not only by cognitive structures but by sociopolitical structures as well. This sociopolitical impediment may be found in economic and linguistic structures, in geographic place, in religious spheres, and in many other ideological public domains. Critical analysts strive to identify these impediments and their effects on how individuals come to see and act on the world (Codd, 1984). For example, no matter how "intelligent" a young woman might be, her identification with a religious sect that viewed women as the metaphorical body and men as the head of humankind would impede transformative action on her part. Such obvi-ous forms of sociopolitical oppression would be exposed by critical analysis. In both the cognitive and the sociopolitical situations, imped-iments serve to impede the disruptive effect of critical accommodation. Critical teacher education would prepare teachers with the skills to map the assimilation and accommodation experiences of their students in relation to the cognitive and sociopolitical interactions that affect these experiences. Learning action research techniques such as semiotics, ethnography, phenomenology, and historiography, prospective teachers would be empowered to uncover the evidence to construct their socio-cognitive maps.

This socio-cognitive mapping of critical teaching consistently involves the revelation of irony at one or more points in the accommodation process. Irony, Hayden White (1978) writes, alerts us to the inadequacy of the theory in question to characterize or account for the elements that don't fit into the order of the explanation. Often in the context of critical accommodation the theory may be an individual's story about her or his self-production, the person's self-identity. Irony may be seen as a linguistic strategy that sanctions skepticism as an explanatory strategy, satire as a form of critique, and agnosticism as an ethical approach. New paradigmatic analysis infatuated with irony, is hard to separate from critical accommodation. Nothing is as closed, self-sufficient, autonomous, or consistent as it seems. All entities are riddled with contradictions. What we think of as real, profound, or stable is merely a reflection of conventions (Hutcheon, 1988; Shapiro, 1992). With this in mind, critical accommodation becomes a critical transformative act as it draws upon ironic recognitions. Paulo Freire characterizes emancipation as risk; so too is critical accommodation. As teachers and students ironically interrogate past understandings, they embark on an agnostic venture into the unknown. Exploring and rereading sedimented meanings, these "geologists" critically accommodate ironic perception into new, albeit tentative, perceptions of reality and self (Greene, 1988, 1995; Grimmett, Erickson, MacKinnon, and Riecken, 1990).

An important aspect of this accommodation of ironic perception into new understandings of reality and self involves the disembedding of personal knowledge from the specific experience in which it developed. Only after this disembedding takes place can accommodations be transferred into new contexts. This critical transference involves a form of anticipatory accommodation that moves beyond a traditional Piagetian notion of formal generalization. The formal thinker, according to Piaget, possesses the ability to construct pristine generalizations from systematic observations. Such a cognitive process accepts a one-dimensional, Cartesian-Newtonian, cause-effect universe. In the formalistic empirical context, for example, all that is needed to ensure transferability is to understand with a high level of internal validity (the extent to which observations of a particular reality are true) something about a particular classroom and to know that the makeup of this classroom is representative of another classroom to which the generalization is being applied. Individuals operating in this tradition argue that the generalization derived from the first classroom is valid in all classrooms with the same population.

When we apply our understanding of critical analysis and disembedding, we begin to see that in everyday situations people don't make generalizations in this formalistic, empirical manner. Our notion of critical accommodation tells us that we reshape cognitive structures to account for unique aspects of what is being perceived in new contexts. Through our knowledge of a variety of comparable contexts we begin to understand similarities and differences—we learn from our comparisons of different contexts. The Cartesian-Newtonian concern with generalization and prediction is not the goal of our disembedding and critical transference, our critical accommodation. Instead, we begin to think in terms of anticipatory accommodation, that is we anticipate what we might encounter in similar situations, what strategies might work in our attempt to bring about emancipatory outcomes (Barrett, 1985; Benson, 1989).

In this context our interpretive strategies become an applied hermeneutics, an effort to use our meaning-making abilities to anticipate what may happen next and what we should do to prepare for such an eventuality. Such anticipation is central to higher orders of intelligence and creativity. Einstein anticipated that the Newtonian rules of physics would change as we approach the speed of light; Bohr and Heisenberg anticipated that at the sub-atomic (quantum) level the rules of Newtonian physics would no longer apply; Marcel Duchamps anticipated that multiple perspectives of reality could be depicted artistically. As they framed the problems they faced, Einstein, Bohr, Heisenberg, and Duchamps drew upon a repertoire of experiences and ways of understanding those experiences. They understood, as did John Dewey, that one function of knowledge of the present involves its kinetic application to the anticipation of what comes next. Dewey argued that fossils, for example, were prophets of the future when read by a creative and intelligent interpreter. Anticipatory accommodation helps us sift through the complexity of reality and eliminate many of the options we must consider. Without such an ability we would be paralyzed, unable to choose among the possible paths on our journey. Understanding the uniqueness of every instance, anticipatory accommodation allows us to escape the present by creating a prereflective grasp. Such an insight empowers us to act in spontaneous ways that those who observe us see as improvisation. The ability to anticipate and improvise is a central dynamic of post-formal thinking (Block, 1995; Munby and Russell, 1989; Hanks, 1991).

General Dynamics of Post-formal Thinking

Before describing post-formal thinking, we need to make sure that the dynamics of mainstream cognitive science are clear. Jean Piaget theorized formal thinking as the highest order of human thought. Such thinking implies an acceptance of a Cartesian-Newtonian mechanistic world view that is caught in a cause-effect, hypothetical-deductive system of reasoning. Unconcerned with questions of power relations and the way they structure our consciousness, formal operational thinkers accept an objectified, unpoliticized way of knowing that breaks an economic or educational system down into its basic parts in order to understand how it works. Emphasizing certainty and prediction, formal thinking organizes verified facts into a theory. The facts that do not fit into the theory are eliminated, and the theory developed is the one best suited to limit contradictions in knowledge. Thus, formal thought operates on the assumption that resolution must be found for all contradictions. Schools and standardized test-makers, assuming that formal operational thought represents the highest level of human cognition, focus their efforts on its cultivation and measurement. Students, teachers, and workers who move beyond formality are often unrewarded and sometimes even punished in educational and work-related contexts.

Moving beyond the certainty and authority of modernist formality is a central goal of a post-formal approach. Liberating teachers and students from authority dependence and the rationalistic chains to conventional practice that accompanies it is also an important goal of a new paradigmatic psychology. Inducing change in the psychological foundations of education involves the adoption of a self-critical stance that sees mainstream cognitive discourses as merely one of many approaches to the analysis of thinking and learning. Such a position leads to a search for new literacies that address the unique interpretive demands of hyperreality's visual imagery (Shor, 1992; Collins, 1994). Modernist cognitive science has too often refused to confront the disciplinary implications of new paradigmatic analysis with its focus on hidden assumptions, false notions of objectivity, and contextualization of scholarly disciplines historically and socially. This new paradigmatic analysis or postmodern critique helps us claim new positions in the web of reality that offer new insights into the subject in question. Many of the great problems of contemporary society are invisible and require an intelligence that moves beyond surface appearances and visual images. In a sense hyperreality forces us to relearn how to learn. Expertise in this context is no longer acquired in a linear step-by-step process where particular tasks are divided into sub-skills and taught outside the context in which they are used (Aronowitz, 1993; Beck, 1992; Block, 1995;

Raizen, 1989). In the modernist context potatoes are best peeled this way:

1. Walk to shelf adjacent to sink and get pot.
2. Walk to storage, carrying pot, and fill it with potatoes.
3. Return from storage, laying pot directly on vegetable preparing surface near sink.
4. Pick up knife (from nail above this surface).
5. Pare potatoes directly into pail (soiling no surface).
6. Wash potatoes and fill pot with water.
7. Wash and hang up knife (on nail above sink).
8. Walk with pot and lay on stove (Allison, 1995, p. 185).

Or cars started in the manner of the hyperrational Vehicle Starting Inventory Checklist (VSIC):

1. Insert key in ignition.
2. Depress clutch.
3. Turn key clockwise until starter engages.
4. Place gear in first (or reverse, depending on the location/placement of automobile and/or preference of driver)
5. Release clutch while simultaneously depressing accelerator.

Understanding the absurdity of hyperrationality, educational psychologists from the new paradigm push the boundaries of Piagetian formality. Many theorists over the last two decades have sought to formulate a post-Piagetian cognitive theory. Too often, however, they have not used a critical theoretical understanding to analyze the ways our consciousness is shaped by the world around us. On the foundation of such understandings we can construct a new vision of cognitive theory, a new conception of what "being smart" entails. We can move beyond Piaget's notion of formal thinking with all of its narrow assumptions about the ways intelligence is expressed. As they move to post-formal thinking, critical educators politicize cognition; they attempt to de-socialize their students and themselves from the conventions of school-based pronouncements of who's intelligent and who's not. In the political context mainstream cognitive psychology often confuses socio-economic privilege with high intelligence and socio-economic marginalization with incompetence. Understanding via feminism the political nature of the personal, post-formal educational psychology appreciates the political dynamics involved with the ways the cultural is implicated in an individual's identity formation (Giroux, 1992; 1997). Economic status, ethnic background, and linguistic conventions are all interrelated and all significant in the production of one's relationship to educational psychology. In this context educational psychology will view individuals as progressively incompetent the farther away they fall from the normalized benchmarks of whiteness, middle-class status, or "standard" English speaking.

As it tenders such observations, post-formality understands its partisanship, its identification with society's marginalized peoples. Aware of its need to contest hidden manifestations of dominant power, new paradigmatic educational psychology draws upon a variety of disciplines to facilitate its democratic attempt to reshape political relations in a more equitable manner. Such a task becomes exceedingly difficult when modernist positivist educational psychology maintains that individual marginalization is a result of personal incompetence. A partisan critical psychology grounds its concern with individual freedom and creativity upon a larger commitment to a politics of social and economic justice. Such a commitment, however, never comes with a blueprint of how specifically it is to be honored. Political action in both psychological and pedagogical contexts is situation specific and idiosyncratic. Just because a particular political strategy worked in the past doesn't mean it will work in the present struggle over a democratic educational psychology. Democratic political action just like post-formality itself never emerges full blown and totally developed. Instead, the political insurgency of a post-formal psychology evolves slowly, always shifting to rearticulate itself in a new context. Given the power-related dynamics of the new psychology, the mainstream response to it will be anything but subdued. Modernist positivist educational psychology on whose pronouncements pedagogical decisions have been rationalized for decades will not surrender its power graciously. In the eyes of modernist positivist psychologists, the post-formal reconceptualization of the discipline will be accurately viewed as a challenge to their world view (Grossberg, 1995; Giroux, 1997; Ferguson, 1984; Block, 1995).

The Interpretive Nature of Post-formal Thinking: Psychological Hermeneutics

Post-formal thinking is concerned with questions of meaning, self-awareness, and the nature and function of the social context. Such concerns move post-formal thinkers beyond formalist concerns with proper scientific procedure and the certainty it must produce. Post-formalism grapples with purpose, devoting attention to issues of human dignity, freedom, power, authority, domination, and social responsibility. Questions of meaning, self-awareness, purpose, and context pull us into the realm of hermeneutics. Concerned with the ambiguous nature of life in general and education in particular, the hermeneutical realm interfaces with the concerns of post-formality. Moving past the boundaries of modern positivist psychology, a critical psychology traces the way power shapes meaning making in those recesses of (un)consciousness hidden to empirical analysts and modernist pedagogies. This desire to go deeper and to gain access to the deepest meanings and experiences is an ability we are capable of as human beings. The critical hermeneutic that post-formality incorporates is a socio-historical analysis that seeks to understand the circumstances under which knowledge and meaning are produced (by scholars and the powerful) and received (by students and other consumers). For example, the manner in which a group of adolescents receive a 501 jeans ad very much depends on the position they occupy in the web of reality. Such an ad with its refusal to "sell" the product in a conventional manner comes across to young people unacquainted with the media as non-sensical, bizarre. Youth anesthetized by constant exposure to television see the ads very differently, as a cool break from the "same old same old." Because of the difference between these ads and other televised ads, because of the 501 jeans ads transgression of the advertising codes, the TV weary young people may be captivated by their different ambiance. The context of reception in this case is very important in understanding the cultural dynamic at work (Slattery, 1995; Giroux, 1992; Capra, Steindl-Rast, and Matus, 1991; Thompson, 1987).

The critical hermeneutic we are describing helps produce a situated knowledge that is aware of the conditions of knowledge production and reception and the power relations between producer and receiver. Knowledge passed between equals takes on a very different character than knowledge transfer from superior to subordinate. For example, information that a teacher receives from a supervisor takes on a different character than information received from a fellow teacher. The two communiqués are situated and transmitted in different power contexts and accordingly will elicit different responses from the receiver—even if the information transmitted is exactly the same. In this communication context, what does it mean to understand and make sense of the two conversations? Without contextual understanding we may be unable to appreciate the various cultural and power-related dynamics at work. To understand the limitations on the modernist positivist view of intelligence and consciousness, post-formal psychologists argue that identity itself must be contextualized. Identity thus is decentered by its social, power-related, and linguistic situatedness. If a critical hermeneutics reveals such socio-psychological dynamics, then we learn that we can only know both ourselves and others through historicization. The psychological implications of such an assertion are dramatic. Notions of innate intelligence or lack of such must be modified by the socially contingent nature of identity formation. Educators, for example, may be far greater equipped to elicit cognitive change in students than previously thought (Damarin, 1993).

Given modernist educational psychological and psychometric tendencies for social decontextualization, post-formal psychologists search for subtle and unrecognized ways the cultural intersects with the psychological. The linguistic/discursive domain emerges as a prime venue for such an intersection. Viewing language as a neutral medium that unproblematically reflects the objective reality that surrounds human beings, modernist positivist psychology has been blinded to the ways that language shapes perceptions of both the world and self. Indeed, linguistic structures may mobilize meaning in a way that sustains unjust power relationships between individuals and groups. The discursive practices, the stories we tell about the world around us sometimes shape our understandings of situations without our conscious awareness. For example, the discursive way in which the term, ethnic, is applied to people other than white moves us to believe that white is not an ethnicity but a normal, pure category. Statements such as "she's too ethnic" or "let's go to an ethnic restaurant" erase the ethnic nature of whiteness. Such a linguistic practice releases white people from confronting their relationship with their own ethnicity. If we agree that the way we see ourselves and the world is shaped by our ethnicities, then white people are released from such a task by these socio-linguistic dynamics. They come to accept their lifestyles, identities, and world views as objective and natural; they often see their biases as an accurate reading of themselves and the world. In this context the need for self-reflection on the construction of their consciousness and of their prejudices is negated.

While upon initial confrontation this psychological hermeneutics may seem conceptually difficult, further analyses reveals its intelligibility and practicality. Psychological hermeneutics specifically addresses the process of understanding the texts that shape human consciousness, subjectivity, and capability. The use of the term, text, in this context does not simply refer to print materials or books but to any entity open to analysis and interpretation. Thus, a classroom could be a text, hyper-reality's array of visual, audio, and electronic knowledge forms can be approached as texts and "read" in a variety of ways. This reading or interpretation process involves the creative construction of meaning—an important basis on which any cognitive psychology is built. A critical psychological hermeneutics, therefore, involves a specific set of activities at least including: 1) the creative reading, the explication of meanings in a particular text; 2) an appreciation of the ways meanings may change given the various contexts the text may be viewed in relation to; 3) an understanding of the ways the meanings constructed may support or subvert existing power relations; 4) a cognizance of the process by which the meanings produced help shape consciousness and identity; and 5) the ways an individual's agency or ability to act in particular circumstances is affected by the texts and the meanings produced (Giroux, 1994; Slattery, 1995; Thompson, 1987).

Critical psychological hermeneutics is deeply concerned with the production of the self and all of the cognitive and pedagogical issues such production involves. As Alan Block (1995) argues in Occupied Reading in his critique of reading education, the act of reading words off a printed page is a sociopsycholinguistic process. By this he means that reading occurs as a transaction involving the cultural and personal psyche of the reader and the verbal text for the purpose of meaning making. In the process a new self is produced in the new meaning made. As Dewey maintained, consciousness is an aspect of meaning making that at any particular time is involved somehow in being transformed. When Block's notion of reading the printed page is expanded to our larger notion of reading the world as a text, the stakes are raised, personal identity production is even more subject to the social. The challenge for a new paradigmatic educational psychology is to incorporate depth hermeneutics into the study of human consciousness, lived experience, and the formation of the self in relation to others. Any psychological hermeneutics that facilitates our understanding of human identity knows that the self is never completely produced or revealed in consciousness. Freud argued that the self can never totally understand its own identity because self-production is not a totally conscious process. Thus, a hermeneutically-informed educational psychology embraces psychoanalysis in order to move beyond the rational dynamics of self-production to the non-rational aspects of the role of the unconscious in the process.

An education emerging in this context induces teachers, students, and democratic citizens to explore what they know and how they came to know it. Understanding contemporary social relations, teachers seek to uncover the ways advertising, for example, sells lifestyles and socially desirable subject positions connected to the product—features in contemporary advertising sold more fervently than the product itself. The Miller Beer drinker is drinking upwardly mobile consumer lifestyles as much as he is drinking beer. The man who uses Brut cologne "smells like macho" as much as he smells like musk. How did the boys in one's tenth grade math class come to hold their view of masculinity? A psychological hermeneutics explores the diverse ways such a socio-psychological, conscious-unconscious process takes place in concrete activities and symbolic engagements. Employing semiotics as part of its interpretive repertoire, psychological hermeneutics explores the ways signs and symbols are employed by individuals to make meaning, to explain their existence. Semiotics provides insight not only into the construction of consciousness but the construction of the unconsciousness as well. Freud's understanding of the unconscious, for example, was a theory of meaning making and signification. Focusing on the symbolic material of dreams, free associations, and the decoding function of the psycho-analytic act, Freudian and post-Freudian theory has revolved around semiotic-based inquiry. Along the same lines, Vygotsky argued that cognitive development is made possible only by an ability to decipher and internalize cultural signs and significations. The use of signs, he concluded, changes psychological operations in the same ways the use of tools expands the range of activities within which the new cognitive abilities can be deployed. Thus, hermeneutics and semiotics take on a very important role in the effort to appreciate the socio-political construction of self, the need to cultivate deeper levels of understanding, and the inseparability of self-production, cognitive development, and the influence of the unconscious on these processes (Trend, 1994; Kellner, 1989; Alvesson and Willmott, 1992; Driscoll, 1994; Henriques et al., 1984; Moll, 1991).

Post-formal Intuition: Grasping Significance
In its perpetual quest to make meaning a post-formal educational psychology holds what has been referred to as intuition in high esteem. While ancients such as Augustine and Aquinas viewed intuition as important, the scientific revolution at the birth of modernity rejected its value in human inquiry and cognition. Because of intuition's lack of

concern with systematic and sequential analysis of formal concepts, Descartes, Newton, and Bacon banished it from the domain of intellectual endeavor. Refusing to equate intuition with the irrational, post-formality prefers to designate it as a non-rational cognitive act that achieves insight not through linear and deductive reasoning but via a more non-linear and holistic mode of thinking. The modernist positivist equation of intuition and the irrational with all of its negative connotations forgot Aristotle's assertion that intuition was not in conflict with reason—conversely, reason was grounded on intuition. Instead of being conflictual, the relationship between intuition and reason is synergistic. Thus, a key feature of the post-formal paradigmatic shift involves the attempt to bridge the rational-intuitive divide, to synergize analysis and synthesis, linearity and non-linearity.

Once synergized by the bridging process, a post-formal intuition is ready to make meaning. In this energized state the intuitive thinker gains the ability to recognize significance or potential significance. When post-formal thinkers follow their intuition, they begin to move on to cognitive pathways that lead to greater insight, they start to assemble ostensibly unrelated fragments of consciousness into unified and consequential wholes. Unlike modernist positivist linear analysis, post-formal intuition perceives qualitative relationships that emerge from the perception of structures so deep that a previously-unseen inner coherence emerges. Unifying mental processes replace digital operations, in the process initiating a previously unimagined dialogue between the whole and parts, panorama and still life, image and sequence. In this intuitive context stories become as important as propositions, for in a post-formal context the story as a whole is greater than the sum of its parts. Such an argument holds dramatic implications not only for cognition but for knowledge production, research, and pedagogy, as it allows for the narrative, poetic, and metaphorical to be employed in the attempt to make sense of and transform self and world. Such aesthetic dynamics or as curriculum theorist James McDonald termed it, aesthetic rationality, puts reason back in touch with feeling, as it listens carefully to and interprets emotional cues.

Intuition understood in this post-formal context lays the cognitive foundation upon which many scientific and mathematical as well as humanistic and literacy innovations are constructed. Einstein talked frequently of his use of intuition to induce a process of visual imagination that resulted in theoretical advances in physics. In order, for example, to develop his theory of light, Einstein imagined how a light wave would appear to someone riding along with it, his theory of relativity was produced via the image of a person in a falling elevator, and his curved four-dimensional continuum of space and time was conceptualized as a suspended rubber sheet stretched taut but imprinted and incurved where massive bodies such as stars or planets were placed upon it. Using intuition in these imaginative ways provides a new vision even when the material is old. Post-formality provides a socio-cognitive context that allows individuals to move from a formal ingenuity that serves the purpose of puzzle solving activities to an intuitive perspective that uncovers puzzles to solve in the mind's journey into the unknown. Conceptualized in this way post-formal intuition is not as much concerned with delineation and categorization as it is with gaining unprecedented insight into the uncharted journey (Courtney, 1988; Capra, Steindl-Rast and Matus, 1991; Voorhees and Royce, 1987; Pinar, et al., 1995).

Cultural Studies' Critique of Disciplinary Delineations: Hyperspecialization, Stupidification, and Individualization

Cultural studies has arisen over the last couple of decades as an inter-disciplinary and counter-disciplinary field that functions within competing definitions of culture. The field asserts that a wide variety of expressions of cultural production should be studied in relation to other cultural dynamics and social and historical structures. We have consistently tried to bring a cultural studies perspective to the analysis of educational and educational psychological discourses—in the process subjecting the academic domains to political, economic, communicative, linguistic, and many other forms of examination. Viewing psychological knowledge in this context entails a discursive deconstruction of the unstated assumptions and tacit rules that contribute to its production and legitimation. Believing that the study of social and psychological phenomena is fragmented among a variety of disciplines, students of cultural studies believe that scholarship in the area(s) becomes fragmented to the point that attempts to make sense of larger socio-psychological processes are undermined. Scholars become so isolated as they work in private, focusing on narrow areas, producing knowledge so specialized that they lose touch with its meaning, application, or social effects. Cultural studies attempts to overcome this fragmentation by highlighting the socio-psychological realm as a living process that shapes the way human beings live, view themselves, and understand the world around them. As students of cultural studies question the ways of seeing that evolve around the "normal science" of psychology as a discipline, they liberate themselves from the unexamined belief structures that limit insight and chain them to familiar explanations.

Thus, a cultural studies encounter with psychology involves a theoretical critique of the authority of psychological knowledge and the paradigm in which it is produced. The modernist psychological paradigm, for example, has ignored the stories, experiences, and life worlds of culturally and politically marginalized groups. A cultural studies-based critique of psychology would force the field to confront the Eurocentric whiteness of the discipline and the ways such a dynamic shapes psychological knowledge. A cultural studies critique challenges mainstream psychology's monocultural value system that reflects the standpoint of a Western modernist empiricism dedicated to the evidence of the senses over speculative, hermeneutical types of knowledge. Such critique is aimed at transcending the paradigmatic blindness and the fragmentary specialization that impedes scholars from critically reading the socio-psychological world. Donaldo Macedo (1994) is very helpful in the attempt to provide examples of the problems with Eurocentric empirically-produced knowledge. Because the defense lawyers for the policemen who beat Rodney King, Macedo maintains, showed white jurors the video of the King beating frame by frame (not at normal speed), the jurors were unable to "feel" the holistic impact of the violence of the beating. In a similar way empirical snapshots of psychological reality taken out of their larger context undermine the cognitive ability to make linkages or to understand the emotional dynamics that provide meaning to a situation.

Empirical decontextualization and hyperspecialization not only subvert meaning making but actually contribute to the stupidification of its victims. Macedo (1994) tells a story illustrating this process about a former colleague of his at MIT whose area of specialization was linguistics. Learning that Macedo was studying pidgin and Creole languages, she asked him what exactly a pidgin language was. Her scholarly work involved the highest-level theory in linguistics possible in the field, yet she had no clue about historical and cultural linguistics. Macedo's colleague was a member of the specialist class (engineers, doctors, professors, etc. . . . .) created by modernist positivist science who knows only one small corner of a specialized area. Anyone who seeks to pursue connection between fields and a larger scheme of knowledge is referred to by such specialists as a dilettante. Cultural studies attempts to interrupt this paradigmatic dynamic by encouraging interdisciplinary studies that connect knowledge to the cultural context in which it was produced and legitimated (Aronowitz, 1993; Giroux, 1997). This fragmentary specialization impulse of modernist empirical psychology also reveals itself in an individualization process. Mainstream psychologists have often refused to employ the sociological strategy of studying individuals in relation to their group identification, choosing instead to highlight individualism. Both the Frankfurt School and the poststructuralist critique of Cartesian-Newtonian science reject this individualization dynamic and the theory of the autonomous rational subject that supports it. Residing at the epicenter of the modernist epistemological universe, this possessive egocentric individual has corrupted Western ways of seeing to the point that manifestations of difference are excluded. Operating in this modernist theoretical galaxy, cognitive psychology validates this individualization impulse as it positions the individual as the nonproblematic unit of scientific analysis. In this context learning is a simple process of absorbing the given while pedagogy is a matter of transmission and assimilation. Such a perspective establishes strict boundaries between the inside and outside of the mind—students take in information from outside themselves. The mindset builds fences between ourselves and other people, borders between our mutual emotional needs—indeed, fragmented knowledge fragments the community (Beck, 1992; McCarthy, 1992; Lave and Wenger, 1991; Bohm and Edwards, 1991).

Understanding the Socially Structured Self:
Escaping the Oppression of Psycholicization

Drawing upon a cultural studies critique of the limitations of the fragmented disciplinary of modernist psychology and the poststructuralist understanding of the need for socio-historical contextualization of any scientific analysis, a post-formal psychology understands that human sociality is a fundamental aspect of the self. Poststructuralist psychoanalysis maintains that the self is never complete, always in process of shaping and being shaped by the socio-cultural and symbolic realms. In this context poststructuralist psychoanalysis replaces the term "self" with its implication of autonomy and unity with the term "subject" with its connotation of the self's production by its interaction with the world around it. In this poststructuralist psychoanalytical context, therefore, the development of mental functions must take into account a wide variety of factors including contextual analysis, the conscious and unconscious production of subjectivity, the subtle dynamics of interpersonal interaction, and an individual or a group's position in the web of reality. Simply put, contrary to the pronouncements of modernist psychology the mind does extend beyond the skin. Intelligence, memory, and thinking are not the possessions of individuals—they are always social processes. With these understandings the primitive nature of psychometric I.Q. testing is exposed with its measurement of cultural familiarity with the discourse of Western schooling and linguistic socialization (Ferguson, 1984; Finke, 1993; Marsh, 1993; Werstch and Tulviste, 1992).

Failure to understand the social structuring of the self leads to a variety of problems, especially for those who are in less powerful, marginalized positions. Without such contextualization individuals from dominant cultural backgrounds are unable to understand that the behaviors of socio-economic subordinates may reflect the structural pressures under which they operate. In addition, men and women from the mainstream often believe that socio-economic success is the result of individual merit and that social hierarchies and bell curves represent the natural dispersion of biological cognitive aptitude. Quite conveniently for the more privileged members of society, such individualized belief structures serve to hide the benefits bestowed by dominant group membership. The same type of concealment by individualization has also taken place in Western cognitive science. The mind, mainstream cognitive scientists have contended, is the "software program" that can be studied in social isolation by fragmenting it and analyzing the parts—a quick and clean form of analysis that avoids the complication of "messy" socio-historical contextualization. Such messiness involves touchy issues such as social values or politics and the intersection of the biological (individual) with the collective. Thus, individualized modernist psychology studies the machine (mind) but not uses to which it is put in the social cosmos of ideological conflict and political activity. Psychologists and teachers like specialists in all fields are educated as technicians who must pursue a critical and contextualized view of the world through their own efforts outside of the professional education (Merelman, 1986; Haymes, 1996; Block, 1995; Macedo, 1994).

These modernist decontextualization processes tend to psychologize the study of cognition or the formation of subjectivity in that analyses of such phenomena are undertaken only as psychological processes, not psychological and sociological, political, economic, and other processes as well. Piaget decontextualized his study of children, often removing questions of cultural context from this observations and analyses. Did children in non-European cultures develop in the same way? In other historical times? Child development in Piaget's work was not examined in these contexts. In the attempt to understand human political behavior, modernist political scientists often neglected to view political beliefs and actions in the context of desire and other emotions, focusing instead on rational dynamics. Such abstraction undermined the larger effort to make sense of such activity. Students of education often approach schooling as an institution that exists outside the cultural, linguistic, or political context. Indeed, the very organization of schooling in America is grounded around the modernist belief that knowledge can be decontextualized. Only in this decontextualized domain can intelligence testing be viewed as an objective, uncontaminated instrument of measurement. To maintain the psychological and educational status quo, social context must be removed from attempts to understand psychological and pedagogical processes (Postman, 1994; Alford, 1993; Lave and Wenger, 1991; Appiah, 1995).

G Spots: The Trouble with Psychometrics

This removal of social context reflects the history of cognitive psychology with its statistical definition of intelligence. The mainstream of educational psychology argued that since intelligence has a biological nature, it can be mathematically measured and expressed. Armed with its circular assertion that intelligence is what I.Q. tests test, psychometrics became the dominant discourse in educational psychology. Initiated by Francis Galton, the psychometric tradition embarked on a perpetual search for an innate mental processing apparatus within which human thinking, emotion, and behavior originated. Obsessed with heredity and genetics, Galton and his followers developed a doctrine of bounded potential that precisely delineated the nature of intelligence. Because of genetic factors, the doctrine held, all people have limits to their intelligence that are fixed throughout their lives. No matter what socio-cultural influences individuals might encounter, these boundaries can never be transcended. Grounded on these assumptions, the science of psychometrics has produced a variety of absurd conclusions including the postulates that Jews are unintelligent, Mediterraneans are inferior to Nordics, and the average mental age of white soldiers in World War I was thirteen (Andersen, 1994; Holt, 1995).

In an era marked by a postmodern critique of the limitations of empirical science, psychometrics reads like an archaic language, a Middle English of research. Ignoring the effects of socio-economic status, psychometrics deploys a biological terrorism that reduces mental operations to genetic determinism. Such an antediluvian view fails to appreciate the relationship between biological and cultural factors. Indeed, genes regulate various human activity but not without relevant social triggers. Without a reflective analysis of the tacit assumptions of the discourse of psychometrics and its disciplinary brother, behavioral genetics, the scholarly work of cognitive psychologists in these disciplinary domains merely reflects their prejudices and predispositions toward particular groups and individuals. The plethora of unexamined assumptions of modernist positivist cognitive psychology were most economically expressed by early twentieth-century statistician Charles Spearman's concept of "g"—a symbol representing general intelligence. Described as the "Rock of Gibraltar" in psychometrics, "g" has been viewed as a type of internal force that supports intellectual ability. Reductionistic to its core, psychometrics employs "g" to argue that contrary to claims of the complexity and ambiguity of general intelligence, it ultimately depends on only one factor—biological/genetic ability (Carey, 1995; Andersen, 1994; McCarthy et al., 1996; Berger, 1995; Gardner, 1995; Sedgwick, 1995; Ryan, 1995; Childley, 1995; Appiah, 1995).

Psychometricians are fond of arguing that "g" is one of the most empirically supported concepts in the science of psychology—a claim that doesn't even come close to reflecting the truth. To read the literature of mainstream psychometrics is to lose sight of any historical factors that might contribute to the formation of subjectivity and intelligence. In much of the knowledge produced by the discipline economic, sociological, and social psychological factors play no role in the development of cognitive skills. One detects a historical erasure that removes from consideration in the conversation about intelligence factors such as unequal access to schooling, unequal schooling, economic disprivilege, racial prejudice, etc. . . . . So many of the most basic questions of psychometrics are sociological, not simply psychological. To remove sociological analysis of the effects of context from consideration is to deny the complexity of humanness; it is to impose a linear scientific explanation on a reality that defies such limitations. If Vygotsky was correct when he argued that higher mental processes involve the internationalization of social meanings coming out of human cultural activities, then by definition psychometrics has historically failed to meet this criterion of a higher mental process. Focusing on the conceptual narrowness of "g" psychometricians lost sight of social meaning making in the context of the construction of subjectivity. Without such sociological insight, the discipline fell victim to the tyranny of unequal access to cultural knowledge valued by educators and psychologist. Lack of opportunity was confused with inability (Gould, 1995; Jones, 1995; Nisbett, 1995; Lincoln, 1996; Slattery, 1996; Marsh, 1993). Undetermined by its cultural blindness, modernist positivist cognitive psychology is a threat to valued notions of democratic community and equal education for all people. As it differentiates between students with low intelligence and students with high intelligence, between students who bring valuable cultural and ethnic experiences to school and those who don't, such a cognitive psychology rewards the privileged and punishes the marginalized. As a science of competition, modernist cognitive psychology shifts analysis from different kinds of mental performances to qualitative differences in performance. With this shift of perspective educational psychologists become identifiers and predictors of difference in ability and success, thus pitting students against one another. In this context "g" takes on a reality, an independent existence of its own that is worth fighting to acquire—a phantom that is imbued with the power to divide us around cultural and psychological lines of demarcation. Blessed by the imprimatur of hard science, modernist cognitive psychology has had the audacity to claim the mental inferiority of the earth's black peoples—measuring in a blatantly decontextualized fashion African I.Q. and determining its median to be about 75 (Andersen, 1994; Gould, 1995; Jones, 1995; Easterbrook, 1995; Herrnstein and Murray, 1994). I am not convinced that all psychometricians do not understand the cultural chasm between African urban residents and tribal Africans—such differences are so obvious that few individuals should miss the inapplicability of particular I.Q. test questions designed from a Western perspective to the lives and conceptual frames of rural African goat herders from Somalia. Psychometricians unable to discern such cultural differences are, bluntly put, exceedingly stupid.

Excluding Difference:
Modernist Psychology and the Crisis of Epistemology
Modernist psychology has been an "excluding" discipline that has sought to canonize the norms of Western white males from the upper-middle class. Intelligence, creativity, mental health, and normality in general have been defined by narrow guidelines that exclude diverse cultural manifestations of such concepts. One standard has worked so far and it is the obligation of the guardians of the discipline to preserve that standard from the multicultural barbarians at the gate. What is obvi-

ous to many is that the standards and guidelines delineated by the discipline are the ones best met by the guardians themselves. America is a Eurocentric country by necessity, gatekeepers such as E. D. Hirsch maintain. So blatantly do Hirsch and his compadres erase the role of non-Europeans in American life and scholarship, one wonders how such scholars convinced themselves that the culture is devoid of African, Asian, and Native American influences. Toni Morrison refers to these absences as so "ornate" they demand our attention. Even those who have understood the impact of history and culture in shaping psychological functions could not escape the broader gravitational pull of Eurocentrism. Though Vygotsky opened an extremely important psychological conversation about the intersection and culture and mind, even he assumed the superiority of European cultural tools and forms of mental functioning to those of other cultures.

Such Eurocentrism when combined with the return of white supremacy and the growing disparity of wealth between whites and non-whites, points to an epistemological crisis of knowledge and human purpose. The way we produce knowledge in the modernist paradigm often focuses exclusively on the macro-level, ignoring the social differences that reside at the micro-level, the domain of the particular. Positivist psychology has assumed that what is statistically most common is, accordingly, most significant. A post-formal psychology seeks out the marginal, the subordinate, and the "deviant," in the process gleaning insights that demand the reconfiguration of the field, the reconceptualization of common assumptions. In this post-formal context the center-margin hierarchies so common to modernist psychology begin to break down. The new psychology forces disciplinary change in light of the exposure of the race, class, and gender-grounding of basic psychological concepts, in the process revealing the ways the field has served to disempower subordinate groups. At the core of the epistemological crisis of modernism is its inability to deal with diversity—a deficiency that takes on exaggerated importance in a globalized culture of hyper-reality (King and Mitchell, 1995; Sedgwick, 1995; Werstch and Tulviste, 1992; Fiske, 1994; Giroux, 1992, 1993).

In schools supported by modernist psychology, marginalized students are often lost and alienated. Unlike students from the dominant culture, they cannot draw upon their personal histories and cultural backgrounds to facilitate their negotiation of school requirements. From the modernist psychological perspective and the pedagogy that emanates from it, such personal and cultural experiences constitute "the problem," the reason for their academic difficulties, their "cultural disadvantage." Consistently confusing intelligence with social advantage (whiteness, middle-classness, and often masculinity), modernist psychology buries knowledge both about individuals from marginalized cultures and the insights they have historically produced. From the perspective of post-formal analysts, modernist psychology, like the whiteness that culturally grounds it, operates as a form of arrogant perception—an epistemological stance that approaches culturally different situations and individuals from a position of power. Thus, white culture uses its science to disseminate images of the world and its people that allow whites to maintain their power position. The arrogant perception of Eurocentric psychology provides white people with a false sense of privilege that undermines their ability to make sense of the world and their relation to it. Such a position in the web of reality blinds individuals to the need for constant self-analysis, for contemplation about one's role in the world. Such inquiries provide the raw material for creative insight. It is obvious that when individuals consider themselves privileged to the point they are exempted from such activity, they offer few compelling insights; they are held captive by the power of the status quo (Raspberry, 1995; Ferguson, 1984; Damarin, 1993; Anthony, 1995).

A post-formal educational psychology refuses to view the psychological domain as separate from the political sphere. Indeed, post-formalists view psychology as a technology of social, economic, and political organization, as it confers both normality and credentials on those who fall within its parameters of acceptability. If more psychologists saw their discipline as a socio-political technology of regulation, they would spend more time uncovering the reasons that the children of the poor and non-white perform as groups so poorly on standardized tests and come to school so often devoid of the skills schools require. Post-formal psychology sees through modernist psychology's "official story" about who we are and what we can do. While understanding evolutionary psychology's analysis of the alienation between the lives we lead and the lives for which we were designed, post-formalists appreciate the fact that power asymmetries render some people more alienated than others—indeed, some alienation has been coerced. Differences are not simply to be tolerated in some liberal celebration of inclusivity but are to be analyzed in light of questions of power and privilege. How does difference shape the socio-educational lives of the marginalized? The privileged? What happens to modernist psychology when the construction of difference and its effects are exposed? Do new definitions of normality and intelligence emerge or do new forms of repression and erasure appear? Post-formal psychologists work to expose the damage caused by the arrogant expression of whiteness, while simultaneously making sure that the positive power of difference is appreciated (Fiske, 1994; Kamin, 1995; Giroux, 1997).

Psychology and Power: Regulating Individuals

Dominant group values must be protected in all institutions. The playing field where this protection takes place is the realm of individual consciousness. Power at the end of the twentieth century involves shaping how individual consciousness experiences the everyday dynamics of social life. If such experiences are generally pleasant, then the social structures with which people identify will experience little pressure to embrace democratic reforms. Discontent at this level of experience, on the other hand, is one of the most important catalysts for social change. Subjectivity, thus, becomes the last frontier of domination. Power is manifested along a spectrum that ranges from the socio-political and economic formation, through education and other social institutions, to the complex subjectivities of individual members of the social order. Post-formal psychology while very sensitive to the impact of all three levels, focuses much of its attention on the level of individual subjectivity. In this context the new psychology emphasizes the impact of power on the 1) intrapersonal—the domain of consciousness; 2) interpersonal—the domain of relationships, social interactions; and 3) corporeality—the domain of the body and behavior, people's physical presence in the social world. Of course, these domains of subjectivity along with social formations and institutions are subtlety integrated in a way that produces cultural reality. As such, one aspect (e.g., subjectivity) cannot be examined in isolation of the others—an assertion that changes the study of psychology forever (Jipson and Reynolds, 1997; Fiske, 1993).

Modernist psychology not only failed to study power relations and the interaction of the social and the individual but was complicit in power's shaping of subjectivity and individual perception. As Foucault argued, contemporary power takes the form of disciplinary power. In this context disciplinary power means not only the prerogative to punish but the ability to transform individuals into "subjects" via the human sciences—psychology in particular. Psychology working in tandem with medicine, criminology, education, and other sciences has facilitated the production of a "normalized society." In the name of caring and humanism practitioners in these disciplines wield a "confessional power" that is able to extract confessions, induce guilt, submit to authority, pry into the deepest recesses of the mind, and induce individuals to consent to their own oppression. Using these disciplines of knowledge the behavior of large numbers of people could be managed. The poor and non-white especially could be stabilized and routinized in a manner that would make their behavior more predictable without the need for overt displays of force on the part of power wielders. Hidden in the disciplinary language of concern, domination could be deployed in a way that avoided evoking the resentment and resistance of the people—it neutralizes the emergence of counter-power with its erratic agitation, rebellion, and popular coalitions.

Few voices in Western culture were conceptually equipped to critique this disciplinary domination—conservative analysts were blinded by their identification with power elites, liberals by their complicity with the fields of study and knowledge production themselves. In such an uncritical context the disciplinary techniques of management, surveillance, and control developed unimpeded, as psychologists unabashedly bandied about and deployed labels such as normality and abnormality. Operating with the imprimatur of hard science, such scholarly activity was naturalized to the point its subjects were unaware of its origins, assumptions, or effects. The twentieth century has observed the steady growth of such disciplines, especially with the emergence of the postmodern condition, hyperreality, with its proliferation of electronic information, high-tech methods of surveillance, and ubiquitous visual media that provide power wielders direct and private access to the formation of individual consciousness. Cartesian-Newtonian science has turned against its inventors just as science fiction writers feared, as authorities have educated, cured, reformed, and punished in compliance with the needs of the power bloc. In this context of "the cure," problems and pathologies are located in the individual. As such a move reflects the abstract individualization of modernist science, it directly shapes the ideology produced by the power bloc with its apologia for the injustice of the status quo—its political economy, its social institutions, and its scientific establishment (Ball, 1992; Ferguson, 1984; Cooper; 1994; Fiske, 1993; Donald, 1993; Denzin, 1987).

When operating most efficiently, modernist psychology creates authority contexts where certified experts impose their interpretation of situations on their subordinates—clients, students, patients, or subjects. Empowered with the right to discern meaning, such experts gain the license to determine what caliber of human beings their subordinates are. This power to define identity helped early twentieth-century pro-gressives, for example, regulate the immigrant poor via therapeutic intervention. Such therapy sought to normalize such families by pro-viding lessons on how to manage a household. In the process such inter-vention sought to change immigrant social behavior through an Americanization process that illustrated the un-American (pathological) nature of European working-class beliefs in anarchism, socialism, labor strikes, and other threats to the social order. Committed to the control-ling and molding of human desire (libido), modernist psychologists saw those who differed from an Anglo-Saxon norm deviant and dangerous. Unlike the "superior" Anglo-Saxons and other northern Europeans, these Eastern and Southern European immigrants needed psychological help in controlling their unbridled desire/libido. In the words of some scholars around the turn of the twentieth century, the new immigrants needed exposure to Anglo-Saxon ways of living, ways of regulating their affect (Abercrombie, 1994; Ferguson, 1984; Fiske, 1993).

Disciplinary Sites, Regulatory Practices

Around such socio-psychological viewpoints regulatory institutions began to develop in order to put disciplinary policies into effect. Through these institutions, bourgeoisie (middle-class) white values of punctuality, emotional restraint, frugality, and rationality could be culti-vated. In this context factories, jails, schools, and hospitals were creat-ed in hopes of molding recalcitrant individuals to the demands of progress. Schools and families were used as disciplinary sites for chil-dren deemed in need of moral guidance and protection. Throughout the twentieth century, schools and families have been used as venues where experts could mold children to the needs of the dominant social struc-ture. The pedagogical strategies evolved in this context were closely tied to the demands of regulation with their pre-determined outcomes and their assumption that the child was defective (not the social order). Pedagogies, accordingly, worked to adjust students to the social order—not vice versa. Working in tandem with these adjustment pedagogies were emerging administrative disciplines with their rule by technique. This rule by technique is defined as the use of standardized means for reaching a predetermined result. Using such an approach, administra-tors, managers, and other leaders were taught to run organizations and bureaucracies by applying linear forms of rationality that defer to effi-ciency as an end in itself. Goals of social change and cultural diversity were by nature inefficient, as standardization demanded narrow and precise objectives that could be quantified for efficient measurability. School principals did not administer schools in a manner that allowed culturally different students to create their own standards for success—there was one correct standard and regardless of background, all students would be held to it.

Given these modernist technicist tendencies, individuals come to learn quickly that there are right and wrong ways of being. As early as kindergarten, children learn that there are culturally correct and incorrect ways of doing things and that the adult way is usually the right way. Individuals in all walks of life devise ways of accomplishing the tasks that confront them. In the context of modernist discipline, such contextualized practitioner understandings or everyday ways of knowing are viewed by technicist administrators and managers as threats. Instead of nurturing and learning from them, organizations and their leaders often attempt to domesticate these "situated knowledges," reconfiguring them to the protocols of bureaucratic culture. When anthropologists, for example, study such situated ways of understanding, they begin to appreciate the cognitive similarity between the knowledge of "plain folks" and the knowledge of experts. Such realizations destroy the modernist illusion, the arrogant perception that certified experts' ways of seeing are obviously superior to the knowledge of the unwashed masses. This is why the techniques of production or teaching produced by the regulators are often viewed by their reality-grounded subordinates as textbook silliness (Christian-Smith and Erdman, 1997; Ferguson, 1984; Block, 1995; Jipson and Reynolds, 1997; Damarin, 1993).

Over the last couple of decades analysts from the new paradigm have launched an assault on the hyperrationality, the unethical nature, and the false-objectivity of modernist disciplinary and regulatory practices. The idea of a neutral detached observer of socio-psychological reality has been discounted over and over again in a variety of disciplines. In psychology, however, (especially in experimental, diagnostic, educational, and cognitive psychology) such provocative insights have not been widely accepted. Clutching the vestiges of Cartesian-Newtonian empiricism, contemporary modernist psychologists echo the belief that they are not involved in the social construction of what is deemed normality or abnormality. These are pre-existing, universalized, natural conditions, modernists contend, that exist separately from psychological perception. Their objective existence can be proven only by detached observation, disinterested control, and value-neutral intervention. Psychologists from the critical new paradigm reject such naturalized objectivity contending that all work in psychology is normatively committed, meaning that it is permeated with values and subjective prescriptions of worthy ways of being. In this normative context theoretical work in psychology always involves value judgments concerning which research topics are the most important to address, diagnostic work in psychology involves substantive assumptions about what constitutes normality and abnormality, and clinical work in psychology (psychotherapies) depends on a variety of value judgments including the distinction between maturity and regression, health and sickness, order and disorder, what (if anything) constitutes human nature, etc. . . .

While constantly denying its subjective status, modernist psychology has for decades been classifying and defining human behavior, even, at times, insidiously instructing people as to the meaning of their existence. As religions have sought to order behavior by delineating between good and evil, modernist psychology has used the dualism of sound-mindedness versus pathology. A cruel irony emerges here given the fact that psychology emerged as a liberatory impulse. Turning on its creators like a sci-fi robot "gone bad," psychology joined religion and government as another technology of hegemony. As a source of domination, psychology came to view normality, maturity, intelligence, and mental health as states of being closely aligned with the needs and values of the existing social order—in this manner sound-mindedness came to involve a conservative political disposition. This is what Nietzsche and Foucault were talking about when they argued that knowledge works as a henchman of power. Psychology served to regulate "dangerous populations" in a way that defined their critical dispositions, their anger at injustice, as pathologies. From this vantage point, privileged with the power of hindsight, the critique of modernist psychology from a new paradigmatic perspective appears justifiable, even necessary. Rationalistic social engineering had to be questioned in the name of democratic and civil-liberty-related values.

Modernist psychology as social regulator works from an instrumentally rational position. Critical analysts from the new paradigm have defined instrumental rationality as a cognitive disease of modernist hyperrationality. Instrumentally rational practices render questions of purpose subservient to questions of techniques. From such a perspective wholes are never more than the sum of their parts; houses are no more than the nails and lumber that go into them, and education is no more than the average number of objectives mastered. As instrumentally rational professionals lose their perspectives on the wholeness of their work or the larger purposes of their efforts, questions of ethics and morality also begin to fall by the wayside. Issues of justice, humanity, and compassion and their relationship to effective practice are irrelevant to instrumentally rational evaluation procedures. The effective practitioner is a master of means—questions of efficiency take precedence over moral vision. When the means/techniques are defined, multiple ways of exhibiting sound-mindedness or intelligence are irrelevant. Questions of difference in general or cultural context in particular in the production of knowledge are equally superfluous. Critical psychologists, rebelling against the ethical indifference and cultural decontextualization of instrumentally rational modernism, have sought a contextually embedded knowledge that is produced with an awareness of its limitations and incompleteness. Such "humble knowledge" is the product of a hermeneutical process, a subjective interpretation limited by the understanding that has emerged from a particular location in the social web of reality.

In light of our analysis of psychology as a regulatory practice, we are reminded of Nietzsche's famous question as to whether life is to dominate science or is science to dominate life. In modernist psychology the latter proposition has undoubtedly been the case. Nietzsche contended that science was a powerful force, requiring constant supervision. In our psychological context, such supervision might involve less interest in the simple production of psychological knowledge and more concern with hermeneutical issues of meaning making, with the ability of human beings to develop more satisfying and meaningful ways of living life and to connect learning, cognitive development, and self-understanding to that process (Levin, 1991; Giroux, 1992). Reflecting his uncanny intuition about knowledge production and the weaknesses of science, Albert Einstein serves as a model for creative ways of supervising science. Einstein sought to undercut "the adult vision" of the world produced by the science of his time. Rebelling against fixed psychological definitions of maturity/normality, Einstein held on to the questions and intuitions of his childhood—a time in his life (a "lower level" of development) when he was unacquainted with the adult perspectives of science. His ability to tap into such ways of seeing and being provided him not only with the cognitive germs of the Theory of Relativity but with a capacity for playfulness and joy repressed by others in the pursuit of a "mature" image and self-concept (Reynolds, 1987).

Naturalizing the Social: Modernist Psychological Magic— Turning Frogs into Princes, Values into Objective Propositions

Modernist psychology from the vantage point of the new paradigm is a fiction, indeed, its underlying assumptions are superstitions that Europeans came to agree upon. The model of the human mind presented by the discipline can be viewed in the same way we examine religious articles of faith—and, as religious dogmas, modernist psychological data often serves the interests of the priesthood, the bishops/scientists who guard the holy scriptures. Along this line, Jacques Lacan, the French psychoanalyst, maintained that psychology's conception of the self is a fiction, just as much an imaginary illusion as science's image of reality as a linear, cause-effect, knowable rational order. Drawing upon the spirit of Nietzsche, Heidegger, and Kafka, new paradigmatic psychology has sought to dismantle the science of the psyche's assumption of the harmonious and Western-defined reality. Despite these reservations modernist psychologists continue to claim objectivity for both their methodologies and the knowledge they produce. Indeed, as Piaget argued, intellectual growth is manifested by an individual grasping reality ever more objectively (King, 1996; Elliot, 1994; Vattimo, 1992; Hauptman and Hauptman, 1987).

Modernist psychology's claim of objectivity ignores the theoretical presuppositions present in any act of knowledge production regardless of whether this theoretical dimension is acknowledged or not. Empiricist psychologists who deny theoretical pre-assumptions in their work are great deceivers, wrapping themselves in the flag of objectivity while often unconsciously promoting specific values, world views, and paradigmatic faiths. Thus, psychologists who desire to counsel, assess, proscribe, research, diagnose, or promote development should engage in an analysis of the theories embedded in disciplinary models and explore how theory shapes the ways the field's hypotheses and truths are generated. To engage in psychological research and/or practice without analyzing the assumptions behind them is to guarantee problems in the long run (Levin, 1991). In the positivistic research that has dominated educational psychology, empirical inquiry has preceded conceptual/theoretical analysis. Without such analysis psychologists fail to understand that modernist empirical science only examines portions of the world—decontextualized portions at that. Indeed, to the empirical psychologist the world of the mind is only what science says it is (McNay, 1988; Yeakey, 1987). Theoretical deconstruction helps us expose the values implicit in both modernist psychology's world view and its perspective on research and knowledge production. Positivistic psychology is chained to the researcher/practitioner's prior theory, interest, and insight—it is "tainted" with subjectivity from the very beginning. Beginning with a question or a case that is important to them, psychological researchers/practitioners formulate a hypothesis or a treatment that is derived from a theoretical construct. The inquiry/procedure is then conducted in a prescribed manner that stays carefully within the boundaries of the established disciplinary procedure.

Nothing is disinterested or without theoretical presupposition in these psychological contexts. The new paradigm challenges these claims of objectivity, directing attention to various ways psychology is a participant in the social reality it examines, measures, and clinically intervenes. From the perspectives of post-formal practitioners psychological practices may disclose more about the discipline's tacit belief structures than they tell us about the individuals under examination. The same is true, of course, with psychological instruments. In many ways an I.Q. test, for example, works better as a cultural artifact than as a measurement of some mysterious innate mental ability. Through their analysis of I.Q. tests future cultural anthropologists might gain profound insights into the nature of success in the late twentieth century, what individuals and groups were more prone to be successful, and how knowledge was produced in the era. Even mainstream psychologists understand the vulnerability of sub-fields such as behavioral genetics to the personal prejudices of psychologists about the groups and individuals being assessed—far too often conclusions mirror assumptions (Levin, 1991; Appiah, 1995; Sedgwick, 1995).

The critique of psychology's unexamined assumptions lays the foundation for the post-formal reconceptualization of the discipline. In this critical (re)interpretive context it is necessary that work in all branches of psychology inform all other branches, not to mention the need for interaction between psychology and the social and cultural disciplinary domains. Educational psychology, for example, with its traditional emphasis on learners, learning, and teaching has often isolated these topics from larger psycho-social, cultural, and philosophical contexts. Using Cartesian-Newtonian empirical methodologies, mainstream educational psychology has attempted to focus on the processes by which information, skills, values, and attitudes have been transmitted from teachers to students. What exciting possibilities recent work in poststructuralist and feminist psychoanalysis could bring to the discourse of educational psychology. Once psychoanalysis is engaged with recent advances in social/cultural theory, questions, for example, of repressed desire will be viewed in the context of power relations and issues of unconscious passion will be studied in relation to the process of cultural reproduction (Elliot, 1994). As a result of such activity, educational psychology cannot remain the same. A critical metamorphosis will take place that moves the discourse to a new level of insight.

The Cultural Inscription of the Psychological Processes

Using a variety of socio-psychological modes of inquiry including post-structuralist psychoanalysis, students of the mind gain new angles from which to make sense of personal life. Lacanian psychoanalysis's emphasis, for instance, on the ways social institutions shape individual subjectivity is essential knowledge for educational psychologists seeking to trace the subtle ways schooling inscribes student consciousness. Vygotskian cognitivism alerts these same psychologists to the ways social relationships and cultural context are not only influential in cognitive development but are the sources of the mind. When the understandings of psychometricians do not include such cultural appreciations, these specialists in measurement/assessment will perceive no problem with standardized tests being prepared by people from only one culture. What's the problem, they may ask, intelligence is intelligence no matter where it's found. In the same sense knowledge is knowledge; so, (as Gilda Radner's Emily Lattella character used to say) "what is all this fuss. . . ?" Because psychology is an important aspect of the social and political world, the discipline has responsibilities to it. The socio-cultural dynamics that shape psychological functions do not alert us simply to methodological features of the scholarly conversation—from a critical perspective they focus our attention on the human damage that results from the cultural blindness of professionals in psychological positions. When cultural difference is confused with, for example, mental deficiency or pathological behavior, serious ethical questions arise.

If we accept Lacan's and poststructuralism's view of the modernist notion of an inner "authentic" self as a fiction and that there is no biological schema that presets behavior in advance, then we will find it difficult to accept Piagetian developmentalism. Post-formal psychology interrogates the foundations on which developmental psychology is grounded, positing that there are: 1) no predetermined stages to human development existing independently of an individual's personal history or social group(s) affiliation; and 2) no genetically-programmed stages of intellectual maturation. Cognitive science's taxonomies are merely heuristic, tools for facilitating understanding—not descriptions, as many assume, of an absolute independent reality. Indeed, post-formal psychology finds nothing wrong with Piaget's efforts to discern patterns in child maturation, William Perry's attempt to identify levels of commonality in adult modes of thinking, or Freud's isolation of syndromes and disorders. There is no difficulty with such academic work as long as the theorists and their faithful followers don't take the insights as the truth. Piaget, Perry, and Freud's work are mere constructs, conceived in particular times and places about individuals carrying particular cultural and historical baggage.

Lev Vygotsky alerted us to these problems of reification (to naturalize that which human beings, social processes, have created) and universalization of cognitive theorizing. Arguing for the need for social contextualization (a contention supported by cognitive scientists such as Jerome Bruner) Vygotsky turned his attention to the ways cognitive development occurred rather than pursuing stage theory. Development is much more complex, constantly changing as it unfolds—a post-formal cognitive psychology views cognitive growth as a dynamic hermeneutic, a process of culturally inscribed meaning making and knowledge production that continues throughout one's entire life. Such a reconceptualization holds dramatic implications for pedagogy, as it rejects traditional developmentalist notions that education should guide students through their natural phases of development. Instruction, Vygotsky maintained, does not follow children's "cognitive unfoldment" to some genetically-programmed developmental plateau. In this pedagogical context post-formal psychology understands the damage that modernist cognitive science's notions of developmental appropriateness inflict on the economically and culturally marginalized. Riddled with ethnocentric and class-biased conceptions of where children should be along the developmental spectrum at any particular age, modernist psychology's discourse of developmental appropriateness makes no allowance for the ravages of poverty, racism, or other forms of disadvantage in many children's lives. In the name of ordering the experiences of students who are "developmentally arrested" compensatory programs overstructure marginalized students' school routines to the point that meaningful self-initiated play and other activities are eliminated. Thus, cognitive psychology through its labeling and pedagogical prescriptions actually creates and perpetuates a disempowered consciousness among the marginalized that exacerbates their academic and vocational disadvantage (Marsh, 1993; Tanaka, 1996; Elliot, 1994; Levin, 1991; Driscoll, 1994; Russell, 1993; Polakow, 1992).

Naturalization and Reductionism

The various branches of psychology formulated within the modernist Cartesian-Newtonian laboratory are some of the greatest perpetrators of the sin of naturalization. Cognitive psychology's presentation of statistical relationships as natural laws, "g" as natural and stable, and I.Q. test scores as intelligence, covers up the human construction of such notions with all their social, political, and economic assumptions. When psychometricians, for example, contend that I.Q. is "normally distributed," they have implicitly assumed that I.Q. scores constitute I.Q. (read, intelligence), this intelligence exists inside the mind as a material entity, and this material mental entity has been proportionally passed out to human beings by nature itself—thus, providing beneficent nature's seal of approval, the validation of naturalization. Mysteriously absent in the public conversation about cognition, however, is the realization that standardized intelligence tests are devised and revised until they produce a normal distribution, a bell curve. Claims of natural cognitive laws ring hollow in this contrived scientific context. Indeed, modernist psychology's use of terms such as natural laws and human nature make it look like the mind is independent of history or culture (Anderson, 1994; Alford, 1993).

The political dynamics of this interrelationship between mind and culture confront us at this point in our reconceptualization of psychology. The political (power-related) dynamics of the social confront us with the role of power in the shaping of consciousness. Our new paradigmatic emphasis on the fiction of the pre-existent, innate self forces us to face some complex problems. Many critical analysts argue that if we deny the existence of an innate, pre- social self then concepts such as ideology lose their meaning, implying as they do that the ideology of the power wielders distorts the socially-pure self. The concept of ideology, I believe, can play a valuable role in understanding both the micro-social production of the individual subject and the macro-social perpetuation of the status quo. If we view ideology as simply one dynamic in a larger socio-political constellation of influences, notions of the production of "false consciousness" do not have to be employed with their implication of a corresponding "authentic consciousness"—i.e., a pre-social self. In this conceptual context we can refute the reductionistic nature of modernist psychology's disposition to naturalization. At this point we can begin to analyze the ways that ideological power complements disciplinary power's shaping of subjectivity.

A well-developed understanding of power is essential in understanding modernist psychology's efforts to naturalize the mind. A postformal psychology is committed to the analysis of the way macro-social processes. To understand the way identity doesn't simply exist but is created, to appreciate the Freudian assertion that reality is not pre-given but is fashioned by human beings to grasp the fact that the unconscious is not a biologically-bounded black box but just as much a social construction as any other aspect of the psyche, one must appreciate the emerging scholarship on social processes and the influence of power. Such new paradigmatic scholarship refuses to accept the reductionism common to mainstream psychology that reduces complex processes to separate syndromes or stages on the basis of a single criterion. This reductionism views psychological truth as a knowledge of discrete and stabilized stages. Typically, such a reductionist psychology is grounded on an epistemology that is unable to deal with transitional states, entities in process—e.g., I.Q. is not genetically fixed but a rather insignificant signpost in an ever-changing, socially-contingent process (Elliot, 1994; Lave and Wenger, 1991; Driscoll, 1994). Such a reductionist science, thus, is blinded to the possibility of growth or breakthroughs that can occur with a change of socio-cultural and political context. It is blinded to the possibility of a pedagogy that refuses to give in to the determinism of psychological classifications. A post-formal educational psychology is a discourse of hope that is optimistic about the ability of humans operating on their own recognizance. In this context the authors of *The Post-formal Reader: Cognition and Education* have written the following chapters about what it means to question educational psychology in a variety of pedagogical and cultural situations. They all agree that it holds great possibility for human potential and great insight into the way power creates human incompetence.

References

Abercrombie, N. (1994). Authority and consumer society. In R. Keat, N. Whiteley, and N. Abercrombie, *The authority of the consumer*. New York: Routledge.

Alford, C. (1993). Introduction to the special issue on political psychology and political theory. *Political Psychology,* 14(2), 199–208.

Allison, C. (1995). *Present and past: Essays for teachers in the history of education.* New York: Peter Lang.

Altrichter, H. and Posch, P. (1989). Does the "grounded theory" approach offer a guiding paradigm for teacher research? *Cambridge Journal of Education,* 1(9), 21–31.

Alvesson, M. and Willmott, H. (1992). On the idea of emancipation in management and organizational studies. *Academy of Management Review,* 17(3), 432–64.

Anderson, M. (1994). The many and varied social constructions of intelligence. In T. Sarbin and J. Kitsuse (Eds.), *Constructing the social.* Thousand Oaks, CA: Sage.

Anthony, C. (1995). Ecopsychology and the destruction of whiteness. In T. Roszak, M. Gomes, and A. Kanner (Eds.), *Ecopsychology: restoring the earth, healing the mind.* San Francisco, CA: Sierra Club Books.

Appiah, K. (1995). Straightening out The Bell Curve. In R. Jacoby and N. Glauberman (Eds.), *The Bell Curve debate: history, documents, and opinion.* New York: Random House.

Aronowitz, S. (1993). *Roll over Beethoven: The return of cultural strife.* Hanover, New Hampshire: Wesleyan University Press.

Ball, T. (1992). New faces of power. In T. Wartenberg (Ed.), *Rethinking power.* Albany, New York: SUNY Press.

Barrett, G. (1985). Thinking, knowledge, and writing: A critical examination of the learning process in schools. Paper presented to the International Writing Convention, University of East Anglia, Norwich.

Beardsley, T. (1995). For whom the Bell Curve really tolls. In R. Jacoby and N. Glauberman (Eds.), *The Bell Curve debate: History, documents, and opinion.* New York: Random House.

Beck, U. (1992). *Risk society: Towards a new modernity.* Trans. M. Ritter. London: Sage.

Benson, G. (1989). Epistemology and the science curriculum. *Journal of Curriculum Studies,* 21(4), 329–44.

Berger, B. (1995). Methodological fetishism. In R. Jacoby and N. Glauberman (Eds.), *The Bell Curve debate: History, documents and opinion.* New York: Random House.

Block, A. (1995). *Occupied reading: Critical foundations for an ecological theory.* New York: Garland.

Bohm D. and Edwards, M. (1991). *Changing consciousness.* San Francisco: Harper Collins.

Bohm, D. and Peat, F. (1987). *Science, order and creativity.* New York: Bantam Books.

Borgmann, A. (1992). *Crossing the postmodern divide.* Chicago: University of Chicago Press.

Capra, F., Steindl-Rast D., and Matus T. (1991). *Belonging to the universe: New thinking about god and nature.* New York: Penguin.

Carey, J. (1995). Clever arguments, atrocious science. In R. Jacoby and N. Glauberman (Eds.), *The Bell Curve debate: History, documents, and opinion.* New York: Random House.

Carlson, D. (1991). Alternative discourses in multicultural education: Towards a critical reconstruction of a curricular field. Paper presented to the Bergamo Conference on Curriculum Theory and Classroom Practice. Dayton, Ohio.

Childley, J. (1995). The heart of the matter. In R. Jacoby and N. Glauberman (Eds.), *The Bell Curve debate: History, documents, and opinion.* New York, Random House.

Christian-Smith, L. and Erdman J. (1997). Mom, it's not real: Children constructing childhood through reading horror fiction. In S. Steinberg and J. Kincheloe (Eds.), *Kinderculture: Corporate constructions of childhood.* Boulder, CO: Westview.

Codd, J. (1984). Introduction. In J. Codd (Ed.), *Philosophy, common sense and action in educational administration.* Victoria, Australia: Deakin University Press.

Collins, A. (1994). Intellectuals, power, and quality television. In H. Giroux and P. McLaren (Eds.), *Between borders: Pedagogy and the politics of cultural studies.* New York: Routledge.

Cooper, D. (1994). Productive, relational, and everywhere? Conceptualizing power and resistance within Foucauldian feminism. *Sociology,* 28(2), 435–54.

Courtney, R. (1988). *No one way of being: A study of the practical knowledge of elementary arts teachers.* Toronto: MGS Publications.

Damarin, S. (1993). Schooling and situated knowledge: Travel or tourism? *Educational Technology,* 27–32.

Denzin, N. (1987). Postmodern children. *Caring for Children/Society,* 32–5.

Donald, J. (1993). The natural man and the virtuous woman: Reproducing citizens. In C. Jenks (Ed.), *Cultural reproduction.* New York: Routledge.

Driscoll, M. (1994). *Psychology of learning for instruction.* Boston: Allyn and Bacon.

Easterbrook, G. (1995). Blacktop basketball and the Bell Curve. In R. Jacoby and N. Glauberman (Eds.), *The Bell Curve debate: History, documents and opinion.* New York: Random House.

Elliot, A. (1994). *Psychoanalytic theory: An introduction.* Cambridge, MA: Blackwell.

Ferguson, K. (1984). *The feminist case against bureaucracy.* Philadelphia: Temple University Press.

Ferguson, M. (1980). *The Aquarian conspiracy: Personal and social transformation in our time.* Los Angeles: J.P. Tarcher, Inc.

Finke, L. (1993). Knowledge as bait: Feminism, voice, and the pedagogical unconsciousness. *College English,* 55(1), 7–27.

Fiske, J. (1993). *Power plays, power works.* New York: Verso.

Fiske, J. (1994). Audiencing: Cultural practice and cultural studies. In N. Denzin and Y. Lincoln (Eds.), *Handbook of qualitative research.* Thousand Oaks, CA: Sage.

Fosnot, C. (1988). The dance of education. Paper presented to the Annual Conference of the Association for Educational Communication and Technology, New Orleans.

Gardner, H. (1995). Cracking open the I.Q. box. In S. Fraser (Ed.), *The Bell Curve wars: Race, intelligence, and the future of America.* New York: Basic Books.

Garman, N. and Hazi, H. (1988). Teachers ask: Is there life after Madeline Hunter? *Phi Delta Kappan,* 69, 670–72.

Giroux, H. (1992). *Border crossings: Cultural workers and the politics of education.* New York: Routledge.

Giroux, H. (1993). *Living dangerously: Multiculturalism and the politics of difference.* New York: Peter Lang.

Giroux, H. (1994). *Disturbing pleasures: Learning popular culture.* New York: Routledge.

Giroux, H. (1997). *Pedagogy and the politics of hope: Theory, culture, and schooling.* Boulder, CO: Westview.

Gould, S. (1995). Curveball. In S. Fraser (Ed.), *The Bell Curve wars: Race, intelligence, and the future of America.* New York: Basic Books.

Greene, M. (1988). *The dialectic of freedom.* New York: Teachers College Press.

Greene, M. (1995). *Releasing the imagination: Essays on education, the arts, and social change.* San Francisco: Jossey-Bass.

Grimmett, P., Erickson, G., MacKinnon, A. and Riecken T. (1990). Reflective practice in teacher education. In R. Clift, W. Houston, and M. Pugach, *Encouraging reflective practice in education: An analysis of issues and programs.* New York: Teachers College Press.

Grossberg, L. (1995). What's in a name (one more time)? *Taboo: The Journal of Culture and Education*, 1, 1–37.

Hanks, W. (1991). Introduction. In J. Lave and E. Wenger, *Situated learning: Legitimate peripheral participation.* New York: Cambridge University Press.

Hauptman, R. and Hauptman, I. (1987). The circuitous path: Albert Einstein and the epistemology of fiction. In D. Ryan (Ed.), *Einstein and the humanities.* New York: Greenwood Press.

Haymes, S. (1996). Race, repression, and the politics of crime and punishment in the Bell Curve. In J. Kincheloe, S. Steinberg and A. Gresson (Eds.), *Measured lies: The Bell Curve examined.* New York: St. Martin's Press.

Held, D. (1980). *Introduction to critical theory.* Berkeley: University of California Press.

Henriques, J., Hollway, W., Venn, C., Walkerdine, V., and Urwin, C. (Eds.). (1984). *Changing the subject: Psychology, social regulation and subjectivity.* New York: Methuen.

Herrnstein, R. and Murray, C. (1994). *The Bell Curve: Intelligence and class structure in American life.* New York: The Free Press.

Holt, J. (1995). Skin deep science. In R. Jacoby and N. Glauberman (Eds.), *The Bell Curve debate: History, documents, and opinion.* New York: Random House.

Hultgren, F. (1987). Critical thinking: Phenomenological and critical foundations. In Ruth G. Thomas (Ed.), *Higher-order thinking: Definition, meaning and instructional approaches.* Washington, D.C.: Home Economics Education Association.

Hutcheon, L. (1988). *A poetics of postmodernism.* New York: Routledge.

Jipson, J. and Reynolds U. (1997). Anything you want: Women and children in popular culture. In S. Steinberg and J. Kincheloe (Eds.), *Kinderculture: Corporate constructions of childhood.* Boulder Colorado: Westview.

Jones, J. (1995). Back to the future with The Bell Curve: Joe Crow, slavery, and G. In S. Fraser (Ed.), *The Bell Curve wars: Race, intelligence, and the future of America.* New York: Basic Books.

Kamin, L. (1995). Lies, damned lies, and statistics. In R. Jacoby and N. Glauberman (Eds.), *The Bell Curve debate: History, documents, and opinion.* New York: Random House.

Kaufman, B. (1978). Piaget, Marx, and the political ideology of schooling. *Journal of Curriculum Studies,* 10(1), 19–44.

Kellner, D. (1989). *Critical theory, Marxism, and modernity.* Baltimore: Johns Hopkins University Press.

King, J. (1996). Bad luck, bad blood, bad faith: Ideological hegemony and the oppressive language of hoodoo social science. In J. Kincheloe, S. Steinberg and A. Gresson (Eds.), *Measured lies: The Bell Curve examined.* New York: St. Martin's Press.

King, J. and Mitchell, C. (1995). *Black mothers to sons.* New York: Peter Lang.

Lave, J. and Wenger, E. (1991). *Situated learning: Legitimate peripheral participation.* New York: Cambridge University Press.

Levin, D. (1991). Psychology as a discursive formation: The postmodern crisis. *The Humanistic Psychologist,* 19(3) 250–76.

Lincoln, Y. (1996). For whom the bell tolls: A cognitive or educated elite? In J. Kincheloe, S. Steinberg and A. Gresson (Eds.), *Measured lies: The Bell Curve examined.* New York: St. Martin's Press.

Macedo, D. (1994). *Literacy of power: What Americans are not allowed to know.* Boulder, CO: Westview Press.

Marsh, D. (1993). Freire, Vygotsky, special education, and me. *British Columbia Journal of Special Education,* 17(2), 119–34.

McCarthy, C. et al. (1996). The last rational men: Citizenship, morality, and the pursuit of human perfection. In J. Kincheloe, S. Steinberg, and A. Gresson (Eds.), *Measured lies: The Bell Curve examined.* New York, St. Martin's Press.

McCarthy, T. (1992). The critique of impure reason: Foucault and the Frankfurt School. In T. Wartenberg (Ed.), *Rethinking power.* Albany, NY: SUNY Press.

McLaren, P., Hammer, R., Reilly, S.,and Sholle D. (1995). *Rethinking media literacy: A critical pedagogy of representation.* New York: Peter Lang.

McNay, M. (1988). Educational research and the nature of science. *The Educational Forum,* 52(4), 353–362.

Merelman, R. (1986). Domination, self-justification, and self-doubt: Some social-psychological considerations. *Journal of Politics,* 48, 276–99.

Moll, I. (1991). The material and the social in Vygotsky' theory and cognitive development. Paper presented at the Biennial Meeting of the Society for Research in Child Development. Seattle, Washington.

Munby, H. and Russell, T. (1989). Educating the reflective teacher: An essay review of two books by Donald Schön. *Journal of Curriculum Studies,* 21, 71–80.

Nisbett, R. (1995). Race, IQ, and scientism. In S. Fraser (Ed.), *The Bell Curve wars: Race, intelligence, and the future of America.* New York: Basic Books.

Pinar, W., Reynolds, W., Slattery, P. and Taubman, P. (1995). *Understanding curriculum.* New York: Peter Lang.

Polakow, V. (1992). *The erosion of childhood.* Chicago, IL: University of Chicago Press.

Postman, N. (1994). *The disappearance of childhood.* New York: Vintage Books.

Raizen, S. (1989). *Reforming education for work: A cognitive science perspective.* Berkeley, CA: NCRVE.

Raspberry, W. (1995). Only racists will cheer this. *Centre Daily Times* (State College, Pennsylvania), September 23, p. A2.

Reynolds, R. (1987). Einstein and psychology: The genetic epistemology of relativistic physics. In D. Ryan (Ed.), *Einstein and the humanities.* New York: Greenwood Press.

Russell, D. (1993). Vygotsky, Dewey, and externalism: Beyond the student/discipline dichotomy. *Journal of Advanced Composition,* 13(1), 173–97.

Ryan, A. (1995). Apocalypse now? In R. Jacoby and N. Glauberman (Eds.), *The Bell Curve debate: History, documents and opinion.* New York: Random House.

Sedgwick, J. (1995). Inside the Pioneer Fund. In R. Jacoby and N. Glauberman (Eds.), *The Bell Curve debates: History, documents, and opinion.* New York: Random House.

Shapiro, M. (1992). *Reading the postmodern polity: Political theory as textual practice.* Minneapolis: University of Minnesota Press.

Shor, I. (1992). *Empowering education: Critical teaching for social change.* Chicago, IL: University of Chicago Press.

Slattery, P. (1995). *Curriculum development in the postmodern era.* New York: Garland.

Tanaka, G. (1996). Dysgenesis and white culture. In J. Kincheloe, S. Steinberg and A. Gresson (Eds.), *Measured lies: The Bell Curve examined.* New York: St. Martin's Press.

Terkel, S. (1972). *Working.* New York: Avon.

Thompson, J. (1987). Language and ideology: A framework for analysis. *The Sociological Review, 35,* 516–36.

Trend, D. (1994). Nationalities, pedagogies, and media. In H. Giroux and P. McLaren (Eds.), *Between borders: Pedagogy and the politics of cultural studies.* New York: Routledge.

Vattimo, G. (1992). *The end of modernity.* Baltimore: John Hopkins University Press.

Voorhees, B. and Royce, J. (1987). Einstein and epistemology. In D. Ryan (Ed.), *Einstein and the humanities.* New York: Greenwood Press.

Werstch, J. and Tulviste, P. (1992). L.S. Vygotsky and contemporary developmental psychology. *Developmental Psychology, 28*(4), 548–557.

White, H. (1978). *Topics of discourse: Essays in cultural criticism.* Baltimore: The Johns Hopkins University Press.

Wirth, A. (1983). *Productive work—in industry and schools.* Lanham, MD: University Press of America.

Wright, R. (1995). The evolution of despair. *Time,* August 28, 146(9), 50–57.

Yeakey, C. (1987). Critical thought and administrative theory: Conceptual approaches to the study of decision-making. *Planning and Changing,* 18(1), 23–32.

Zunker, V. (1986). *Career counseling: Applied concepts of life planning.* Monterey, CA: Brooks/Cole Publishing.

CHAPTER TWO

A Tentative Description of Post-formal Thinking: The Critical Confrontation with Cognitive Theory

Joe L. Kincheloe and Shirley R. Steinberg

Postmodern analysis, though diverse in the ways it is conceptualized, has consistently laid bare the assumptions of Cartesian logic by exposing the ways that the structure of traditional science constructs imaginary worlds. Science, like a novel, is "written"; both the novel and science operate according to the arbitrary rules of a language game. Such postmodern understandings confront us with a dramatic socio-educational dilemma: how do we function in the midst of such uncertainty?

The contemporary debate over postmodernism is often framed in all-or-nothing terms—we can either completely accept or completely reject Western modernism. In our work, we have sought a middle ground that attempts to hold onto the progressive and democratic features of modernism while drawing upon the insights postmodernism provides concerning the failure of reason, the tyranny of grand narratives,[1] the limitations of science, and the repositioning of relationships between dominant and subordinate cultural groups.[2] In such complex and changing times, we, as critical educators, turn to our emancipatory system of meaning, grounded as it is in feminist notions of passionate knowing, African American epistemologies, subjugated knowledges[3] (ways of knowing that have been traditionally excluded from the conversation of mainstream educators), liberation-theological ethics, and the progressive modernist concerns with justice, liberty, and equality. As we temper our system of meaning with a dose of postmodern self-analysis and epistemological (or maybe post-epistemological) humility, we move to a new zone of cognition—a post-formal way of thinking.

Formal thinking à la Piaget implies an acceptance of a Cartesian-Newtonian mechanistic worldview that is caught in a cause-effect, hypothetical-deductive system of reasoning. Unconcerned with questions of power relations and the way they structure our consciousness, formal operational thinkers accept an objectified, unpoliticized way of knowing that breaks a social or educational system down into its basic parts in order to understand how it works. Emphasizing certainty and prediction, formal thinking organizes verified facts into theory. The facts that do not fit into the theory are eliminated, and the theory developed is the one best suited to limit contradictions in knowledge. Thus, formal thought operates on the assumption that resolution must be found for all contradictions. Schools and standardized testmakers, assuming that formal operational thought represents the highest level of human cognition, focus their efforts on its cultivation and measurement. Students and teachers who move beyond formality are often unrewarded and sometimes even punished in educational contexts.

This article attempts to define the type of thinking that might occur when individuals, and teachers in particular, move beyond the boundaries of Piagetian formality. Many theorists (Lave, 1988; Walkerdine, 1984, 1988) over the last two decades have sought to formulate a post-Piagetian cognitive theory. Too often, however, they have not used a social theoretical analysis to construct a critique and a new vision of cognitive theory. In some ways, Piaget anticipated our theoretical project as he and Rolando Garcia (Piaget and Garcia, 1989) discussed the impact of social and epistemic paradigms in shaping cognitive systems. Unfamiliar, however, with critical postmodern analysis of subjectivity and power, Piaget was limited as to how far his intuitions could take him. Even with such limitations, Piaget often understood far more than many of his students about the situated nature of cognition (Walkerdine, 1984, 1988). Nevertheless, he did not connect this situatedness with any effort to break the confines imposed by the abstract rationality of the formal stage. Grounded in an understanding of critical and postmodern advances in social theory, we attempt to develop a *socio*-cognitive theory that draws upon the evolving discourses and moves beyond the monolithic essentialism[4] of the past.

Moving to post-formality, critical educators politicize cognition; they attempt to disengage themselves from socio-personal norms and ideological expectations. The post-formal concern with questions of meaning, emancipation via ideological disembedding,[5] and attention to the process of self-production rises above the formal operational level of thought and its devotion to proper procedure. Post-formalism grapples with purpose, devoting attention to issues of human dignity, freedom, authority, and social responsibility. Many will argue that a post-formal mode of thinking with its emphasis on multiple perspectives will necessitate an ethical relativism that paralyzes social action. A more critical post-formality grounded in our emancipatory system of meaning does not cave in to relativistic social paralysis. Instead, it initiates reflective dialogue between critical theory and postmodernism—a dialogue that is always concerned with the expansion of self-awareness and consciousness, never certain of emancipation's definition, and perpetually reconceptualizing the system of meaning. Critical theory, in brief, refers to the tradition developed by the Frankfurt School[6] in Germany in the 1920s. Max Horkheimer, Theodor Adorno, and others attempted to rethink the meaning of human self-direction or emancipation, to develop a theory of non-dogmatic social transformation, to expose the hidden social relationships of the everyday world, and to analyze the problems of social theories that celebrated social harmony without questioning the assumptions of the larger society. In a sense, the dialogue between critical theory and postmodernism produces a theoretical hesitation, a theoretical stutter.

One of the main features of post-formal thinking is that it expands the boundaries of what can be labeled sophisticated thinking. When we begin to expand these boundaries, we find that those who were excluded from the community of the intelligent seem to cluster around exclusions based on the premise that some people are intelligent and others aren't (Case, 1985; Klahr and Wallace, 1976). Intelligence and creativity are thought of as fixed and innate, while at the same time mysterious qualities found only in the privileged few. The modernist grand narrative of intelligence has stressed biological fixities that can be altered only by surgical means. Such an essentialism is a psychology of nihilism that locks people into rigid categories that follow them throughout life (Bozik, 1987; Lawler, 1975; Maher and Rathbone, 1986). Howard Gardner's work, thought not situated in the postmodernist tradition, has criticized this type of rigid modernism. This article positively draws from Gardner's critiques and theories. At the same time, it attempts to move beyond some of Gardner's ideas by connecting the political realm to the cognitive (Gardner, 1983, 1989, 1991).

The developmentalism of Piaget, while claiming a dialetical[7] interaction between mind and environment, still falls captive to the grand narrative of intelligence. The theory walks into its own captivity because it views intelligence as a process that culminates in an individual's mastery of formal logical categories—a mastery born of thinking that is separate from, disconnected from, the external environment. This conception reflects the innate fixity of earlier Cartesian-Newtonian views of intelligence as a specter emerging from innate inner structures. The early Piaget, in particular, maintained that the desired pedagogical course was to move students' development away from the emotions so rationality could dominate the progress of the mind. Stages were thus constructed around this logocentrism—stages that would become key supports in the commonsense, unquestioned knowledge about intelligence (Piaget, 1970, 1977; Piaget and Inhelder, 1968).

Feminist theory challenges this meta-narrative,[8] arguing that cognizance of social construction of individuals and the inseparability of rationality and emotion causes us to question essential categories of human development. Feminists ask us to examine the difference between masculine and feminine ways of knowing (Belenky, Clinchy, Goldberger, and Tarule, 1986). The masculine, of course, represents the "proper" path for human cognitive development. Proposing that intelligence be reconceptualized in a manner that makes use of various ways of thinking, feminist theorists teach us that intelligence is not an innate quality of a particular individual but, rather, something related to the interrelationship among ideas, behaviors, contexts, and outcomes (Bozik, 1987; Lawler, 1975; Walkerdine, 1984).

Developmental psychological principles have become so much a part of teacher education programs that it is hard to see where questions about them might arise. Not understanding the etymology of cognitive developmentalism, educators are unable to see it as a system of scientific classification. Developmentalism hides behind its claim of "freeing the child" from traditional methods of instruction, protecting its identity as an order of regulation on which child-centered pedagogy has been established. Critical constructivism (a constructivism grounded on an understanding of critical theory and postmodernism) along with post-formal thinking seeks to expose developmentalism as a specific socio-historical construction grounded in a specific set of assumptions about the mind. Developmentalism is not the only way to view intelligence. As we have come to see individualized instruction and child-centered pedagogy as a set of regulated and normalized progressive stages, we have missed the rather obvious point that individuals operate simultaneously at divergent cognitive stages. For example, an eight-year-old may employ particular skills with a computer that certainly reflect a formal-like thinking, while his or her understanding of US politics reflects a more concrete-like cognitive stage. Indeed, is what Piaget described as formal thinking a "universal" stage in cognitive development? When we examine the percentage of adults who "fail" when assessed by this formal standard, its universality is brought into question. The irony in the twentieth century's history of developmental psychology is that in its concern with individual freedom and the production of a rationality that could save human beings in their struggle for survival, it produced a system of cognitive and pedagogical apparatuses that delimited and rigidly defined the normalized individual. The biological capacities developmentalism has designated have ensured that even progressive teachers often view the child as an object of scientific pronouncement and, in the process, have undermined the liberation promised (Maher and Rathbone, 1986; Riegal, 1973; Walkerdine, 1984).

Indeed, the child in the developmentalist discourse is often viewed, within an ethic of Lockean individualism, as an isolated entity. Critical studies (Bourdieu and Passeron, 1977; McLaren, 1986; McLeod, 1987) have long maintained that children come to school with disparate amounts of cultural capital[9] or awareness that can be traded in for advantage in the school microcosm. Knowledge of white middle-class language, concern for academic success, and the ability to deport oneself in a "courteous" manner all contribute to one's advantage at school. Metaphorical constructs and meaning-making frameworks brought to school by African American, Latino, or other children who do not come from white middle-class backgrounds are often dismissed as developmentally inappropriate. Because developmentalism fails to ground itself within a critical understanding of the power relationships of dominant and subordinate cultures, it has often privileged white middle-class notions of meaning and success (O'Loughlin, 1992). Liberatory outcomes are far from the consciousness of many curriculum makers who ground their work in the discourse of child development.

Liberatory intent is also betrayed when we fail to address the critical-constructivist concern with the social construction of mind. In the same way that Cartesian-Newtonian science strips away the layers of the social from our analysis, cognitive development is essentialized. The social features (race, class, gender, place) that influence patterns and definitions of development are ignored, allowing what are actually social constructions to be seen as natural processes. Here rests the practical value of the postmodern critique with its decentering[10] of the subject. Not allowing for a pre-existent essence of self, postmodernism

denies the existence of men and women outside of the socio-historical
process. The grand narrative of liberal individualism is thus subverted,
for objects of any type (especially knower and known, self and world)
cannot be defined in isolation to one another. Cognitive development,
then, is not a static, innate dimension of human beings; it is always
interactive when the environment, always in the process of being
reshaped and reformed. We are not simply victims of genetically determined, cognitive predispositions (Lawler, 1975; Walkerdine, 1984).

The postmodern critique not only undermines cognitive essentialism, it also subverts socio-cognitive reductionism.[11] The normalization
of social control along the lines of scientifically validated norms of
development and conduct implicit within developmentalism is not the
outcome of some repressive power broker determined to keep individuals in their place. Power manifests itself not through some explicit
form of oppression but via the implicit reproduction of the self. Thus,
advocates of critical thinking will operate within the boundaries of
developmentalism with its predetermined definitions of normality;
these advocates teach and learn within its gravitational field. The task
of those who understand both the social contextualization of thinking
and the postmodern critique of its discursive practices is to overthrow
these reductionistic views of the way power works. When we view the
effect of power on the way we define intelligence or when we construct
consciousness as some simple cause-effect process, we forfeit our grasp
on reality and lose our connection to the rhythms of social life (de
Lauretis, 1986; Walkerdine, 1984). Post-formal thinking attempts to
conceive cognition in a manner that transcends the essentialist and
reductionist tendencies within developmentalism, coupling an appreciation of the complexity of self-production and the role of power with
some ideas about what it means to cross the borders of modernist thinking.

Since one of the most important features of post-formal thinking
involves the production of one's own knowledge, it becomes important
to note in any discussion of the characteristics of post-formality that few
boundaries exist to limit what may be considered post-formal thinking.
Post-formal thinking and post-formal teaching become whatever an
individual, a student, or a teacher can produce in the realm of new
understandings and knowledge within the confines of a critical system
of meaning. Much of what cognitive science and, in turn, the schools
have measured as intelligence consists of an external body of informa-

tion. The frontier where the information of the disciplines intersects with the understandings and experience that individuals carry with them to school is the point where knowledge is created (constructed). The post-formal teacher facilitates this interaction, helping students to reinterpret their own lives and uncover new talents as a result of their encounter with school knowledge.

Viewing cognition as a process of knowledge production presages profound pedagogical changes. Teachers who frame cognition in this way see their role as creators of situations where students experiences could intersect with information gleaned from the academic disciplines. In contrast, if knowledge is viewed as simply an external body of information independent of human beings, then the role of the teacher is to take this knowledge and insert it into the minds of students. Evaluation procedures that emphasize retention of isolated bits and pieces of data are intimately tied to this view of knowledge. Conceptual thinking is discouraged, as schooling trivializes learning. Students are evaluated on the lowest level of human thinking—the ability to memorize without contextualization. Thus, unless students are moved to incorporate school information into their own lives, schooling will remain merely an unengaging rite of passage into adulthood.

The point is clear: the way we define thinking exerts a profound impact on the nature of our schools, the role that teachers play in the world, and the shape that society will ultimately take. As we delineate the following characteristics of post-formal thinking, each feature contains profound implications for the future of teaching. Indeed, the post-formal thinking described in the following section can change both the tenor of schools and the future of teaching. Self-reflection would become a priority with teachers and students, as post-formal educators attend to the impact of school and society on the shaping of the self. In such a context, teaching and learning would be considered acts of meaning making that subvert the technicist[12] view of teaching as the mastering of a set of techniques. Teacher education could no longer separate technique from purpose, reducing teaching to a deskilled act of rule-following and concern with methodological format. A school guided by empowered post-formal thinkers would no longer privilege white male experience as the standard by which all other experiences are measured. Such realizations would point out a guiding concern with social justice and the way unequal power relations in school and society destroy the promise of democratic life. Post-formal teachers would no longer passively accept the pronouncements of standardized-test and curriculum makers without examining the social contexts in which their students live and the ways those contexts help shape student performance. Lessons would be reconceptualized in light of a critical notion of student understanding. Post-formal teachers would ask if their classroom experiences promote, as Howard Gardner puts it, the highest level of understanding that is possible (Gardner, 1991).

Our search for such understanding is enhanced by a delineation of the following four features of post-formal thinking: *etymology*—the exploration of the forces that produce what the culture validates as knowledge; *pattern*—the understanding of the connecting patterns and relationships that undergird the lived world; *process*—the cultivation of new ways of reading the world that attempt to make sense of both ourselves and contemporary society; and *contextualization*—the appreciation that knowledge can never stand alone or be complete in and of itself.

Etymology

The Origins of Knowledge
Many descriptions of higher-order thinking induce us to ask questions that analyze what we know, how we come to know it, why we believe it or reject it, and how we evaluate the credibility of the evidence. Post-formal thinking shares this characteristic of other descriptions of higher-order thinking but adds a critical hermeneutic[13] and historical epistemological dimension to the idea. In order to transcend formality, we must become critically exposed to our own tradition (and other transitions as well) so that we may understand the etymology of the cultural forms embedded within us. Antonio Gramsci (1988) noted that philosophy cannot be understood apart from the history of philosophy, nor can culture be grasped outside the history of culture. Our conception of self and world, therefore, can only become critical when we appreciate the historicity of its formation. We are never independent of the social and historical forces that surround us—we are caught at a particular point in the web of reality. The post-formal project is to understand what that point in the web is, how it constructs our vantage point, and the ways it insidiously restricts our vision. Post-formal teachers struggle to become aware of their own ideological inheritance and its relationship to their own beliefs and value structures, interests, and questions about their professional lives (Cherryholmes, 1988; Codd, 1984; Daines, 1987; Greene, 1988).

As historical epistemologists, post-formal thinkers understand the etymology of knowledge, the way that knowledge is produced and the specific forces that contribute to its production. The *Zeitgeist* influences knowledge production as it directs our attention to certain problems and potentialities—for example, the questions of equality emerging from the civil rights movement or the nature of religious fundamentalism coming from the rise of the New *Zeitgeist* changes or as multiple *Zeitgeists* complete in the same era, some bodies of information go out of fashion and are forgotten for the time being. Other bodies of knowledge are shelved because they seem to be tied to one particular research methodology and are not amenable to extension into different contexts. Thus, social and educational knowledge is vulnerable to the ebb and flow of time and the changing concerns and emotional swings of different eras. This vulnerability to the temporal will probably continue, for social science shows no sign of developing consistent universal strategies for evaluating the validity of these various forms of knowledge. Indeed, such a strategy would be positivistic[14] and suggest regression to a more formalistic mode of thinking (Fiske, 1986).

Post-formal thinkers concerned with epistemological etymology and their own subjective etymology have identified with Michel Foucault's (1984) notion of genealogy. By epistemological and subjective etymology, we are referring to: 1) the process by which social forces shape our understanding of what constitutes knowledge (is it a scientific process or are there other legitimate ways of knowing?); 2) the process by which social forces shape our subjectivities or, less subtly, our identities. Foucault uses the term "genealogy" to describe the process of tracing the formation of our own subjectivities. By recognizing the ambiguities and contradictions in the construction of their own subjectivities, post-formal teachers can better understand the complexities of their students' consciousnesses. As they engage in self-critical geneology, draw on our critical system of meaning, and employ action-research techniques, post-formal teachers become "ungrounded" and "unrigorous" from the perspective of the technicists who wag their fingers at their lack of technical procedure and formal systemization. Indeed, the self-critical genealogy and the critical action research that has grown out of it constitute an emancipatory "rite of post-formal passage," as teachers leave behind their cognitive past (Kincheloe, 1991). Exercising new insights, they come to formulate more penetrating questions about their classrooms, decipher connections between sociocultural meanings and the everyday life of school, and reconceptualize what they already "know." As post-formal teachers grow to understand the etymology of the race, class, and gender locations of the students and others they study, they come to appreciate their own etymology, their location, and the social relationships such as locations produce (Aronowitz, 1992; Miller, 1990; Reinharz, 1982).

Thinking about Thinking—
Exploring the Uncertain Play of the Imagination

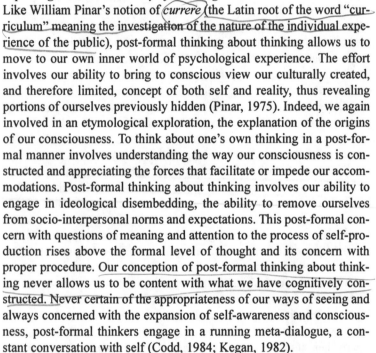

Like William Pinar's notion of *currere* (the Latin root of the word "curriculum" meaning the investigation of the nature of the individual experience of the public), post-formal thinking about thinking allows us to move to our own inner world of psychological experience. The effort involves our ability to bring to conscious view our culturally created, and therefore limited, concept of both self and reality, thus revealing portions of ourselves previously hidden (Pinar, 1975). Indeed, we again involved in an etymological exploration, the explanation of the origins of our consciousness. To think about one's own thinking in a post-formal manner involves understanding the way our consciousness is constructed and appreciating the forces that facilitate or impede our accommodations. Post-formal thinking about thinking involves our ability to engage in ideological disembedding, the ability to remove ourselves from socio-interpersonal norms and expectations. This post-formal concern with questions of meaning and attention to the process of self-production rises above the formal level of thought and its concern with proper procedure. Our conception of post-formal thinking about thinking never allows us to be content with what we have cognitively constructed. Never certain of the appropriateness of our ways of seeing and always concerned with the expansion of self-awareness and consciousness, post-formal thinkers engage in a running meta-dialogue, a constant conversation with self (Codd, 1984; Kegan, 1982).

Ancient Greeks mythologically portrayed this dialogue with self. They were fascinated by the lulls of profound silence that periodically spread across a room filled with conversation. The Greeks postulated that at such moments Hermes had entered the room. By silencing the everyday babble, Hermes allowed the Greeks to tap their imaginations, fears, hopes, and passions. Through this awareness they were freed from acting out socially constructed expectations they really didn't understand. Hermes came to symbolize the penetration of boundaries— boundaries that separated one culture from another, work from play, fantasy from reality, and consciousness from unconsciousness. As he connects us with the unconscious, Hermes becomes another in a long line of trickster gods whom ancients associated with the power of the imagination.

Post-formal thinking about thinking draws upon the boundary trespasses of Hermes and the playful parody of postmodernism to transgress the official constraints of our consciousness construction, to transcend modern convention by exposing its etymology and its ironic contradictions (Bohm and Peat, 1987; Combs and Holland, 1990; Hutcheon, 1988; Kramer, 1983; Van Hesteran, 1986). As Peter McLaren explains the postmodern double reading of the social world, he writes of a teaching disposition that encourages students to think about their thinking in a post-formal manner. Students learn to construct their identities in a way that parodies the rigid conventions of modernism, thus assuming the role of postmodern stand-up comics, social satirists (McLaren, forthcoming). Hermes, the playful trickster, mysteriously pops up everywhere with his fantasies, surprise inspirations, and other gifts of the imagination; they are ours for the taking if we can hold onto the silence long enough to listen to him, if we have not let social expectations crush our propensity for play (Kristeva, 1980).

Asking Unique Questions—Problem Detection
The technical rationality of modernism has long ignored the ability to ask unique questions and to detect problems as important aspects of higher-order intelligence. This modernist tradition has often reduced intelligence and, in turn, the work of teachers to problem-solving. Such cognitive reductionism restricts teaching tot he level of formal thinking and captures practitioners in a culture of bureaucratic technicalization where they simply seek solutions to problems defined by their superiors (Munby and Russell, 1989; Schön, 1983). When the work of teachers is reduced to mere problem-solving, a practitioner's ability to identify the problems of the classroom and to ask unique questions about them is neglected. Indeed, pedagogies of problem-solving and tests of intelligence that focus upon problem-solving ignore the initial steps of questioning and problem detecting, which are prerequisites to creative acts of learning and post-formal thinking (Courtney, 1988). Problem detecting is a far more holistic act than problem-solving, in that problem detecting demands understanding the goals of social justice and the etymology of those forces that undermine them. Such etymological appreciations shape our post-formal ability to detect contradictions, conflicts in the social order.

Problem detecting is undoubtedly a necessary precondition for technical problem-solving, although problem detecting is not itself a technical problem—it cannot be approached in a formalist procedural (technical) way. As a problem is detected, questions are formulated about a situation. In the process, a coherence is imposed on the situation that exposes asymmetries and helps cultivate an intuition for what might need to be changed about the situation. The context is framed in which an observation will be made. A body of past experiences and understandings is applied in this framing process to the situation in question. Problem detecting and the questioning that accompanies it become a form of world making in that the way these operations are conducted is contingent on the system of meaning employed. For example, a teacher in a multicultural education classroom may find that the texts recommended and the conception of the classroom conveyed by the course description encourage students to ask questions about the cultural identity of a variety of minority groups. Though it is not framed as a problem in the traditional conversation about multicultural education, the post-formal teacher might detect a problem in the discourse's erasure of "whiteness" as a ethnicity—indeed, an ethnicity with a cultural identity. Raising the issue as a problem might open a new window of insight into the ways that white ethnocentrism is constructed and how the power of dominant culture reveals itself. Such problem detecting exposes the ways white people are sometimes shielded from forms of self-reflection that might reveal the origins of condescending views of "the other." With their focus on meta-awareness, post-formal thinkers are cognizant of the relationship between the way they themselves and others frame problems and ask questions about the nature of the system of meaning they employ. They possess an understanding of the etymology of frames, even when the individual involved fails to recognize the origin of a question or a problem.

Without this meta-awareness of a system of meaning, we, as teachers and administrators, may learn how to construct schools but not how to determine what types of schools to construct. We will not grasp the connection between political disposition and the types of education that are developed. Grounded on an understanding of such connections, post-formal teachers, administrators, and teacher educators realize that school problems are not generic or innate. They are constructed by social conditions, cognitive assumptions, and power relations, and are uncovered by insightful educators who possess the ability to ask questions never before asked, questions that may lead to innovations that promote student insight, sophisticated thinking, and social justice (Munby and Russell, 1989; Ponzio, 1985; Schön, 1987).

Pattern

Exploring Deep Patterns and Structures—Uncovering the Tacit Forces, the Hidden Assumptions That Shape Perceptions of the World
Physicist David Bohm helps us conceptualize this aspect of post-formal thinking with his notion of the "explicate" and "implicate" orders of reality (Bohm and Edwards, 1991; Bohm and Peat, 1987). The explicate order involves simple patterns and invariants in time—that is, characteristics of the world that repeat themselves in similar ways and have recognizable locations in space. Being associated with comparatively humble orders of similarities and differences, explicate orders are often what is identified by the categorization and generalization function of formal thought. The implicate order is a much deeper structure of reality. It is the level in which ostensible separateness vanishes and all things seem to become a part of a larger unified structure. The implicate order is a process, an enfolded sequence of events like the process of an oak embedded in an acorn. The totality of these levels of enfolding cannot be made explicit as a whole. They can be exposed only in the emergence of a series of enfoldings. In contrast to the explicate order (which is an unfolded order) where similar differences are all present together and can be described in Cartesian-Newtonian terms, the implicate order has to be studied as a hidden pattern, sometimes impenetrable to empirical methods of inquiry (Bohm and Peat, 1987).

Post-formal thinking's concern with deep structures is, of course, informed by an understanding of the implicate order. Many have speculated that at a higher level of human consciousness, we often peek at the implicate pattern. Profound insight in any field of study may involve the apprehension of structures not attainable at the explicate order of reality. At these points we transcend common sense—we cut patterns of the cosmic fabric (Combs and Holland, 1990). "Artists don't reproduce the visible," Paul Klee wrote; instead they "make things visible" (Leshan and Margenau, 1982). Similarly, Albert Einstein often referred to his physics as based on a process of questioning unconscious assumptions as to reveal the deep structures of the universe. The theory of relativity itself emerged from his probing of the tacit assumptions underlying classical physics, in particular, absolute conceptions of time and space (Reynolds, 1987). As Einstein exposed deep physical structures of the shape of space, he was at least approaching an implicate order of the physical universe.

Post-formal thinking works to get behind the curtain of ostensible normality. Post-formal teachers work to create situations that bring hidden assumptions to our attention and make the tacit visible. For example, an American history teacher can create a hermeneutic atmosphere, a safe learning situation where students are encouraged to seek meaning, to interpret, even to be wrong at times. In this context, the teacher could point out the implicate patriarchal order of the required U.S. history text. Predominately a story of male triumph in the political and military spheres, the book is arranged as a story of exploration, a conquest, consolidation of power, and the problems of ruling the expanding empire. Questions of women's history, the history of poverty, racial justice, moral self-reflection, the history of ideas and culture, if addressed at all, are secondary. What may be the most important dimensional classroom may involve the post-formal uncovering of hidden assumptions of U.S. textbook publishers. Post-formal students come to recognize exclusion, identifying historical themes or events that are typically erased from the "American Pageant." Virginia Woolf argued that artists possess many of these same abilities: they uncover hidden realities and communicate them to their readers. These hidden realities are inseparable from implicate orders that ultimately are to be found at the base of all experience. Formal thinking has not been attuned to such a reality, possibly because the expansionist, conquest-oriented goals of the Cartesian-Newtonian paradigm emphasized the explicate order of things. The social world is in many ways like an onion—as we peel off one layer, we find another beneath. An outside layer of socio-educational reality is the standardized test performance of a school. A second layer is the assumptions behind the language that is used in discussing the curriculum. A third layer is the unspoken epistemological assumptions of the curricular reforms. A fourth layer is the body of assumptions about learning that students bring to school, ad infinitum (Bohm and Peat, 1987; Briggs, 1990; Greene, 1988).

Unfortunately, the formalist analysis of school is grounded in the explicate order in which deep structures remain enfolded and out of sight. The dominant culture's conversation, not only about education but also about the political process, racism, sexism, and social-class bias, is formalist and focuses on the explicate order. Educators come to understand, for example, that the most damaging form of racism is not an explicate "George Wallace in 1963" variety but an institutional racism built into the enfolded structure of schools, corporations, professional sports, and other institutions. Critical postmodern theory has taught us that little is as it appears on the surface (Giroux, 1992; Kanpol, 1992; McLaren, 1989; Pagano, 1990). When post-formal observers search the deep structures that there are to be uncovered in any classroom, they discover a universe of hidden meanings constructed by a variety of socio-political forces. These meanings often have little to do with the intended (explicate) meanings of the official curriculum. A post-formal analysis of curriculum is grounded in the recognition that there are implicate orders of forces that shape what happens in schools—some complementary, others contradictory, some emancipatory, others repressive. When this post-formal analysis of deep structures is applied to education, the implications for change are infinite. Imagine the way we might post-formally reconceptualize evaluation, supervision, administration, and so on. The reduction of the explicate approach to these areas would be overthrown.

Seeing Relationships Between Ostensibly Different Things— Metaphoric Cognition.
Post-formal thinking draws heavily on the concept of the metaphor. Metaphoric cognition is basic to all scientific and creative thinking and involves the fusion of previously disparate concepts in unanticipated ways. The mutual interrelationships of the components of a metaphor, not the components themselves, are the most important aspects of a metaphor. Indeed, many have argued that patterns of relationships, not objects, should be the basis of scientific thinking (Gordon, Miller and Rollock, 1990; Grumet, 1992; Rifkin, 1989). When thinking of the concept of mind, the same thoughts are relevant. We might be better served to think of mind not in terms of parts, but in terms of the connecting patterns, the dance of the interacting parts. The initial consciousness of the "poetic" recognition of this dance involves a non-verbal mental vibration, an increased energy state. From this creative tension emerges a perception of the meaning of the metaphor and the heightened consciousness that accompanies it. Post-formal teachers can model such metaphoric perception for their students. Such perception is not simply innate, it can be learned (Bohm and Peat, 1987; Fosnot, 1988; Talbot, 1986).

Pondering the question of what is basic in education, Madeleine Grumet (1992) argues that the concept of relation, of connecting pattern, is fundamental. Ironically, she argues, it is relation that we ignore when asked to enumerate the basics. Education involves introducing a student to modes of being and acting in the world that are new to his or her experience. Grumet concludes that it is the relation, the dance between the student's experience and knowledge, that separates education from training or indoctrination (Grumet, 1992). Post-formal thinkers recognize that relationships, not discrete objects should be the basis for definitions in the sciences and humanities. From this perspective, the physical and social worlds are seen as dynamic webs of interconnected components. None of the parts of the webs are fundamental, for they follow the dance of their relationship with the other parts. The nature of their interconnections shapes the form the larger web takes. The educational implications of such a realization are revolutionary. The uncovering and interpretation of the dance becomes a central concern of teachers and students. Curricular organization, evaluation techniques, teacher education, and definitions of student and teacher success cannot remain the same if this post-formal characteristic is taken seriously (Capra, 1982; Fosnot, 1988; Talbot, 1986).

In the attempt to understand more than the explicate order of school, post-formal thinkers might draw upon the perspectives of oppressed peoples (Welch, 1991). Taking a cue from liberation theologians in Latin America, post-formal analysts begin the cognitive process of understanding the way an institution works by listening to those who have suffered most as a result of its existence. These subjugated knowledges allow post-formal thinkers to gain the cognitive power of empathy—a power that enables them to take a picture of reality from different angles, to analyze the deep patterns and structures of oppression. The intersection of these angles and the connections of deep patterns allow for a form of analysis that moves beyond the isolated, fragmented analysis of modernity. With these ideas in mind, post-formal thinkers seek a multicultural dialogue between eastern cultures and western cultures as well as a conversation between the relatively wealthy northern cultures and the impoverished southern cultures (Bohm and Peat, 1987). In this way, forms of knowing that have traditionally been excluded by the modernist West move post-formal teachers to new vantage points and unexplored planetary perspectives. Understanding derived from the perspective of the excluded or the culturally different allows for an appreciation of the nature of justice, the invisibility of the process of oppression, and the recognition of difference that highlights our own social construction as individuals.

In this spirit, post-formal teachers begin to look at their lessons from the perspectives of their Asian students, their black students, their

Latino students, their white students, their poor students, their middle- and upper-middle-class students, their traditional successful students, their unsuccessful students. They examine their teaching from the vantage points of their colleagues or outside lay observers, which helps them reveal the hidden patterns and assumptions that shape their approaches. Thus, they step out of their teacher bodies and look down on themselves and their students as outsiders. As they hover above themselves, they examine their technicist teacher education with its emphasis on bulletin board construction, behavioral objective writing, discussion skill development, and classroom management. They begin to understand that such technicist training reflects a limited formality, as it assumes that professional actions can be taught as a set of procedures (Nixon, 1981).

Uncovering Various Levels of Connection Between Mind and Ecosystem—Revealing Larger Patterns of Life Forces
As a result of a dinner conversation with Albert Einstein, Carl Jung theorized his notion of synchronicity, the meaningful connection between causally unconnected events (Combs and Holland, 1990). Jung maintained that at the center of the mind a level of consciousness existed that connected the inner world of the psyche with the outer world of physical reality. The inner world of the psyche, Jung argued, is a mirror of the outer world—thus, the origin of his notion of the collective consciousness or deep unconsciousness as a collective mirror of the universe. Such a theory implies a level of connection between mind and reality or ecosystem that opens a realm of cognition untouched by cognitive science. Peter McLaren (forthcoming) taps this post-formal level of cognition when he writes of the realm of "impossible possibility" where teaching begins to move beyond the Cartesian-Newtonian borders in the explosion of our postmodern cognitive revolution, we begin to transcend our current disposition of being-in-the-world, our acceptance of boredom, alienation, and injustice. In a way, we become the science fiction writers of education, imagining what is admittedly not yet possible; yet if we can conceive of it, like sci-fi writers who imagined trips to the Moon, we make what we can imagine possible (Combs and Holland, 1990).

Post-formality is life-affirming as it transcends modernism's disdain and devaluation of the spiritual. Post-formalism, in its postmodern deconstructive manner, contests the "meaning of life"—that is, the actual definition of life. In the process of deconstruction, it begins the task of reshaping on multiple, possibly contradictory levels, the definition of living. Transcending Cartesian-Newtonian fragmentation, post-formal thinkers understand that life may have less to do with the parts of a living thing than with patterns of information, the "no-thing" of the *relations* between parts, the "dance" of a living process—that is, life as synchronicity. Postmodernism is the consummate boundary crosser, ignoring the no-trespassing signs posted at modernism's property line of certainty. It is possible that postmodernism and its socio-cognitive expression, post-formality, will lead us across the boundary dividing living and non-living. Those characteristics that modernism defined as basic to life are present in many phenomena in the universe—from subatomic particles to weather to seahorses. Because all life on the planet is so multidimensionally entwined, it is extremely hard to separate life from non-life. Indeed, some scientists have already begin to argue that the best definition of life is the entire Earth. Seen from this perspective, modernism's lack of concern with ecological balance is suicidal on many levels (Talbot, 1986). Post-formal teachers can design lessons that illustrate the physical and spiritual connections between self and ecosystem. For example, a post-formal biology teacher might design a research project that seeks to define where animate objects end and inanimate objects begin. Students would be encouraged to define "life-force" and to develop an alternative taxonomy of living entities.

The world around us (maybe more precisely, the world, an extension of us) is more like an idea than a machine. Post-formality's concern with etymology, pattern, process, and contextualization expresses a similar thought on the social level. Human beings cannot be simply separated from the contexts that have produced them. Post-formality assumes the role of the outlaw, as it points out modernism's tendency to fragment the world. Indeed, post-formality recognizes none of the official boundaries that define our separateness. This post-formal transgression of boundaries that define our concept of connectedness writes large (Belenky, Clinchy, Goldberger, and Tarule, 1986) a holistic connectedness that opens cognitive possibilities previously imaginable only by the dreamers. As a hologram, the brain may interpret a holographic universe on a frequency beyond Newtonian time and space (Ferguson, 1980). The only definition left for life in the postmodern world is not some secret substance or life force but an information pattern. This definition of life as an information pattern elevates the recognition of relationship from cognitive to spiritual realm, for it is the relationship that is us. The same is true for consciousness; that is, sensitive intelligence is present wherever an entity can tune into the woven mesh of cosmic information, the enchanting pattern, the implicate order of the universe. From this definition, then, the ecosystem is conscious—the "nothing" of perceived pattern is the very basis of life and mind. Post-formal thinkers thus become ambassadors to the domain of the *pattern*. The cognitive revolution initiated by post-formality reshapes the school in a way in which life and its multi-dimensional connectedness resides at the center of the curriculum. Thinking is thus conceived as a life-sustaining process undertaken in connection with other parts of the life force.

Process

Deconstruction—Seeing the World as a Text To Be Read
The post-formal thinker reads between the lines of a text, whether the text be, as with a physical scientist, physical reality or, for a teacher, the classroom and students. Thus, a text is more than printed material, as it involves any aspect of reality that contains encoded meaning to be deconstructed (Scholes, 1982; Whitson, 1991). Deconstruction can be defined in many ways—as a method of reading, as an interpretive process, and as a philosophical strategy. For post-formality, it involves all three of these definitions since it views the world as full of texts to be decoded, to be explored for unintended meanings. Jacques Derrida (1976) has employed deconstruction to question the integrity of texts, meaning he refuses to accept the authority of traditional, established interpretations of the world. He has characteristically focused on elements that others find insignificant. His purpose is not to reveal what the text really means or what the author intended but to expose an unintended current, an unnoticed contradiction within it (Culler, 1981, 1982).

When post-formal teachers view the world as a text, deconstruction can revolutionize education. No longer can the reader be passive, a pawn of text producers. Whether the text is produced by an author or by tradition, "areas of blindness" are embedded within it. When these areas are exposed, they reveal insight into the nature of how our consciousness is constructed. All texts are silent on certain points, and the task of deconstruction is to reveal the meanings of such silences (Scholes, 1982). Operating in the spirit of deconstruction, post-formal thinkers come to realize that what is absent is often as important, or maybe more important, than what is present in a text. Employing the deconstructive process, post-formal teachers and students gain a creative role that transcends the attempt to answer the attempt to answer correctively questions about what the author meant. After deconstruction, we can never again be so certain and comfortable with the stability of the world's meanings. Here rests a key element of post-formal thinking. Aware of the instability of meaning, post-formal thinkers abandon the quest for certainty, for closed texts. Unlike more formal thinkers in search of solutions to logical problems, post-formal thinkers are not uncomfortable with ill-structured problems with ambiguous answers.

Deconstruction represents the contemporary postmodern extension of a century of attempts in art, literature, psychology, and physics to penetrate surface appearances, to transcend the tyranny of common sense, to expose the unconsciousness of a culture. Within a deconstructive framework, consider what has happened to the Cartesian-Newtonian concept of reality in the twentieth century. The work of Albert Einstein, Werner Heisenberg, Sigmund Freud, and Carl Jung planted mines in the sea of modernity. Lying dormant until armed by the postmodernists, the mines were detonated by the ships of absolute truth. In the explosions, certainty was destroyed. In the wake of the destruction, the postmodern critique has taught us that, like fiction, science is a text. It produces "truth" no more absolute than the truth of Mozart or Dickens—it is an inventive act, a creative cognitive process.

Connecting Logic and Emotion—
Stretching the Boundaries of Consciousness
Feminist theory, Afrocentrism, and Native American ways of knowing have raised our consciousness concerning the role of emotion in learning and knowing (Jensen, 1984; Myers, 1987; Nyang and Vandi, 1980). In Afrocentric and Native American epistemologies, reality has never been divided into spiritual and material segments. Self-knowledge lays the foundation of all knowledge in these traditions, and a unified process of thinking has moved these traditions to appreciate the continuum of logic and emotion, mind and body, individual and nature, and self and other. Such appreciations have often caused great historical problems. ~~Such appreciations have often caused great historical problems.~~ It is only in the last thirty years that some European peoples have begun to recognize the epistemological sophistication of the African and Native American paradigms, with their recognition of unity in all things. Thus, from the post-formal perspective, that which is deemed primitive by Western observers becomes a valuable source of insight in the attempt to attain higher levels of understanding (Kincheloe, 1991).

Feminist constructivists have maintained that emotional intensity preceded cognitive transformation to a new way of seeing. Knowing, they argue, involves emotional as well as cognitive states of mind. As such, emotions are seen as powerful knowing process that ground cognition (Mahoney and Lyddon, 1988). Formal thinkers in the Cartesian-Newtonian lineage are procedural knowers who unemotionlly pay allegiance to a system of inquiry—indeed, they often see emotion as a pollutant of reason. Post-formal thinkers grounded in feminist theory unite logic and emotion, making use of what the emotions can understand that logic cannot. Emotionally committed to their thoughts, post-formal thinkers tap into a passion for knowing that motivates, extends, and leads them to a union with all that is to be known. Feminist scholar Barbara DuBois describes passionate scholarship as "sciencemaking, [which is] rooted in, animated by and expressive of our values" (cited in Belenky, Clinchy, Goldberger, and Tarule, 1986, p. 141).

Using a cognitive process created by the union of reason and emotion, feminist thinkers have revealed unanticipated insights gleaned from the mundane, the everyday lived world. They have exposed the existence of silences and erasures where formal thinkers have seen only "what was there." Such absences were revealed by the application of women's lived experience to the process of analysis, thus forging new connections between knower and known. Cartesian-Newtonian formalists had weeded out the self, denied their emotions and inner voices, in the process produced restricted and object-like interpretations of social and educational situations. Using empirical definitions, these formalist object-like interpretations were inferior, merely impressionistic, and journalistic. Feminist theorists came to realize that the objective process described by Piagetian formality was released from any social embeddedness or ethical responsibility. Objectivity in this sense became a signified for ideological passitivity and an acceptance of a privileged socioeconomic position. Thus, formalist objectivity came to demand a separation of logic and emotion, the devaluation of any perspective maintained with emotional conviction. Feeling is designated as an inferior form of human consciousness—those who rely on logical forms of and operate within this framework can justify their repression of those associated with emotion or feeling. Feminist theorists have pointed out that the thought-feeling hierarchy is one of the structures historically used by men to oppress women. In heterosexual relationships, these theorists assert, if a man is able to represent a women's position as an emotional perspective, then he has won the argument—his is the voice worth hearing (Belenky, Clinchy, Goldberger and Tarule, 1986; Reinharz, 1979).

The way of knowing ascribed to "rational man" defines logical abstraction as the highest level of thought—symbolic logic, mathematics, signifiers far removed from their original function. Piaget's delineation of formality fails to appreciate these androcentric forces of decontextualization. Unlike Piaget's objective cognition, women's ways of knowing are grounded on an identification with an organism's life and its preservation. Rational man contends that emotions are dangerous because they exert a disorganizing effect on the progress of science. Informed by feminist perspectives and critical constructivist epistemology, post-formal teachers admit that, indeed, emotions do exert a disorganizing effect on traditional logocentric ways of knowing and rationalistic cognitive theory. But, they argue, such disorganization is a positive step up in the attempt to critically accommodate our perceptions of ourselves and the world around us. Emotions thus become powerful thinking mechanisms that, when combined with logic, create a cognitive process that extends our ability to make sense of the universe (Fee, 1982; Mahoney and Lyddon, 1988; Reinharz, 1979).

Non-Linear Holism—
Transcending Simplistic Notions of the Cause-Effect Process
Post-formality challenges the hegemony[15] of Cartesian-Newtonian logocentric formality, as it reverses the hierarchy of cause-effect, the temporality of modernist cause-effect rationality. In formalist thinking, cause has always been considered the origin, logically and temporally prior to effect. Post-formality upsets the certainty of this easy process by asserting that effect is what causes the cause to become a cause. Such a displacement requires a significant re-evaluation of common sense in the mundane, in everyday language. In this context, we begin to understand that while the formal operational orientation functions on the basis of the Cartesian assumption of linear causality, the post-formal perspective assumes reciprocity and holism (Kramer, 1983; Van Hesteran, 1986). Holism implies that a phenomenon can't be understood as part of an organic whole. A film is the process, the totality—not a succession of discrete images (Bohm and Peat 1987; Talbot, 1986). This returns us again to David Bohm's conception of the implicate order. The implicate order of a film, or a piece of music, or a painting is constantly unfolding from an original perception in the mind of the artist. More traditional conceptions of the creative process use a machine model, implying that the whole emerges out of an accumulation of detail—the whole is built out of a set of pieces. Thus, we see an

important distinction between formal and post-formal thinking: creative unfolding representing a post-formal act and the sequential accumulation of detail representing a formal act. In any creative act there is an implicate order that emerges as an expression of the creator's whole life. The formal attempt to separate this holism into parts misses the essence of the creative process. Indeed, the attempt to teach based on this formalist, linear assumption will contribute little to the cultivation of creativity (Bohm and Peat, 1987).

Thus, creative thinking originates in the holistic depths of an implicate order. Such an order does not operate in a Newtonian universe of absolute, linear time. Events happen simultaneously rather than in a particular order of succession. When Einstein or Mozart or Da Vinci saw whole structures of physics, music, or art in a single flash of insight, they grasped the implicate order, the overall structure of a set of relationships all at once. Cognitive theorists have spoken simultaneity for years, but they have rarely dealt with how to accomplish it. Post-formality can be more specific as it reconceptualizes the process of analysis. The flash of insight where all things are considered at once involves connecting to the current of the implicate order. It is not easy to teach products of Cartesian-Newtonian consciousness construction to think in terms of this simultaneous cognitive process and the holism it implies. Modernist thinkers have become accustomed to thinking that formal cognition with its scientific method is the zenith of human consciousness. We learn in the formal milieu to direct our attention to partial aspects of reality and to focus on a linearity consistent with our metaphors for time. In this formalist partiality we leave the whole stream of continuity, as we separate the humanities from the sciences, work from play, love from philosophy, reading from painting, the private from the public, and the political from the cognitive. The cognitive process as conceptualized by post-formalism invokes deconstruction to undermine the simple literalism of intended meanings. At the same time, this process embraces a holism that subverts post-formal thinking's notion of cause-effect linearity. Teachers who employ this post-formal cognitive process will be far better equipped to "read" their classrooms and the requirements of educational bureaucracies. Such teachers will be prepared to articulate the contradictions between society's educational and social goals and the realities of school practice.

Contextualization

Attending to the Setting

The development of a context in which an observation can assume its full meaning is a key element in the construction of a post-formal mode of thinking. The literal meaning of context is "that which is braided together." Awareness of this braiding induces post-formal thinkers to examine the ecology of everything, as they realize that facts derive meaning only in the context created by other facts. For instance, only in recent years has the medical profession begun to examine the context of disease—some physicians even argue that we should study the milieu and not simply the symptoms (Ferguson, 1980). In the same way, post-formal educators have begun to acknowledge that the contextualization of what we know is more important than the content. In response to technicist educators who argue the importance of content, the need to "master" the basics as an initial step of learning, post-formal thinkers maintain that once a fabric of relevance has been constructed, content learning naturally follows (Ferguson, 1980).

An example of the way meaning is dependent on context might involve a listener who lacks adequate context to understand the "order" of a musical form. In many cases, such a listener will judge an avant-garde composition as meaningless. Europeans, upon hearing African music, for instance, attempted to assess it in the terms of another musical form. Unable to appreciate the context that gave meaning to the African music, the Europeans did not hear the intentions of the composers and performers with their subtle rhythms and haunting melodies. They heard primitive noise (Bohm and Peat, 1987).

Cartesian-Newtonian thinking fails to convey a valuable perspective on cognition and teaching as it fails in its reduction to account for context. In modern empirical research, so-called scientific controls contribute to a more perfect isolation of the context being investigated. Attention to circumstances surrounding the object of inquiry must be temporarily suspended. This suspension of attention is based on the assumption that these extraneous circumstances will remain static long enough to allow the study to be validated. Of course, these extraneous circumstances never remain static. They are constantly interacting and shaping. To exclude them is to distort reality (Longstreet, 1982). In settings such as schools, student and teacher behavior cannot be understood without careful attention to the setting and the individuals' relationships to the traditions, norms, roles, and values that are inseparable from the lived world of the institutions. The inability of Cartesian-Newtonian researchers to say very much that is meaningful about school life is due in part to their lack of regard for the context—the often invisible but foundational aspects of organizational life (Eisner, 1984; Wilson, 1977). John Dewey (1916) long ago argued that many thinkers regard knowledge as self-contained, as complete in itself. Knowledge, Dewey contended, could never be viewed outside the context of its relationship to other information. We only have to call to mind, Dewey wrote, what passes in our schools as acquisition of knowledge to understand how it is decontextualized and lacks any meaningful connection to the experience of students. Anticipating our notion of post-formality, Dewey concluded that an individual is a sophisticated thinker to the degree to which he or she sees an event not as something isolated "but in its connection with the common experience of mankind" (Dewey, 1916).

Understanding the Subtle Interaction of Particularity and Generalization

Grounded in the Cartesian-Newtonian universe, formal thinking often emphasizes the production of generalizations. The post-formal teacher's concern with the particular, the unique experience of each learner, *every day* seems rather unscientific to the modernist educational scientist. To the *life* post-formal thinker, the scientism, the obsession with generalization of the formal thinker are not especially helpful in the everyday world of the classroom. Formal generalization is out of sync with the rhythm of everyday life with its constant encounters with the novel and the unexpected—the particular.

When thinking is captured by Cartesian-Newtonian generalization, the nature of the particular is missed when it is treated as a sample of a species or a type—it is not itself, it is a representative. Viewed in this way, the particular, the individual has no proper name; it is alienated and anonymous. Children are interesting to the empirical researcher only as they represent something other than themselves. Joe Kincheloe and William Pinar's (1991) theory of place, which grounds post-formality's transcendence of mere generalization or mere particularity, fights formality's reductionist tendency. Place, as social theory, brings the particular into focus but in a way that grounds it contextually in a larger understanding of the social forces that shape it. A sense of place sharpens our understanding of the individual and the psychological and social forces that direct her or him. Place, in other words, grounds our ways of seeing by providing the contextualization of the particular—

a perspective often erased in formal forms of abstract thinking. Such contextualization connects post-formal thinkers with the insight of the visceral—its lust, fear, joy, love, and hate. Post-formal thinking returns the particular to the educational conversation. Existing educational research focuses, for example, on public activities. Questions of social justice are public questions, often uninterested in the particularity of individual or family experience. As we are acculturated by the school, such tendencies induce us to repudiate the intimacy of our own autobiographies. Concepts as personal as epistemology are transformed into the height of abstraction, as our way of knowing becomes a public word connected with abstract theory. Indeed, the mere implication that epistemology is personal raises collegial eyebrows. In such a context, concern with the general and the abstract turns us away from place. The particularity, for example, of our home lives marked by thrilling, frightening, shameful, and proud moments is out of bounds in the public discourse of generalization. Such notions are translated into the everyday practice of schooling. As our children progress to the upper grades, too often they are taught to leave the "real work" of school. Teachers who let themselves be known too well by students are immediately under suspicion. The curriculum is a public domain, as education leads us out of our intimate place to a world of public anonymity. Post-formal teachers fight such tendencies by drawing on student autobiography, theater, and literature to connect public knowledge to our private lives, to the formation of our subjectivities (Grumet, 1992).

Uncovering the Role of Power in
Shaping the Way the World Is Represented
The way we make sense of the world around us is not as much a product of our own ability to assimilate information as it is the result of dominant ideologies[16] or forces of power in the larger society. This dominant power insidiously blocks our ability to critically accommodate. As it blocks our recognition of exceptions, it undermines our attempt to modify our assimilated understandings of ourselves and the world. When educational leaders use particular words, metaphors, and models to design programs and policies, they reflect the effects of the influence of power. When teachers unquestioningly accept these models and metaphors and employ them to ground their instructional practices, they unwittingly allow power to shape their professional lives. Power, as Foucault (1980, 1984) argued, has served to censor and repress like a

great superego, but, he continues, it serves to produce knowledge, creating effects at the levels of the formation of consciousness. As a censor in our thinking as practitioners, power serves to reward particular ways of seeing and acting. For example, teachers who desire to be recognized as successful learn to follow particular norms and conventions that they have little to do with teaching and learning per se. When teachers internalize these norms and conventions, they allow power to create a context that dictates their views of appropriate "ways of being" (Cherryholmes, 1988; Giroux, 1992, McLaren, 1989).

Post-formal thinkers, operating at a meta-cognitive level, are able to understand the way power shapes their own lives. Post-formal teachers realize that in school, power often silences the very people that education purports to empower. This is the great paradox of contemporary schooling and teacher education: educators speak of empowerment as a central goal but often ignore the way power operates to subvert the empowerment of teachers and students. Failing to ask how curricular knowledge is produced, educational analysts infrequently address which social voices are represented in the curriculum and which voices are excluded. When such questions are not asked, the attempt to move to a higher order of cognition is undermined as both teachers and students fail to explore the ways that social forces have contributed to the production of their identities, their ability to function in the world (Giroux and McLaren, 1988). Does it matter that we come from rich or poor homes, white or non-white families? These questions are not recognized as cognitive questions of power—indeed, they are often not recognized at all. In the post-formal attempt to contextualize cognition, such questions of power must be seriously considered.

Conclusion

If knowledge and consciousness are social constructions, then so is post-formal thinking—for it also emerges from a particular historical and social location. Recognizing post-formal thinking as historically situated, we in no way intend for it to be portrayed as an essential list of what constitutes higher-order thinking. We offer it simply as a heuristic, an aid to further one's thinking about cognition. Post-formal thinking always includes an elastic clause—a rider that denies any claim of the objective existence of a post-formal way of thinking. It is one perspective from a particular point in the web of reality; a mere starting point in our search for what constitutes a higher level of understanding.

Endnotes

1. Grand narratives represent any macro-theories that attempt to explain social reality in its entirety. Such explanations, subsuming every aspect into one narrowly defined lens, are overly simplistic in that they suppress differences into homogenizing schemes. For example, the Marxist notion that class struggle is the unifying principle of human history is a totalizing narrative. Where there is a monopoly on the power structure in a particular social order, some of these theories *(master narratives)*, such as the modernist claim to universality, have a large impact on the structure of society and generally go unquestioned and unchallenged.

2. Subordinate cultural groups refers to groups that are politically, socially, and economically disempowered in the greater society. As Lilia Bartolomé describes, "While individual members of these groups may not consider themselves subordinate in any manner to the White 'mainstream,' they nevertheless are members of a greater collective that historically has been perceived and treated as subordinate and inferior by the dominant society. Thus it is not entirely accurate to describe these students as 'minority' students, since the term connotes numerical minority rather than the general low status (economic, political, and social) these groups have held" (p. 230).

3. Subjugated knowledges are the excluded, silences, or marginalized histories, memories, and experiences of subordinated populations. Critical pedagogy calls for learners to become active participants in the reconstruction and transformation of their own identities and histories.

4. Essentialism ascribes a fundamental nature or a biological determinism to humans (i.e., men are naturally aggressive, and women are naturally nurturing) through attitudes about identity, experience, knowledge, and cognitive development. Within this monolithic and homogenizing view, categories such as race and gender become gross generalizations and single-cause explanations about individual character. These authors point out that cognitive development is not logical and that it is affected by other environmental influences.

5. Disembedding in this sense refers to the process of identifying, challenging, and transformating the ideologies that structure particular bodies of knowledge and social practices. "Knowledge" in the modernist sense is seen as "objective." Critical pedagogues argue that buried (embedded) in all social constructions are values and interests. Kincheloe and Steinberg are calling for a process of extracting such ideologies so that they can be engaged.

6. This German institute of social research, frequented by the likes of Marcuse, Fromm, Horkheimer, Adorno, Habermas, Arendt, Brecht, Lukacs, and a great many others, had an enormous impact on the sociological, political, and cultural thought of this century. It was from this institute that the term "critical theory" and its ideas evolved.

7. While there are a number of definitions and interpretations of dialectics, for the general purposes of critical pedagogy, this concept refers to the interconnecting and contradicting relationships that constitute a particular phenomenon, for example, among the economic, political, social, and cultural dimensions of society. A dialectical analysis is also often used to show how every idea or force has its opposite/contradiction. For example, the dialectic of "oppressor" is the reality of the "oppressed." Such an analysis holds both "oppressing" concepts together at once to see how they interconnect and play off each other.

8. A meta-narrative analyzes the body of ideas and insights of social theories that attempt to understand and make understood a complex diversity of phenomena and their interrelations.

9. Cultural capital refers to Pierre Bourdieu's concept that different forms of cultural knowledge, such as language, modes of social interaction, and meaning, are valued hierarchically in society. Critical pedagogues argue that only those characteristics and practices (i.e., cultural wealth) of the dominant paradigm will facilitate academic achievement within mainstream schools and reflect that dominant and exclusionary ideology.

10. This notion of decentering is a rebuttal to the modernist (central) notion that the autonomous self (the individual being outside of social and historical influences) exists.

11. To be reductionistic is to simplify a particular phenomenon so as to mask its complexity. For example, arguing that social reality is shaped solely by socioeconomic status and class conflict obscures the multiple and interconnecting relationships of other significant human experiences (such as race, gender, and sexual orientation) and their effects on perception and struggle.

12. Emanating from the positivist tradition, technocratic models, which conceptualize teaching and leaning as a discrete and scientific undertaking, embrace depersonalized methods for educating students that often translate into the regulation and standardization of teacher practices and curricula and rote memorization of selected "facts" that can easily be measured through standardized testing. As such the role of the teacher is reduced to that of a technician— an uncritical, "objective," and "efficient" distributor of information.

13. Hermeneutics refers to the ongoing process of interpreting text for understanding the significance of lived experience as opposed to believing that meaning is evident or understandable without need of interpretation.

14. Associated with the Enlightment and modernism, positivism refers to a belief system or paradigm that makes claims to objectivity, truth, and certainty in defense of a scientific basis for the study of culture. As such, knowledge and reason are seen as neutral and universal rather than as social constructions that reflect particular interests and ideologies. This uncritical call to science has resulted in an obsession with finding and using the "right" technique to understand a phenomenon or solve a problem. For example, "technocratic" models, which conceptualize teaching as a discrete and scientific undertaking, embrace depersonalized methods for educating students that often translate into the regulation and standardization of teacher practices and curricula, and rote memorization of selected "facts" that can easily be measured through standardized testing. As such, the role of the teacher is

reduced to that of an uncritical, "objective," and "efficient" distributor of information.

15. Hegemony, as derived from the work of Italian theorist Antonio Gramsci, is used to express how certain groups manage to dominate others. An analysis of hegemony is especially concerned with how the imposition of particular ideologies and forms of authority results in the reproduction of social and institutional practices through which dominant groups maintain not only their positions of privilege and control but also the consensual support of other members of society.

16. Dominant ideologies are bodies of ideas held by cultural groups that are politically, socially, and economically in positions of power and are therefore able to impose on the greater society, through various social institutions and practices, particular traditions, bodies of knowledge, discourse styles, language uses, values, norms, and beliefs, usually at the expense of others.

References

Aronowitz, S. (1992). *The politics of identity: Class, culture and social movements*. New York: Routledge.

Bartolomé, L. (1996). Beyond the methods fetish: Toward a humanizing pedagogy. In P. Leistyna, A. Woodrum and S. Sherblom (Eds.), *Breaking free: The transformative power of critical pedagogy*, Reprint Series No. 27 (pp. 229–252). Cambridge, MA: Harvard Educational Review.

Belenky, M., Clinchy, B., Goldberger, N. and Tarule, J. (1986). *Women's ways of knowing: The development of self, voice, and mind*. New York: Basic Books.

Bohm, D. and Edwards, M. (1991). *Changing consciousness*. San Francisco: Harper.

Bohm, D. and Peat, F. (1987). *Science, order, and creativity*. New York: Bantam Books.

Bourdieu, P. and Passeron, J. (1977). *Reproduction: In education, society, and culture*. Beverly Hills, CA: Sage.

Bozik, M. (1987, November). *Critical thinking through creative thinking*. Paper presented to the Speech Communication Association, Boston.

Briggs, J. (1990). *Fire in the crucible*. Los Angeles: Jeremy Tarcher.

Capra, F. (1982). *The turning point: Science, society, and the rising culture*. New York: Simon and Schuster.

Case, R. (1985). *Intellectual development: Birth to adulthood*. New York: Academic Press.

Cherryholmes, C. (1988). *Power and criticism: Poststructural investigations in education*. New York: Teachers College Press.

Codd, J. (1984). Introduction. In J. Codd (Ed.), *Philosophy, common sense, and action in educational administration* (pp. 8–28). Victoria, Australia: Deakin University Press.

Combs, A. and Holland, M. (1990). *Synchronicity: Science, myth, and the trickster*. New York: Paragon House.

Courtney, R. (1988). *No one way of being: A study of the practical knowledge of elementary arts teachers*. Toronto: MGS.

Culler, J. (1981). *The pursuit of signs: Semiotics, literature, deconstruction*. Ithaca, NY: Cornell University Press.

Culler, J. (1982). *On deconstruction: Theory and criticism after structuralism*. Ithaca, NY: Cornell University Press.

Daines, J. (1987). Can higher order thinking skills be taught? By what strategies? In R. Thomas (Ed.). *Higher order thinking: Definition, meaning and instructional approaches* (pp. 3–6). Washington, DC: Home Economics Education Association.

de Lauretis, T. (1986). Feminist studies/critical studies: Issues, terms, and contexts. In T. de Lauretis (Ed.), *Feminist studies/Critical studies* (pp. 1–19). Bloomington: Indiana University Press.

Derrida, J. (1976). *Of grammatology*. Baltimore: Johns Hopkins University Press.

Dewey, J. (1916). *Democracy and education*. New York: Free Press.

Eisner, E. (1984). Can educational research inform educational practice? *Phi Delta Kappan, 65*, 447–452.

Fee, E. (1982). Is feminism a threat to scientific objectivity? *International Journal of Women's Studies, 4*, 378–392.

Ferguson, M. (1980). *The Aquarian conspiracy: Personal and social transformation in our time*. Los Angeles: J. P. Tarcher.

Fiske, D. (1986). Specificity of method and knowledge in social science. In D. Fiske and R. Shweder (Ed.), *Metatheory in social science: Pluralisms and subjectivities* (pp. 61–82). Chicago: University of Chicago Press.

Fosnot, C. (1988, January). The dance of education. Paper presented to the Annual Conference of the Association for Educational Communication and Technology, New Orleans.

Foucault, M. (1980). *Power/knowledge: Selected interviews and other writings, 1972-1977* (Ed. Colin Gordon). New York: Pantheon.

Foucault, M. (1984). *The Foucault reader*. (Ed. P. Rabinow). New York: Pantheon.

Gardner, H. (1983). *Frames of mind: The theory of multiple intelligences*. New York: Basic Books.

Gardner, H. (1989). *To open minds*. New York: Basic Books.

Gardner, H. (1991). *The unschooled mind: How children think and how schools should teach*. New York: Basic Books.

Giroux, H. (1992). *Border crossings: Cultural workers and the politics of education*. New York: Routledge.

Giroux, H. and McLaren, P. (1988). Teacher education and the politics of democratic reform. In H. Giroux (Ed.), *Teachers as intellectuals: Toward a critical pedagogy of learning*. Granby, MA: Bergin and Garvey.

Gordon, E., Miller, F., and Rollock, D. (1990). Coping with communicentric bias in knowledge production in the social sciences. *Educational Researcher, 19*(3), 14–19.

Gramsci, A. (1988). *An Antonio Gramsci reader* (Ed. David Forgacs). New York: Schocken Books.

Greene, M. (1988). *The dialectic of freedom*. New York: Teachers College Press.

Grumet, M. (1992). The curriculum: What are the basics and are we teaching them? In J. Kincheloe and S. Steinberg (Eds.), *Thirteen questions: Reframing education's conversation*. New York: Peter Lang.

Hutcheon, L. (1988). *A poetics of postmodernism*. New York: Routledge.

Jensen, K. (1984). Civilization and assimilation in the colonized schooling of Native Americans. In P. Altbach and G. Kelly (Eds.), *Education and the colonial experience* (pp. 155–179). New Brunswick: Transaction Books.

Kanpol, B. (1992). *Towards a theory and practice of teacher cultural politics: Continuing the postmodern debate*. Norwood, NJ: Ablex.

Kegan, R. (1982). *The evolving self: Problem and process in human development*. Cambridge, MA: Harvard University Press.

Kincheloe, J. (1991). *Teachers as researchers: Qualitative paths to empowerment*. New York: Falmer Press.

Kincheloe, J. and Pinar, W. (1991). Introduction. In J. Kincheloe and W. Pinar (Eds.), *Curriculum as social psychoanalysis: Essays on the significance of place* (pp. 1–23). Albany: State University of New York Press.

Klahr, D. and Wallace, J. (1976). *Cognitive development: An information processing view.* Hillsdale, NJ: Erlbaum.

Kramer, D. (1983). Post-formal operations? A need for further conceptualization. *Human Development, 26,* 91–105.

Kristeva, J. (1980). *Desire in language: A semiotic approach to literature and art* (Ed. Leon S. Roudiez). New York: Columbia University Press.

Lave, J. (1988). *Cognition in practice.* Cambridge, Eng.: Cambridge University Press.

Lawler, J. (1975). Dialectical philosophy and developmental psychology: Hegel and Piaget on contradiction. *Human Development, 18,* 1–17.

Leshan, L. and Margenau, H. (1982). *Einstein's space and Van Gogh's sky: Physical reality and beyond.* New York: Macmillan.

Longstreet, W. (1982). Action research: A paradigm. *The Educational Forum, 46(2),* 136–149.

Maher, F. and Rathbone, C. (1986). Teacher education and feminist theory: Some implications for practice. *American Journal of Education, 94(2),* 214–235.

Mahoney, M. and Lyddon, W. (1988). Recent developments in cognitive approaches to counseling and psychotherapy. *The Counseling Psychologist, 16(2),* 190–234.

McLaren, P. (1986). *Schooling as ritual performance: Towards a political economy of educational symbols and gestures.* London: Routledge.

McLaren, P. (1989). *Life in schools.* New York: Longman.

McLaren, P. (forthcoming). Postmodernism/post-colonialism/pedagogy. *Education and Society.*

McLeod, J. (1987). *Ain't no makin' it.* Boulder, CO: Westview Press.

Miller, J. (1990). *Creating spaces and finding voices: Teachers collaborating for empowerment.* Albany: State University of New York Press.

Munby, H. and Russell, T. (1989). Educating the reflective teacher: An essay review of two books by Donald Schön. *Journal of Curriculum Studies, 18(1),* 72–85.

Myers, L. (1987). The deep structures of culture: Relevance of traditional African culture in contemporary life. *Journal of Black Studies, 18(1),* 72–85.

Nixon, J. (1981). Postscript. In J. Nixon (Ed.), *A teachers' guide to action research*. London: Grant McIntyre.

Nyang, S. and Vandi, A. (1980). Pan Africanism in world history. In M. Asante and A. Vandi (Eds.), *Contemporary black thought: Alternative analyses in social and behavioral science*. Beverly Hills: Sage.

O'Loughlin, M. (1992, September). Appropriate for whom? A critique of the culture and class bias underlying developmentally appropriate practice in early childhood education. Paper presented to Conference on Reconceptualizing Early Childhood Education: Research, Theory, and Practice, Chicago.

Pagano, J. (1990). *Exiles and communities: Teaching in the patriarchal wilderness*. Albany: State University of New York Press.

Piaget, J. (1970). Piaget's theory. In P. Mussen (Ed.), *Manual of child psychology, vol 1*. (pp. 703–732). New York: Wiley.

Piaget, J. (1977). *The essential Piaget* (Eds. H. Gruber and J. Voneche). New York: Basic Books.

Piaget, J., and Garcia, R. (1989). *Psychogenesis and the history of science* (Trans. H. Feider). New York: Columbia University Press.

Piaget, J., and Inhelder, B. (1968). *The psychology of the child*. New York: Basic Books.

Pinar, W. (1975). The analysis of educational experience. In W. Pinar (Eds), *Curriculum theorizing: The reconconceptualists*. Berkeley: McCutchan.

Ponzio, R. (1985). Can we change content without changing context? *Teacher Education Quarterly, 12(3),* 39–43.

Reinharz, S. (1979). *On becoming a social scientist*. San Francisco: Jossey-Bass.

Reinharz, S. (1982). Experiential analysis: A contribution to feminist research. In G. Bowles and R. Klein (Eds.), *Theories of woman's studies* (pp. 162–191). Boston: Routledge and Kegan Paul.

Reynolds, R. (1987). Einstein and psychology: The genetic epistemology of relativistic physics. In D. Ryan (Ed.), *Einstein and the humanities* (pp. 169–176). New York: Greenwood Press.

Riegel, K. (1973). Dialectic operations: The final period of cognitive development. *Human Development, 16,* 346–370.

Rifkin, J. (1989). *Entropy: Into the greenhouse world*. New York: Bantam Books.

Scholes, R. (1982). *Semiotics and interpretation*. New Haven: Yale University Press.

Schön, D. (1983). *The reflective practitioner: How professionals think in action.* New York: Basic Books.

Schön, D. (1987). *Educating the reflective practitioner.* San Francisco: Jossey-Bass.

Talbot, M. (1986). *Beyond the quantum.* New York: Bantam Books.

Van Hesteran, F. (1986). Counseling research in a different key: The promise of human science perspective . *Canadian Journal of Counseling 20(4),* 200–234.

Walkerdine, V. (1984). Developmental psychology and the child-centered pedagogy: The insertion of Piaget into early education. In J. Henriques, W. Hollway, C. Urwin, C. Venn, and V. Walkerdine (Eds.), *Changing the subject* (pp. 153–202). New York: Methuen.

Walkerdine, V. (1988). Redefining the subject in situated cognition theory. Paper presented to the American Educational Research Association, San Francisco.

Welch, S. (1991). An ethic of solidarity and difference. In H. Giroux (Ed.), *Postmodernism, feminism, and cultural politics: Redrawing educational boundaries* (pp. 83–99). Albany: State University of New York Press.

Whitson, J. (1991). *Constitution and curriculum.* New York: Falmer.

Wilson, S. (1977). The use of ethnographic techniques in educational research. *Review of Educational Research, 47,* 245–265.

CHAPTER THREE

The Education of Meaninglessness and the Meaninglessness of Education: The Crisis of the Human Psyche at the Birth of the Second Millennium

Danny Weil

> Today's social ugliness, which makes the bizarre seem normal, is no longer just a surrealist fantasy, a proto-surrealist spin-off, or a Baudrillardean rehearsal for a futureless future. This scenario is the present historical moment, one that has arrived in a body bag—unraveled and stomped on by the logic of the fascist's steel-toed boot. Serial killer Ted Bundy has donated his multiple texts of identity to our structural unconscious and we are living them.
>
> —Peter McLaren, Rhonda Hammer

Cynicism, disillusionment and alienation have all been words used to describe the loss of meaning and sense of hopelessness and despair experienced by many citizens in advanced capitalist industrialized countries in the battered stages of the late twentieth century. For many, existential uncertainty has degenerated into hollow existence and collapsed into a debilitating sense of pessimism. Postmodern capitalism, with all its emphasis on material acquisition at the expense of human sovereignty and dignity, has created a society whereby heroes and heroines have been replaced by celebrities, artists replaced by producers, and citizens replaced by consumers. It is a society marked by insipid individualism, rabid consumption, material acquisition, and a collective loss of reason and historicity. The logocentric hyper-reality of postmodern capitalism, with its deification of technology and commodification and *imagineering* of identification and representation, has virtually torn asunder humanistic meaning—replacing it instead with hyperrational engineered and *imagineered* cognitive and emotional impulses. In short, it can be characterized as a social system gone mad.

In the *imagineering* culture, a culture that technologically colonizes imagination through the creation of needs and wants, emotion and desire are lured into malleable submission and endlessly wooed by market forces bent on colonizing subjectivity in the interests of profit. Individual and social output lays claim to commodification, as personal and collective identification finds currency only in the commercial barter and the exchange of *things*. For many, the journey is little more than an anesthetized indentureship which promises fulfillment but instead delivers little more than alienation reified and cloaked in despair. Emotional and aesthetic enjoyment, production, and fulfillment transmogrify into synthetic reproduction. Here, appearance victimizes reality in the interplay of stultified symbolic misrepresentations where signifier and signified melt into the obscurity of imagery; the consumer-viewer of the *spectacle* becomes implicated as an active participant in the production and reproduction of a simulacrum existence writhing in the throes of historical uncertainty.

The imagineering culture dialectically relates to a process of representation and identification particular to actual existing post-modern capitalism. Here, the meaning of life changes and mendacity as opposed to veracity becomes reality. In a certain video made in Japan:

> It's family time in a suburb in Tokyo. A couple and their three-year-old son greet the wife's eighty-year-old grandmother at the train station and escort her back to their home for an afternoon of Japanese noodles and warm conversation. Grandson kisses Grandma, and daughter holds her hand as they talk about all living together again (*Los Angeles Times*, 1992).

The only problem with this video is that the people, save Grandma, are actors. At the cost of $1,125, customers can avail themselves of a service called Japan Efficiency Corporation that allows them to produce a video to experience the warmth of a simulated three-hour family visit, or other similarly benign encounters with loved ones. Because Grandma's real daughter is a working mother of two and cannot see her mother regularly, Grandma can fill her emotional void by *renting* another person. An elderly husband and wife when explaining how they felt when they *rented* a couple and a child to *play* the role of a second son and family commented:

I had no feeling that they were strangers. When I saw my thirty-one-year old "second son," I thought, "How tall he is!! How manly he is!!" When I met his "wife," I thought she was a very open hearted person—that she really was my daughter-in-law!!

Here, emotion is commodified and packaged in a vicarious virtual reality where the spectacle, ones' own life, is *dramatized* and sold back to the subject. Joy is produced precisely as pseudo-joy—as reason, memory, history, and emotion unite in an image of happy unification surrounded by misery and loneliness—encased in the heart of a techno-disorder inebriated with its own image. The submissive consumer is lured into his or her own emotional and rational captivity where the increasing isolation of postmodern life, coupled with an idolization of youth, render maturation and aging a painfully lonely and alienated process.

Technocentric-evangelism helps define subjective thought in ways unheard of in earlier industrial times, precisely because of the control of information and dissemination of mis-information—a communication that is unilateral. Where capitalism was once dependent on a public, de-politicized realm, it is now embarked on the privatization of all public life replacing a de-politicized public realm with an ideologically dependent privatized social reality. To this end, the information revolution is gearing up for the further de-politicization of daily life by *re-politicizing* the masses with a sense of private gratification and a possessive individualism founded on market civilization values and dispositions. This de- politicization has now become *re-politicization* as the project of technological innovation helps to glorify the object at the expense of the subject. Virtual reality and artificial intelligence become more important than human reality and human intelligence; the interest in *machines* forces humanistic intellectuals out of universities in favor of technocratic intellectuals held hostage to research grants and favoritism from large corporations; science and math are advanced as disciplines over music and the arts, as more and more people become road kill on the information superhighway. Here, corporate promises of *opening communication* through technological information linkage become the metaphorical equivalent of mendacity disguising itself as a benign, progressive extension of society and self. In reality, it is more probable that in control of a few, this *open communication* will become the symbolic equivalent of censorship and control as a virtual handful of corporations control, contrive, and disseminate unilateral information serving their self-vested economic and ideological interests.

The importance of these insights have direct bearing on intelligence and educational practice and theory; this is especially true in light of rapid changes in the forces of production and the consequent blistering of emotion and reason. I will argue that the only medium where rational critical discourse can emerge is within the public realm—the realm unfettered by the motor-driven need for marketization and increased accumulation. Without critical public discourse with and among students, parents, educational workers, and community regarding popular culture, media, representation, and identity, social change harvested through compassionate reason will be forever an elusive reminder of our own alienation and occupation by the forces of ideological and material domination. Yet in a culture that deifies technology while restricting social public discourse, technology assumes the omnipotent, omniscient features associated with a "new religion." The distinct and purposeful action of human beings becomes transferred to the deification of the *machine*. When the machine is controlled by a handful of technocrats, cognitive elites, and their bourgeoisie masters, then we see the disintegration of human communication in favor of a medium of technocratic possibility divorced from discussions of human purpose—an insipid instrumentalism. So, we find many children exploring computers but not their neighborhoods or viewing animal species on CD-ROMS while these species vanish on earth. In this way, the human being becomes not simply the object of technological device and order but is integrated both ideologically and materially in its reproduction and perpetuation into new forms of techno-control and subjective colonization. Subjective freedom is sacrificed in face of a more insidious yet comfortably secure objectification. And of course, the role of the state in this situation is to idealize technocratic and technological capabilities while at the same time assuring financial support for their realization.

The Meaninglessness of Education

Whatever significance schooling might once have held for the majority of youngsters in our society, it no longer holds significance for many of them. Most students (and, for that matter, many parents and teachers) cannot provide compelling reasons for attending school. The reasons cannot be discerned within the school experience, nor is there faith that what is acquired in school will actually be utilized in the future. Try to justify the quadratic equation or the Napoleonic wars to an inner city high school student—or his parents! The real world appears elsewhere: in the media, the marketplace, and all too frequently in the demimonde of drugs, violence, and crime. Much if not most of what happens in schools happens because that is the way it was done in earlier generations, not because we have a convincing rationale for maintaining it today. The often heard statement that school is basically custodial rather than educational harbors more than a grain of truth.   —*Howard Gardner*

As the *deliquescence of community*, accompanying loss of meaning, social pathology, and painful psychic hemorrhaging stain human existence, school as presently structured, fails to hold the promise of joy, creativity, and meaning for too many students and educational workers. Most students find little resonance within the four walls of schools, preferring instead to "hang-out" or socialize with friends. They see little or no purpose in what they study, what they are forced to learn, and the people who are responsible to teach them. Because ideological representations within school life operate to disseminate and legitimate larger social practices—both corporate and political—without critical exploration into this legitimizing ideology of schooling, teachers laboring within the educational setting easily fall prey to a form of pedagogical alienation. They fail to come to understand their role as agents of either social conformity or social change and the role played by texts and curriculum as objects of political/economic interests deserving unwavering scrutiny and critical analysis.

Because schooling as it is presently structured treats knowledge as a commodity (a set of skills and attitudes to be consumed in the "free" market of ideas), the role of schools, teachers, administrators, and students becomes nightmarishly synonymous with the multiple alienated roles existent in the *free market life* of the factory. The regimented classroom becomes the metaphorical equivalent of the tyranny of the Tayloristic assembly line. Students and their subjective lives are carried "kicking and screaming" along a pedagogical conveyor belt where *teacher-workers,* consciously or unconsciously, are bent on inculcating dominant and authoritarian societal culture, attitudes, and skills while they labor piecemeal with fragmented curricula—revealing the way both the product and the worker become emotionally and rationally alienated from the entire process of material, mental, and social production. The school principal is metaphorically transformed into the managerial equivalent of the "on-line-production-manager," assuring through pedagogical "time-and-motion-studies" (in the form of orchestrated seven-step "lesson plans") that the "worker" and the "product" produced conform to quality control standards adopted by still *another* layer of educationally divorced administrative bureaucracy. This *"quality control"* in pedagogical life finds itself to be the expression of nothing more than raw authoritarian power accomplished through culture-dominant standardized teaching, normative individualistic testing of rote memorization, inauthentic teacher evaluations, consequent levels of achievement claims, implications, assumptions, and conclusions. Efficiency and production, or the coverage of greater and greater content, becomes the dynamic engine which acts as a vehicle for perniciously driving schooling further and further away from human values, self-dignity, and conscious individuality. Workbooks and page numbers comprise student assignments as the factory-classroom grows in size due to lack of societal commitment to democratic educational ideals, thereby causing classroom managerial problems that often run roughshod over even the most enthusiastic, strident and critically conscious educator as the material and psychological limitations of classroom production function as an obstacle to critical and creative opportunities.

The Cognitive Dis-ease

> The limitation of the early infancy researchers (including Piaget) lay in an underestimation of what the infant knows—information that can be elicited when the infant is "questioned" more directly and more appropriately about specific bodies of information or knowledge.
> —*Howard Gardner*

The techno-rationalist, instrumentalist approach to understanding educational theory and practice segments the world in order to understand it. Theory is divorced from conceptualization as the planning and design of curriculum proceed uninformed. Texts add to this failure by generally offering the dominant narrative of reality on issues of contemporary and historical concern, thereby offering little opportunity to see the world from alternative cultural and economic points of view. Texts suggest and provide lesson plans to teachers that require not independent thinking on behalf of students or teachers but merely rote dissemination and memorization opportunities alienated from the discourse of everyday life. I call this "anorexic-bulimic learning." Students starve themselves until test time, then attempt to cram as many factoids as possible in their heads and regurgitate them without the benefit of intellectual digestation. We know what happens to the body when this occurs—it atrophies and dies—and so too does the mind.

This type of divorced instruction—the instruction of accommodation and trivialization, of decontextualization and alienation, of subjugation and domination—can have no appreciable effect on human growth and potential and can certainly never act as a catalyst for transforming the human mind or world in which we live. It is an anaesthetized approach to learning that claims *social and political neutrality* as the playground of educational practice—a neutrality that presumes education is not a form of *"political"* expression but rather *generic* or *value free*. The *generic curriculum* fraudulently pretends to serve as *wide appeal* to most students while conveniently separating emotion from reason, shunning controversy, depersonalizing learning, and trivializing reality. Giroux suggests some valuable questions we as teachers would profit from asking:

> What relationship do my students see between the work we do in class and the lives they live outside of class? Is it possible to incorporate aspects of students' lived culture into the work of schooling without simply confirming what they already know? Can this be done without trivializing the objects and relationships important to students? And can it be done without singling out particular groups of students as marginal, exotic, and "other" within a hegemonic culture? (Giroux, 1989, p. 243)

However, the skill-driven curriculum that fragments knowledge into curricular categories promotes the teaching of *subjects* as opposed to *subjectivity*. Relevancy and motivation of both students and teachers are sacrificed to the exigencies of technical questions and skill-driven abilities. In his introduction to this book, Kincheloe refers to this crisis as *the cognitive illness*; I will use the term *cognitive dis-ease*.

The *cognitive dis-ease* is nurtured and encouraged by a a formalist psychology—a positivistic modernistic theory that diminishes pedagogical, psychological, and socio-economic issues to technical questions which can only be answered within the logic of its own monologue. This apologetic theory of formalist psychology perceives cognitive and emotional forces as divorced from historical and social reality; *emotion* as a noun and the infinitive *to emote* are relegated to the sphere of irrationality in explaining human intelligence and thinking. Falsely separating emotion from reason and feelings from rationality, this psychology born from market civilization's *attempt to explain itself* has sought to colonize the former and subject the latter to little more than abstract scientific inquiry. Yet unfortunately, the pseudo-pedagogical understandings born from formalistic pedagogical theories have served to guide both the development of students and teachers. In the judgment of many, this has led to a cultivation of meaninglessness at educational sites among both teachers and students subsequently harvesting an individualism devoid of *individuality*. The bi-polarization and false bifurcation of reason and emotion which underlies formative psychology have had the effect of separating our understanding of human feeling from rationality, thought from passion. Thus, formalistic pedagogical theory is neither interested nor equipped to imagine or render solutions to pedagogical problems, nor can it cultivate resistance to oppressive conditions.

Only what Kincheloe refers to as a post-formal pedagogy informed by critical multicultural literacy, feminist theory, disenfranchised narratives, and multiple epistemologies can promise to forge educational theater for all community members. Post-formal pedagogy concerns itself with social responsibility, power, authority and control, civic courage and the common struggle for human dignity, and the logic of oppression. It is a pedagogy forged in the fires of constructive *discourse,* where ideas and narratives are exchanged in an atmosphere of civility, a discourse where not simply cognition but the values and dispositions *of* cognition engage all members in self-questioning as opposed to self-righteousness. A post-formal pedagogy recognizes the need to cultivate intellectual reciprocity, empathy, humility, integrity, fairmindedness, courage, imagination, curiosity, independent critical thinking, and personal and social responsibility in the interest of liberty, human emancipation, and critical sensibility. In this mission, post-formalist pedagogy recognizes that all learning and teaching is political—that post-modern criticism must of necessity encompass a realistic vision of despair precisely because a portrait of private lives tormented by public oppression has reached Marcusean levels of episodic, nightmarish proportions.

Cognition as Knowledge Generation

> The test of a first-rate intelligence is the ability to hold two opposed ideas in the mind at the same time, and still retain the ability to function.
> —F. Scott Fitzgerald

In a society where intelligence has been traditionally defined by instrumentalist rationality and mastery over specific Cartesian-Newtonian cultural ways of knowing, multiple intelligences and multiple narratives are far too often excluded from the definition of what it means to be intelligent (Gardner, 1991). The result is not simply the loss of epistemological opportunities but is even more insidious—it symbolizes the meaninglessness of schooling and the schooling of meaninglessness by marginalizing students' and teachers voices, repressing the affective dimension of their learning, and teaching in favor of the cultivation of a rationalistic cognition, thereby denying both students and teachers emancipatory and self-productive opportunities that connect their subjective lives to the world and the socio-historical construction of the mind and organizing them into a geriatric curriculum of condescension and dis-interest.

Education loses its legitimacy and status as a form of critical discourse when dialogue fails to address issues of mass ideology, culture, issues of gender and class, and material reality. Cast in this role, education operates as the de-politicization of the masses by conforming dialogue to one-dimensional discourse. On the other hand, teachers familiar with post-formalist theory would organize their classes so that students' lives worked *with* and *within* a problem-posing curriculum that deconstructed the orchestration of identity and representation. These teachers would think of themselves as thought provocateurs as opposed to intellectual chauffeurs—as midwives helping their students give birth to knowledge, knowing that they cannot go through the labor process for them. This means developing forms of pedagogical practices that involve an understanding of the principles and strategies of critical thinking and the ability to implement them within classroom life (Paul, p. 319). Of necessity, these understandings arise from the language of critique, but their actual internalization and implementation in the dialogue of educational discourse can only come about through their utilization—by radically transforming the way teachers and students come to view the role and process of education. This includes how students are questioned, what materials and experiences should constitute the object of critical examination and reflection, the infusion of critical thinking strategies and principles in an active curriculum of critical social discourse and dialogical and dialectical examination, and an understanding of the significance of subjective experience, power, domination, and social and economic justice. Making the lived experiences of our students the lively subject of public and private debate means offering legitimacy to such experiences—thus giving those who live them affirmation and voice; it means offering critical educational opportunities for students to articulate their language, dreams, hopes, values, and encounters with others; it heralds reflection, metacognition, and insight into these experiences both on the part of students and teachers—while offering the promise of countless opportunities for critical thinking about social and personal issues.

The American Association of University Women in their June 1992 Report entitled *Creating a Gender-Fair Multicultural Curriculum* states that:

> It is therefore imperative that the formal curriculum which conveys the central messages of education, provides students with "mirrors" reflecting their experience as well as "windows" revealing those of others. But for most students, particularly girls and minorities, "the present curriculum provides many windows and few mirrors" (AAUW, p. 1).

Students need to see that the purpose and implications of schooling go beyond the classroom—as something more than a marriage that ends in annulment at age eighteen or earlier. Education, as presently structured, remains so disconnected from the lived struggles in the mind, community, neighborhood, religious institutions, and the workplace that students are deceived into thinking that being educated has nothing to do with social institutions or their daily lives. How we define thinking and intelligence will provide us with underlying assumptions and conclusions from which to analyze and evaluate the role of teachers, the conditions of our schools, educational practices, and how students, parents, teachers, workers, and community negotiate reality on a daily basis. By opening cognition to socio-political and personal concerns, we recognize and utilize historical materialist, feminist, and indigenous theories as well as theories and insights from peoples of color in an attempt to promote critical thinking and critical action. Both our definition of thinking and intelligence and our realization of how schools are implicated in a postmodern capitalist society can offer profound suggestions and strategies for teaching and society in general.

Redefining Our Roles as Educators: From Technicians to Organic Intellectuals

> I do not say, of course, that schools can solve the 10 problems of poverty, alienation, and family disintegration. But schools can *respond* to them.   —*Neil Postman*

I have attempted in this essay to ask the critical question of how we as educators might help our students and ourselves find our voices while dealing with meaningless and despair in the interest of hope and trans- formative metacognition, how we might develop a post-formal educa- tional psychology—one grounded in historical and political under- standing—a theory and practice that can advance our ability to struggle against irrational and pathological institutional and personal relation- ships and forces. The answers to these complex questions are not easy, and although various theoretical solutions have been put forward, one of the purposes of this essay is to ground our understanding of post- modern capitalism within both *objective* and *subjective* conditions that affect the construction of human psyche and consciousness and impact on the production of knowledge as well as the values and dispositions associated with critical thinking and learning. Postformal pedagogy must embrace an understanding of how objective conditions impact on subjective concerns. Equipped with an understanding of both historical materialism and the educational and psychological insights born from the contributions of postmodernism, we can begin to define a pedagogy that addresses both the *subjective* and *objective* issues facing educa- tional institutions, students, workers, parents, and civil society in gen- eral. From there, we can begin to develop strategies of resistance at school sites that confront both external and internal forces.

It is important in the development of a post-formal pedagogy that we define the concepts *objective* and *subjective*. A discussion of the objective conditions of late postmodern capitalist relations as they appear generally in society and specifically at school sites would con- cern the material conditions of existence—historical, economic, institu- tional, and political arrangements as they affect distribution of opportu- nity, wealth, power, patriarchy, racism, authority, and control. Subjective issues would address these issues within cultural, psycho- logical, and educational arenas. I will use the term *critical pedagogy* to define a Post-formalist pedagogy interested in the dialectical relation- ship between both subjective *and* objective conditions. Politicizing ped- agogy through objective understandings brings an awareness of class, history, gender, racial, and capitalist relations to cultural and psycho/educational concerns and thus holds a promise for both materi- al and individual transformation. Politicizing and personalizing peda- gogy through subjective understandings brings with it a knowledge of the prevailing psychic dis-order and its relationship to the affective and cognitive dimensions of human existence. My position is that both sub- jective and objective conditions must be perceived in the definition of a critical pedagogy—both are necessary for an understanding of the educational domain as simply one irrational institution among many.

In a Society That Doesn't Value Family, There Can Be No Family Values

> Many poor families manage by cutting back on food, jeopardizing their health and the development of their children, or by living in substandard and sometimes dangerous housing. Some do without heat, electricity, telephone service, or plumbing for months or years. Many do without health insurance, health care, safe child care, or reliable transportation to take them to and from work. Confronted with impossible choices and inadequate basics, and lacking any cushion of savings or assets, many are just one illness, job loss, or family crisis away from homelessness or family dissolution.
> —*Children's Defense Fund*

An analysis of the objective conditions of postmodern capitalism would begin with issues of material reality, specifically as these issues impact on children, communities, teachers, parents, and society in general. It would concern itself with how poverty and lack of opportunity impact on learning and teaching—and it would help define a critical pedagogy interested in the relationship between the *empty* stomach and the *full* head.

According to national statistics, the number of children living in poverty increased by 2.2 million between 1979 and 1989. Not only are there 14 million children living in poverty in the U.S., the highest number for any industrialized nation in the world, but when it comes to providing family support, the U.S. ranks in the lower half of all Western industrialized countries. Couple with this increases in child abuse nationally, suicide as the leading cause of death amongst teenagers, and homelessness and Dickensian lifestyles, and the United States is beginning to resemble Brazil in its division of rich and poor, with the top 1% of the population controlling more than 40% of the wealth, and 5% controlling more than 77% of all equity holdings in stocks including individual shares, pensions, and all defined contribution funds such as Keogh's and IRA's. The bottom 80% of households—roughly 4 out of 5—own just 1.8% of the total value of all stocks and bonds (*Business Week*).

This is the same society where black teenagers face unemployment rates of 57%, where an *injustice system* imprisons, keeps under surveillance, or otherwise places on probation one in three black men in their twenties; and a society where youth is increasingly divorced from the cognitive and affective dimensions of thinking necessary to sustain a democracy and public discourse.

The current trend, for those who are fortunate enough to afford it, is to seek private solutions to social problems. As a result, public institutions and accompanying civic and community life have been increasingly ceded to increased privatization. So, for example, we live in a reality whereby Barnes & Noble now is open longer than our public libraries and has better lighting and seating; the super mall has replaced public parks and public gatherings in many locales as a source for enjoyment and community congregations; Federal Express, if one has the means, promises far superior delivery service than the U.S. Post Office; private security police remain one of the fastest-growing industries in American society; and private schools and their "voucher" proponents along with home schooling advocates threaten one of the nation's the last national treasures—public schools and the Jeffersonian commitment to a common school for all citizens.

. The objective conditions of post-capitalist relations find their expressions in school sites both in terms of oppression and resistance to this oppression. Inadequate resources, regressive property tax funding, decaying buildings, non-working toilets, metal detectors, dog search-and-seize units, school uniforms, underpaid staff, overcrowded classrooms, workers who have lost power, authority, and control, overburdened curricula, and disenfranchised parents are just a few of the obvious oppressive problems that schools are grappling with. These objective expressions of postmodern capitalism are implicated in pedagogical theories and practices as they work to dialectically impact on the way schooling is organized, controlled, and negotiated on a daily basis both within a community and within and outside of classrooms. Control and power in the outside world become translated within classrooms. Educational practices, for example, formalist or developmental classroom management, although wedded to a particular didactic theory of teaching and learning, are little more than organizational managerial expressions attempting to maintain docile tranquillity among students through an extrinsic reward system—thus satisfying the obedient educational work force and those who oversee them.

Objectively, we can also speak of laws that have recently impacted on school sites and what it means to be an educator and learner within this judicial climate. Recently, Proposition 187 was passed in California, mandating that schools would become policemen for the

Immigration Naturalization Service by reporting kids with no legal status in the country. Although this is being challenged, new laws regarding affirmative action and enrollment were slated to be voted on by California residents in November of 1997. In Arizona, voters approved an initiative that makes it illegal for workers in the public sector to speak anything but English on the job. This is being challenged in the U.S. Supreme Court, but there is little doubt that the scapegoating, racist, anti-immigrant laws are reflective of the objective conditions of postcapitalism. And of course, Clinton's *end of welfare as we know it,* as opposed to *ending poverty as we know it,* promises to do away with 60 years of a federal commitment to the poor, add 1.2 million children to the poverty roles, and disadvantage millions and millions others by limiting health care, nutrition programs, and lunch programs.

There is little doubt that more than children, or family, or public community, profit, wealth and greed constitute the real values of postcapitalist society. What is important here for pedagogical purposes is to recognize and analyze how the forces of privatization and consumption work to construct citizens so that they might deal with a reality devoid of individual and social meaning, personal and social responsibility, and the moral, emotional and cognitive compasses necessary for democratic living.

The Poverty of Pedagogy and the Promise of Possibility

> The paradox of education is precisely this—that as one begins to become conscious one begins to examine the society in which he is being educated. The purpose of education, finally, is to create in a person the ability to look at the world for himself; to make his own decisions, to say to himself this is black or this is white, to decide for himself whether there is a God in heaven or not. To ask questions of the universe, and even to learn to live with those questions, is the way he achieves his own identity. But no society is really anxious to have that sort of person around. What societies really, ideally, want is a citizenry which will simply obey the rules of society. If a society succeeds in this, it is about to perish. The obligation of anyone who thinks of himself as responsible is to examine society and try to change it and fight it—no matter at what risk. This is the only hope society has. This is the only way societies change.   —*James Baldwin*

Much of what has been written in North America and elsewhere concerning problems associated with educational forms and practices has been weighted heavily on the side of critique, accurately arguing that a critical examination and analysis of the *poverty of pedagogy,* both in the social relations of production and within the bankruptcy of current and past curriculum and pedagogical practices, is essential. However, it is only recently that educational theorists have turned their attention to the *promise of possibility* and the *possibility of promise,* correctly arguing that forms of collective empowerment appear among both educational workers and students as they engage in and critically reflect upon issues of domination, power, and social relations, while simultaneously developing a body politic concerned with morality and the common struggle for human dignity and freedom. This realization has profound implications for students, parents, teachers, and society as a whole.

To begin with, as educators we need to struggle to embody and exemplify the politics of hope and optimism as we go about our daily activities as teachers. In face of drastic pay cuts, intolerable working conditions, excessive bureaucracy, an over-population of technocrats divorced from the classroom, increased violence within the schools, parent alienation, racism, sexism, and the wide range of problems facing our society and public schools, it is often difficult to maintain and resonate a sense of hope towards the future of our students and the democracy we are attempting to build. It is difficult to transcend the politics of despair and there is no question that we confront real institutional blocks of despondency and melancholy that limit our hopes for freedom each and every day. I know that as an educator, I must confront the depths of misery in pondering both a better world and a corresponding pedagogy that exemplifies and conveys critical thinking opportunities for my students. I don't want to be cursed with the politics and polemics of nihilism or consumed with the negative side of the dialectic. I want to search out new meanings of expression and hope that we can make relevant and liberatory "educational theater" for the masses of people in this country, that we can struggle to make transformative metacognition—a commitment to a critical sensibility and the rethinking of our thinking in the interest of social change—an actual and integral part of personal reflection and daily activity. An intellectual understanding of the negative devoid of hope and without a commitment to embracing the positive can become a crippling and disabling metaphor for despondency.

For Sharon Welch, the pedagogical notion of hope is embodied in a theology that combines a vision of liberation with an understanding of oppressive conditions both past and present. She remarks:

This theology emerges from the struggle to create, not merely to proclaim, a human community that embodies freedom. The verification of this struggle is not conceptual, but practical: the successful process of enlightenment and emancipation, a process that is open and self-critical. This theology emerges from an effort to live on the edge, accepting both the power and peril of discourse, engaging in a battle for truth with a conscious preference for the oppressed. . . . It is a discourse imbued with a particular tragedy of human existence—the dangerous memory of despair, barrenness, suffering—and with the particular moments of liberation—the equally dangerous memory of historical actualizations of freedom and community. . . . [This] type of theology . . . affirms with Bloch "that learned hope is the signpost for this age—not just hope, but hope and the knowledge to take the way to it" (Welch, p. 214).

By embracing pedagogical hope, teachers can become to view themselves as more than simply school teachers—but rather as *intellectuals*. Giroux has commented:

Viewing teachers as intellectuals also provides a strong theoretical critique of technocratic and instrumental ideologies underlying an educational theory that separates the conceptualization, planning and design of curricula from the process of implementation and execution. It is important to stress that teachers must take active responsibility for raising serious questions about what they teach, how they are to teach, and what the larger goals are for which they are striving. This means that they must take a responsible role in shaping the purposes and conditions of schooling. . . . If we believe that the role of teaching cannot be reduced to merely training in the practical skills, but involves, instead, the education of a class of intellectuals vital to the development of a free society, then the category of intellectual becomes a way of linking the purpose of teacher education, public schooling and inservice training to the very principles necessary for developing a democratic order and society (Giroux, p. 126).

I would also add that this conceptualization affords teachers a new-gained respect and integrity, both for themselves as agents of social change and for the profession of pedagogy in general. Redefining ourselves as intellectuals affords us a dignity and a sense of self-esteem which is so viciously expropriated by the power relationships within the educational system.

   Schooling in a profound sense is an institution dependent on external social and economic forces. One need only to witness the dramatic debate over public and private school funding, vouchers, and so-called "Choice." Visions and struggles for transformations in educational sites and pedagogical practices will of necessity be forced to address these wider economic and social concerns. For educators in oversized classrooms, saddled with inadequate resources, impeded by biased assessment processes, disdained by administrators conceptually divorced from what it means to be an educator or an educated person in today's rapidly changing global reality, victims of ill-conceived and deficient training programs, laboring without sufficient quality educational preparation time or resources, and burdened with time constraints and content-driven curriculums, this in itself represents an enormous educational challenge. But if we are to imagine and create centers of learning available to all members of society, then we must begin to rethink our role as educators, to become to think of ourselves as *active organic intellectuals* in the construction of the material and ideological preconditions of the pedagogical utopia we seek.

Through our educational and political organizations and diverse community involvement, both teachers and students need to address issues involving the broader function of schooling. Issues having to do with questions of power, community involvement, philosophies of knowledge acquisition, social theory, and political ideology all must become the object of critical examination. Schooling as an institution must be recognized as a political site and pedagogical practices as political practices. By imagining a vision of schooling informed by compassion, faith in the human being, and the obligation for struggling to create a better world, we as educators can help students to constitute this language of critique from which can be born the practical *promise of possibility.*

References

American Association of University Women (June,1992). *Creating a gender-fair multicultural curriculum.* Washington, DC: 1.

Baldwin, J. (1988). A talk to teachers. Reprinted in R. Simonson and S. Walker (Eds.), *The Graywolf annual five: Multi-cultural literacy.* St. Paul: Graywolf Press.

Business Week (April 22, 1996). Soaring stocks: Are only the rich getting richer? New York: McGraw Hill.

Children's Defense Fund and Northeastern University's Center for Labor Market Studies (1992). *Vanishing dreams: The economic plight of American young families.* Washington DC: Children's Defense Fund.

Fitzgerald, F. S. (1935). The crack up. In A. Mizener (Ed.), *The Fitzgerald Reader* (p. 405). New York: Charles Scribner's Sons (1963).

Gardner, H. (1991). *The unschooled mind.* New York: Basic Books.

Giroux, H. A. (1989). *Critical pedagogy, the state, and cultural power.* Albany: SUNY Press.

Giroux, H.A. (1988). *Teachers as intellectuals: Toward a critical pedagogy of learning.* South Hadley, MA: Bergin and Garvey Publishers. .

McLaren, P. and Hammer, R. (Winter, 1992). Media knowledges, warrior citizenry, and postmodern literacies. *Journal of curriculum theorizing, 57.*

Paul, R. (1990). *Critical thinking: What every person needs to survive in a rapidly changing global world.* Center for Critical Thinking and Moral Critique. Sonoma: Sonoma State University.

Postman, N. (1995). *The end of education.* New York: Knopf.

Title unknown (1992). California: *Los Angeles Times.*

Welch, S. (1985). In E. Bloch (Ed.), *The Principle of Hope, III* (pp. 1366-67). Cambridge, MA: MIT Press.

CHAPTER FOUR

Constructivist Theory in the Age of Newt Gingrich: The Post-formal Concern with Power

Lourdes Diaz Soto

Piaget's Constructivist Paradigm

"What is REAL?" the Rabbit asked the Skin Horse in the children's story, *The Velveteen Rabbit*.

> "Real isn't how you are made," said the Skin Horse. "It's a thing that happens to you. When a child loves you for a long, long time, not just to play with, but REALLY loves you, then you become Real" (Williams, 1981, p.14).

Borrowing from Piaget, the Skin Horse's background and expectations shaped her perceptions. What appeared to be objective reality is merely what her mind constructed since within the constructivist paradigm "[human] beings do not find or discover knowledge so much as construct or make it" (Schwandt, 1994).

As I reviewed the literature on constructivism and thought about this talk I also shared some thoughts with my students. Pei, a graduate student from the Taiwanese traditions warned me, "Don't do it, Dr. Soto, after all Piaget and psychology are just too much a part of the early childhood research literature. It will not be good for you!" Her consejo/advice was well intentioned and reminded me of our many years of acceptance and support of "taken for granted" knowledge evolving from one particular world view and one particular way of seeing and experiencing the world. My intent is to assume a critical voice that questions the consequences of this "taken-for-granted knowledge" that historically and currently shapes our profession. I maintain that silence and voicelessness are no longer necessities for early childhood practitioners within a critical constructivist paradigm that acknowledges multiple ways of knowing. The creation of knowledge within the field is not just for "elitist researchers only" but for all of the members of our community, thereby leading to a place where a greater moral vision of social justice and equity will be evident.

On behalf of young children and families, it is crucial to critically analyze the constructivist paradigms by asking about their ties to psychology, genetics and biology. Who drives this knowledge base? Whose definition of normative? Why are issues of power and voice so blatantly absent?

I asked Pei to think about the biological, genetic and psychological origins of the constructivist paradigm. We examined Piaget's *Limnaea stagnalis* and the importance of Vygotsky's contributions (our dialogue is in progress). We also found it important to think about the sociohistorical context of the "great male theoreticians." Issues of context, gender, race, socioeconomic status, and the scientific and political climates of the time no doubt influenced these thinkers. Vygotsky, who was influenced by Marxist theory, is Pei's favorite but she confessed that it is not always prudent to bring a sociocultural approach to discussions with "Piagetian worshipers." In Pei's mind, Piagetian followers are clearly blinded by what they maintain to be "indisputable and scientific truths" and find it hard to move beyond Piaget.

Constructivism is a theory of learning, not a description of teaching. It is at once a theory of knowing and a theory of coming to know. The theory of knowing was first articulated by Piaget and is essentially biological in nature and attempts to reveal how the "organism" encounters new experiences and therefore seeks to assimilate knowledge into the existing cognitive structures or to accommodate, thereby adjusting the new information. These cognitive structures evolve as individuals interpret, understand, and come to know (Piaget, 1970). The individual, the organism, the evolution, the mechanism of equilibration, the accommodation, the assimilation, the biological, the genetic epistemology are evident throughout these writings.

Piaget's writings have appeared for over half a century. A remarkable body of research, yet it is the work done in the last decade of his life that serves as the psychological basis for constructivism. He and his colleagues focused on the mechanism of learning and on the process that enabled new constructions—new perspectives—to take place. In his later research, Piaget returned to the mechanism of equilibration, an idea he formulated earlier in his career. Piaget's early work as a biologist studying *Limnaea stagnalis* (snails) is important because it helps to explain his interpretation of the mechanism of equilibration. Piaget showed a fascination for the snail's adaptation (Fosnot, 1996). Piaget studied three separate groups of snails—those that live in still tranquil waters; those that live in mildly disturbed waters agitated by waves; and those that live in severely disturbed waters agitated by high winds and waves. Piaget maintained that behavior drives the evolution of new structures because the development of new behavior causes an imbalance in the genetic structures, thereby causing a mutation. He proposed through much of his research that the mechanism promoting change in cognition was the same as that in evolution—equilibration. It may be, however, that we are not all snails, that some of us are lobsters and others are jellyfish! Piaget noted that his early explanations were limited and began to describe equilibration as a dynamic "dance" of progressive equilibria but continued to maintain and emphasize that "they resemble above all . . . the biological dynamic equilibriums" (Piaget, 1977, p.4).

Piaget does not completely overlook the social elements and refers to the interplay of the operations: "there is no longer any need to choose between the primacy of the social or that of the intellect; the collective intellect is the social equilibrium resulting from the interplay of the operations" (Piaget, 1970, p.114). Recent research (Fosnot, 1996; Lambert, et al., 1995; Perret-Clermont et al., 1991; Resnick, et al. 1991, and Wertsch, 1991) has helped us to gain additional understandings of the theory of constructivism as it relates to children's cognitive development. The theory of constructivism relies on the theories of Piaget, Vygotsky, and the semiotic interactionists to a great extent since these provide the basis for this psychological theory of learning.

According to Piaget, a change of developmental stage occurs as a result of a combination of four factors, maturation, physical and logico-mathematical level, social experience, and equilibration and is thought to be a slow process. Yet the work conducted by Perret-Clermont, et al. (1991) with elementary school children shows how participants were observed to progress from one stage to another in a very short time (from 5-10 minutes). These researchers note, "these observations show that research paradigms built on supposedly clear distinctions between what is social and cognitive will have an inherent weakness, because the causality of social and cognitive process is, at the very least, circular and is perhaps even more complex" (p. 50). The notion of individual testing is noted to be a complex social interaction where children access a wealth of social knowledge and skills. Contemporary biologists also note that the biological and the social are not separate but complementary (Lewontin, Rose and Kamin, 1984). Recent research is showing that we cannot understand cognition without observing the interaction within a context, within a culture. Cobb, Yackel, and Wood (1992) note that knowledge within a culture is "taken-as-shared."

Vygotsky's emphasis on the sociohistorical aspect of knowledge is an important contribution to this knowledge base. Vygotsky, like Piaget, believed in the idea that learning is developmental but distinguished between "spontaneous" (naturally occurring learning) and "scientific" (structured learning) concepts. His now-famous ideas include among others, the "zone of proximal development," the formation of inner speech and dialogue. Bruner extended Vygotsky's work with the notion of "scaffolding." Although not all constructivists agree with these theories, the work of Piaget, Vygotsky, and others helps to form the basis for the constructivist paradigm. Newly evolving terminology is evident and includes a distinction between the "cognitive constructivism" and "social constructivism."

> Implied in all of these ideas is that human beings have no access to an objective reality since we are constructing our version of it, while at the same time transforming it and ourselves. The important question to be asked is not whether the cognizing individual or culture should be given priority in an analysis of learning but what the interplay between them is (Fosnot, 1996, p.23).

In Resnick's et al. (1991) book introducing the idea of socially shared cognition, Wertsh notes that Piaget, Werner, and Vygotsky all place the genetic analysis at the very foundation of the study of the mind. In Vygotsky's case, the genetic method was in part due to his goal of creating a scientific psychology compatible with the Marxism-Leninism of the 1920's. Vygotsky also emphasized the development of the individual and formulated a "general genetic law of cultural development" stating that:

> Any function in the child's cultural development appears twice, on two planes. First it appears on the social plane, and then on the psychological plane. First it appears between people as an interpsychological category, and then within the child as an intrapsychological

category. We may consider this position as a law in the full sense of the word. Social relations or relations among people genetically underlie all higher functions and their relationships (Vygotsky, 1981, p. 163).

The major goal of his approach was to create an analysis that recognizes the historical, the cultural, and the institutional. Wertsch (1991) maintains that Vygotsky did not meet this goal but that others have added complementary knowledge. Wertsch also sees a need to search for theoretical constructs that will extend beyond psychology and among other disciplines. It will not be enough for contemporary researchers to extend psychological accounts to small interactions since there is a need

> to search for theoretical constructs and units of analysis that ensure a fundamental compatibility between the analyses conducted in psychology and other disciplines . . . we need to formulate issues under the heading of socially shared cognition in such a way that concrete empirical studies can be conducted that do not reduce inquiry to the exclusive language of a single discipline (Wertsch, 1991, p. 98).

Berk and Winsler (1995) also note that developmental psychologists and educators are beginning to embrace the idea that both the social and the cognitive are essential to one another. The idea that the background and the expectations of the individual shape their perception is a monumental contribution; yet as Kincheloe and Steinberg (1993) note in their theory of post-formalism that

> Developmental psychological principles have become so much a part of teacher education programs that it is hard to see where questions about them might arise (p. 171).

There is no doubt that Piaget and the cognitive psychologists have added tremendous knowledge to our field and have transformed modernist notions by indicating that there is no truly objective reality. One of the problems with Piaget's version of constructivism, however, is that it includes reductionist analytical reasoning, coinciding with the Cartesian dualism that splits the human experience into the "in here" and the "out there." Critical constructivism, on the other hand, asserts that human thought, human feeling and human actions are all interrelated. Constructivism may be a necessary prerequisite in order for education to experience a sociohistorical shift from modernism to post modernism (Kincheloe, 1993).

The objectivist perspective of the modernists maintains that students should be socialized within an efficiency model that fosters economic productivity. In a recent talk at Franklin and Marshall College in Pennsylvania (November 13, 1996), Newt Gingrich maintained that education needs to shift its focus to a free enterprise, technologically driven system that relies less on educators and more on monetary rewards similar to the "Learning by Learning" program that pays children $2 for every book they read.

Issues of power have been notably absent from the constructivist paradigms with the exception of those of critical theorists (Kincheloe and Steinberg, 1993; Kincheloe and McLaren, 1994; Kincheloe, 1993; 1995); and feminist theorists (Belensky, Clinchy, Goldberger and Tarule, 1986; Gilligan, 1982; Longino, 1981; Maher, 1987; Weiler, 1991). In our own field the politics of early childhood developmentally appropriate practices have been valiantly analyzed and critiqued by early childhood educators such as Janice Jipson (1991), who sees the need to examine the increasingly individualistic and positivist nature of early education, and Sally Lubeck (1994) who indicates that it is

> time to move beyond the narrow confines of the environment paradigm and time to confront the irony of the idealized curricular approach that discourages critical reflection on—and fair and open dialogue about—practice. At issue is the question of whether cherished beliefs in pluralism and democracy will be manifest as rhetoric or as reality, a question of whether the distant voices of those too long silenced will be heard (p.38).

In early childhood education, the issue of power relates both to young children's daily realities in a conservative America and to our child care teachers' low wages. Practitioners caring for the greatest responsibility of our nation—our young children—earn wages often below poverty levels and often lack medical coverage. Our child care teachers have been relegated to an underclass as our nation sacrifices the lives of young children and the lives of child care teachers for its own economic benefit. All of these issues of power and oppression are clearly absent from the sterile and sanitized psychological paradigms that have been blinded to issues of equity and social justice in contemporary America. As Kincheloe aptly indicates in his introduction to this book:

Empiricist psychologists who deny theoretical pre-assumptions in their work are great deceivers, wrapping themselves in the flag of objectivity while often unconsciously promoting specific values, world views, and paradigmatic faiths.

In a recent article, Gary Natriello (1996) also begins to unmask how our political and corporate leaders at the National Education Summit (1996) have diverted attention from the conditions in American schools by proposing recommendations that have little relevance on our understandings about schools. This effort to distract us from paying serious attention to the real issues facing our schools and our learners will prove costly. Natriello notes that in states throughout the nation parents and students are seeking legal remedies from state governments that have been actively participating and supporting educational systems that privilege some while oppressing others. The corporate sector has also contributed to the problem by abandoning U.S. cities, and like our government leaders, corporate leaders express neither regret nor show any signs of change. Natriello sees the need for educational researchers to begin to ask the difficult questions about "how and why political discourse has become detached from the reality of American schooling" (p. 8).

The conservative modernists' willingness to worship scientific methods and traditions has helped to establish the separation of the cognitive from the emotional and the spiritual. Children's issues include a variety of domains. Goleman (1995) notes the importance of emotional intelligence, and teachers working with young children have long understood their emotional and spiritual needs.

Early childhood practitioners have shown a willingness to become advocates on behalf of young children. The practitioners' voices have often been drowned however by the "experts," the elitist thinkers, and politicians whose quantifiable and objective knowledge is somehow more valued. Kincheloe and McLaren (1994) point to the importance of legitimating worker knowledge since the practitioner is less likely to distort reality by being closer to the everyday realities. Our nation and our field have created a cadre of "elitist" researchers and politicians obsessed with the scientific quantification and statistical measurement of discrete and "objective" variables quite distant from the daily realities of young children, teachers, and families.

Critical constructivism, on the other hand, asserts that human thought, human feelings, and human actions are all interrelated. Critical constructivists maintain that the whole is more important than the discrete in education and

> reject reductionist task analysis procedures . . . [as well as] definitions
> of intelligence grounded upon a quantitative measurement of how
> many facts and associations an individual has accumulated; critical
> constructivists maintain that there are as many paths to sophisticated
> thinking as there are sophisticated thinkers. The best way to teach one
> to think is to research particular students, observing the social context
> from which they emerge and the particular ways they undertake the
> search for meaning. In this process critical constructivist teachers set
> up conditions that encourage self awareness and reflection
> (Kincheloe, 1993, p.115).

Self-reflection not only promotes self-knowledge but also affords teachers an opportunity to initiate a cultural and educational critique. Critical constructivism as a theoretically grounded form of "world making" allows teachers to step back from the "taken for granted knowledge" and to view ways that our perceptions are constructed through our language, culture, and power.

In order to determine what constitute valid constructions of reality Kincheloe (1993) proposes some guiding principles for critical constructivism:

1. that the constructions are consistent with a critical postmodern system of meaning;
2. that the constructions are helpful to emancipatory goals;
3. that the constructions are internally consistent;
4. that the constructions contribute to the ability of humans to function and survive;
5. that the constructions are appropriate for inquiry; and
6. that the constructions avoid reductionism by recognizing the complexity of the situation.

As the field of early childhood education embarks on a journey beyond Piaget toward a "critical constructivist paradigm" that acknowledges multiple ways of knowing, the foundation for post-formal thinking needs to emerge.

> The task of the advocates of critical thinking—those who understand
> both the social contextualization of thinking and the postmodern cri-

tique of its discursive practices—is to overthrow these reductionist views of the way power works (Kincheloe, 1993, p.128).

The issue for early childhood educators is to uncover how children and child care teachers have been silenced and oppressed by the more powerful elements of our nation who are driven by the Cartesian scientific genetic traditions and motivated by an ego-centric economic self-interest. When early childhood educators view, examine, and critique how issues of power are affecting their lives and children's lives, they will also see the need to map an early childhood utopian dream in solidarity and within our characteristically caring traditions. As Maxine Green (1996) notes that,

> for those of us who teach the young [this is a] peculiar and menacing time. Perhaps we might begin by releasing our imaginations and summoning up the traditions of freedom in which most of us were reared. We might try to make audible again the recurrent calls for justice and equality (p.28).

Children in Conservative America

An NPR story about the South Bronx gave listeners a vivid aural portrait of common school conditions by including recordings of children's audible wheezing as well as a school nurse's labored breathing as she climbed the stairs to her office ("Asthma," 1996). The story detailed how children attending P.S. #20 and living in the South Bronx are being affected by the environmental pollution of an industrial waste site. Hoping to make their voices heard, the children in the school wrote letters to the President of the United States explaining their problem. If local industry and local politicians were unable or unwilling to tackle the problem, they reasoned, then the President of their nation would surely respond.

Close your eyes and imagine that YOU live in the South Bronx and that these are YOUR children. How would you feel if your child's health was being affected on a daily basis by the fumes, the thick waste, and the odors emanating from the proximity of this industrial garbage. We should all be outraged that children's health and voices are not being attended to and that an increasingly mean-spirited political context continues to disregard children's needs.

Children growing up in the South Bronx, children growing up in the housing projects of Chicago, children growing up in the ghettoes of Philadelphia, children growing up in reservations throughout America, children growing up in Appalachia, all of our poor children, our black children, our Latino children, our Asian children, our white children, our brown children are all being neglected, forgotten, abused in this richest nation of the world. The Children's Defense Fund (1996) shows that it is not only the South Bronx children and the Chicago children but 15.3 million children. Our youngest children comprise the poorest children (1:4 younger than six); while the richest one fifth of American families received 11 times as much income as the poorest one fifth. This constitutes the widest economic gap since 1947. The child poverty rates in the United States of America are the highest among 18 industrialized countries, according to the Luxembourg Income Study. Bilingual children, immigrant children, and women are also caught in the politically conservative net of our leaders:

• WHEN California continues to approve mean-spirited propositions (Proposition 186, Proposition 209);
• WHEN Presidential candidates openly support English-only measures;
• WHEN a Texas judge seriously considers taking a child away from a home-language-speaking mother;
• WHEN a conservative radio talk show host Rush Limbaugh continues his relentless attacks on women calling us "femme-Nazis" while denigrating and objectifying people of color.

All of these attacks continue until our lives are ridiculed, dehumanized, and devalued. As Henry Giroux (1995) maintains, our nation is experiencing a popular construction of a

> national identity that is read as white, heterosexual, middle class, and allegedly threatened by contamination from cultural, linguistic, racial, and sexual differences (p. 48).

This mean-spirited conservative agenda is being disseminated publicly and privately by powerful elements like Newt Gingrich, the corporate sector (e.g., Texaco), the Rush Limbaugh worshipers, and the religious right who is infiltrating our schools with school board appointments. The political saviness of these players is evidenced as they continue to acquire power and influence our schools, our government, our legal system, and our politicians.

Our nation already has a sad history of intolerance and oppression as exemplified by:

- the Massachusetts Colony anti-Quaker provisions;
- the removal of the Cherokees from Georgia, later known as the Trail of Tears;
- the United States' Constitution's willingness to define a slave as the equivalent to three-fifths of a free man;
- the city of "brotherly love's" violence against Catholics, Irish, and African Americans;
- the Chinese exclusion laws in California that were not repealed until 1952;
- the Japanese internment camps;
- the Indian wars;
- the myth of a Jewish conspiracy and continued antisemitism;
- the lynching and killing of Tejanos;
- the refusal of the Three Rivers community to bury Felix Longoria, a Tejano killed in the line of duty who was later buried in the Arlington National Cemetery with full military honors due to efforts of then-U.S. Senator Lyndon Baines Johnson of Texas;
- the Ku Klux Klan's reign of terror showing that by 1993 there were over 300 different white supremacist organizations actively recruiting in the U.S.; while a former grand dragon of the KKK, David Duke, ran for the Presidency of the United States of America;
- and the fact that today gays and lesbians are the most frequent target of hate crimes (Carnes, 1995).

In spite of progress in this area the Southern Poverty Law Center documents how Skinhead, Ku Klux Klan, and Neo-Nazi organizations are an integral part of our nation with over 300 hate groups scattered throughout America. Between 1990 and 1993 alone there were 108 bias-motivated murders, thousands of assaults, cross-burning and acts of violence and intimidation. In addition Jim Carnes states:

> Equally troubling is the willingness of so many people to look the other way. In a 1992 survey of high school students, 30 percent said they would participate in racist incidents, and 17 percent said they would silently support them. These numbers suggest that we still have much to learn from the bitter harvests of our past—that our democracy is still a work in progress (p.128).

Is this the America early childhood educators have been dreaming about? Is this the legacy American children will want to inherit? How can professionals in our field relate to all of these complex issues? What role does a constructivist paradigm and post-formal thinking play in all of this? Why shouldn't we critically examine the long-held Cartesian scientific genetic traditions and visions of our profession?

Will the field of early childhood education see the moral imperative to move beyond existing scientific, biologically derived, genetically based paradigms in this era that is so willing to disregard the needs of children and child care teachers?

An Early Childhood Dream of Social Justice

President Clinton talks about building a bridge to the twenty-first century. As we envision the future of our nation we need to ensure that it is more than an economically driven and scientifically based society. Historically the powerful elements of our nation have relied on the notion of "rugged individualism" based upon a pioneer mentality. The complex issues facing our children signal a need for additional wisdom from many voices. The many ways of seeing the world from many perspectives can be built upon with additional voices, with the additional wisdom of a "critical constructivist paradigm," with multiple voices and multiple ways of knowing.

As my students and I have continued to read and discuss these and other issues, I asked my students to think about the knowledge and wisdom that is needed in contemporary society. These students have read and discussed the socio-cultural and socio-historical issues impacting linguistically and culturally diverse people throughout the world. They have read about linguistic human rights, the documents emanating from the United Nations, and the ways nations of the world handle issues of language and culture. They have noted that most nations of the world include second-language learning as an integral part of the curriculum. In Luxembourg, for example, teachers speak five languages as a part of the certification process. My students have been perplexed at America's continued insistence on a monocultural, monolingual, English-only, "tongue-tied" conservative perspective.

Since my students represent various nations of the world and a variety of linguistic and cultural traditions I asked them, "What is the one piece of advice/consejo, or wisdom that you would give to Americans?"

"Kerjasama," the notion of collaboration and solidarity has become a common theme in our discussions. The idea of re-examining outdated and outmoded notions of "rugged individualism" and male-dominated paradigms opens up a space for a spirit of solidarity. The idea advocated by my students has also been shown to be an integral part of the Native American traditions. Philips (1983) as well as Au and Jordan (1981) have noted the importance of collaborative ways of interacting in early childhood settings. My students from eastern traditions, especially from Taiwan, emphasized the importance of loving one another and stressed how highly regarded friendships are. "A friend would give her life for you, a friend would give you her child if you needed one," Jiam told us. One student from Papua New Guinea shared the idea of unity, "bungwantaim," and friendship, "wantok." Their conclusion has been that these are "matters of the heart." By "matters of the heart," they mean love, solidarity, and the willingness of human beings to reach out to one another and create a significantly better world.

It IS possible for communities to choose a critical constructivist humanism as opposed to economic and scientific paradigms. It is also possible for communities to initiate power models in the spirit of "kerjasama," "wantok," and "bungwantaim." One such example is the Pro-Canada network described by Peter Findlay (1994). A coalition of groups was initiated within the context of a global economic restructuring. When a major policy initiative called for the signing of a major trade agreement, various community groups organized themselves. The vision included organizing the economy to meet the human need rather than the capital accumulation. This meant rethinking a variety of relationships including ethics, the economy, and the society. As Findlay notes:

> The loose coalition of individuals and groups which had formed to combat the trade initiative . . . includes labor, farmers', women's, anti-poverty, aboriginal, environmental, peace, church, cultural and senior citizens' groups and its purpose is to continue the struggle to ensure that the future of Canada is shaped by and for people not profits. The Pro-Canada Network is committed to the principles of decentralized participation, conscientization, cultural struggle and praxis (p.114).

Paulo Freire's ideas about conscientization were pertinent to the Pro-Canada Network in light of his call for the union of ideas and practice within liberating struggles and the "importance of their role of subjective in the process of making history or of being made by the history" (Freire cited in Findlay, 1994, p. 121).

The many culturally and linguistically diverse families I have met over the years have shown far more wisdom and knowledge than the school administrators and school board leaders responsible for their children's schooling. Puerto Rican mainland families, for example, interviewed in a study reported elsewhere (Soto, 1997), revealed very specific educational knowledge consistent with research evidence while the more powerful elements of the school and the community overshadowed their knowledge and silenced their voices. Educational leaders may want to humbly examine the idea that they are not the only knowledge brokers.

Throughout history when people wanted answers to life's questions they relied on the wisdom of their forefathers, written documents, or myths if they were an oral people. Contemporary societies have now turned to modern science and have disregarded alternate and multiple ways of seeing the world. Smith (1994) notes that

> It is a signal feature of our century's close that we recognize that this turn to science was mistaken. Not entirely mistaken, for science (and its spin-off, technology) have their place. What was mistaken was to expect science to answer ultimate questions, for its method doesn't connect with them (p. 10).

Smith adds that

> Modern science . . . must be reassessed in light of the changing times and the continuing struggle for social justice. But if we single out their conclusions about reality and how life should be lived, they begin to look like the winnowed wisdom of the human race (p. 246).

Science does indeed become the "winnowed wisdom of the human race" when we critically examine the complicated issues facing children, families, and educators in increasingly complex context. The daily realities faced by young children and families in an increasingly conservative context help us to realize just how much of a moral imperative an early childhood dream of social justice has become.

The life of Janusz Korczak of Poland (Brendtro, Brokenleg, Van Bockern, 1990) portrays the actions of a teacher loved by his children. The *Velveteen Rabbit* would find Korczak to be very REAL, as a writer, teacher, and the director of a school and orphanage for Jewish children of the street. His school was moved to the Warsaw Ghetto when the Nazis occupied Poland. He chose to remain with his 200 children and when it became evident that he and his children would be sent to a death camp, "he prepared them for what was to come." They prepared a play based on Rabindrinath Tagore's *Post Office*, a story about a dying Hindu boy. The day the soldiers arrived they were dressed in their best and marched behind the biggest boy who led them carrying a green flag. This children's parade made its way to the chlorinated box cars and ultimately to the gas chambers of Treblinka.

There are no buildings in the place where Korczak and his children met their death, only trees, grass, and a circle of stones. The only individual name on any one stone reads "Janusz and children" along with names of the cities and countries of the victims of this holocaust. A manuscript entitled *Ghetto Diary* was recovered by Korczak's friends behind a brick wall in the children's home. He summarized the meaning of his life by stating, "I exist not to be loved and admired, but to love and to act."

My students immersed in "kerjasama" and "bungwantaim," *The Velveteen Rabbit*, Janusz Korczak, and many early childhood educators have shown that the wisdom we need to hold on to relates to matters of the heart. The wisdom includes solidarity and love. Love for humanity and love for ourselves. Early childhood educators have been loved by children for a long, long time. This love has made us REAL and unwilling to become transfixed mannequins hypnotized in our daily lives as spectators of the prevailing conservative whims of our politicians. It is evident that conservative forces fear that educators may actually be teaching children to critically analyze deplorable conditions like the ones Jonathan Kozol (1995) reveals. We should be optimistic, however, that our profession with the advent of post-formal thinking and multiple ways of knowing can fashion a caring early childhood utopian dream. It seems to me that if we are willing to take the risk in solidarity, we CAN find a space of hope and possibility where issues of equity and social justice will become the more powerful elements for our mutual benefits.

References

Asthma in the South Bronx (May 23, 1996). *All things considered.* Washington, DC: National Public Radio.

Au, K. and Jordan, C. (1981). Teaching reading to Hawaiian children: Finding culturally appropriate solutions. In H. Trueba and G. Guthrie (Eds.), *Culture and the bilingual classroom: Studies in classroom ethnography.* Cambridge, MA: Newbury House.

Belensky, M., Clinchy, B. Goldberger, N. and Tarule, J. (1986). *Women's ways of knowing: The development of self, body, and mind.* New York: Basic Books.

Berk, L. and Winsler, A. (1995). *Scaffolding children's learning: Vygotsky and early childhood education.* Washington, D.C. : National Association for the Education of Young Children.

Brendtro, L, Brokenleg, M., and Van Bockern, S. (1990). *Reclaiming youth at risk: Our hope for the future.* Indiana: National Educational Service.

Carnes, J. (1995). *Us and them: A history of intolerance in America.* Montgomery, AL: Southern Poverty Law Center.

Children's Defense Fund. (1996). *The state of America's children: Yearbook 1996.* Washington, D.C.: Author.

Cobb, P., Yackel, E., and Wood, T. (1992). Interaction and learning in mathematics classroom situations. *Educational Studies in Mathematics, 23,* 99–122.

De Vries, R. and Kohlberg, L. (1987). *Constructivist early education: Overview and comparison with other programs.* Washington, D.C.: National Association for the Education of Young Children.

Findlay, P. (1994). Conscientization and social movements in Canada: The relevance of Paulo Freire's ideas in contemporary politics. In P. McLaren and C. Lankshear (Eds.), *Politics of liberation: Paths from Freire.* New York: Routledge.

Fosnot, C. Twomey (1996). *Constructivism: Theory, perspectives and practice.* New York: Teachers College Press.

Freire, P. (1985). *The politics of education: Culture, power, and liberation.* MA: Bergin and Garvey.

Gilligan, C. (1982). *In a different voice.* Cambridge: Harvard University Press.

Giroux, H. (1995). National identity and the politics of multiculturalism. *College Literature, 22*(2), 42–57.

Giroux, H. and McLaren, P. (1986). Teacher education and the politics of engagement: The case for democratic schooling. *Harvard Educational Review, 56*(3), 213–238.

Goleman, D. (1995). *Emotional Intelligence.* New York: Bantam Books.

Green, M. (1996). In search of a critical pedagogy. In P. Leistyna, A. Woodrum, and S. Sherblom (Eds.). *Breaking free: The transformative power of critical pedagogy.* Cambridge, MA: Harvard Educational Review.

Jipson, J. (1991). Developmentally appropriate practice: Culture, curriculum, connections. *Early Education and Development*, 2(2), 120–136.

Kincheloe, J. (1993). *Toward a critical politics of teacher thinking: Mapping the postmodern*. Westport, CT: Bergin and Garvey.

Kincheloe, J. (1995). *Toil and Trouble*. New York: Peter Lang.

Kincheloe, J. and McLaren, P. (1994). Rethinking critical theory and qualitative research. In N. Denzin and Y. Lincoln, *Handbook of Qualitative Research*. Thousand Oaks, CA: Sage Publications.

Kincheloe, J. and Steinberg, S. (1993). A tentative description of post-formal thinking: The critical confrontation with cognitive theory. *Harvard Educational Review*, 63(3), 296–320.

Kozol, J. (1995). *Amazing grace*. New York: Crown Publishers.

Lambert, L., Walker, D., Zimmerman, D., Cooper, J., Lambert, D., Gardner, M., and Slack, P. J. Ford (1995). *The Constructivist Leader*. New York: Teachers College Press.

Lewontin, R, Rose, S., and Kamin, L. (1984). *Not in our genes*. New York: Pantheon.

Longino, H. (1981). Scientific objectivity and feminist theorizing. *Liberal Education*, Fall, 187–195.

Lubeck, S. (1994). The politics of developmentally appropriate practice. Exploring issues of culture, class, and curriculum. In B. Mallory and R. New (Eds.), *Diversity and developmentally appropriate practices. Challenges for early childhood education*. New York: Teachers College Press.

Maher, F. (1987). Toward a richer theory of feminist pedagogy: A comparison of "liberation" and "gender" models for teaching and learning. *Journal of Education*, 169(3), 91–100.

Natriello, G. (1996). Diverting attention from conditions in American schools. *Educational Researcher*, 25(8), 7–9.

Perret-Clermont, A., Perret, J., and Bell, N. (1991). The social construction of meaning and cognitive activity in elementary school children. In L. Resnick, J. Levine, and S. Teasley (Eds.), *Perspectives on socially shared cognition*. Washington, DC: American Psychological Association.

Philips, S. (1983). *The invisible culture*. New York: Longman Press.

Piaget, J. (1970). *Structuralism*. New York: Basic Books.

Piaget, J. (1977). *Equilibration of cognitive structures*. New York: Viking.

Resnick, L., J. Levine, and S. Teasley (Eds.) (1991). *Perspectives on socially shared cognition.* Washington, D.C.: American Psychological Association.

Schwandt, T. (1994). Constructivist, interpretivist approaches to human inquiry. In N. Denzin and Y. Lincoln, *Handbook of qualitative research.* Thousand Oaks, CA: Sage Publications.

Smith, H. (1994). *World's religions: A guide to our wisdom traditions.* New York: Harper.

Soto, L.D. (1997). *Language, culture, and power.* New York: SUNY. Press.

Vygotsky, L. S. (1981). The genesis of higher mental functions. In J.V. Wertsch (Ed.), *The concept of activity in Soviet psychology.* New York: Sharpe.

Weiler, K. (1991). Freire and a feminist pedagogy of difference. *Harvard Educational Review,* 61(4), 449–474.

Wertsch, J. (1991). A sociocultural approach to socially shared cognition. In L. Resnick, J. Levine, and S. Teasley (Eds.), *Perspectives on socially shared cognition.* Washington, D.C.: American Psychological Association.

Williams, M. (1981). *The Velveteen Rabbit or How Toys Become Real.* Philadelphia, Pennsylvania: Running Press.

PART TWO
THEORY

CHAPTER FIVE

Emotion
Educational Psychology's Pound of Flesh

Patricia H. Hinchey

In Shakespeare's *Merchant of Venice,* the moneylender Shylock offers a loan to the merchant Antonio if the merchant will agree to forfeit a pound of his flesh should repayment be late. Sure that his ships would return well before the loan came due and confident that, even if they didn't, he could live after losing a mere pound of flesh, Antonio signs a legal document committing himself to the terms. When his ships are lost and Shylock demands his due—a pound of flesh, which he specifies must be cut from around the merchant's heart—Antonio learns too late that he had undervalued his flesh and that the real cost of the bargain was his very life.

For me, this familiar plot offers an instructive metaphor for the influence of educational psychology. Those rich in prestige, position, and power—the experts in scientific research, in educational psychology—have willingly offered practitioners the benefit of their expertise. For years, they have shared their prescriptions for "effective" teaching and learning, their formulas for exactly what a teacher should do, when, and how often. In return for these gems of practical classroom wisdom, practitioners have been expected to pay deference to expert opinion, forfeiting a measure of their own pedagogical freedom. At one time—when formalist thinking structured the world of schools so authoritatively and crisply—the price must have seemed small (assuming, of course, that expert advice would indeed serve to help teachers become more "effective").

Only recently—now that post-formalist thinkers have begun remapping the shape of the sharply delineated formalist world, have begun identifying borderless realms of shadowy territory where positivists assumed natural, sacrosanct boundaries—have the terms of educators' original bargain come into question. Theorists pushing against the boundaries of accepted practice have reflected growing misgivings about the value of expert "scientific" advice. As Schön (1987) noted in his highly influential text on teacher education: "In recent years there has been a growing perception that researchers, who are supposed to feed the professional schools with useful knowledge, have less and less to say that practitioners find useful." Not only may educators have received less than we bargained for, but the cost has surely been higher than practitioners ever anticipated.

The Real Cost

As Antonio never dreamed Shylock would use their agreement to attempt murder, most educators never anticipated that experts in educational psychology would work to reduce the teacher's role to that of a mere functionary executing others' plans. Nor did they imagine the impact of expert influence on the life of their classrooms.

The Loss of Teacher Authority

As education struggled to establish itself as an academic discipline entitled to the same legitimacy and prestige enjoyed by the physical sciences, educational researchers adopted the same kind of methodology as physical researchers studying rocks and plants (somehow managing to ignore the blatantly obvious differences between seaweed and six-year-olds). They insisted on splintering human complexity into discrete components (even if a child can't be forced to leave fury outside the classroom door). They did much of their work in laboratories (as if the heat of human feelings could be regulated like room temperature) and with animals (although six-year-olds are as different from rats and doves as they are from seaweed).

As reverence for the resulting, authoritative technical formulas grew (as how could it not, with so many incomprehensible statistical calculations offered to "validate" them?), the knowledge that teachers themselves developed from practice was valued less and less, even by teachers themselves. Only comparatively recently has it begun entering theoretical discussions, embodied in such concepts as Schön's "knowing-in-action" and Polyani's "tacit knowledge." Outside the realm of such revolutionary thinking, however, we remain at a place where many experts not only discount practitioner knowledge but also voice thinly veiled contempt or hostility toward teachers who dare to have opinions and ideas about good practice for themselves.

Consider, for example, some revealing statements from a widely used textbook in educational psychology. In the preface, the authors validate the importance of material presented not in terms of its benefit for teachers and students in classrooms but in terms of whether or not other experts agree it's important. The authors pause to note that "for many years this text is *(sic)* more often cited and used than almost any other, as necessary for preparing for Ph.D. qualifying or certification exams in psychology" (Bower & Hilgard, 1981). If the information is related to the certifying of expert researchers, then it must be important. (What do teachers say about it? Who cares!)

Moreover, the text's last chapter makes clear the mechanical role assigned to classroom practitioners: the teacher's job is to follow instructions. If practice remains ineffective, it's because practitioners are unreasonably resistant or even lazy:

> Once the basic-science principles have been established and the applications validated in practice schoolrooms, their more widespread adoption is by no mean guaranteed, nor, if the adoption is forced, is there assurance that the desired results will be forthcoming. Abstractly, the steps of innovation are clear enough: (a) provide a sound research-based program, validated in tryout; (b) have the program packaged in such a way that it is available, as in good textbooks, supplementary readings in the form of pamphlets, films, programs for teaching machines, and guides for the teacher; (c) provide testing materials by which it can be ascertained if the objectives of the program have indeed been realized with appropriate normative data on these evaluative instruments; (d) provide service training of the teacher to overcome the teacher's resistance to new methods and materials and to gain his enthusiastic acceptance of the program as something valuable, as well as to train him in its use; and (e) be sure there is support for the program from the community, school boards, parents, and others concerned with schools. To cite one example, the resistance to widescale adoption of PSI [Personalized Systems of Instruction] teaching methods comes from teachers who do not want to expend the effort, or who love to lecture, and from administrators upset with the high grades of PSI students (p. 575-6).

Entirely missing from this picture is the possibility that teachers' resistance might be valid, as it might be if they disagreed with the *goals* of new programs as being too narrow, or perhaps with assumptions about which information is most important for their particular students to master. This "if it doesn't work, don't blame us" stance, as it dismisses teacher thinking as irrelevant or obstructive, is patronizing and patriarchal. So, too, is a subsequent suggestion that teachers be allowed at least a little voice, phrased thus:

> Teachers could have a voice in saying whether or not they wanted the new devices, or in selecting among various possibilities. Usually no harm would be done in waiting for a while if teachers were not ready, for methods imposed on teachers are unlikely to prove successful. (p. 76)

Teachers might be given a voice about adopting innovations not so much because they might be knowledgeable evaluators of new methods, but because they are likely to petulantly undermine the new methods if they aren't offered at least a token voice.

This stance privileges a kind of knowledge that assiduously avoids being contaminated by the real world and the real people which it presumes to shape (the *empirical decontextualization* and *hyperspecialization* post-formalists critique, processes that result in the *stupidification* of everyone involved). Little wonder that its credibility has been waning.

The Subjugation of the Non-Rational
As they splintered the complex human endeavor of teaching and learning into the discrete parts necessary for "scientific" inquiry, researchers conceptualized the interaction between teachers and students as a mechanical and logical enterprise: if teachers did *a*, then *b* would result (the mindset post-formalists call *instrumental rationality*). Research focused on identifying which variables might affect the process and then telling teachers how to manipulate each variable in order to produce desired results (usually something equivalent to earning good test grades, some performance that could be scored in numbers).

This determination to divide the teaching/learning experience into researchable components and the accompanying view of teaching/learning as a mechanical process generated an educational world view that routinely denied the complexity of human experience. Once the goal of "teaching" was established as "student learning" and once "learning" was accepted as being much the same as "acquiring knowledge," the boundaries of educational psychology were set: it would explore how a specific teacher treatment would affect student "knowledge." In this "scientific" realm, there was no place to accommodate the question of how the *feelings* humans bring to a classroom might affect the process. Too subjective. Not part of rational science.

When some particularly insightful researcher *did* acknowledge that a student's feelings might influence the learning process in some way (noting, for example, that a hungry child might be expected to pay less attention to a math lesson than a child who has just had a good break-fast), the resulting inquiry generally tried to pummel freewheeling human emotion into some shape that fit mechanistic conceptions rather than to rethink the assumptions that underpinned them. Instead of acknowledging emotion as an unavoidable complexity of classroom life, positivist educational researchers tucked it neatly into the category of "motivation," which they then cast as just another variable to be manipulated by certain teacher treatments. The very language used to discuss the concept suggests the extent to which researchers have lost sight of the complex humanity of their subjects:

> Motivation . . . determined which aspects of the environment would be attended to by the organism. For example, the hungry organism would attend to food-related events. (Hergenhahn and Olson, p. 296)

> Another [important variable is] the organism's conviction that it can successfully execute the behavior required to produce the outcomes. (Bower and Hilgard, p. 470)

These specialists think not of *children,* but of *organisms.* They think not of the importance of a child's mental well-being, but of how a mental state might influence *which aspects of the environment would be attend-ed to by the organism.*

Not surprisingly, discussions of the motivational impact of negative emotions (like anger, reluctance, or anxiety) are usually tied to the question of how they might be treated. There is little or no suggestion in common discussion of negative emotions to explore what conditions in the classroom, school, home, or community might be triggering them, and/or whether those conditions need to be addressed. Instead, the focus is simply on "fixing" whatever it is the researchers decide is broken (the process of *regulating* individuals, working to reduce any inclination to challenge the status quo):

> One advantage of conceptualizing emotions in this way is that it sug-gests therapeutic techniques for alleviating depression, shyness, unhappiness, and anxiety. A basic procedure is to attack the inappro-

priate thoughts of the patient in order to demonstrate the illogicality of the inferences, and to suggest substitute rules that will lead to more realistic and less disabling appraisals. (Bower and Hildegard, p. 468)

Again, if the desired outcomes aren't forthcoming, look for problems in the people involved, not for any inadequacy in the researcher's world view. If a student is angry or anxious about a grade or a class, let's go to work showing him that his thinking is illogical—rather than exploring whether there are things (unfair testing, humiliation by teachers and peers, inadequate school supplies) he might be legitimately angry or anxious about.

The work of educational psychologists to date has been limited by an extraordinary flaw: of all the variables that might be productively manipulated to improve classrooms, there is one that they've ignored for decades. That is, few researchers have pondered the possibility that their very conception of that educational psychology is—what it should be and should do—is inadequate.

The Results

In short, at every turn experts staked out classrooms as places where unsophisticated teachers would execute sophisticated research prescriptions for using variable a to produce outcome b. All outcomes were assumed to fall into the category "knowledge acquisition" and to relate exclusively to logical thinking. If the subject of emotion had to come up, then it would be allowed in only as the variable "motivation," which would be subject to the same sort of experimentation and prescription as other variables (like time on task). If expert plans didn't improve classroom learning, then the failure was probably due to some defect in teachers, administrators, or students.

The intent of the experts we bargained with has consistently been to reduce the interaction of unique and complex human beings to a thoroughly mechanical, dehumanized process. And like Antonio, only now that the deal has been consummated are we coming to understand what the terms actually required. Ultimately, we agreed to renounce our own authority, and we simultaneously endorsed both a mechanical conception of teaching and the trivializing of the non-rational. And those terms have cost us the very life of our classrooms.

In the name of "achievement," experts have set students to mastering decontextualized and impotent bits of information year after year (more *stupidification*). In the name of "effectiveness," they have set teachers to imposing plans and tasks designed by distant others who think of students not as "children" but as "organisms" (*individualization,* the insistence that a human might be, in Kincheloe's words, a *nonproblematic unit of scientific analysis*). In the name of "standards," they have imposed conformity (to Eurocentric norms). In the name of "rationality," they have crowded out individual voice and passion (again in Kincheloe's words, the *logocentric masculinization of thinking*). As a result, teachers and students alike have become robotic drones with little energy or enthusiasm for the business of schools. Classrooms are dead places, lacking human energy, creativity, invention or excitement. Too often, they are antagonistic sites of hopelessness as well. Like Antonio, we unknowingly agreed to sacrifice the very heart of what we do.

Rethinking the Role of Emotion

The extent to which classrooms feel like dead places lacking passion and purpose argues vehemently that we need to think again about the split between intellect and emotion (among other things). Is it possible to contain the volatility of human feelings within the tidy package of "motivation"? No. Should we want to, even if we could? No. When conceptualize emotion as a variable that is important only as it impacts on "knowledge acquisition," and when we maintain that we can manipulate it at will, we concurrently ensure that our efforts will be both inadequate and wasteful.

We Can't Fence Our Feelings Out

The most obvious argument against isolating emotion as a controllable variable is simply this: often, it cannot be done. A teacher can know full well that it's considered "unprofessional" to dislike John or to well up with frustration during that rowdy last-period class—but what human being can rationally *decide* that they will stop disliking so-and-so or stop feeling frustrated by thus-and-such? If we could put our feelings aside at will, it's likely that there would be far fewer feuds among in-laws about seating arrangements at weddings and far fewer arguments between spouses about asking for directions when lost. Intelligent employees wouldn't be sarcastic to stupid bosses, and responsible people would stop loving louses. Even comics—some of whom, like the fools in early dramas, are astute observers of the human condition—know that issues of the heart and head are often inextricably tangled. For example, consider Richard Pryor's observation about this heart/head matter: "Marriage is really tough because you have to deal with feelings and lawyers." Anyone who doubts that how people feel often trumps what logic dictates ought to try negotiating a prenuptial or divorce agreement—logically and unemotionally.

However much positivist psychologists would like to divide and subdivide and sub-subdivide humans into discrete components, and however desirable such division might be for scientists or divorce lawyers or parents or folks in love, the reality is simply that the human heart habitually refuses to take orders from the head. Choosing an action logically is one thing, but actually preventing our emotions from influencing our actions is quite another. To think that feelings can be effectively and scientifically managed by logical prescriptions is wishful thinking indeed.

I don't need to look far into my own experience for examples. I clearly remember reading an assigned novel for a graduate course and flinging it across my bedroom when I came to the part where a child died unexpectedly and the survivors grieved. Reading it too soon after my father's unexpected death brought my own overwhelming anger and grief to the surface immediately, and I was so upset that I thought seriously about not attending the class when the book would be discussed. I finally did go but only because I promised myself that the minute anyone said anything that made me uncomfortable I would simply walk out of the room. The class was my first with my doctoral advisor and so was particularly important to me. I had, in fact, every reason to be "motivated" to go and to fear not going. (Would I miss important information? Would the instructor think me "unmotivated"?) I tried hard to control my feelings and just do what logically needed to be done. It was impossible. There was no way to leave my feelings about my father's death out in the hallway while I attended class. Who could?

Seeking "Objectivity" Ensures Inadequacy
Because it's frequently not possible to control our feelings rationally, insistence that students subjugate their feelings to logical classroom requirements is likely to result in procedures that are partial, handicapped, distorted. This is readily evident in the example above. Could my advisor have adequately assessed my performance if she concerned herself only with the fact that I had missed or fled from one of her classes? What should she have said to me if I visited her during office hours to explain the circumstances? Here's one objective response she might have offered: "Well, in classrooms we have to keep our feelings in control. I can only consider empirical data when I evaluate your performance—and that includes an absence. I'm afraid that your feelings are

the domain of therapists, not professors." What further emotional response might that have generated in me and with what impact on my graduate education? And if we tried to make room for feelings in the existing paradigm, what would we do? Have students rate their depression on a scale of 1 to 10? What empirical evidence would we require before factoring the motivation variable into a grade? Humans are just not that simple.

My own children have gone to school dealing with grief from the death of grandparents and friends; my own students have come to class while trying to decide whether to divorce, how to avoid parental abuse on a given night, or whether they were gay or straight. Or bisexual. Insisting that students leave such issues and their attendant emotional upheaval at the classroom threshold or that they logically order their feelings to behave all but ensures that the teacher's performance will be inadequate (and inhumane) and that students will violate the absurd regulations.

Instead of issuing impossible edicts and treating students as if they *were* rats in a maze, we would do well to give more thought to the various roles emotion plays in the classroom and to start talking together about how we might integrate concern for emotional well-being into school life.

Emotion and Learning

Whether students engage in classroom activity and pursue learning depends a great deal on how they feel about themselves, about the classroom, and about school in general. While traditional educational psychology acknowledges this reality in its discussions of motivation (in such concepts as Bandura's "self-efficacy judgments"), its focus on regulating student feelings and behavior is far too limiting. We need to look not only at how feelings affect behavior but also—instead of presuming a fault in the child—at what factors may be triggering emotions in particular circumstances. We need, as post-formalists so vehemently argue, to consider children and schooling in a social context.

Feelings About Classes and Teachers

Reading theorist Frank Smith often makes the point that people don't do things that they don't believe they can do or that they just can't imagine themselves doing. How we feel about a task has everything to do with how we approach it—or whether we agree to approach it at all. Daily life offers countless examples affirming this observation. How often do we all make statements beginning with the words "Oh, I'm just not the kind of person who could ever . . ."? Men who are frightened of hurting a baby or who dread being perceived as less macho than the Marlboro man refuse to learn the simple task of changing a diaper. Women who fear that they'll blow up a car engine and/or maim themselves if they so much as touch a hood refuse to learn to jump start a car or to check its oil. Shy people who are afraid to look others in the eye or to say something stupid in public make excuses and skip social events. People who were made to feel stupid in high school don't attempt college, and graduate students intimidated by self-important professors leave graduate school. Of course, refusing to try something ensures that we won't in fact learn it—and so teachers had better be very concerned about how students *feel* about their ability in a subject.

Some useful work in this area has come out of the behaviorist paradigm, to be sure. The issue of test anxiety, for example, has already been widely explored. Several strategies have been devised, and workshops on how to deal with test anxiety have become common and have helped many students overcome the problem. What is worrisome about the traditional therapeutic approach, however, it that it may lead to treating what is actually a symptom as if it were the problem itself. For example, when I was taking my qualifying exams for my doctorate, a friend of mine passed out cold immediately after reading her exam, despite the fact that she was well prepared and eventually composed a sterling response. As her body thudded to the floor, many other test takers started rushing to her aid—only to pause and ask the proctor if he'd allow a few extra minutes for the good samaritans. How can we be sure that the problem here is more with students who exhibit such extreme anxiety than it is with a tyrannical educational system that finds it reasonable to judge the whole of the knowledge a student has "acquired" from twenty texts in a three-hour written exam?

If a student comes into class terrified of failing or of offering a wrong answer, might it not be more productive to ask about experiences that child had with earlier teachers? Or about what consequences the child suffers at home for poor grades? To "fix" the child's "anxiety" about math while ignoring its possible causes (which might well include abusive behavior by other adults) is to cultivate an arrogant, self-imposed blindness.

Feelings About School

An enormous complication for a teacher trying to work *with* student feelings is that often, students exhibit hostility toward a subject or teacher that is evidence of a general disenfranchisement with schooling. Such hostility often signals *resistance*, a phenomenon that extends well beyond the four walls of a particular classroom.

In poor areas, where schools are underfunded, unemployment is high, and qualifying for a teaching position may require only the ability to breathe and the willingness to work in a dangerous area, many students perceive schooling as an injustice and a type of fraud that they refuse to endorse. When a school in a Hispanic or African American community has textbooks that have been outdated for decades (if they happen to have textbooks at all) and a school in an affluent area of the same district has current texts and a computer for every student as well, poor students clearly see that they are neither valued nor treated fairly by their society. Jonathan Kozol, of course, demonstrates such disillusionment eloquently and in great detail in *Savage Inequalities*.

Why should students cooperate with classwork that is rarely challenging, unrelated to their interests and needs, ill-supported materially, and imposed by unskilled and unqualified teachers? When they graduate, if they bother to graduate, they will not be able to compete with students who have attended generously funded schools. A high school diploma from an inadequate school guarantees nothing but a license to apply for menial, repetitive jobs. Students who attempt more are likely to have enormous difficulty acquiring the skills needed to survive a college career, and when they do succeed, they may be told that success came because of skin color rather than ability and hard work. Moreover, along the way it is likely that they will be required to agree that the speech of their homes is inferior and be advised to stop sounding like their mothers and brothers and to start sounding like the newscaster reporting that the average salary of a Super Bowl attendee is over $70,000.

Of course, noting the realities in difficult schools is not to suggest that no good work is being done in them or that many people who work in them do not care passionately about the welfare of their students (the courage of the Oakland School District in taking its public stance on Ebonics comes to mind). But systemic funding inequities ensure that their good work will be significantly undermined by realities beyond practitioners' immediate control. If teachers are not to blame the victim in cases where recalcitrant students are exhibiting resistance or if teachers themselves are not to burn out from trying to solve individually problems that extend far beyond their classrooms, then the impact of social context on mental health must be closely examined.

Emotion and Teaching

Given the messiness of human emotion and given earlier criticism of taking a strictly reactive stance, how do we begin to move toward a proactive position? How do we begin thinking about emotional concerns as we try to plan energized and productive classrooms? How can we begin repairing the unnatural rift between cognitive and emotional domains?

Emotional Objectives in Our Plans

First, a disclaimer and word of caution: in Pennsylvania, where I live and work, there has been enormous public controversy over whether or not schools have any right to concern themselves with anything beyond disciplinary subject matter. Nationwide, I know, parents are concerned about what they perceive as the state's attempt to usurp the parents' rights in relation to students' character formation and values system. The issue is a serious one, not to be dismissed as rabble rousing by a few radicals. The line between the parents' right to control values education and the state's right to promote some values essential to democratic citizenry is not easily drawn.

Still: few parents of any political persuasion will argue that a child who hates school is unlikely to perform as well as a child who loves school. We *can* make persuasive arguments for being concerned with emotional elements in the classroom—we just need to make them very carefully, now that our reverence for scientific objectivity has persuaded the public that it's possible to separate feeling and intellect in the first place. I intend here a word of caution as we try to redefine classroom boundaries, not to discourage the effort. We need to insist on reintegrating emotional concerns—but we need to do it carefully and thoughtfully.

So, where to begin? I would argue first that we need to begin thinking about emotional objectives and prerequisites as routinely as we do cognitive ones. We need to begin our plans by asking about the emotional state of our students: are they likely to fear this assignment or course? Then first we have to alleviate that fear—remembering that we can make good plans for that *only* when we've openly explored a variety of factors that might be prompting it. (After all, if our policy is to give tests that intelligent and hardworking students routinely fail, as has been the case in my daughter's calculus course, then it might make more sense to change the tests or teaching than to try to change the students.) Are students likely to experience frustration in this project? Do they have the self-confidence it requires to keep trying after repeated failures? If not, we may have to provide constant encouragement—or more help with finding materials, or a willingness to extend deadlines in the face of good faith effort, or schedule one-on-one conferences for individual assistance. It's time we started considering what will ensure the mental well-being of our students as routinely as we consider what will ensure their physical well-being in a science lab.

It's not so much that positivists are mistaken when they relate emotion to motivation as that they simply take far too limited a view of its sources and its power and assume we can prescribe teacher reactions. No problem can be efficiently and effectively solved if its causes are misdiagnosed. Presuming that a defect in the student always and everywhere accounts for resistance assures that often our diagnosis will be wrong and our "treatment" inadequate—especially in the case of disadvantaged students, who are not taken seriously into account in this literature. For example, one ed psych text notes that "children's basic needs are adequately taken care of in our society" and another that "given the comforts of our affluent society, compelling external forces rarely move us." Essentially, one presumption of existing motivation research is that children's actions in learning situations will not be motivated by the need for food, safety, or shelter since those needs will already have been met. Given that we *know* that's a faulty assumption, the inadequacy—and delusional potential—of this work are evident.

Moreover, we need to try to avoid triggering disabling emotions in the first place. The teacher who ridicules student responses teaches students to fear voicing an idea. The teacher who is proud of inspiring fear teaches students to be hostile toward a self-proclaimed enemy. The teacher who delights in tricky questions on multiple-choice tests teaches students to distrust teacher motives.

We need to think about such factors more often, more openly, and more complexly than we have to date.

Emotion as a Window of Opportunity

When we begin to accept emotion as an integral part of classroom complexity, we can hear more clearly the voices of non-traditionalists, like Schön, who have been thinking about how we might use emotional responses to trigger learning processes. Perhaps an example from my own professional development most readily clarifies how such a process might work.

Once when I was in charge of logistics for a week-long retreat for graduate students, I announced that every student would contribute a fixed amount to a grocery fund, which staff would use to provision the retreat house. Soon after, two students visited my office to request—with the greatest possible reluctance, humility and tact—that they be exempted from the collection and allowed to purchase their own groceries. They were devout Jewesses who ate only kosher foods and wanted to survive the week without developing malnutrition. I immediately apologized for not having anticipated special dietary needs; I also told them that they would have to contribute to the fund, but that they should turn in a list of what foods they wanted us to buy for them. "We're shopping for the *group*," I told them, "and since you're part of the group we're shopping for you. You shouldn't have to do work others don't just because you happen to hold different religious beliefs."

Their highly emotional response to my decision led to an indelible lesson for me, one I've returned to over and over again in my professional life. They were actually moved by what I said and grateful far beyond, it seemed to me, what such a simple action merited. They couldn't thank me enough and went on and on about how much they appreciated being treated as if they were "just normal students." *My* emotional reaction to their reaction was nearly as strong: I was so surprised that I was stunned and couldn't think about anything else for some time after they left my office (extreme *cognitive dissonance*, for sure). Puzzled, I pondered for a good long time why such a small thing should be so important to them.

Eventually I realized that their gratitude probably meant that they were quite used to having to apologize for being different, to being in situations where there was no food for them to eat, where everyone was assumed to match some picture of "normal" which they didn't fit. If they couldn't be accommodated, why then, that was *their* problem, not a problem for anyone else. Suddenly, I was appalled by years and years of my own insensitivity. I learned that by *not* remembering that not everyone fits the majority mold, I had thoughtlessly set some students apart as "different" by not taking their needs into account; I contributed to the isolation and sense of "otherness" that students from nonmainstream groups so often feel.

Suddenly, I started paying attention to what kind of foods were routinely offered to students at school events. Were there foods Jewish students might eat? Vegetarians? Could everyone find *something* being offered that they could share? I watched for new things I could include to expand the menus I planned myself, and I called exclusionary practices to the attention of others who weren't lucky enough to have had an enlightening experience like mine. I know I've behaved differently because I thought through my students' excessive gratitude and my own surprise, and I know I've influenced others to behave differently as well—the ultimate proof of effective learning (and also an accessible demonstration of *critical accommodation* and *praxis*).

Surprise, our reaction when something happens we didn't expect and calls our attention to our assumptions if we allow ourselves to pay attention to it and if we try to think it through. Or, in Schön's more sophisticated description of the process,

> Surprise leads to reflection within an action-present . . . asking ourselves, as it were, "What is this?" and, at the same time, "How have I been thinking about it?" Our thought turns back on the surprising phenomenon and, at the same time, back on itself. (p. 28)

The teacher is surprised when most of the class fails a test she thought was easy. What does that mean? Did she expect these students to pass because other students always had, or did she have other evidence that led to her assumption? Why did she miscalculate their probable performance? Did they all seem to misunderstand the same areas? Which ones? Did the test actually focus on areas she'd stressed in class, or was there a mismatch in emphasis? Is it conceivable her answer sheet was off somehow, that the teacher herself had made mistakes in correcting? Pursuing such questions allows for teachers to learn something about their own practice and/or also about student needs. Teachers who routinely assume that any surprise signals a defect in students—"I was really surprised you all failed, class. Make sure you study hard for the next exam to make this grade up."—are less effective than they might be if they put more thought into finding more possible causes.

Students can also learn more about themselves and how they understand something by exploring their emotional reactions. In my educational theory class, for example, I assign a reading about the removal of Native Americans to tribal reservations and the destruction of effective tribal educational systems, replaced by government schools which repeatedly reversed themselves in mission and which have, on the whole, failed dismally. When students come into class, I ask them how they *feel* about the reading. Invariably, they are very, very angry that they had never encountered the information before. I ask them to explain why they're angry, and they talk about feeling cheated by their high school history books, about feeling angry because certain information had been kept from them. In the course of this discussion, a great many unconscious assumptions about what American schools are and do become explicit. We go on to use their assumptions to think about the historical and potential purposes of public schools, about the roles public schools can and should play in a democratic society. In effect, their anger prompts my students to voice their unconscious assumptions about school (*schools are supposed to tell the truth; schools exist for the benefit of students*) which we then use for further academic inquiry.

Emotional reactions can kick-start any number of discussions that lead to lessons relative to cognitive development. Following the lead of theorist Louise Rosenblatt, many English teachers use a similar approach to literature study, referred to as a *reader-response* approach. In this approach, classroom discussions of a piece routinely begin with the questions "How do you feel about this work? What were you thinking when you finished reading?" Such questions lead to discussions both about the specific values the student brings to the work (which are usually societal and unconscious) and about the students' reading and interpretive skills.

One short story I've frequently taught, for example, recounts an afternoon's spontaneous adultery during a rain storm (Kate Chopin, "The Storm"). The final line of the story reads "And so the storm passed, and everyone was happy." My students routinely said they hated the characters and were glad they'd suffer later. What always struck me was that there was no doubt in their minds that the characters *would* suffer later despite the apparently happy ending. The students' comments revealed their own values regarding fidelity, of course, but they also prompted a valuable classroom discussion about what it means exactly to say that a text can have multiple readings and what it means to *think* about an idea. I frequently used this opportunity to explain that while a reader can doubt whether something a writer invents could actually happen in real life, they may *not* doubt the writer's word *in the story* (that is, no reading can contradict a text). In this case, readers are bound to accept the writer's word that, in fact, the affair caused no harm; students learned that their reading could not be based on what they thought was right but on what the writer *said*. They learned about the difference between judging a story by established societal norms and thinking about an alternative value system a story may propose. (That is, instead of making autopilot evaluations based on their largely unconscious values, they were encouraged to see their own *cognitive dissonance* as an opportunity to think about the effect of the shape their society has imprinted on them).

If we start thinking about our emotional reactions as signals to start thinking deeply about something, I've no doubt every day will yield a wealth of food for thought to nourish our classroom efforts.

Emotion and Life

A word of caution as we ponder how to infuse emotional concerns into our classroom thinking: given the erratic and often passionate souls of human beings, there is just so much we'll ever be able to do in the way of planning for and around student feelings. Never, never will I forget an early morning Spanish class during my junior year of college—although I didn't hear a single word that the professor (whom I adored) said to us that day. I had been head-over-heels in love with a tall, dark, and handsome man (who came equipped with a new, red, splashy convertible) for over two years, but while we spent a lot of time together, he had assiduously avoided what all very young lovers know as "those three words." On the morning in question, I discovered on my Corvair's windshield (windshields being a vehicle for messages when our schedules didn't allow for real-time conversation) a scrap of paneling with a message formed from ragged lengths of black electrical tape: "I love you." I grinned ear to ear not only on my way to school and through that class, but nonstop until I risked my parents' insisting on a psychiatric examination.

Some days, student souls will be AWOL, taking the intellectual capacity of their hosts along for the ride. I think we just need to learn to live with that—and even, from time to time, to give thanks for what makes us uniquely human.

Undoing the Damage

OK—so Shylock wanted more than Antonio could afford to pay. OK—so we can't afford an educational psychology based on an extraordinarily mechanical, dehumanized world view. What does that mean?

First, it would be nice if we could manage not to throw the baby out with the bath water. It was rather startling and useful for positivist research to call to our attention to the fact that teachers were routinely waiting some infinitesimal amount of time for students to answer questions. It was helpful when, as a result, they urged teachers to give students time to *think*. If we deny such contributions and reject what's been done as having *nothing* of value to offer, then we are guilty of the same arrogance and self- righteousness as those we criticize. We may want to filter what we accept as useful carefully, but there is an open-mindedness in allowing for such filtering that we (who so frequently urge inclusiveness) need to maintain.

What we might do, as constructivist researchers have urged, is to trade in the image of research as yielding prescriptions for the image of research as producing plain old food-for-thought: "Does John never answer because I don't wait long enough for him? I hadn't thought of that! Then again, I've never seen him talking to anyone casually in the cafeteria, either. Hmm . . . ." Of course, those of us working toward a new conception of schooling entirely will find much of the work that's already been done oversimplified or aiming for goals we don't endorse—but still. We ought to look around pretty thoughtfully before putting torches to any bridges.

Also, we need to keep working (as this text does) toward a more inclusive post-formalist theory of educational psycholoogy that we can use as a foundation for a radically different kind of practice. It's not enough for us to tear down; we need an alternative conception—incomplete and in need of refinement as it will always be—to offer in its stead. We need to regain what we've lost and to refashion learning communities on a post-formalist foundation, establishing schools as purposeful and fluid learning communities, nurturing both mind and spirit of their members. We need, in short, to just keep at it.

References

Bower, G. and Hilgard, E. (1981). *Theories of learning*, fifth edition. Englewood Cliffs, NJ: Prentice Hall.

Hergenhahn, B. R. and Olson, M. (1993). *An introduction to theories of learning*, fourth edition. Englewood Cliffs, NJ: Prentice Hall.

Lefrançois, G. (1994). *Psychology for teaching*, eighth edition. Belmont, CA: Wadsworth Publishing.

Polyani, M. (1967). *The tacit dimension.* New York: Doubleday.

Rosenblatt, L. (1968). *Literature as exploration.* New York: MLA.

Schön, D. (1987). *Educating the reflective practitioner.* San Francisco: Jossey-Bass Inc.

CHAPTER SIX

Spirituality
Post-formal Thinking, Spiritual Intelligence and the Paradox of the Developmental Journey

Aostre N. Johnson

Including the Spiritual in Post-formal Thinking

Kincheloe and Steinberg's theory of post-formal thinking (1993) provides a context for re-visioning human cognition which furthers the recognition and appreciation of diverse ways of knowing. They utilize a critical interdisciplinary perspective that allows us to step outside of the assumptions of positivistic developmental psychology's views of intelligence. Cognitive growth is seen as a dynamic hermeneutic with pattern making as one of its hallmarks. All intellectual work, all theories, illustrate the mind's predilection to search for meaning by constructing patterns out of perceptual phenomena. We build models to "capture" some aspect of reality and then get caught in our own conceptual traps. The tendency to reify theories is characteristic not only of psychology but of every discipline. Unlike formal operations, post-formal operations require that we see any theory, including itself, as historically situated and only relatively true, as "one perspective from the particular point in the web of reality" (p. 317).

I believe that the "potentially unlimited mind" called for by post-formal theory will be greatly illuminated by the concept of spiritual cognition, which offers fertile theoretical ground as a perspective for expanding our understanding of the nature of thinking. The existence of a spiritual mode of consciousness has been largely obscured by the limited view from the conceptual traps inherent in the modern mind. But to exclude this dimension is to suppress the experience and beliefs of the majority of human beings across cultures and throughout history, including those of original cultures, traditional religious cultures, and indigenous peoples. Its inclusion allows for an expanded understanding of the mysterious journey of consciousness from birth to death experienced by all human beings and a greater appreciation of children's ways of knowing.

The concept of spiritual intelligence will highlight paradoxical thinking, the embracing of apparent contradictions without a rational resolution, which contributes to establishing the place of post-formal operations in the middle ground between modernism and postmodernism. Or in other words, perhaps the contradictions between modernism and postmodernism can be partially resolved/dissolved in spirit.

I am speaking here of spirituality rather than religion, but their meanings overlap. While religions have been constructed to come to terms with the same questions at the core of spirituality, those of origin, purpose, and ultimate meaning, the word religious is often used to refer to the concerns of specific established religions, organized around particular deities. I use the word *spiritual* in a more general sense, reaching within, across and outside of religious boundaries, derived from the Latin *spiritualis*: of breathing, of wind, breath of god, inspiration.

Modernist biases have limited us to symbolic uses of *spiritual* connoting "nonspiritual spirit," including: a lively, brisk quality, a vitality; a temper or disposition of mind, i.e., in good spirits; a mental disposition characterized by firmness or authenticity and a special attitude or frame of mind, such as courage, hope or compassion. These symbolic meanings can all be seen as aspects or qualities of the spirit, but the following definitions come closest to the sense in which I use *spiritual* here: "the immaterial, intelligent or sentient part of a person"; "relating to, or consisting of spirit, an animating or vital principle held to give life to physical beings"; and "relating to sacred matters," with *sacred* derived from the Latin *sacrare*, meaning *holy*, from the Old English *halig* or *hal*, meaning "more whole." Following from these, *spiritual* can be seen as an aspect of life that is the essence of intelligence, a force animating and connecting all beings and things so that all of life is seen as a sacred whole.

This way of understanding the spirit is characteristic of many traditional indigenous cultures. For example, in speaking of current Native American spiritual beliefs, Cajete (1994) says:

> Most Indian tribes share basic understandings about sacred knowledge. These include the understanding that a universal energy infuses everything in the cosmos and expresses itself through a multitude of

manifestations. This also includes the recognition that all life has a power that is wondrous and full of spirit. That is the Great Soul or Great Mystery or the Great Dream that cannot be explained or understood with the intellect, but can be perceived only by the spirit of each person. The next perception is that all things and thoughts are related through the spirit. (p. 44)

What is the relationship of *soul* to *spirit*? The soul is a particular embodiment of the spirit, a metaphorical construction of self arising from spirit. The soul can be seen in counterpoint to the ego form of self; both are ways of being, roughly corresponding to communion and agency.

A Brief History of Consciousness: The Downfall of Immanence

Although we can only theorize about historical changes in consciousness, particularly in ancient history, this approach has potential for shedding light on spiritual cognition. Human thinking is sometimes characterized as a shifting from a more "wholistic" to a more fragmented way of viewing the word which is referred to as "despiritualization" (Capra, 1983; Kovel, 1991) or "disenchantment" (Berman, 1984). I utilize four major paradigms to trace this shift: original, premodern, modern, and postmodern.

Barfield (n.d.), Berman (1984), and Sloan (1983) characterize the consciousness of the original era as one of participation, in which perception and thought were experienced as a body-based, active, physical, and emotional relationship with an essentially undivided world. Sloan (1983) describes it as "a knowing that comes not from a detached looking on, but an immediate participation in the known, a kind of indwelling in the surrounding reality of nature and the cosmos . . . which is expressed in myth, symbol and image" (p. 85). Moreover, the symbols and myths themselves were *living*, seen as actively participating in the reality they represented. Although the individual self was partially distinguished from "other," self and other also intermingled. The community (the tribe) rather than the individual was the dominant reference point.

In original societies people did not have a concept of the nonspiritual, did not make a distinction between spiritual and nonspiritual aspects of life, so that "virtually all activities were conducted with regard to spirit as a vital, intangible principle which suffused human experience and indeed the whole universe" (Kovel, 1991, p. 18). Sexuality, art making, food producing, and religious ceremony were woven together as expressions of the spirit. Spirituality was intermeshed with social structure,characterized by an absence of state and social class. Eisler (1987) suggests that males and females were partners, with no sense of inferiority and superiority. The divine assumed both masculine and feminine forms.

This consciousness can be called *immanent*, perceiving the divine within life. Immanence is non-hierarchical, with everything in the universe and every moment seen as spiritual; the material world, including the body, is an expression of spirit. Body, emotion, mind, and spirit exist as continuities in "a seamless whole." Life is experienced as a web connecting all beings so that spirit seems to be communal rather than individual.

Premodern societies shared with original societies the view that the world of the senses is rooted in Mind (or Intelligence), the primary ground of being, called variously Great Mystery, God, Goddess, divine wisdom, and many other names. This mind was seen as the source of qualities such as meaning, value, harmony, and creativity and as the living matrix of material forms, united in "cosmological harmony."

Despite this similarity, fundamental differences about the nature of the cosmology arose during the premodern era with the suppression of female power and symbols and the emergence of male-dominated religious institutions and cultures, accompanied by the formation of statist societies and social class distinctions. The shift itself took many forms, sometimes violent ones, and the various religions also struggled for control and dominance: "Indeed, history details a perpetual struggle to the death of spiritual systems and doctrines, because spirituality itself was a matter of life and death, the mythopoetic framework which made existence intelligible" (Kovel, 1991, p. 8). Participatory thought still dominated consciousness but gradually faded. The world became less numinous and symbols less alive, with a gradual separation of self from world. The suppression of the feminine resulted in an overvaluing of ranking over equality; heaven over earth; culture over nature; mind over nature; mind over body; rationality over emotions, intuition and imagination; and achievement over affiliation. This imbalance would intensify in modernity.

Pre-modernism could be characterized as a gradual shift from immanent to transcendent consciousness. The transcendent world view assumes a separation between matter, mind, and spirit. Transcendence often results in hierarchy, with mind taking precedence over body and matter—and spirit over mind. In transcendent religions, God is "the other," perfect and self-sufficient, outside of the realm of ordinary experience; divine love or grace is necessary to complete or redeem us.

In the modern era we see the rise of science, with its separation from morality, art and religion, and an increasingly socially stratified, materially based society. The shift in thinking from participation to objectification, from unity to fragmentation, from spiritualized to despiritualized matter continued. As mind rejected spirit and detached from body, the world lost its magic and the individual ego, rather than the communion of beings, became the reference point. The universe, no longer the living mind of God, was seen as a hierarchical series of machines. Objectivist rationality emerged as the only legitimized way of knowing, directed towards the control and domination of nature. Knowledge based on intuition, feeling, and imagination was suppressed by both science and religion. Bodies became objects to be controlled, satiated, decorated, used, and discarded.

What has happened in terms of the immanent and the transcendent? Traditional religions opted for an increasingly transcendent God, often branding as heretics those mystics who experienced themselves and the cosmos as One. Rather than struggling for control, religion and science went their separate ways. Empirical reason can also be seen as transcendent, since it values unifying rational categories over particular forms or mind over matter, but it legitimizes a very limited ascension: "Ascend to reason, but not further" (Wilber, 1995, p. 373). The despiritualized transcendent turned its attention to the material world, which "was not isolated and emphasized and pressed into service as a research agenda" (Wilber, 1995, p. 400). No longer a manifestation of spirit, nature became a flat surface composed of quantities rather than qualities, with the new salvation based on measuring and controlling the material world. A small minority carrying the torch of the spiritualized immanent, the Romantics rebelled against both science and religion. They idealized nature, diversity, radical uniqueness, imagination, and pure human feeling; communing with nature became the ultimate spiritual experience.

The Paradox of Immanence and Transcendence
The immanent/transcendent duality between this world and another "higher world" can be seen as:

> the great dualism of all dualisms. . . . It has infected our spirituality, our philosophy, our science . . . it is the cause of bitter, bitter acrimony between the two camps, with each formally accusing the other of being the epitome and essence of evil (literally). (Wilber, 1995, p. 345)

In the modernist struggle the "great dualism" continues with the despiritualized transcendent consciousness gaining control. Immanence is the unity and connectedness of all forms in spirit, transcendence the "separating from or rising above" (rather than "spiritual as opposed to material"). Seen negatively, transcendence suggests the repression and devaluing of that which has been transcended as clearly seen in modernity. However, in a positive sense, transcendence is a separation which allows for a different perspective on experience. The creation of God(dess) as "other" permits spirit to be known and loved in new ways. The evolving constructions of the conceptual mind result in novel ways of understanding and shaping the world. The transcendent and the immanent are paradoxical concepts about a nondual mind/reality, both of which are necessary to understand it.

The Modernist Developmental Version: The Transcendence of Ego

The first version of the development of consciousness, although told as history, can also be seen as an individual journey. It represents the "romantic" theory of development of self and society, the fall from the state of grace, nature condemned by culture. The original era was cast as perfect mother/nature/spirit and the premodern era as her weaker daughter apparently slain by the villainous modern transcending male.

But suppose instead of dying, she has gone underground? Suppose the male is not the other but another side of herself and her journey underground part of her quest for greater wholeness. Suppose that original mother/nature/spirit was not perfect and complete but lacking in the ability to choose to be other than what she was, not wholistic but merely undifferentiated? Suppose rationality/individuality is savior rather than slayer? This version, slanted towards the transcending ego and accompanying rationality, represents the developmental psychology paradigm. While the modernist stages of development are generally applied to the individual, a number of theorists (Wilber, 1995; Habermas, 1979; Campbell, 1968; Neumann, 1954) also apply them to societies.

Developmentalism, based on the assumption of progress and evolution through predictable, sequential, increasingly complex stages, has been called the "cultural symbolic" of modernity. Inherent in this perspective is the inadequacy of the "lower" (the child's/earlier society's) stages, since a more-developed state is more valuable than a less-developed state. Two distinct paradigms have shaped the field of human development.

The psychoanalytic approach is based on the concept of a biological energy, libido, present at birth and moving to various areas of the body in a predetermined timing that defines developmental states. Freud's theory of libido as the erotic force behind development is often reduced to a narrow notion of sexuality; however, Freud understood sexuality as eros, or desire, the universal drive for connection. Psychoanalytic theory is inherently psychosocial in that intense emotions arise from libidinal energy within the developing child's family. Since the objects and forms of the childhood desire are seen as threatening to culture, early childhood emotions are repressed and then appear as the unconscious component of adult minds. From this perspective the mind is controlled by emotion, which is seen as the critical force in the developing human being. However, the goal of development is the "unmasking" of the unconscious so that rationality can tame bodily-based desire.

A second paradigm, cognitive developmentalism, posits mind as the organizing force with stages of mental growth resulting from the dialectic between the pattern-seeking mind and the environment. Although humans are included in the environment, they are objectified so that critical inquiry seems to take place between mind and material world. Reality is constructed through the mind's interactive equilibration between assimilation—shaping events to fit existing cognitive structures—and accommodation—restructuring cognitive structures with the goal of reaching the stage of formal operational thinking, which separates "objective" from "subjective" reality, individuals from context and objects from consciousness.

Despite their differences, both theories emphasize the initial global perceptions and egocentrism of infants and young children, gradually vanquished by the differentiation of self from others and objects with a resulting emphasis on separation, rationality, and abstraction. Ironically, the birth of the ego is seen to permit a move beyond egocentrism, by allowing for a sense of a separate self with increased ability to detach from personal emotions and see others' perspectives.

The magic-animistic/pre-operational stage corresponds to the original era. Participation as the primary mode of consciousness is now considered inaccurate. Although mind and body are somewhat differentiated, consciousness is still experienced as bodily based. The self continues to be emotionally fused with objects and others, particularly mother and society as matriarch. The ego individuality, born as the ability to think symbolically through imagination, allows for the gradual separation of self from world. However, symbols are perceived as alive and magic because they are confused with the objects themselves and mental intentions are believed to magically alter the world. On a societal level, people live in and identify with a tribe but are often in conflict with other tribes. Thus egocentrism is not individual but tribal.

In the mythic/concrete operational/premodern stage, the self internalizes symbolic thought sufficiently to work with rules which operate on concrete symbols and to see others' perspectives. The ego emerges more fully with greater ability to tame libidinal desire. The individual/society adopts and depends on external (parents'/society's) laws, norms or moral codes so that egocentrism is replaced by ethnocentrism. Identification shifts from body/earth matriarchy to mind/culture/patriarchy and shared cultural myths can unite many tribes in a statist society.

The reflective rationality of the formal-operational/modern period permits the creation of multiple possibilities and thus the potential for grasping mutual interrelationships, which allows a move beyond ethnocentrism. A fully formed ego structure includes internalized values and independent moral reasoning. Mind has separated and subdued body and emotion. Formal operational thought and an independent ego are seen as making possible liberty, equality, and fraternity for all people, even without shared, unifying mythologies. These developments also allow for creative individual pursuits in all areas of human endeavor, resulting in progress, both personal fulfillment and a higher quality of life for more people.

The Paradox of Development

Which version of the drama, rational mind as villain or hero, is "true?" Well. . . neither. . . and both. Each tells a version which seems to partially capture the human story, yet each by itself is simplistic, a caricature of history and development. In the first version, the rise of rationality and ego is cause of the "fall" of humanity; in the second, it is the savior. The first is the story of the importance of loss of immanence and the second the story of the necessity for transcendence.

The paradox of the two stories raises many questions. Can we construct a rational mind without identifying with it completely, without separating and repressing body/emotions/spirit? Can we use conceptual structures as tools while viewing their paradoxical nature? Can we develop an ego without the loss of soul? Can we remain connected with and care for others and the world while living our individual journeys? Is a participatory mode of formal operations possible? (Is this what is meant by post-formal operations?) Can we reunite the immanent and the transcendent?

The development of transcendent individuality or ego is not in itself the root of modernity's downfall. Rather, the ego, becoming intoxicated with its ability to create the world in its own image, went too far and declared itself Ego, replacing first its own soul, and then the spirit which binds all things, losing the potential for many voices, pathologically repressing other forms of thinking.

What perspectives have been repressed in the developmental story? The rigidity of stage theory forced categorizations that resulted in the misunderstanding and devaluing of many individuals. Because cognitive researcher's questions were based on the assumption that the formal operational view of reality is the only "right one," it was inevitable that a hierarchy with children and traditional societies on the bottom would emerge. In addition, current research suggests that aspects of development proceed at varying rates; for example, mathematical understanding may be far more advanced than musical conceptualization in a particular person. Thus unitary stages evolving into higher ones at specified ages don't really exist, or they exist in a relative sense as tendencies under certain conditions.

Since the approaches focus on either isolated individual development or development contextualized in the nuclear family, the effects of larger social forces, such as socio- economic class, gender, and race are ignored or understood as isolated influences on the individual. Pathologies are seen as rooted in individuals, not in the social forces that impact them. Further, because most studies were conducted on males in Western cultures, the data itself compounds the powerful unacknowledged modernist biases. Thus we have a body of knowledge focussed on autonomy and independence, abstract logical thought and the morality of abstract justice. We know little about empathy, interdependence, intimacy and intuitive, personal, emotion, imaginative and connected ways of knowing.

Freud's focus on emotion/desire as central was no doubt shaped by the modernist era's need for rational control of body/emotions. The validity of bodily based and emotional knowing was dismissed as "irrational." However, recent theories about brain functioning and intelligence (e.g. Gardner, 1983; Goleman, 1995) validate kinesthetic and emotional intelligence. The more rational neocortex is linked to the limbic system or the emotional brain through myriad neural connections; all cognition is embedded in sensation and emotion.

Piaget saw imaginative and symbolic play as based on egocentric thinking:

> The child who plays with dolls remakes his own life as he would like it to be . . . he compensates for and completes reality by means of a fiction. Symbolic play is not an attempt by the subject to submit to reality but rather a deforming assimilation of reality to the self. (Piaget, 1968, p. 23)

This quotation illustrates how Piaget misunderstood not only imagination but creativity, which can be seen as changing the environment, rather than adapting to it—or accommodation, not assimilation. Formal operational thought privileges assimilation, forcing the outside world to conform to decontextualized thinking, further isolating self from world. The rational distancing from/denial of imaginative aspects of knowing has led to a misunderstanding and devaluing of creativity, ironic and inaccurate since the imagination allows for discovery in science as well as in the arts.

Nor have developmental perspectives been sympathetic to the spirit. Cognitive developmentalism, not recognizing the validity of nonrational thinking, has ignored the topic. Classical psychoanalytic theory views all spiritual experience as regression to infantile thought in which the narcissistic infant, without a developed ego structure, psychically merges with the mother in a kind of "oceanic" union. "Transcend to the mind, but no further" seems to characterize developmental psychology.

Entering the Postmodern Era

Overall, postmodernism seems to represent a shift back towards the immanent with the fall of empiricism allowing for more participatory modes of consciousness. A loosening of the grip of transcendental meta-narratives opens the doors to the valuing of multiple voices and meanings. Investigations of interior and qualitative dimensions with emphasis on situatedness, relatedness, particularity, meaning and subjectivity allow for the possibility of respiritualizing the world.

The spiritual impulse could not remain suppressed in a human history characterized by god(dess)-making, for the search for origin, meaning and purpose of being seems to be a defining aspect of humanity. Popular culture's obsession with spiritual matters is frequently noted. Participation in traditional as well as non-traditional religious and spiritual organizations is rising. The debate between conservative and "new

age" religious perspectives often translates into profound disagreement
about a transcendent God versus an immanent spirituality.

The battle between immanence and transcendence continues in
many forms. On the immanent side, "holists" of every shape and kind
urge our embrace of some form of "whole systems" world view with an
emphasis on the interconnections between everything. Many voices call
for a balancing of the patriarchal modernist era with a return to values
and ways of knowing connected with nature, earth, relationship, the
body, emotions, imagination and intuition and spirit. An "ecological
postmodernism" (Spretnak, 1991; Jardine and Field, 1996) asks us to
return to "an old, earth(l)y wisdom of wholeness, interdependence, patterns: Multiple, interweaving voices and a certain generativity and spirit" (Jardine and Field, 1996, p. 56).

Meanwhile, some critics of these perspectives warn of dangerous
regression, fearing that rationality will become an endangered species,
resulting in increasing fascist religious and political forces. Others see
them as no more than the restless movement of desire seeking fulfillment in varied forms, blown by the political winds with no ultimate des-
tination but in our capitalistic society likely to end up as some form of
egoistic spiritual materialism. Bellah (1986) and Kovel (1991) warn that
the current upswelling of imminent spirituality may result in greater isolated individualism:

> spirituality arises . . . and turns inward, to the only frontier left open—
> to the self itself. That is, it becomes subjective. Subjectivity is like a
> black hole in contemporary culture, pulling everything into itself.
> Thus when the modern American thinks in spiritual terms, the frame
> of reference is . . . personal fulfillment. (p. 209)

On the other hand, deconstructive versions of postmodernism allow
for the dismantling of the politically and socially imposed metanarra-
tives of modernism. This ideological disembedding can free the soul
just as spiritual traditions can expose the illusory nature of our constructed world view. But destruction of conceptual reality taken to its
extreme with no other place to go is also the destruction of spirit and
soul. With the ground of existence as language rather than thought or
spirit, and the only reality that which is constructed by discourse, meaning is only possible through fleeting personal glimpses or false truths
tyrannically imposed:

> In a justifiable reaction to the violence associated with the metaphys-
> ical tradition, the notion of a transcendent signified—a reality beyond
> signification—has been refused. Thought turns even further in upon
> itself, and since it knows itself to be inadequate yet cannot let go of
> logos, it continually tears itself to shreds like a mythical beast.
> (Kovel, 1991, p. 168)

Thus extreme forms of deconstruction ultimately represent the transcendent egoic modernist paradigm they attempt to destroy, exhibiting
"deeply ingrained cultural norms of separateness, reactive autonomy
and self-absorption" (Spretnak, 1991, p. 15).

"Constructivist" versions of postmodernism seek to reunite
dichotomies between subjective and objective, fact and imagination,
secular and sacred (Doll, 1993), immanent and transcendent. Yet, it is
difficult to achieve this synthesis without the construction of yet another metanarrative. However, the inclusion of a spiritual perspective may
permit acceptance of the paradoxes inherent in these dichotomies.

If our culture of separation arises partially from an overemphasis
on the intellect and the ego, then the rebalancing of spirit and rationality are necessary at this stage of human history to forge the types of
social structures necessary to nurture life. Obviously, spirituality is
inseparable from history and politics; as Kovel says: "to paraphrase
Marx, we make spirituality; not as we choose, but rather according to
the history into which we have been thrown. And we make history as
we make spirituality" (Kovel, 1991, p. 198). Our spirits make history as
political players making moral choices, and our particular relationship
with spirit influences the power we exercise in the decisions we make,
the ways in which we care (or do not care) for self, others, and world.

Spiritual Intelligence

As we have seen, for much of history, people understood intelligence as
rooted beyond individuals, in the "mind of the universe." Classical
philosophers from the Greeks to Hegel saw intelligence as an attribute
of being or God. Plotinius referred to the divine and the intellect syn-
onymously in contrast to discursive reasoning, and many Christian theologians, including Saint Augustine, have understood it in this way:
"The prime author and mover of the universe is intelligence" (Gardner,
1983, p. 6). Tillich (1951) calls this type of intelligence "ontological
reason" in contrast to logical reason, and he warns that when logic is
elevated to mean the only type of reason, human intelligence is gravely

misunderstood as has been true in the last several centuries of intellectual thought.

Traditional Buddhist thought refers to our three natures or three types of knowing. The first is our unconditioned or absolute nature, the inherent wholeness and purity of the world, the felt or intuited ground of intelligence. Out of the first rises the second, our relative or conditioned nature, the result of cause and effect, the inherent phenomenal structure of the world, or the realm of forms which we know perceptually. The third, our conceptual knowing, comes from the second. The goal is to understand our beliefs and concepts as partial, paradoxical truths so that the conditioned can be seen as an aspect of the unconditioned. When conceptual reality is deconstructed, the ground it rests on is being or intelligence.

I use "spiritual intelligence" in this sense, to refer to the capacity of the mind that is the basis of intelligence, the essence of consciousness, the knowing faculty. The consciousness of unconditioned being makes possible the perceptual or conceptual consciousness of phenomena. Spiritual intelligence can be seen as a uniting mode of thought which underlies and energizes the various forms that specific intelligences take in the world, the capacity to solve problems and create new knowledge. Imagination can be seen as a bridge between spiritual intelligence and the rational mind because it both allows the rational mind to connect to the spirit through image and translates spiritual knowing into specific intelligences or frames.

Howard Gardner's (1983) theory of multiple intelligences suggests that intelligence is not a unitary entity but rather is comprised of multiple "frames," each consisting of unique problem-solving abilities, all of which are potentially equally valuable to human communities but actually variously culturally valued. His original theory proposed seven intelligences with the potential for others to emerge. Logical-mathematical and linguistic intelligences are the backbone of traditional intelligence theories, including Piaget's developmental theory. Bodily kinesthetic, spatial, and musical intelligences legitimize the importance of the body and the arts as ways of knowing and offer a psychological underpinning for the existence of aesthetic rationality. The personal intelligences emphasize the importance of emotional and social knowing and self-reflection.

Multiple intelligence theory loosens the straitjacket of modernism's narrow views of intelligence, allowing for the recognition and honoring of culturally and individually diverse ways of knowing. As such, it has liberating potential as a basis for pedagogy. (However, the social and political implications of the theory, especially in their potential for co-option and misuse, are often left unexamined. It could easily be used to justify racial and class stereotyping and insidious forms of tracking.) Gardner (1995) has hinted at the possibility of a spiritual intelligence joining his current list of eight intelligences. Since multiple intelligence theory does not posit any underlying or organizing self, when Gardner discusses the search for a spiritual intelligence, he seems to be referring to it on the same level as the others. He has suggested that it could be an aspect of the personal intelligences with a value component added, a kind of culturally relative moral intelligence (1995).

Gardner uses eight "signs" or criteria as measures of the suitability of a candidate intelligence for inclusion on his list. While I will postpone a comprehensive discussion of the relevance of these criteria, the following search for signs of a spiritual intelligence in three contexts does correspond to several of them.

Modernist psychology drew its metaphors and models for the workings of the mind from its science. New scientific paradigms demand new metaphors and models. If spiritual intelligence arises from the "ground of being," we can investigate that ground, considering the contributions of science as we attempt to discover clues about our minds in the "mind of the universe."

1. We can also examine the evidence from individual mystics, mystical cultures and religious meditative traditions.
2. When perceptual or conceptual objects of consciousness are removed, as in mystical or meditative experience, intelligence is "thrown back on itself" to experience itself directly.
3. Thus, mystics are the pioneer investigators of spiritual intelligence.
4. Another way of saying this is that mystics intuit the "hidden" nature of thought and the universe.

And we can consider children's minds, before the development of formal operational thinking. Of course, the validity of this approach will be denied by those who are biased towards a transcendent perspective. As Wilbur (1995) says:

> the productions of, say, the preoperational mind initially look very holistic, very interconnected, very "religious" in a sense, until we scratch the surface and find the whole production supported by ego-centrism, artificialism, finalism, anthropocentrism, and in dissocia-

> tion. . . . before we can say what higher development is, what genuine
> mystical or contemplative or spiritual experience is, we have to know
> what it is not. And above all else, what it is not is . . . infantile indis-
> sociation. (p. 209)

I will argue that this view is limited by its failure to recognize immanent
spirituality.

Postmodern Science

Fritjof Capra (1983), a physicist, suggests that modern physics, including quantum theory and relativity theory, shares a very similar world
view to that of mystics of all ages and traditions. He describes this
world view as one in which

> all things and events perceived by the senses are interrelated, con-
> nected, and are but different aspects or manifestations of the same
> ultimate reality . . . the cosmos is seen as one inseparable reality—for-
> ever in motion, alive, organic, spiritual and material at the same time.
> (p. 24)

This "new physics" posits both individual particles and wave-like
patterns of probabilities of interconnectedness. The individual particles
can be "seen" to rise out of this background, but they do not lose their
wave-like patterns. The Cartesian notion that the world is comprised of
independent parts is reversed. Quantum interconnectedness becomes
the ultimate ground for particular forms. The "particle picture" and the
"wave picture" are each only partially correct and both are necessary for
a complete description of the physical world. Physicist David Bohm
(1980) suggests an implicate order which underlies the structure of the
physical universe, a state in which everything is infolded, unified, connected. The explicit order of the world as external structure emerges
from the deeper implicate order. In the explicit order, things unfold and
become manifest in an upsurge, like an individual wave arising from the
ocean.

Applying quantum metaphors to understanding thinking, we could
say that the mind itself thinks in both holistic, wave-like patterns which
directly intuit the implicate order and provide a context for grasping
paradoxical truths (spiritual intelligence) and in particular, specific, par-
ticle-like patterns corresponding to the explicate order which define and
delineate experience indirectly by dividing it into distinct objects, prop-

erties, relationships, theories. Both types of thinking are necessary for understanding ourselves and our world.

"New physics" theory also tells us that the existence of the observer is necessary to account for the properties of the observed. In other words, things do not exist independently of our perceptions of them, or at least they do not exist in the same ways that they exist when we perceive them. The observer is a part of the entire interconnected process. The idea of separate, objectivist knowing is illusory.

Ilya Prigogine (1980) won the Nobel Prize for his theory of chaos or dissipative structures, according to which all life in the universe is seen as part of a dynamic state that fluctuates between rest and perturbation. Periodically, living systems become so perturbed that they seem to dissipate, and, in fact, their existing form is destroyed. At that point, they either die altogether or are recollected in a state with a more coherent, more complex order of organization. Thus living structures are like the mythical phoenix, continually creating new selves from the old. This theory of self-organizing capacity, applied to cognitive structures, validates stage theory's formulation of increasingly complex structures—but not its lockstep sequencing of those structures.

Mystics' Thinking

The study of mysticism is extensive, inter-religious, multicultural and interdisciplinary, based on the examination and interpretation of numerous personal accounts from many cultures and religions throughout history. The word "mysticism" is derived from a Greek root meaning "to close," especially referring to closing the eyes and lips. Having been initiated into the secret esoteric knowledge of a religion, the mystic vowed to keep silent about it. A later derivation added the meaning of closing the mind to external reality (Smith, 1980, p. 19).

Many scholars of mysticism suggest that mystical doctrines from diverse religious traditions and historical periods are remarkably similar. However, there is an ongoing debate in the field of comparative mysticism about similarities and differences among mystical experiences and the extent to which they are bound by culture and tradition.

William James (1980) creates a context for understanding mystical knowing as a mode of cognitive perception potentially available to all people: "States of mystical experience may be only very sudden and great extensions of the ordinary field of consciousness" (p. 215). He suggests that mystical experience is the "uncovering" of aspects of reality hidden from but connected with our everyday consciousness.

The mystic "knows" by attaining a deep state of feeling often described as love or ecstacy. "He may be reached and held close by means of love, but by means of thought, never," says the anonymous author (Trans., Progoff, 1983) of *The Cloud of Unknowing*, one of the best-known mystical tracts. The mystic's love is the love of being and her intense desire is the desire for being, a longing for connection with the source of self. Like all other experiences of eros, mystical experiences are bodily based, but the nature of mystical eroticism is often unrecognized or misunderstood. A feeling of heightened significance or meaningfulness associated with mystical experience often remains long after the immediate experience.

Mystics claim a unique type of perception or cognition. Margaret Smith (1980) says that mysticism . . . "denies that knowledge can be attained only by means of the senses or the intellect . . . and claims that the highest knowledge can be attained by this spiritual sense of intuition" (p. 21). Moreover, this intuition seems to confirm a knowledge already possessed, an uncovering rather than an adding. "Spiritual knowledge is revealed, not learned" (Smith, 1980, p. 21). The logic of spiritual knowledge is best described as paradoxical. For example, God is frequently described as "nothing, both existing and not existing as the same time as the mystic attempts to convey the paradoxical consciousness of the unconditioned/conditioned nature of God/reality."

Mystics can be seen as "radical empiricists," searching for clues about the nature of the universe in the mind of God, but they are also aestheticists, claiming that God is the ultimate subjective experience. "This God is to be approached through the imagination and can be seen as a kind of art form, akin to the other great artistic symbols that have expressed the ineffable mystery, beauty and value of life" (Armstrong, 1993, p. 396). The mystic uses imagination in two ways. She tries to convey her experience of God through paradoxical imagery or artistic forms. But imagination can also function as a ladder on which to climb towards God: by imagining a deity, she can experience some aspect of the actual deity until the experience overwhelms the image and the "ladder" is no longer necessary.

In the study of mysticism, many classification systems, cutting across religions, are based on the immanent/transcendent distinction, and forms of the familiar battle exist here, too, between scholars who debate the relative validity of various mystical experiences. R.C. Zaehner (1980) distinguishes between theistic or transcendental experiences and monistic or immanent experiences. In the transcendental, the mystic is absorbed in the deity, distinct from the objective world, in nature. But these are the rational classifications of mystical experiences by scholars or the self-understandings of the mystics after their experiences, used to explain the relationship of their vision to their theology. The mystical experience itself is one of unity, making the transcendent God immanent or merging with the immanent many into the One. Thus, mysticism can be seen as a resolution of the duality.

Although mystical experiences may be fleeting, they flourish in communities as a result of disciplined spiritual experience. Practices from many traditions, including diverse forms of meditation, attempt to uncover the spiritual nature of intelligence, allowing an escape from the rational mind by challenging habitual and often superficial conceptualizations. Thus spiritual practice can be a tool for attaining greater perspective on the situatedness of ordinary rational consciousness. By simultaneously realizing our conditioned and unconditioned natures, we relativize the conceptualizing process.

Young Children's Thinking

It is difficult to sort out what is known about young children's thinking from the theoretical biases inherent in the research. Generalizing about this area is also problematical, given the fact that I am relativizing stage theory. The following discussion should be seen as an attempt to balance the picture in light of the imbalances inherent in prevailing developmental perspectives.

Above all else young children are characterized as highly egocentric, as seeing themselves at the center of reality because they are not fully aware of themselves as being separate from it. But of course this is deceptive since the belief that individuals are separate from the rest of reality reflects the dominant modernist rationality. Some aspects of young children's "egocentricity" could be attributed to their accurate sense that they are connected rather than separate beings.

Cognitive developmental theory describes young children as unable to de-center, to see the world from others' perspectives. Yet there is evidence that this aspect of the theory is misguided. In *Children's Minds* Margaret Donaldson (1978) argues that the research tasks Piaget (and other researchers who followed him) used to measure de-centering were constructed in ways that didn't make sense to children. Adults emphasize abstract thinking while children function in contextualized action. When young children are assigned active tasks, they are frequently quite capable of decentering, taking multiple perspectives and behaving with social maturity. All people, adults and children, act in egocentric ways in some situations and not in others.

In a way, psychology "has it backwards." Seeing children as egocentric, isolated entities is at least partially a projection of adult noncontextualized thinking. Young children interact naturally in a social context. They spontaneously bond, play and explore with others. Although "socialization" fulfills a necessary function in terms of the continuity of cultural morals, mores and morale, it also reproduces cultural biases. Western cultures emphasize the development of individual ego and achievement and teach children to disconnect from others, shaping them towards egocentrism and then characterizing them as "naturally" egocentric.

According to Piaget, young children's thinking is defined by animism, artificialism and finalism. Animism endows everything in the world with consciousness and intention. Artificialism is the understanding that humans or a divine being created the world and finalism is the belief that there must be a reason for everything, "there is no chance in nature and everything is 'made for' man and children according to an established and wise plan" (Piaget, 1968, p. 25). Not only little children but some quantum physicists understand the world in similar ways:

> Life is not accidental. On the contrary, Wheeler asserts that "quantum physics has led us to take seriously and explore the directly opposite view that the observer is as essential to the creation of the universe as the universe is to the creation of the observer." Though man is not at the center of the universe he appears to be at the center of its purpose . . . a universe aimed at the production of man implied a mind directed it. For matter on its own cannot aim at anything. Hence . . . a mind that directs the whole universe, all the laws of nature and all the properties of matter, to a goal. (Augros and Stanciu, 1986, p. 70)

Even during infancy, the child's exploration of the world is fueled by emotional curiosity; this is often described as wonder and awe. Infants and young children see the world "as a text to be read." They are not concerned with the end point but with the ongoing fascinating, emotion-driven process of exploring and relating to the people, objects and situations around them. Virtually everyone understands young children's thinking as characterized by participation, a bodily based merging of emotion and cognition with objects of consciousness, but developmental perspectives have interpreted this as preventing children from seeing the world objectively—as it "really is." Piaget also sees *partici-*

pation as the inaccurate belief that two beings or phenomena—without any clear causal connection between them—are believed to influence each other. Yet, quantum physics theories remind us of the connections between all phenomena. The participatory nature of children's thinking allows for a more aesthetic experience of the nature of the world, "true" in different ways than formal operational thinking.

The human mind seems to come equipped not only with the desire but the capacity to make meaning, to find patterns and relationships. Infants and young children could be said to be obsessed with a desire to "map out" the physical and social worlds. Their meaning making capacity has been continually underestimated by developmental theorists.

It is noteworthy that "pre-operation," the name Piaget chose to designate a stage of young children's thinking, is based on his perception of a deficiency in their logical-mathematical thinking. Because he focused on that intelligence and because his scientific world view was based on Cartesian rationality, he seemed to dismiss the extraordinary imagination and creativity of young children's thinking, based on rapid growth in ability to understand and express symbols. Rather than a "deforming assimilation," imaginative symbolic play can be understood as a unique task of childhood which may be the prototype of later genius.

Young children can demonstrate amazing perception in their ability to reflect on themselves, others and their origins—to grasp and express subtle philosophical and religious concepts. They are interested in penetrating the surfaces. Wellman's (1992) extensive studies demonstrate that, in contrast to the traditional Piagetian view, young children's theories of mind are remarkably like those of adults.

In his book *Philosophy and the Young Child*, Gareth Mathews (1980) discusses young children's ability to reason and to grapple with complex philosophical issues:

> for many young members of the human race, philosophical reasoning—including, on occasion, subtle and ingenious reasoning—is as natural as making music and playing games, and quite as much a part of being human. (p. 36)

Mathews, a philosopher, critiques *The Child's Conception of the World*, showing how Piaget (1983) actually discouraged children from doing philosophy in the way he asked the questions. Whereas Piaget says real understanding of philosophical issues cannot take place until adolescence, Mathews says that young children are more likely to "do philosophy" because genuine philosophical questions are the basic and important ones about life that young children naturally ask but which may come to seem naive as we grow older and are socialized not to raise.

Edward Robinson (1983) used data from an Oxford University study of religious experience in which about 600 adults who had experience of "some power beyond themselves" in their childhood years wrote accounts of the experiences and the effects that they had on their lives. This study led Robinson to believe that Piaget typically underrated childhood capacities for religious insight and understanding, and it also led him to formulate "the original vision of childhood," a intuitive holistic form of knowing that is indispensable to later adult knowing.

Revisioning Thinking and Development

Although modernist developmental theories denied the validity of spiritual perspectives, this was only an apparent vanquishing of the spirit. The spirit was never absent, it was only our ability to perceive it that waned. What are the contributions of the "non-spiritual" theories to a psychology of spirit?

Freud demonstrated the centrality of bodily based emotion or desire to human experience. Desire can be seen as longing to experience and express the nature of being—"the pre-verbal voice of praxis as it breaks loose from and then reapproaches the plasma of our being" (Kovel, 1991, p. 170). It is spirit as life force which drives the process of individuation in its urge to connect and to create and recreate itself.

Piaget's genius was his insight into the expression of the interactive organization and reorganization of external and internal forms created as spirit expresses itself in the process of differentiation. Cognitive developmental theories demonstrate the self-organizing, self-constructing capacities of transcending spirit, although the bias of the theory limits the extent of the transcendence.

Robert Kegan (1982) is one of very few academic psychologists who have attempted to integrate theories of mind and emotion. He sees meaning making as the organizing force in development with neither emotion nor thought as dominant but both as subject to the more basic experience of meaning making and considers that this meaning-making capacity may have a spiritual basis:

> The making and surrendering of meaning, it is suggested, is a "universal" activity, but not because Someone remembers to make each person this way. It is universal because it is a single activity, there where the dance is, an activity which may itself be the Someone. (Kegan, 1980, p. 437)

From this perspective, meaning is inherent in spirit which gives rise to the human activity of making meaning. Immanence and transcendence are both aspects of this meaning-making process, with immanence understood as the embodied felt or intuited experience of the implicate being that makes transcendence possible and transcendence as the creation of explicate states in order to understand and express the implicate in unique ways.

A number of theories express this (or something similar to it) in other terms. The word intuition is frequently used to denote a type of knowing contrasting to logical knowing. In *The Encyclopedia of Philosophy*, Richard Rorty (1967) gives "immediate apprehension" as the broadest definition of intuition and goes on to say that apprehension can mean either sensation or knowledge or mystical union. Bruner (1982) sees intuition as "the act of grasping the meaning, significance or structure of a problem or situation without explicit reliance on the analytic apparatus" (p. 102). It acts as a broad map, intimating new areas of thinking that we will later define and refine using logical methods. Dewey (1931) describes qualitative thinking as the "ground" out of which quantitative thinking arises. Every explicit thought is derived from underlying, prior qualitative thinking, experienced as feeling/intuition. Qualitative thinking has a shaping and integrating power that provides the meaningful context for quantitative thoughts, energizing and guiding them in patterns that allow us to make explicit sense of our experiences. Polyani (1967) suggests a tacit power of knowing that shapes and integrates explicit bits and pieces of information into wholes capable of comprehension, the power "by which all knowledge is discovered and, once discovered, is held to be true" (p. 6). Creative discovery is impossible without the tacit sense of the presence of a hidden reality, of "yet undiscovered things." Sloan (1983) distinguishes imaginative fancy, which recycles old images and ideas in a mechanical way, never rising above the explicit state, and insight/imagination, which is rooted in the implicit and allows for the anticipation of new ideas and events, the creation of new possibilities.

Those who write about development as a spiritual process recognize the necessity for some form of ego development and movement from global to differentiated cognition but they differ on the extent to which these must occur, the value of earlier forms of cognition, and the relationship of these earlier forms to later adult or modern consciousness. Some see the more global consciousness as the source and origin of all later spiritual experience and thus view the total replacement of global consciousness as neither desirable nor inevitable. These theorists value "non-rational" types of knowing, seen as physical, emotional, imaginative, and/or intuitive. Others see rationality as a pre-condition for true spirituality and classify early global consciousness as a "primitive" state with little or no relationship to later adult spiritual consciousness so that its dissolution is seen as both inevitable and desirable.

Ken Wilbur (1986) suggests a nine-stage system based on structures that include body, mind, emotions, and spirit. Wilbur's first four stages of consciousness correspond directly to Piaget's and the last four are "higher levels" that include spiritual understanding. Humans begin by developing the rational mind and then may attain "higher" modes of consciousness. As we have seen, he explicitly rejects the idea that young children's thinking has any spiritual basis. Wilbur (1983) also proposes the "pre/trans fallacy" to explain the errors made by various psychologies when viewing religious or spiritual experience. The "pre" and "trans" stand for prerational or prepersonal and transrational or transpersonal states of consciousness. He says that because they are both nonrational states, they are confused by the undiscerning. The pre-fallacy occurs when "authentic" adult spiritual experience is reduced to a lower state of development, as in the classic psychoanalytic position on mystical experience. The transfallacy results from elevating the global consciousness of children or an archetypal experience to the level of genuine spiritual experience.

But I suggest that it is Wilbur's bias towards transcendent mind and spirit that leads him to dismiss global consciousness as non-spiritual. The ultimate stage of his system is the ground of being: "Strictly speaking, the ultimate is not one level among others, but the reality, condition, or suchness of all levels." (Wilbur, 1986, p. 7) If this is so, then the suchness can be accessed from the pre-rational or pre-egoic mind even if the experience is not consciously understood as such. While Wilbur's theories are extremely useful for understanding adult mysticism of the contemplative traditions, I believe that they misrepresent the spiritual nature of childhood experience as well as many types of adult experience (including the shamanism of indigenous cultures, understood as less advanced than forms of yogic, Buddhist, or Christian mysticism) as a result of undervaluing the embodied emotional/intuitive experiences of immanence.

A.H. Almaas (1986) integrates neo-Freudian ego psychology with stages of spiritual growth. Libido becomes *essence* seen as the subtle, powerful, energy of being or spirit. Babies and young children embody this essence. While the construction of ego is potentially healthy, the developmental process typical of our culture encourages overidentification with the ego personality, accompanied by a gradual weakening of connection with essence. In fact, our ego representations fill the holes previously filled by essence until we identify completely with them, resulting in the loss of our subtle spiritual perception. Spiritual or inner development consists of freeing our awareness or essence. In this sense we return to our early childhood essence, but we experience and understand it differently as a result of development. This perspective suggests a way to value both the experience of immanent spirituality and what is gained by transcendence.

Resolving the Paradox

The whole of existence can be seen to consist of explicating the implicate order or changing the formless into diverse forms and then continually reforming the forms, becoming separate while remaining whole. The developmental journey is also about explicating the implicate order: the spirit as a virtuality becomes a reality as ourselves as the existential world configures itself in each of us in a unique way. We are continually recreating ourselves and our worlds and as we do, we contribute to the universe; our individual and social expressions add something unique to existence. Behind it all is the passion, desire, and will to understand and create, to express our sense of the meaning of existence.

Modernist cultural conditioning encourages our rational minds to continually destroy our intuition of the meaningfulness and connectedness of our lives, and to think of ourselves, our thoughts and the world as isolated, static states. Actually, our thoughts are broken off fragments of a deeper process of thinking and everything, including ourselves, is connected but constantly changing. Although the experiences we have in life may obscure our relationship with living spirit, it is as close as our own breath.

Spirituality can be seen as the deepest dimension of ourselves, the source of life which both finds and allows for individuality and creativity. We are both separate and that which is beyond separate, conditioned and unconditioned, implicit and explicit, immanent and transcendent. This mystery is not fully understandable by the rational mind because it includes the rational mind as tool of the spirit for explicating the implicit.

If spiritual intelligence, or mind as fabric of universe, is the underlying source of cognition, then infants come to the world with the ability to know and to experience connection—to think post-formally fully operative. This intelligence provides a context for making sense of the world. Another way of saying this is that intelligence begins as an innate power of reflection manifesting through the body as a powerful drive to seek and create meaningful patterns and relationships. It is the imma- nent background which provides a sense of connectedness and unites emotion, body, senses, perception and action in the quest for under- standing and creating. The child knows spirit through feeling and intu- ition but may not know that she knows, or, if she does, she cannot always express it. However, at age three my daughter offered this insight: "The difference between Elsie (the cow) and me is that even though God is inside us both, she doesn't know it, but I do."

The transcendental aspect of development arises from the desire to understand and express the nature of being. The challenge is to con- struct an effective rational mind and a healthy ego that represents self without sacrificing soul. Since everyone is continually structuring and restructuring themselves, any stage theory can be seen as arbitrary, yet there are certain loose constructions of self, with many variations, that many individuals can be seen to manifest in a particular order and rhythm. These can be called "stages," if they are seen as metaphorical constructions, paradoxically existing and not existing in the same way that particles exist as continually restructuring potentials against the background of waves.

Development is inherently a paradoxical process, uniting the immanent and transcendent aspects of our being. Starting from a feel- ing of unity, we appear to separate so that we can contribute our partic- ular qualities to the whole and fully realize our unity. We enter into duality to understand and express the unity but then we have to give up dualism to become it and in becoming the dualism, we can overcome it. We journey from the spirit to the spirit, returning with ourselves as uniquely configured to offer back to the whole—without ever having left. The spirit is always fully present during the journey, but the chang- ing nature of our expression and awareness of it change the nature of the journey.

Young children are not fully conscious of themselves as creators and connectors. Their minds inherently represent the vitality, variety, and bonding nature of spirit. Their thinking naturally reflects the nature of the implicit, unconditioned, immanent dimensions of the universe. The passion with which they approach learning about the conditioned nature of the world results in the rapid construction of the mind with its various forms of problem solving and creating abilities, an effective tool to further their knowledge, especially if its construction doesn't disconnect them from the spiritual nature of knowing.

Most adults in our culture are dually conditioned—they reflect not only the conditioned nature of the universe but the cultural conditioning that disconnects them from the unconditioned so that their rational thinking embodies a limited and disconnected dimension of life. The values of some contemporary indigenous cultures allow adults with fully developed rationality to remain connected with the spiritual nature of their intelligence which also connects them with the world. Those with a bias towards transcendent spirituality or rationality may mistakenly view these cultures as pre-rational.

Adult "geniuses" consciously master some domain of conditioned intelligences while they simultaneously, although often unknowingly, stay connected to the implicit nature of mind and universe. Mystics can be seen as geniuses of the unconditioned being, attempting to understand and describe its nature while they intensify their experience of it. Of course, knowing *about* the spiritual nature of intelligence is very different from unconsciously reflecting it.

The process of individuation includes recognizing and gaining control of our unique gifts, both as individuals and as cultures. We are each (individually and culturally) expressions of various intelligences, all of which are expressions of the intelligence of spirit. Maturity involves taking responsibility for our abilities, utilizing them to make a better world, expressing connections with and caring for other individuals, cultures and forms of life. It also includes our responsibility to recognize and nurture the spirit in others. Teachers of spirit recognize every being, and the gifts of being in the process of becoming; they allow all beings to feel special, valued, whole, and holy.

References

Almaas, A.H. (1986). *Essence*. York Beach, ME: Samuel Weisner.

Armstrong, K. (1993). *A history of god*. New York: Alfred A. Knopf.

Augros, R. and Stanciu, G. (1986). *The new story of science*. Toronto: Bantam Books.

Barfield, O. (n.d.). *Saving the appearances*. New York: Harcourt, Brace and Jovanovich.

Bellah, R. (1986). *Habits of the heart*. New York: Harper and Row.

Berman, M. (1984). *The reenchantment of the world*. New York: Bantam Books.

Bohm, D. (1980). *Wholeness and the implicate order.* Boston: Routledge and Kegan.

Bruner, J. (1982). *On knowing.* Cambridge, MA: Harvard University Press.

Cajete, G. (1994). *Look to the mountain: An ecology of indigenous education.* Durango, CO: Kivaki Press.

Campbell, J. (1968). *The hero with a thousand faces.* New York: World Press.

Capra, F. (1983). *The Tao of physics.* Boulder: Shambala Press.

Dewey, J. (1931). *Philosophy and civilization.* New York: Minton, Balch and Co.

Doll, W. (1993). *A postmodern perspective on curriculum.* New York: Teachers College.

Donaldson, M. (1978). *Children's minds.* London: Fontana Press.

Eisler, R. (1987). *The chalice and the blade: Our history, our future.* New York: Harper and Row.

Gardner, H. (1982). *Art, mind, and brain.* New York: Basic Books.

Gardner, H. (1983). *Frames of mind.* New York: Basic Books.

Gardner, H. (1993). *Multiple intelligences: The theory in practice.* New York: Basic Books.

Gardner, H. (1995). Reflections on multiple intelligences. *Phi Delta Kappan,* 77, 200–209.

Goleman, D. (1995). *Emotional intelligence.* New York: Bantam Books.

Habermas, J. (1979). *Communication and the evolution of society.* Boston: Beacon Press.

James, W. (1980). A suggestion about mysticism. In Richard Woods (Ed.), *Understanding mysticism* (pp. 215–22). Garden City, NY: Image Books.

Jardine, D., and Field, J. (1996). On postmodern shadow of whole language: Theory and practice and the ecological wisdom of good work. *Holistic Education Review,* 9, 54–58.

Kegan, R. (1980). There where the dance is: Religious dimensions of a developmental framework. In *Toward Moral and Religious Maturity.* Morristown, NJ: Silver Burdett.

Kegan, R. (1982). *The evolving self.* Cambridge: Harvard University Press.

Kincheloe J. and Steinberg, S. (1993). A tentative description of post-formal thinking. *Harvard Educational Review* 63, 296–320.

Kovel, J. (1991). *History and spirit.* Boston, MA: Beacon Press.

Mathews, G. (1980). *Philosophy and the young child.* Cambridge, MA: Harvard University Press.

Neuman, E. (1954). *The origins and history of consciousness.* Princeton, NJ: Princeton University Press.

Piaget, J. (1968). *Six psychological studies.* New York: Vintage Books.

Piaget, J. (1983). *The child's conception of the world.* Totowa, NJ: Rowman and Allanheld.

Polyani, M. (1967). *The tacit dimension.* Garden City, NY: Doubleday.

Prigogine, I. (1980). *From being to becoming.* San Francisco: Freeman.

Progoff, I., Trans. (1983). Author anonymous. *The cloud of unknowing.* New York: Dell.

Robinson, E. (1983). *The original vision.* New York: The Seabury Press.

Rorty, R. (1967). Intuition. In P. Edwards (Ed.), *The Encyclopedia of Philosophy,* Vol. 4. New York: Macmillan.

Sloan, D. (1983). *Insight-imagination: The emancipation of thought and the modern world.* Westport, CT: Greenwood.

Smith, M. (1980). The nature and meaning of mysticism. In Richard Woods (Ed.), *Understanding mysticism.* Garden City, NY: Image Books.

Spretnak, C. (1991). *States of grace: Recovering meaning in the postmodern age.* San Francisco: Harper.

Tillich, P. (1951). *Systematic Philosophy, Vol. I.* Chicago: University of Chicago.

Wellman, H. (1992). *The child's theory of mind.* Cambridge, MA: MIT Press.

Wilbur, K. (1983). *Eye to eye.* Garden City, NY: Doubleday.

Wilbur, K. (1986). *The spectrum of consciousness.* Boston: New Science Library.

Wilbur, K. (1995). *Sex, ecology and spirituality.* Boston, MA: Shambala Press.

Zaehner, R.D.. (1980). Mysticism sacred and profane. In Richard Woods (Ed.), *Understanding mysticism* (pp. 56–77). Garden City, NY: Image Books.

CHAPTER SEVEN

Creativity
Creativity, Art, and Aesthetics Unraveled Through Post-formalism: An Exploration of Perception, Experience, and Pedagogy

Leila Villaverde

Ever since I was in grade school I wondered about the purpose of what I was being taught. One subject which exemplified this for me was geometry. I found its meaning to be the essence of abstraction and explanation, which was applicable to a variety of areas in life and society. This insight, if I can call it that, didn't materialize until the second time taking the course. This was largely possible through the teacher who continuously referred to the larger picture of geometry. I started to analyze the process of geometry, the particular way my mind had to operate in order to understand the theorems, proofs, and logic. Despite geometry's limitations or its linearity, the analytical process I had to implement to search for the meaning helped substantially, not only in geometry but elsewhere. Basically, it was the combination of the teacher's application of the terms and how it challenged me to analyze the process to understand it better that facilitated a meta-awareness. Through his passion, I was able to see the potential implications of the opposite and plural within the singular. I understood the irrational of the rational. Understanding some of the how's, if's and then's helped me formulate a deeper meaning in a critical perspective of probing deeper and deeper into unanswered questions and possibilities.

Later on in my undergraduate education, I realized how important it was to search for a purpose and how it helped relieve some of the anxiety when I didn't understand something. Locating a purpose also fueled the motivation to go further as I pursued my educational endeavors. I decided to relinquish the hesitation and hiatus I had taken from producing my own art. My parents began framing my artwork in the second grade, and I continued on and off with my art until I started taking it more seriously in college where I realized it was a vital part of who I am. I had become disenchanted with art in high school, because of the singularity in which it was presented to me. What was praised and considered talented were photorealistic images, mimicking almost faultlessly what we considered reality. This became very frustrating to me as I never saw an end to the obsession of getting it right, without mistakes; so I quit. Art lost its magic when it was reduced to the mastery of technical skills; I just did not have the patience. It was not until college that I experienced alternative expressions within art.

The more I probed the essence of the art, the more intimate I became with its process and product. I localized the seed initiating the gestation of the entire process, the seed of creativity. Creativity is the essence of producing meaning, questions, aesthetics, thought, and action which all encompass deep-rooted emotions compelling inclinations to sway one way or another. It is imperative to develop a pedagogy of creativity within an era that almost seems apathetic to the disconnection it generates within the individuals that constitute it. I am suggesting that we have neglected our creative seed, and the seed is planted deep inside, enveloped by multiple almost impenetrable layers. Our creativity is suppressed by the social conditions which deem compliance and non-individuality, making creativity obsolete, bypassing its cultivation and thus harvest. The concept of rekindling or nurturing any creative seed, of patiently witnessing its unfolding, may seem unproductive in a society thriving on immediate gratification. Creativity is imponderable knowledge subjected to the quantifications and qualifications of an era that recognizes its importance but in the process of exposing its benefits, advantages, and necessity ironically demeans its fluidity and flexibility. I am not exactly absolved from the above statement either. The very nature of this chapter is to lay out at least a notion of what creativity could be. But I hope that my explanation does not limit the possibility, expansiveness, and richness creativity offers. On the contrary, I want to highlight its fluid and flexible nature so that the reader can amplify its use and meaning. This chapter will offer readers ways to negotiate their agency with the increased awareness of the limits imposed and a critical investigation of working within and through the boundaries.

The arts and creativity have been closely aligned if not thought of as one in the same for quite a long time. Yet even the arts often neglect an in-depth study of creativity. The arts are objectified and reduced to techniques. Art, whatever it may be and however it may be expressed, requires techniques, emotions, thoughts, a way of seeing, conceptualizing, dialoguing, and acting, all interrelating and never isolated from one another. But one element is not enough; everything occurs simultaneously and exists non-linearly.

In the scope of this chapter, we will take a look at how we can use post-formal thinking to redefine art, creativity, and aesthetics in relation to power, subjectivity, and consciousness construction. In doing so, we will also examine how art, creativity, and aesthetics can further expound on post-formalism, how it is understood, enacted, and applied. The chapter is divided into four sections: first, I will discuss several definitions of creativity that were formed within a formal paradigm, then appropriate elements of these definitions to develop a theory of creativity that is post-formal. Second, the realms where creativity, art, and aesthetics intersect will be explored and challenged. Third, symbolism is examined as it renders a language which helps to encode and decode our ways of seeing, feeling, and thinking, enhancing a critical analysis of being and specifically of learning and teaching. Fourth, post-formal thinking is envisioned through the arts curriculum as well as examining its necessity within education. Throughout the chapter I will stress not only the importance of understanding the parameters and boundaries of the concepts and realms we will address, but also the crucial necessity of traversing these boundaries, finding ways to invert them, and utilizing their elements in multidirectional ways. In this chapter, post-formal thinking is used to interrogate the standards in which we perceive, experience, and teach art, creativity, and aesthetics through ways that inescapably require post-formalism to also be questioned in order to clarify how the arts and post-formalism inform and redefine each other creating various pedagogical experiences.

Creativity in a Post-formal vs. Formal Paradigm

Creativity may not be the easiest concept to verbalize or define, but as Torrance (1988) states, "It involves every sense—sight, smell, hearing, feeling, taste and even perhaps the extrasensory. Much of it is unseen, nonverbal, and unconscious" (p.43). The intangible nature of creativity makes it difficult for those trying to understand or experience it. The crucial aspect, I believe, is allowing oneself to reach that point of accepting something new. Creativity is not something outside or inside the individual exclusively, undoubtedly it is the woven interaction of the two localities which produces the possibility of creativity. The goal is not to find a locality within or outside of ourselves for creativity but rather to understand that it is fluid, flexible, and existent everywhere.

What I will attempt to do is give a sense of what creativity may encompass, but ultimately the definition lies in the synthesis of what the circumstances and individual (the reader) prescribe. These definitions and attempts at logically describing creativity often limit the way in which we can understand such a concept if we do not deconstruct what is presented to us in critical fashion in order to extrapolate other meanings. Barron (1988) lists six "ingredients" as he designates the elements of creativity:

1. Recognizing patterns
2. Making connections
3. Taking risks
4. Challenging assumptions
5. Taking advantage of chance
6. Seeing in new ways

Although I don't agree with a recipe approach due to its assumed static nature, realistically even literal recipes are open to variation. The ingredients above, on their own, pose and require some interesting action-oriented behaviors. The ingredients describe the natural processes the mind engages in, regardless of any conscious participation from the individual. So to alleviate some of the anxiety that comes along with trying to grasp a new concept, what I am saying is that this, the nature and process of creativity is not something new, really, but something that we already engage in to different degrees. In becoming aware of it, we can utilize it to increase our agency. The behaviors described in the ingredients are inherent in the process of how we perceive, internalize, store, recollect, and enact what we see, feel, and experience. It is important to grasp a substantial Gestalt (an awareness of an organized concept, thing, schema, system, or unit)[1] in order to branch out into the related issues that will allow us to comprehend the relevance of the aesthetic and creative in post-formal thinking and pedagogy.

Creativity if nothing else provides a vast range of possibilities, of different avenues that are equally valid and plausible. In a 1960 unpublished report titled *Definitions and Criteria of Creativity* from the Dow Chemical Company, L. C. Repucci thematically categorized definitions of creativity. These categories are relevant to mention since they highlight what creativity is often associated with and follows suit to some of the issues we are discussing in this chapter. There are six differential classifications:

1. "Gestalt" or "Perception" type definitions wherein the major emphasis is upon the recombination of ideas or the restructuring of a "Gestalt."
2. "End Product" or " Innovation" oriented definitions resulting in novel works or productions.
3. "Aesthetic" or "Expressive" definitions emphasizing self-expression unique to the individual.
4. "Psychoanalytic" or "Dynamic" definitions describing creativity in terms of the id, ego, and superego.
5. "Solution Thinking" stressing the thinking process itself rather than the actual solution of the problem.
6. "Varia" entails a variety of definitions which combine the subjective reaction, the individual, and the environment, as well as other definitions not characterized by the other categories.

The fourth category deals with psychoanalytic theory exclusively. Repucci might have found only these type of definitions to explain the connection between creativity and personality, but psychoanalysis is barely the end-all source of reference for theories of personality. I find the essentialism of psychoanalytic theory problematic. Defining the individual in terms of a tertiary axiom, such as the id, ego, and superego seems deterministic and counterproductive to the applicability of the other definitions. It also limits the discourse in which one can explore creativity and the individual. There are many other schools of thought-rendering theories of personality examining familial and societal circumstances for a more comprehensive view of the individual, context, and history.[2]

The last category is interesting because it represents the vast number of definitions that could not be characterized by any of the other categories and therefore warranted a separate place of its own. Creativity can not be neatly categorized, defined, or delineated. Some of the definitions that comprise the last category stress interaction and subjectivity, both vital to the existence and development of creativity. The process that allows an event to take place, a feeling to be felt, a stimulus to be interpreted, is extremely complex and multi-faceted. Things do not happen in a vacuum, one does not live in isolation, interaction is a basic social process, and subjectivity is influenced and constructed through a variety of experiences. There are several functions just within one's being that take place simultaneously in order for other things to occur, from simple reaction to complex thoughts and actions. It is this interactive component which produces a space for the subjective, creating a necessary exchange between the individual and society. This, in turn, yields to pedagogical experiences allowing a variety of texts to come together in one site. There needs to be a space where intellect, emotions, physicality, consciousness, and unconsciousness reside so that expressive and communicative elements can produce insight and creativity. Aesthetic or Gestalt "aha" experiences can also transform familiarity to unfamiliarity and vice versa, consequently expanding the notion of what is real. There is a level of freedom and will inscribed in all of this providing a vast range of possibilities for the individual to maximize his or her own experiences within the limits placed by economic or class hierarchies or finding ways to transgress them.

I propose that the definitions of creativity utilized in this section were designed out of a formal operational thought model (Piaget's highest order of thinking) because the authors continually try to logically lay out creativity, devising rules and standards to explain this phenomenon. The mere act of attempting to systematize creativity preordains the level in which our thoughts, feelings, perceptions, and experiences can be conceptualized and expressed. Therefore, throughout this section I critically analyze the elements within these definitions that can be challenged into higher modes of thinking, i.e. post-formal thinking. In the fashion that I dissected the definitions, posed questions, alluded to other possibilities, and created new formulations in thinking about and employing creativity, made creativity post-formal. Kincheloe (1993) asserts, "One of the main features of post-formal thinking is that it expands the boundaries of what can be labeled sophisticated thinking"(p. 125). In getting one to think about how one is thinking and what constructs what one is thinking about, two fields intersect, critical theory and constructivism. Kincheloe (1993) adds:

> This notion of critical constructivism allows teachers a critical consciousness, that is, an ability to step back from the world as we are accustomed to perceiving it and to see the ways our perception is constructed through linguistic codes, cultural signs, and embedded power. Such an ability constitutes a giant step in learning to teach, indeed, in learning to think (p. 109).

In the ways in which we gain and use this meta-awareness, we can employ creativity in realms usually devoid of the richness it can espouse. Creativity then coupled with the arts and aesthetics can offer a multitude of avenues for thinking, expressing, and teaching. Teachers, particularly, can use post-formal thinking and creativity to increase the meaning-making process in their practice.

Creativity, Art, and Aesthetics Intersect

So why is the creative almost always associated with the artistic? Art, the term, is a modern construction. Art has existed throughout history, never formally designated as "art," as something outside of the ordinary or the necessary, or even outside daily life. Art has thus been mystified and clouded only to allow those who are innately creative or artistic, who have the talent to belong in that world. As Kincheloe and Steinberg (1993) state, "Intelligence and creativity are thought of as fixed and innate, while at the same time mysterious qualities found only in the privileged few" (p. 298). This only alienates art from one's life instead of permeating every aspect of it.

Creativity and art have been closely related because artists have been deemed creative, possessing something unique, different, producing objects or a way of life, self-expressing and searching for some type of meaning or connection to what they do, feel, and inhabit. All of the above cover the wide range of classifications of the definitions of creativity. It becomes something vague, inexplicable at times, what motivates artists and fuels their creativity. The notion of having something "special" can create a cycle of sorts, a self-feeding one, either creating an ego that might facilitate producing art for the sake of producing it, or limiting the creation of art to solely a private sphere instead of a public one, where again alienation is pivotal as artists intensely feel the chasm between themselves and society. Art is still looked at as an "other" given its exclusive designation of who is and isn't an artist. Then those deemed as artists are left somewhat vulnerable to the external definitions of art, as they bear the burden of limited representations. These definitions are constructed by modernist ideologies of art which become hegemonic in perpetuation of a singular view in defining art and artist and acquiring a wide consensus of these definitions. The modernist ideological perspective judges art on its pleasing aesthetics, assigning aesthetics the standards to demarcate the boundaries between high and low art as well as inscribing a superficially removed quality to experiencing art. Yet contemporary art has changed modernism's perspectives to some extent, redefining what art is and where it is. Giroux (1992) proposes:

> As an antiaesthetic, postmodernism rejects the modernist notion of privileged culture or art; it renounces "official" centers for "housing" and displaying art and culture along with their interests in origins, periodization, and authenticity. Moreover, postmodernism's challenge to the boundaries of modernist art and culture has, in part, resulted in new forms of art, writing, film-making, and various types of aesthetic and social criticism. (p. 58)

Moving away from the good, clean pleasure people usually received from looking at artwork for its prettiness to an aesthetic experience that could displace them from their own reality, I think, has been quite difficult.[3] I refer to aesthetic experiences as the visceral reaction possible from engaging with any type of art which can then, challenge perceptions, overwhelm with emotion, provide food for thought or simply reduce the space between the viewer and the art. In incorporating the study of the arts and all its ramifications into a postmodern pedagogical paradigm, the possibilities for the individual to seek and experience expand almost instantaneously, possibilities and questions flourish. Attempts to provide the immediate or singular answers and solutions to what lies ahead are done away with, shedding uncertainty from its negative connotations and instead exploiting its exploratory potential, basically actively seeking participation, recognizing the inherent struggle, and not shying away from work.

Creativity is not the magic formula for artistic expression, although undoubtedly it has a lot to do with it. Artistic expression includes all the senses, lived and imagined experience, feeling, intuition, and creative momentum that propels the individual or group to move in some direction through a multitude of venues with the freedom and will to pursue wherever it takes them. Art requires a deeper involvement with the self, forcing one to interrogate the why's and how's of the phenomena that surrounds the self in order to know, philosophize, and express. Franklin (1992) states, "When creating art one can not help but look inward and participate in decision making that is targeted at the resolution of various emotional and cognitive processes" (p. 79). Art is paramount in influencing self-formation, consciousness, and power dynamics. As McNiff (1995) discusses the need for an inverted perspective, which he attributes to Adolf Arheim:

The creative process thrives on the inversion of habitual thoughts. When I reverse a fixed point of view, such as the location of value exclusively in the light and not in the dark, I open to alternate ways of looking, and I see how custom and bias can hinder a more comprehensive interpretation of a particular situation. (p. 163)

He further states how things can not be seen from only one vantage point and discusses how education has been afflicted by this "illusion of linear reality." This is exactly what I'm proposing to abandon, given the three-dimensionality of ourselves and our environment. I would venture to say, we have the capacity to enter into a fourth dimension by engaging in the space between ourselves, others, and things.

The fourth dimension is the world of our imaginative capabilities, aesthetic experiences, and pedagogical insights which help us transcend from one state to another. In order to explicate this fourth dimension further, I will employ Jaynes' (1976) discussion of the nature of consciousness and Kincheloe's (1993) critical analysis of it. Jaynes maintains that consciousness has six parts, three *(the analogue "I," the metaphor "me," and narratization)* of which are pertinent to our discussion of the fourth dimension. *The analogue "I"* is our imagined self, *the metaphor "me"* is seeing ourselves as a character in our imaginings in the third person, and *narratization* is the ability to narrate or construct a story about our integration into the environment that surrounds us, therefore conceptualizing a whole picture of ourselves in our imagination. All three elements work together in the fourth dimension, offering the space to play with different ideas, actions, and possibilities. It allows us the freedom to assume different roles and to grapple with the coalescence of intangible and tangible realms, concepts, and experiences. The *"I"* is embedded in the *"me,"* and vice versa creating different spaces in which to engage the self, allowing the self to reflect on past and future decisions and memories, and increasing self-confidence in the growing visual representations of the self expanding itself. An individual's ability to exercise his or her imagination to this extent fosters continual reinvention of the self in a multitude of scenarios that produces a hybrid identity imperative to cross the complex and overlapping borders in society.

In a society of visual, intellectual, physical, affective, and kinesthetic multiplicity, three dimensions are insufficient in fulfilling our needs and desires. The fourth dimension allows us to suspend the imaginative capabilities, aesthetic experiences, and pedagogical insights long enough to expand the sensation and factors involved in order to intersect them, slice them with other discourses or possibilities creating or extrapolating new understandings, hopes, and purposes to inform our view of the world and our view into others' worlds. Particularly for teachers and students, the exercise and utilization of the fourth dimension seems almost indispensable as both groups are encountered with a variety of interpretations and meanings, often without translators or common denominators. The ability to transcend into to somebody else's interpretations or views is facilitated by use of the *"I," "me,"* and *narratization* discussed previously. Kincheloe (1993) critically expands Jaynes's conceptualizations:

> As we critically reconceptualize Jaynesian consciousness in our move to post-formal connected consciousness, we uncover the analogue "you" and the metaphor "us." In this connected consciousness we not only "see" ourselves in the imagined situations and outcomes of the analogue "I," we can also "see" others—we "see" what they "see." This is the analogue "you." When we see others in our "mind's eye" and imagine their actions based on a contextualized appreciation of their personal histories, we have discovered the metaphor "us." The critical empathy transcends merely "seeing" another's point of view; it also involves an understanding of why they hold that point of view. (pp.135-136)

Often our bodies feel and confront the fourth dimension before our mind does. The fourth dimension can house the inexplicable tension or gaps between people that we cannot necessarily articulate but can affectively mark and that our imagination can struggle with, decipher, comprehend, and address. These capabilities allow us to play with possibility and hope, two things which underlie agency and the creative process. It can help us navigate in, out, and through a variety of disciplines and planes that our socialized actions and thoughts are bound by.

There is also an energy which can generate from these capabilities and realms often suppressed consciously but exerted unconsciously through some of our dreams, symbolic language, and fluctuating mood states. Carl Jung (1964) termed this energy "numinosity," believing the continual repression of this energy led to neurosis. Not that it is a simple equation (nor do I think Jung suggested that), given the complexities within each individual, varied coping skills, biological predispositions, and societal factors which markedly influence how the energy is repressed and its consequences. Jung considered dreams a large component of our lives as they served to unravel what happened in our waking life and helped to integrate our archetypes with the present, investigating our collective unconscious and furthering our journey to self-actualization. But to Jung self-actualization was not a pinnacle one reached but rather a process that was always in place, integrating, recollecting, and transforming what we embody and what we are connected to. It requires a level of awareness of what exists, a comprehensive view of who we are, where we are, and where we are going. Every step requires a negotiation, weighing the options and possibilities. McNiff (1995) stated, "The moral life requires the freedom to err, reflect, and adjust" (p. 188). The moral life, I equate with the creative, symbolic and imaginative elements of our life, where we are given room to play and grow.

The components of a moral life involve a level of responsibility undoubtedly intertwined with the freedom and will to make decisions, yet often this responsibility seems frightening to some because of the linear or singular possibilities of correctness and validation. At one time or another we all have obsessed about doing the "right thing" or getting things "right," guided by some ethical referent. But who defined or constructed the ethical referent? Seldom do we take it upon ourselves to define what we need at that particular point, knowing ethics fluctuate given the circumstances and people involved. We cannot discard what has constructed our way of thinking to this point or what has forced us to deviate, but that cannot continue to prescribe a one-dimensionality in our thinking and being. Many times the external restrictions placed on our ability to choose limits our freedom and will; therefore, it is extremely important that we are critically aware of the contextualization of our agency.

Schooling and the production of curriculum kits do not help to bridge the gap between learning and "real life." This affects every aspect of the student's life. The arts sometimes provide an outlet for students to explore the void and consequently find meaning somewhere with something, but it is still limited to the arts. Students can only exert their creativity in the arts, the only place they may be validated and own their voice, whether it's through their sketchbook, paintings, sculptures, performances, songs, dances, poems, or writings. Of course this, too, depends on the school, teacher, circumstances, etc. Although the arts could have allowed me to develop many sides of myself, I was not able to because of the emphasis on techniques, leaving me without even a thought of other possibilities. So one wonders why art and creativity are so easily woven together, largely because of the marginalization they have in the curriculum.

There has been an attempt to incorporate the arts into other areas of the curriculum, with a very controlled insertion of specified tasks and outcomes. This is not unexpected, since discipline and structure are the keys to education, according to the vast array of books and curricula designed to manage every minute of the class and every student. There is no recipe or method, no one way of creating a more well-rounded educational experience or student. It takes thought, intuition, and passion to act in the here and now and respond to what the students need and what society, schools and their families expect. Our imagination can supply the time and space to unravel and explore the possibilities an integrative approach imbues. Our imagination can be the playground for what we experience in the outside world as well as intrapersonally, since it is largely made up of those things which we perceive and internalize through a variety of experiences. The imagination is an encyclopedic library of sensory experiences coupled with the associated feelings and thoughts. By sensory experiences, I refer to what we see, feel, smell, hear, and taste, which become cues to other things and can provide access into vivid memories and insights. The imagination also captures the essence of an aesthetic experience, which may sometimes seem inexplicable, but has somehow moved and touched our inner being. Being cognizant of the capacities of the imagination, one can take full advantage of its existence to maximize any encounter. By interjecting this into the classroom, the meaning and purpose of what is being learned and left out can be facilitated for the students (including teachers, since they are students as well). It is important to acknowledge the weight of the imaginary and peripheral sensations carried on in our imagination and in our being. Our imagination exercises post-formal thinking and post-formal thinking relies on the imagination to force our questioning of the way we learn, what we learn, how we are tested, etc.

Post-formal thinking, just like creativity, does not have to be an alien concept or the current trend to be incorporated into education. They are not alien concepts but venues to expand the possibilities of perception and interpretation within the curriculum, our teaching, and our being. If a student is having problems understanding something, the teacher can use post-formal thinking and creativity to search for other ways to explain or demonstrate the lesson or concept. The teacher can also encourage the student to utilize both post-formal thinking and creativity to investigate other perspectives of viewing the lesson or concept as well as different ways to tackle the barriers that prevent the student from facilitating pedagogical insight. Through the struggle alone some insight will surface, further expanding the fund of knowledge for the teacher and student.

Critical awareness is not always easy; one may be privy to that which may seem uncomfortable, but the implied safety of passivity is overrated. Progress and motion take energy, both positive and negative, and the greatest constant of reality is that it is a paradox, a permanent inclusion of extremes. One must be at a point in which he or she is ready to accept such a challenge, to take the risk to exercise freedom. Greene (1988) states, "Education for freedom must clearly focus on the range of human intelligences, the multiple languages and symbol systems available for ordering experience and making sense of the lived world" (p. 125). Making sense of the world involves interpretation and transcendence, allowing a relationship to take place with things to further study their place and effects and our consequent affect. Kincheloe (1993) states, "Comfort with uncertainty allows us the freedom to experiment and to be transformed by the process. We are free to be fallible and learn from our infallibility" (p. 144). In the process of socialization subtle controlling agents permeate our thinking and acting, so there needs to be an understanding of the power dynamics that shape or mold our identity and sense of agency.

Judith Rubin (1984) describes a "framework for freedom" where an amiable existence of extremes provides the freedom and structure necessary for creative growth. She quotes Kubie (1958) as he discusses the creative process requiring, "flexible alternation of roles [because] it is impossible to produce free associations, to be freely imaginative, to be freely creative, if at the same time and in the very moment of 'freedom' one attempts to maintain a watchful, critical, scrutiny of what one is producing" (Rubin, 1984, p. 54). So the structure is basically a critical awareness of the contextual circumstance as opposed to a confining boundary. Rubin also refers to Barron's (1966) description of this alternation as an "incessant dialect and essential tension between two seemingly opposed dispositional tendencies: the tendency towards structuring and integration and the tendency towards disruption of structure and diffusion of energy and attention" (Rubin, 1984, p. 88). This seeming paradox provides the components to the intricate balance between the extremes whatever they may be. Rubin believes art does this naturally, "Art itself offers a kind of protective framework, a boundary between reality and make-believe, which enables the [individual] to more daringly test [him/herself] and more openly state [his/her] fantasies than is possible without its aesthetic and 'psychic' distance" (28). It is her belief as well as mine and many others, that we have an "inner creative potential," and it is this which will give us the greatest mobility in our sense of agency.

Symbolism as a Language of Interpretation

Symbolic language, as mentioned previously, is crucial to understand in relation to consciousness construction and how we situate ourselves in the context of where we live and what we do. Fromm (1951) defines it as a "language in which inner experiences, feelings and thoughts are expressed as if they were sensory experiences, events in the outer world" (p. 7). Deri (1984) believed the ability to form symbols provides the basis for communication within the self, bridges inner and outer worlds, and creates order and connectedness. Both Eric Fromm and Carl Jung discussed that however our symbols manifested themselves, whether through dreams, art, language, myths, fantasies, etc., we could deepen our understanding of our personality, because the symbols housed information concerning how we processed perception and memory.

Symbol formation is a way of producing meaning based on perceiving something and translating it into the familiarity of memory so that it becomes meaningful and completes the Gestalt.[4] Deri (1984) believed it originates in perception but also thinks the reverse is true, that our own personal storehouse of internal symbols bestows order and meaning on our perception of the world. It is a meaning-making process, where the act of creating is paramount in establishing connections or networks between internal and external material.[5] To further explain symbolization, we can use the metaphor of the world as an incomplete canvas. There are structures and things already in place that we must make sense of as well as work with to imprint our meanings in completing the canvas. In order to closely align the parallels between the canvas and our lives, we should understand the work of art is a continual process, as is life; it is never quite complete or singularly defined. Here the correlation to art is twofold, not only because the process is continual, but also because art can concretize our thoughts and feelings. It can act as a mirror for cognitive and emotional processes as it bridges inner and outer worlds. We must also take into consideration that although we utilize the existing symbols in our repertoire as well as have the capacity to create new symbols, we are subject to changing their meaning as we live through different experiences within the guiding forces of perception and memory.

Langer (1953) states that memory is the great organizer of consciousness, simplifying, and composing our perceptions into units of personal knowledge. She further states that to remember an event is to experience it again but not in the same way as the first time, because memory is a special kind of experience, composed of selected impressions. So even our personal history, she adds, as we conceive it, is, then, a construction of our own memories, reports of other people's memories, and assumptions of causal relations among things, people, or places. Between the explanations that both Deri and Langer provide, we have two ways to theorize perception and memory that are not so dissimilar but highlight different points of origination. Yet another viewpoint is Wilson's (1985), where she states that perception of reality is shaped by mental representations in significant ways. She believes we often do not respond to the external stimuli but rather the mental representations activated by it and these mental representations can be the product of many distorting and mediating forces that include feelings, memories, and cognition. In my opinion, the distorting or mediating forces Wilson discusses do not always carry a negative connotation. Feelings, memories, and cognition can be the very things that provide the link in the meaning-making process and produce the impetus to push beyond the alleged limits of our agency. Beres and Joseph (1970) define mental representations as, "a postulated unconscious psychic organization capable of evocation in consciousness as symbol, image, fantasy, thought, affect, or action" (p. 2). There are various ways to explain the ways we see the world, how we process this information, and how it affects who we are, but all these theories involve memory, perception, imagination, and creating. The reoccurrence of these elements is extremely important pedagogically, since they offer the possibility of action and the application of history.

So then how does all of this relate to how we contextualize ourselves? We create a meaningful lifespace, interpreting and forming meaning from the impersonal material by which we find ourselves surrounded.[6] We are part of larger social structures that become interactive texts as they define the hierarchal and power dynamics we mimic, resist, or restructure to what suits our identity and politics. Through understanding the ways in which we produce symbols and what functions they provide in our own consciousness construction, perception, and memory, we further understand how we interact with others and the environment. Basically, we learn about the construction of our individual and collective identities. The pedagogy in symbolization may not be in tracing the specific translation of one concept, idea, or thing into memory but in understanding the process external material undergoes as we perceive and internalize it without being conscious of it, as we undoubtedly seek to complete the Gestalt (the organized, completed whole). Symbol formation helps to situate what we encounter with what we know. The entire process reaffirms the importance of historicity, contextualization, awareness, and possibility. All of these are crucial elements in the chain of events of deconstructing and uncovering the unjust power relations that oppress and marginalize difference.[7] We can, then, discern students' frames of reference to increase all levels of communication and begin a discourse where the students are active in their own symbolic process, increasing their understanding of the self and social relations which is imperative to meaningful existence, agency, power, and identity.

Post-formal thinking is intricately wedded to symbolism and the processes in which we perceive and internalize information. In fact, post-formal thinking facilitates the capacity to engage in symbol formation and utilization of those symbols as we develop in our thinking and processing. Kincheloe (1993) maintains:

> post-formal thinking is not objective, it is unabashedly subjective with its celebration of intimacy between the knower and the known. . . . Post-formal thinking is interested in the ability to see problems where others see tranquility. Instead of focusing on the solution to the puzzle everyone recognizes as a puzzle, post-formal thinking wonders where the puzzle came from and who recognized it as being in need of a solution. (p. 143)

At this point an analysis of the various functions symbols serve provides insight into how symbolization applies to our consciousness construction and everyday lives[8]:

1. BRIDGING-OVER FUNCTION:
   - links person to environment and provides a basis of communication within the self
   - helps us to get in touch with ourselves, uniting or connecting parts of ourselves
   - meets the external environment and takes what one knows from previous experiences allowing him or her to understand concepts such as future and hypothetical situations

2. ORGANIZING FUNCTION:
   - makes sense of the world, leading away from external chaos toward articulated order
   - promotes homeostatic equilibrium with completing gestalts within the organism

3. STIMULUS BARRIER FUNCTION:
   - allows us to protect ourselves from overstimulation
   - we use our perception to condense stimuli and form symbols

4. TRANSLATING FUNCTION:
   - the human brain is constantly carrying on a process of symbolic transformation of the experiential data that comes into it, allowing it to change to fit the accepted language of different regions

It's important to note here where we first attempt to symbolize. Symbolization is first utilized in infancy when we begin to cope with the concepts of time, hope, and trust using our imagination to soothe the needs that are not immediately cared for. The acceptance of time allows us to trust in the hope that possibility exists. Creativity is then born out of the weave between time, hope, trust, and possibility. Deri (1984) contends that hope underlies the creative process. Hope instills hypotheticals that can be transformed into reality through the different ways we exercise our creativity. We can use our imagination as a huge sketch pad where various possibilities play themselves out.[9] Before discussing how art can easily foster the symbolization process, let's define symbols.

There are three types of symbols that warrant specification in teasing out symbols from signs. We have discussed the process of symbol formation but not the variety of symbols that play into that process which is important to understand. Eric Fromm (1951, pp. 12-18) delineated these descriptions out of the specific connection between the symbol and that which it symbolized.

1. CONVENTIONAL: This type of symbol is the best known since it is employed in everyday language. It is the convention learned through connection, by repeated experience of hearing the word or recognizing a picture in reference to an object, such as seeing the object that we call chair and knowing it is a chair, "chair" is the conventional symbol for the corresponding object.

2. ACCIDENTAL: It is the opposite of conventional in that it is circumstantial, because there is no intrinsic relationship between the symbol and that which it symbolizes. It cannot be shared by anyone else as we relate the events connected with the symbol.

3. UNIVERSAL: The only type of symbol in which the relationship between the symbol and that which it symbolizes is not coincidental but intrinsic. It is rooted in the experience of the affinity between an emotion or thought and a sensory experience.

A symbol is something that stands for something else; it may represent and express an intuition, idea, feeling, or action consciously or subconsciously. It is also important to note, symbols can have multiple meanings that change, signs on the other hand, tend to represent one singular thing. Deri (1984) succinctly states, "Symbols represent something absent. Signs indicate something present. . . . Symbols evoke the conception of a thing that is absent . . . and signs announce their object and trigger a rigidly performed, immediate response"(pp. 162-163). Signs function similarly to stereotypes, curtailing the possibility for multiplicity. Signs almost dangerously simplify, universalize, and essentialize meaning which is counterproductive to the ways post-formal thinking pushes beyond modernism's rigid paradigm. In artistic expression, however, both symbols and signs are employed for multiple reasons. It is significant to delineate the limitations and purposes of each, symbol and signs, in order to maximize and reformulate their potential. Understanding symbol formation, symbols, and artistic creation produces a meta-awareness of one's thinking, interpretation, and expressive processes, necessary for a critical perspective on one's existence. This critical perspective and meta-awareness would not be possible within a modernist paradigm.

Modernism is concerned with scientific methods and answers, cause-effect relationships, and singular perspectives. Formal operational thought is limited to the same constructions (see the first section of this essay), yet post-formal thinking is comfortable with uncertainty, contradiction, and dissimilarity. Post-formal thinking allows the individual to see multiple perspectives and methods of approaching, interpreting, or synthesizing any phenomena. It is a way of thinking that allows the functions of the symbolization process to take place, suspending barriers in our consciousness long enough to challenge and baffle with existing and new information, therefore producing a struggle that will open other possibilities and pedagogical insights. It also allows students and teachers to mobilize the barriers of their knowledge and perceptions to transcend their existence , utilizing what they know to travel into other people's perceptions and ways of seeing the world. In a classroom setting, post-formal thinking allows the teacher to utilize his/her position of power and knowledge to aid the learning process of his/her students, making the methods of teaching more flexible and encompassing. It challenges student's creativity in researching, interrogating, problem solving, and synthesizing. By expanding their knowledge repertoire within a classroom environment that fosters the freedom to explore in multiple ways, students' learning is increased and expanded as every member of that class is faced with the responsibility of investigating the connections between each other, the relationships between the knower and the known, and recognizing the borders waiting to be crossed and redefined. Without the ways in which post-formalism affords us the space to reconceptualize our thinking processes, consciousness construction, and knowledge production within the larger sphere of power relationships, we would not be able to entertain, much less use, the language of symbolism or its contributions to our meaning making process.

Art lends itself to the flexibility needed in the symbolization process; language can, too, but it requires more cognitive than visceral or intuitive processing through engaging with the art media and struggling through the process. Both art and language have the ability to capture affect which can subsequently rearticulate thoughts and actions. The visceral components in art and language resonate with our specificities in the abstract. We are able to identify with the ideas or emotions they convey regardless of whether they are directly about us or not. It is the transcendent quality or potential both art and language may possess that provides an aesthetic experience and ruptures the traditional paradigm of aesthetics. Engaging in aesthetic experiences, the individual explores different ways of defining the experience and translating it into a new definition of aesthetics. The recognition or creation of visual imagery and the articulation of this process through language make the aesthetic experience possible, organize it, and express it.

Another realm—our dreams—which we briefly discussed earlier, is often neglected but vital to the fashion in which we function and the frames of reference which we work from. Dreams, like art, express and bridge our inner and outer worlds as a result of the symbolism inherent in both. Our dream life is belittled for the most part, and the wealth of information housed in the act and products of dreaming is overlooked. Our dreams are as varied as our experiences, feelings, and thoughts, yet the synthesis of these three may facilitate resolutions to perceived or felt conflicts. Jung, in particular, discusses dreams and their relationship to the symbolic process. He points out that symbols arise through archetypes consisting of both images and emotions simultaneously, and this produces "numinosity" or psychic energy as previously discussed. He further states, "The general function of dreams is to try to restore our psychological balance by producing dream material that re-establishes, in a subtle way, the total psychic equilibrium" (Jung, 1964, p. 50). Dreams affect our functioning whether we are conscious of it or not. The mental activities which take place while we sleep influence our moods when we awake. It is important to acknowledge that we do dream and that these experiences affect us. According to Jung, it is the only way to move into an integration of the whole person.

We often have this essentialized idea that if we didn't see, hear, remember, or somehow sense it, it didn't happen. Unless we qualify it consciously it isn't valid to us, but we absorb and process information at all levels and sub-levels of consciousness. We need to acknowledge this process regardless of our control over it. Dream material helps to understand all parts of one's personality as does art, providing depth to our existence and fueling active imagination. Jung (1964) states, "The modern [individual] does not understand how [his/her] rationalism (which has destroyed [the] capacity to respond to numinous symbols and ideas) has put him/her at the psychic 'underworld'" (p. 94). Rationalism and the obsession with explaining everything and making even the subjective objective has dehumanized society and alienated realms that enhance the understanding of our historicity and contextualization. In postmodern society, a shift continues to include and accept the subjective and multiple realities, but the shift is not global and not effective enough to minimize sufferings or disparities produced by the categorical rationalism of modernity.

For at least the past fifteen years of my life, I have seen what art has offered. For the latter six years I have seen its influence in education. And, during the last two years as I completed a Masters in art therapy, I saw the benefits it provided through therapy. Art can be the vehicle to self-reflection as individuals enter into a relationship with the art, increasing their empowerment in reshaping or solidifying self-images. Art can also aid an impaired capacity to symbolize as well as language development (since language is a symbolic system); both are central to our experiences and consciousness construction. Lusebrink (1990) states, "Expression through art media concretizes the symbolic images, giving them a specific form which has structural, imaginal, and affective components" (p. 57). She further states that artistic expressions provide a means to portray multileveledness, and this quality makes them well suited for the expression of symbols. The "multileveledness" is not only inherent in the artwork and symbolization but in the aesthetic experience, as the individual has the capacity to grasp the expression on several levels, such as (1) imaginal/structural, (2) affective, (3) sensory, and (4) kinesthetic.[10]

Throughout our discussion of creativity, production, interpretation, reception, and experience in the arts and symbolism, we have alluded to the necessity of expression. It is important to understand the multileveledness (to borrow Lusebrink's term) of expression. The acknowledgement of its fragments does not take away from its totality. The notion of something as a whole is important as we have alluded to previously in this chapter in reference to Gestalts, but its parts or levels are equally important. Art is both expression and impression as it provides multiple ways to convey or represent what we have retained from our experiences. As we explore the pedagogical interventions accessible through the arts and creativity, it's important to understand the unity of the whole and the unity within the parts or fragments of the whole, i.e. the non-linear sequence of emotions, thoughts, interactions, and interpretations that lead to what is, in fact, a need to create and express. Betensky (1995) stated:

> Expression is a given propensity which answers a human need to portray in individual ways feelings and thoughts being about what one is or, in certain cases, what one aspires to be, these feelings and thoughts being human experiences. . . . The given need of expression is manifest in another given propensity, that of using some visible or audible means to make the expression tangible. (p. 30).

Art, symbolism, aesthetics, and dreams help us compensate the void sometimes felt in society, but it requires the study of how all these elements coincide and revolve around a creativity axis to comprehend their importance and necessity. The study of symbolism, creativity, art, and aesthetics is also imperative to the overall cognitive and emotional development of the individual, inadvertently abetting the individual's capacity to learn. Art and dreams, in particular, can offer tangible exploratory experiences into underlying ideologies of what we see, feel, and do. They can take us into a fourth dimension of integrating our knowledge into some cohesive or noncohesive whole where we find meaning and purpose, setting the ground for a type of pedagogy that truly engages the individual and resonates with their knowledges and experiences, then pushes them further.

I believe it is essential to be aware, critically so, of what we do, how we do it, where we are, and where we can go. It is almost unbelievable that students are not allowed spaces to interrogate and investigate their surroundings, what they are learning or how. How do we lessen the confusion postmodernism allegedly fosters through its fragmentation and deconstruction? There isn't only one solution, obviously, but by bringing up the concepts we have discussed in this essay through post-formal thinking, the dialogue can at least begin.

Post-formal Thinking in the Arts and Education

As far as learning, all areas of education have devised theories based on stages that chart development, whether cognitive, emotional, moral, social, or artistic. We know these stages are not fixed or exist as neatly one after the other, nor are as applicable to all individuals as suggested by their creators. In the scope of this book, we challenge Piaget's highest order of thinking, the formal level of operation through Kincheloe and Steinberg's (1993) "post-formal thinking." Post-formal thinking proposes what the arts have also offered, mainly the ability to reconfigure and probe what is, as opposed to accepting it because it just is. These qualities have not been part of the mainstream in education and other disciplines. We can no longer settle for conformity if we are to propose that people search for ways to make the meaning process productive for themselves. What post-formal thinking facilitates is the creation of the structure of freedom, as Kincheloe and Steinberg (1993) state, "Post-formal thinking and post-formal teaching become whatever an individual, a student, or teacher can produce in the realm of new understandings and knowledge within the confines of a critical system of meaning" (p. 301). Both the student's and teacher's sense of agency and mobility are expanded, so that they can explore the dynamics behind the nature in which they learn, what constructs and produces knowledge, what they internalize, and how it influences their subjectivity.

So how do the arts embody post-formal thinking and vice versa? How can we integrate the importance and necessity of the aesthetic into pedagogical interventions? How do we water the seed of creativity? How does post-formal thinking challenge notions of creativity and artistic renditions? I think what this requires is rearticulating or constructing a pedagogy of creativity exploring how pivotal a position creativity, art, aesthetics, symbolism, and dreams have in the production, reception, and construction of knowledge and in self-formation. These elements also espouse a responsibility to accompany their production as well as challenge definitions of democracy and work. The reason why I think art is an arena for critical pedagogy and cultural studies is largely due to the nature of art, its multiplicity, and inclusivity. One, of course, questions what is the nature of art or even what is art? The answer is there isn't just one answer, but it's a synthesis of the artist, agenda, project, philosophy, emotions, media, genre, society, politics, class, race, etc. What it elucidates is the complexity that resides in one site, whatever that site may be, particularly an individual's historicity, meaning-making processes, and agency. Art may provide the struggle necessary for pedagogy, pushing and challenging the development of an idea or process against its own grain. Lewis and Simon (1986) discuss the basic conditions for a process of pedagogy as "a struggle over assigned meaning, a struggle over discourse as the expression of both form and content, a struggle over interpretation of experience, and a struggle over self" (p. 469). The pedagogical tool in the arts can be illustrated through the individual or group artists explicating their art, unraveling the need to create, and locating the motivation fueling such an endeavor, all of which engages the multiplicity of self and its contextualization. Producing art for art's sake is nearly impossible since the art reflects something about the artist or his or her positionality. The art, too, has a voice and the image or creation contains volumes of information.

Michael Franklin (1992) eloquently describes the parallels between the art-making process and life's processes:

> The unformed materials, much like the notion of tabula rasa, begin to take shape as the artist engages in a decision-making process that documents change. To work with art materials is to transform their physical and symbolic potential. Thus, art may be considered a simultaneous process of reformulating the self through the active formation of an object. (p. 79)

Art requires the four features of post-formal thinking Kincheloe and Steinberg (1993) delineate: "*etymology*—the exploration of the forces that produce what the culture validates as knowledge; *pattern*—the understanding of the connecting patterns and relationships that undergird the lived world; *process*—the cultivation of new ways of reading the world that attempt to make sense of both ourselves and contemporary society; and *contextualization*—the appreciation that knowledge can never stand alone or be complete in and of itself" (p. 302). In this sense we could look at art through the intercontextual axes of aesthetics, creativity, symbolism, and dreams, equating aesthetics with etymology, creativity with process, and symbolism and dreams as patterns. Aesthetics has been the standard through which art has been viewed, demarcating high and low art and alienating the viewer and creator of art from an intimate relationship with the arts. It has also provided a discourse of distance to discuss the superficiality of how the art adorns and decorates. Aesthetics then becomes an arena where the standards our culture constructs and validates are interrogated and redefined, subsequently expanding the active engagement and discussion of art. Creativity provides the space to cultivate innovation for the individual or group, shedding the burden and limited definitions of originality. Using creativity in a postmodern fashion does away with a universalizing essentialism of knowledge, emotions, needs, desire, and expression. Symbolism and dreams can facilitate the understanding of the patterns that construct and maintain the lived world, as they can also inform our ways of reading the world and our existence in it. The fluidity of art, creativity, and aesthetics lends itself to travel discourses, injects possibilities previously not considered, and ruptures existing stasis.

At the beginning of this chapter, I state the necessity of a pedagogy of creativity. At this point I feel the need to explain why I highlighted creativity over art, aesthetics, and symbolism. Creativity seemed like the one element that could truly spark the needed unrest in any discipline without the anxiety of supposedly taking on a different discipline, such as art, that has numerous connotations and singular definitions outside of art itself. Creativity can disguise itself as an enhancement to any field as opposed to a threat, which then opens many doors and might reduce the defense against change or modification. The anxiety and defense against change must be considered in an attempt to revamp anything radically. Creativity offers the accessibility necessary to hybridize other discourses with the elements in art, aesthetics, and symbolism that enrich, politicize, question, and challenge existing paradigms. The possibilities this entails, particularly in the schools, to reinstate the hope, meaning, purpose, and motivation that many students have lost or never owned, are invaluable. Art classes can nurture this hope so that it can be applied to the student's interests, those spaces where art can become the vehicle to a meta-awareness and critical perspectives on the production of knowledge, power dynamics, self-formation, and consciousness construction without being limited only to the realm of art. In this manner individuals can exercise a critical democracy in their sense of agency and can feel competent and fulfilled in their work.

Here we encounter the intersection of two fields that in their union offer each other all that we have described above—art and cultural studies. The literature that has emerged from cultural studies over the last two decades needs to be inserted into the discourses and literature in the art world. For a couple of reasons: to sever the alienation between the art world and society; and to allow students or anybody else to utilize the literature in the meaning-making process of their own art in order to situate themselves and connect with a wider audience. Carol Becker (1996) reiterates the importance of presenting the issue of an audience and who the audience is:

> it is art's separateness from an expanded audience that has allowed it to become a vulnerable subject of narrow-minded attacks... The relationship of the artist to society and the conflict between the artist's sense of art's function and that of the general public have not been adequately addressed by the art world or within art schools. (pp. 58, 57)

It is paramount for students to have the knowledge of the nexus of the two fields, art and cultural studies, in order to begin to address their art (whatever it may be), with a critical consciousness that is political, democratic, passionate, subversive, informed, and informative.

bell hooks (1995) discusses the notion of using art as a space to exercise one's freedom:

> Art should be, then, a place where boundaries can be transgressed, where visionary insights can be revealed within the context of the everyday, the familiar, the mundane. Art is and remains such an uninhibited, unrestrained, cultural terrain only if *all* artists see their work as inherently challenging to those institutionalized systems of domination (imperialism, racism, sexism, class elitism, etc.) that seek to limit, co-opt, exploit, or shut down possibilities for individual creative self-actualization. Regardless of the subject matter, form, or content, whether art is overtly political or not, artistic work that emerges from an unfettered imagination affirms the primacy of art as that space of cultural production where we can find the deepest, most intimate understanding of what it means to be free. (p. 138)

Here, hooks delineates not only what art is, but the potential for what it holds to be, or rather how it can work to engage a critical discourse to understand and create freely. Art can serve as part of a counternarrative of emancipation in which new visions, spaces, desires, and discourses can be developed that offer students the opportunity for rewriting their own histories differently within rather than outside of the discourse of critical citizenship and cultural democracy.[11] Along the same line, Giroux (1994) discusses how politics of representation can be taken up by cultural workers and how representational pedagogy allows students to interrogate the historical, semiotic, and relational dynamics. Art works and processes can address the politics of representation and the vast array of representations that permeate society through art and about art and the artist. Again it is projects like these which can grow out of the intersection of these two fields. And ultimately this leads to a connection to performing good work, with a sense of responsibility, initiative, and creativity[12]; engaging with learning through art, we come to see a purpose in what we are taught and a use for it as well: to critically transform our existence.

This process can also facilitate the location and application of eros, as hooks (1994) discusses in *Teaching to Transgress,* because it can provide an epistemological grounding informing how we know what we know. We briefly discussed this earlier in the chapter with Betensky's "unity of the body" in dealing with sexuality. Eros needs to be displaced from its association only with sexuality while simultaneously using its location in the body to incorporate the body demystifying and crossing the boundaries surrounding the body. Eros fosters the excitement and passion to fully engage in one's project and to play with a multitude of possibilities that our imagination can store as if it were a warehouse and play out as if it were the stage of our own theater.

What I have done in this chapter is unfold an idea, challenge its proposal and entertain its application through an emotive and cognitive process that post-formal thinking allows us to exercise. Post-formal thinking opens the door that we thought was closed; it changes the lens of the microscope to a higher exponential power magnifying what is deemed real and unreal, demystifying reality's illusion of impenetrable wholeness. Paralleling and intersecting post-formalism and art helps to expand, inform, and redefine each realm. The correlation of the two and all that encompasses post-formalism and art dictate a confrontation and interrogation of the visual representations we express, perceive, internalize, contest or conform to as well as the politics of those representations.

The necessity, function, and possibilities of art are made explicit in the previous discussions of creativity, aesthetics, symbolism, and dreams. I agree with the notion that art is not accessible to the general public but only to a few who are peripherally cognizant of it or are integrally in the center creating art. This must be changed. Art, images, simulacra, symbols, and dreams are part of our everyday life; they permeate and cohabit the same spaces we do. We cannot continue to pretend their existence does not involve us nor can we immediately use morality to censor art. Art, aesthetics, creativity, symbolism, and dreams must be taken up critically to understand them and how they reflect historical and contemporary realities to maximize our meaning-making process and continually rearticulate our self-formation through the varying dynamics of power and knowledge production. We can work to demystify the art world through post-formal thinking (and vice versa) to lessen the anxiety as it probes forsaken boundaries to increase its accessibility as pedagogy and in society.

Endnotes

1. To further explain "Gestalt", Deri (1984) refers to Gestalt theorists such as Wertheimer (1923), Kohler (1929), and Kofka (1935). I also must add the founding father of Gestalt psychology, Frederick Perls, M.D., Ph.D. Gestalt psychology targets basic questions such as: How does the organization of our perceptual field occur? Why do we see segregated "things"? What are the laws governing the order of our visual world? Under what conditions are "things" perceived as a cohesive, unified "group"? (Deri, p. 32), dealing with the concepts of figure/ground formation facilitation methods to get in touch with our bodies, emotions, and ourselves.

2. For further reference on other theories of personality, or just different psychological models: Hall and Lindzey (1978) *Theories of Personality* (3rd ed.); Corey (1991) *Theory and Practice of Counseling and Psychotherapy* (4th ed.).

3. On a side note, it is not surprising that people want to have something pretty to look at (given society's obsession with beautification) or something that just makes them smile (given the preoccupation with somehow having a carefree, "don't worry be happy" attitude, and the attention towards goodness through a pleasing, non-offensive demeanor) as opposed to something that might rupture, baffle, question in some way or attract them for reasons other than its polished look. People seek comfort and security, the cer-

tainty that modernism has made so palatable. Sometimes in search for these things, people forego enriching experiences, choosing a limited participatory stance in their own lives. This also ties into the unity that we search for or need in the Gestalt process, wanting to make connections to something familiar so we can reduce the anxiety associated with the unknown.

4. How is symbol formation a Gestalt forming process? According to Deri (1984, pp. 38, 51, and 61), it's as follows: Perception by its nature tends to see forms in terms of maximum possible completeness, closure, simplicity, regularity, and symmetry. These Gestalt-forming tendencies are considered "givens"of human perception. They harbor psychological dangers as well as the seeds of creativity. All the well-known perceptual "illusions" are based on laws of Gestalt perception. The preference for closed figures, regularity, symmetry makes us see an unclosed c-shape as a closed circle; "the law for good continuation" accounts for our "overlooking" some "unfitting" change of direction or gap in a line, since a straight line is perceived as a more stable structure than a broken line (pp. 37-38). We also see here how modernism's paradigm and scientific experiments have supported these notions. Deri also refers to Plato, as he contends that *homo sapiens* is an essentially split organism; we are human because we are incomplete (yeah right). In any event, Deri continues by adding that the wish to experience total unity with the physically separate "other" remains an ever-present human desire. We see this every day through popular culture as it tries to satisfy desire with external stimuli. We, then, search for union and completeness not only through physical contact but also through various symbolic forms in the world of ideas, art, and religion.

> To reiterate: the symbol is a guide toward the missing half that will complete a gestalt. In the act of perception, recognition takes place when a memory image, matching the present perception, separates itself out of the mass of existing internal representations exactly because it is symmetrical with the outside pattern. This gestalt-forming process by pairing formation is the act of recognition. It manifests itself in the experience of knowing, i.e. the feeling of "clicking" is the moment when the internal lotto picture, the image-symbol finds its matching "other half" in the outside world. (pp. 51-52)

The last point is that symbols pointing beyond themselves, towards what cannot be directly reached, reflect a need for some explicit connection to what is outside (p. 61). Even our unconscious reaches toward the outside, so we could never successfully dismiss that we are both social and individual beings.

5. Deri (1984) points out that the perception is not just a point-by-point registration process of external stimuli but a process of selectively organizing what we see (p. 69). It is important to note this is not a passive process in the least. This discussion also relates to media studies and the potential influences of the media which does not suggest a passive registration of what one sees or is exposed to either. Other axes intersect in our reception to determine the influence of what we see, feel, or experience and its negative or positive consequences.

6. To further define "lifespace," Kurt Lewin (1935 and 1936) first coined the term and defined it as the intrinsic unity of the person in his environment as one dynamic Gestalt system. In his theory the person comprises numerous intrapsychic regions, just as the environment consists of various environmental regions. These regions are separated by boundaries with different degrees of permeability, or rigidity. Boundaries that don't allow some permeability are barriers. He called his theoretical system "topological and vector psychology" (Deri, pp.29-30).

   In Deri's definition of a lifespace: a person's total lifespace includes past, present and expected future—an organic and organized Gestalt; its creation is predicated on the capacity for expressive symbol formation; and, each person's total lifespace is a unique pattern (p. 41).

7. Difference is usually marginalized, and we need to be weary of falling prey to a binary system in which the mainstream is essentialized. There is a wealth of information residing both in the center and margins of society and in our psyche that create necessary combinations which enhance our intellect, affect, and being.

8. The functions are a compilation of various works in symbolism— Deri (1984); Fromm (1951); Wilson (1985); Jacobi (1959); and Lusebrink (1990).

9. I have used metaphors in my explication of symbolism because the use of metaphor can facilitate meaning through imagery, experience and parallels that jog something familiar in what seems unfamiliar, enabling understanding. There is an extensive list of literature in this area as well.

10. I would venture to say that the theoretical or intellectual could be grouped within the first level, but these are not organized in any particular order. The order may vary with each aesthetic experience. The multileveledness explanation is part of Ch. 3 of Lusebrink's *Imagery and Visual Expression in Therapy*, pp. 51, 57, and 58, which provides a comprehensive explanation of her theories of visual expression.

11. I inserted "art" into this excerpt from Giroux's piece "Living Dangerously: Identity Politics and the New Cultural Racism," p. 51 in Giroux and McLaren's *Between Borders*. I saw a natural fit between what Giroux discussed and what I propose for the arts that created a powerful statement.

12. This comes from the notion of performing good work in Kincheloe (1995) *Toil and Trouble*, p.30.

References

Barron, F. (1966). Creativity in children. In H.P. Lewis, *Child art: The beginnings of self- affirmation*. Berkeley: Diablo Press.

Barron, F. (1988). Putting creativity to work. In R.J. Sternberg, *The nature of creativity* (pp.76–98). Cambridge: Cambridge University Press.

Becker, C. (1996). *Zones of contention: Essays on art, institutions, gender, and anxiety*. Albany, NY: SUNY.

Beres, D. and Joseph, E. (1970). The concept of mental representation in psychoanalysis. *International Journal of Psychoanalysis,51*, 1–9.

Betensky, M. G. (1995). *What do you see? Phenomenology of therapeutic art expression*. London: Jessica Kingsley Publishers.

Deri, S. (1984). *Symbolization and creativity*. Connecticut: International Universities Press.

Franklin, M. (1992). Art therapy and self-esteem. *Art Therapy: Journal of the American Art Therapy Association, 9*(2), 78–84.

Fromm, E. (1951). *The forgotten language: An introduction to the understanding of dreams, fairy tales and myths.* New York: Grove Weidenfeld.

Giroux, H. (1994). Living dangerously: Identity politics and the new cultural racism. In H. Giroux and P. McLaren (Eds.), *Between borders: Pedagogy and the politics of cultural studies* (pp. 29–55). New York: Routledge.

Giroux, H.A. (1992). *Border crossings: Cultural workers and the politics of education.* New York: Routledge.

Greene, M. (1988). *The dialectic of freedom.* New York: Teachers College Press.

hooks, b. (1995). *Art on my mind: Visual politics.* New York: The New Press.

hooks, b. (1994). *Teaching to transgress: Education as the practice of freedom.* New York: Routledge.

Jacobi, J. (1959). *Complex, archetype, symbol in the psychology of C. G. Jung.* New York: Pantheon Books.

Jaynes, J. (1976). *The origin of consciousness in the break-down of the bicameral mind.* Boston: Houghton Mifflin Co.

Jung, C.G. (1964). *Man and his symbol.* New York: Doubleday.

Kincheloe, J. (1993). *Toward a critical politics of teacher thinking: Mapping the postmodern.* Westport, CT: Bergin andGarvey.

Kincheloe, J.L. (1995). *Toil and trouble.* New York: Peter Lang.

Kincheloe, J.L. and Steinberg, S.R. (1993). A tentative description of post-formal thinking: The critical confrontation with cognitive theory. *Harvard Educational Review,63* (3), 296–320.

Kubie, L. (1958). *Neurotic distortion of the creative process.* New York: Noonday Press.

Langer, S.K. (1953). *Feeling and form: A theory of art.* New York: Charles Scribner's Sons.

Lewis, M. and Simon, R.I. (1986). A discourse not intended for her: Learning and teaching within patriarchy. *Harvard Educational Review, 56* (4), 457–472.

Lusebrink, V.B. (1990). *Imagery and visual expression in therapy.* New York: Plenum Press.

McNiff, S. (1995). *Earth angels: Engaging the sacred in everyday things.* Boston: Shambhala.

Repucci, L.C. (1960). Definitions and criteria of creativity. Unpublished report, Dow Chemical Company.

Rubin, J.A. (1984). *Child art therapy: Understanding and helping children grow through art*, second edition. New York: Van Nostrand Reinhold.

Torrance, P.E. (1988). The nature of creativity as manifest in its testing. In R.J. Sternberg, *The nature of creativity* (pp. 43–75). Cambridge: Cambridge University Press.

Wilson, L. (1985). Symbolism and art therapy: Symbolism's relationship to basic psychic functioning. *American Journal of Art Therapy, 23,* May, 129–133.

CHAPTER EIGHT

Knowledge and Power
The Learning Organization: Recovery of Control

Sharon L. Howell

The learning organization is ". . . where people continually expand their capacity to create the results they truly desire, where new and expansive patterns of thinking are nutured, where collective aspiration is set free, and where people are continually learning how to learn together" (Senge, 1990a, p. 1). "Post-formal thinking" could replace "learning organization" in this definition with one very important difference. Post-formal thinking recognizes the political dimensions found at all levels of social organization, analyzing how power is produced and distributed (Kincheloe, 1995, p. 122). Failing to address the political context of the workplace and issues of power allows organizations to use learning organization tools to increase control over workers' thoughts and actions. However, post-formal workers understand these unstated power strutures and social context of the workplace, allowing space at the margin to challenge this control.

The Learning Organization and the Post-Industrial Age
In the face of rapid technological change and increasing global competition, management literature of the 1980s and 1990s has co-opted the language of critical theory and postmodernism. The literature includes references to intuition and the telling of stories, the need to understand connecting patterns and relationships as well as system archetypes, the involvement of employees at all levels as active producers of knowledge, the collective nature of thought, generative learning and creative tension, and critical reflection. These are all elements of post-formal thinking which explore the origins of knowledge and deep patterns and

structures, metaphoric cognition and holistic thinking, the connectedness of logic and emotion, dialogue and collective learning, as well as focusing on problem detection not just fragmented problem solving.

Realizing the inadequacy in the organizational structures from the industrial age and the workplace training that supported these structures, top management is looking for a master plan to replace the fragmentation of Cartesian-Newtonian instrumentalism where management was responsible for thinking and workers were responsible for doing. The emerging paradigm represents the attempt to integrate personal and work-related development with a focus on lifelong learning within a framework of collaboration and teamwork to support the institutional goal of quality and customer satisfaction. Learning is the construction and reconstruction of meaning for continuous transformation of the organization. A learning organization, according to its advocates, is the ideal organizational model to meet the fast pace of change necessitated by the movement from the industrial age to the post-industrial age and the requirements of global realignment and competition.

Post-formal Thinking and the Learning Organization

Post-formal thinking and the learning organization are both attempts to move away from Cartesian-Newtonian mechanistic view of the world which dominates educational and corporate discourse, respectively. Kincheloe (1995) outlines four features of post-formal thinking which are paralleled in the literature of the learning organization. These four features of post-formal thinking are etymology, pattern, process, and contextualization.

Etymology, the first component of post-formal thinking, is the awareness and understanding of the source of intuition and feelings, the collective awareness of why a culture values certain forms of knowledge and not others. To grasp an understanding of the origins of knowledge, the post-formal thinker will not only ask questions of "what," "how" and "why" certain things are known but will also question the historical origins of knowledge from a critical perspective. Thinking about thinking explores the psychological experience of thinking, the origins of consciousness, socially constructed hidden mental models and the ability to participate in critical dialogue which leads to play with new ideas. Asking unique questions, problem detection not just problem solving, involves the use of past experience and understanding to frame problems in a holistic manner through the use of archetypes, general types of problems, and dialogue (Kincheloe, 1995, pp. 196-204).

From the learning organization literature, the word dialogue is derived from the Greek word *dialogos* meaning "when a group of people talk with one another such that the meaning moves through" (Senge, 1993, p. 21). Dialogue is a search for a deeper meaning. Discussion comes from the words *percussion* and *concussion* which imply a competition with a winner and a loser (Senge, 1993). Dialogue is very important to the concept of the learning organization since employees are to challenge the established norms. Freire's use of dialogue is applicable to the learning organization. "Freire's method of dialogue and problem posing involves people in a critique of their own taken-for-granted reality so that they can reexamine what they believe to be problematic in their lives and take action, usually with a group, to change the underlying conditions that have shaped their beliefs" (in Marsick and Watkins, 1990, pp. 28-29). While the authors do not recommend the type of revolution Friere advocated in the Third World, the transformation which dialogue potentially produces can seem revolutionary in a traditional corporate culture.

Senge (1990b) identifies several new tools needed by leaders in a learning organization, one of which is a step-by-step method to use a form of dialogue as a means to transform the organization. Confronting core dilemmas uses a seven-step process: 1) identify the opposing values, 2) position the opposing values on either end of an axes and have managers identify where they stand on the axes, 3) describe the axes as a process, 4) have each side provide the context for the other so that neither is seen as superior, 5) think in terms of process not static position, 6) recognize that both values may get worse as learning takes place and still end up with both at a higher level, and 7) work together to create improvement along all axes.

Critical reflection involves probing for the assumptions, values, and beliefs underlying all actions. Simple reflection is the examination of one's experience to assess effectiveness, what works and what does not work in cause-effect relationships. Critically reflective learners ask why things are done in a certain way, what values are espoused, what discrepancies exist, and what type of force is used to shape the outcomes (Mezirow in Marsick, 1988a). Reflection and critical reflection are a part of single-loop and double-loop learning respectively. Argyris and Schön (1978) define single-loop learning as occurring when ". . . members of the organization respond to changes in the internal and external environments of the organization by detecting errors that they then correct to maintain the central features of organizational theory-in-use" (p.18). The organizational performance is kept within the established norms. Success is measured by the effectiveness and the efficiency in responding to and in correcting deviations from the organizational norms. Senge's (1990b) adaptive learning is equivalent to single-loop learning. Argyris and Schön (1978) define double-loop learning as ". . . organizational inquiry that resolves incompatible organizational norms by setting new priorities and weightings of norms or by restructuring the norms themselves together with associated strategies and assumptions" (p.24). Inquiry must take place to determine if the error can be corrected by doing the same thing better or if a restructuring of the organizational norms is necessary. Incompatibility of the norms is generally expressed through conflict among individuals within the organization. For double-loop learning to occur, these conflicts must be resolved. Senge (1990b) refers to this type of learning as generative learning.

The second component of post-formal thinking is to understand the often invisible patterns and relationships which link all components of the lived world, uncovering tacit forces and hidden assumptions which shape our perceptions. Simple patterns that repeat themselves and have recognizable locations in space represent the explicate order. The implicate order consists of deeper patterns characterized by a large unified structure within which separateness blurs. Unconscious assumptions are questioned and hidden realities brought to the surface, resulting in profound insights. Recognizing the relationship between different things, the post-formal thinker utilizes metaphors to connect seemingly dissimilar concepts in unanticipated ways. The focus is on relationships rather than objects. Also, larger patterns are revealed from a psychological perspective through the connection between the inner world of the psyche and the outer world of physical reality, a holistic view of the universe (Kincheloe, 1995, pp. 204-212).

The literature on the learning organization makes extensive use of metaphors. Individuals bring different experiences, understandings, and contexts to the organization. The use of metaphors offers a new way of expressing ideas and concepts common to all members of the organization that fosters greater commitment. Metaphors that are common to the literature include the term "learning organization" itself as well as references to systems, the art, and sports.

The arts provide many metaphors to describe and define the learning organization. The learning organization is a tapestry or weaving with the beauty of the final product equaling more than the sum of the color and texture of the individual threads. Each individual thread is significant, but taken as a whole the final product has a greater impact on the viewer (Ellerington, Marsick, and Dechant, 1992). Music also provides a metaphor. The individual members of the orchestra bring their talents to the group. The final product is better than each one playing their own instrument separately. Each must know how to interact creatively with the others in the group to create the whole (Marsick, 1988a). These examples provide short descriptions of the ideal organization, one that is continually learning.

Watkins and Marsick (1993) take the metaphor of the arts much further. The title of their book, *Sculpting the Learning Organization*, is based on the work of a sculptor, Elisabet Ney (1833-1907). A sculptor has a mental image of the form before starting to create a work of art. Gradually this mental model forms and becomes a reality, a creation for all to see and experience. The raw materials used by the sculptor compare to the human and capital resources available to the organization, along with the organizational culture, history, and circumstances. The vision that inspires the work of art and the vision that inspires the learning organization present challenges and jolts along the way. Both the sculptor and the learning organization chip away at obstacles that inhibit learning. Various angles and perspectives provide different views of reality. Both the learning organization and the sculptor start with a vision and gradually transform the materials. Paradoxically, both are permanent and yet both are ever-changing.

The concept of the learning organization is also a metaphor. Terms normally associated with individuals, such as action, behavior, intelligence, and memory, also describe organizations. Expressions referring to an organization's learning or failing to learn are common in the literature. Organizations don't act, think, remember, or learn. Individuals who make up the organization do the acting, thinking, remembering, and learning. However, the metaphor provides a framework to distinguish between organizations that are just collections of individuals and those who work together collectively (Argyris and Schön, 1978).

Another common metaphor is sports related. Individualism is subordinated to the interests of the team and the organization. Learning laboratories provide opportunities to learn how to work as teams, how to play the game. Also, learning provides a competitive advantage, the ability to compete in the global market place (DeGeus, 1988; Stata, 1989).

The third element of post-formal thinking is "Process—the cultivation of new ways of reading the world that attempt to make sense of both ourselves and contemporary society . . . to rethink thinking in a way that repositions men and women as active producers, not passive receivers of knowledge" (Kincheloe, 1995, pp. 195-96). Through a process of deconstruction, the meaning of silences is exposed, the instability of meaning is recognized, and surface appearances are penetrated. Logic and emotion are connected resulting in an expanded notion of what constitutes knowledge which includes feminist, Afrocentric, and Native American epistemoloiges of reality. Emotions are recognized as an important factor in how we know the world, moving beyond the androcentric, logocentric world view of Western modernism. Pushing beyond linear causality, non-linear holism and integration replace fragmentation and reductionism. Post-formal thinking is placed within the web of reality characterized by multiple interacting forces (Kincheloe, 1995, pp. 212-222).

The common metaphor in use for organizations based on the industrial age model is the machine. The dominant social organization of the workplace, and the one that determines most training models, is hierarchical with many rules, procedures, and controls in place. The whole is equal to the sum of the parts with a direct cause-effect relationship. This system is based on functional rationality within a fixed system and with a fixed purpose guiding its work. Like a radio, if one part is defective, the whole will not operate effectively or efficiently, if it operates at all. With the rapid pace of change in the post-industrial age and the need to look at new ways of doing business, another metaphor is now popular to describe the ideal social organization for the workplace. Studies of the brain show that memory is distributed throughout, and if destroyed in one part memory can be recreated in another part. The hologram represents the complexity of the brain. The hologram is a picture that allows one to see the whole picture from any viewing angle. Like the brain, a single part functions throughout the whole, and the whole finds representation in every part. The ideal organization is one in which all members have a broad view of the organization, not just a view of one little piece for which they alone are responsible. Cross training within work teams allows any individual job to be shaped by the particular problems facing the entire organization at any given time. The organization is self-organizing, or substantially rational, with each part questioning, defining what is appropriate, and making adjustments (Morgan and Ramirez, 1983).

Contextualization, the fourth component of post-formal thinking, is the realization knowledge is not complete by itself but must include an examination of the setting, the interaction between the particular and the general, and the role of power. Knowledge must always be viewed in relationship to other information and relationships, the social relationships which shape it, and a recognition of the power structures which shape the world. "Post-formality. . . focus on elasticity and expansion allows it to transcend total reliance on previously generalized categories so that unique, particularistic expressions of creativity and intelligence can be included in the discourse about higher order cognition" (Kincheloe, 1995, p. 225).

According to Senge (1990), learning is a natural function for human beings. Children explore and experiment, learn to walk, to talk, and to master spatial relationships. But this natural curiosity and impulse to learn is inhibited early in life. The prevailing culture is to control rather than reward learning. Rewards come from getting the "right" answer and from avoiding risks which might lead to mistakes. Intrinsic motivation is replaced by extrinsic motivation. By focusing on performance to gain someone else's approval, performance can only be mediocre at best. The learning organization requires two types of learning, adaptive and generative. The first stage in moving toward a learning organization involves adaptivity, the ability to cope, or in terms of the total quality movement making the product reliable. The next stage is generative learning which requires seeing the systems which control events, meeting the needs of the customer before the customer realizes the need exists. The principle of creative tension illustrates the difference between these two types of learning. Adaptive learning uses problem solving to move away from the current reality that is undesirable, a form of extrinsic motivation. Generative learning provides intrinsic motivation, using the energy for change which comes from having a vision of what people might find more important than the current state. Analysis can not be substituted for vision. Utilization of creative tension creates the energy needed to move reality toward vision. "The principle of creative tension has long been recognized by leaders. Martin Luther King, Jr. once said 'Just as Socrates felt that it is necessary to create a tension in the mind, so that individuals could rise from the bondage of myths and half truths . . . so must we . . . create the kind of tension in society that will help men rise form the dark depths of prejudice and racism'" (Senge, 1990, p. 9).

Watkins and Marsick (1993) approach learning from the adult education perspective. The traditional organization focused on formalized training to provide workers the specific skills needed to perform a specific task. The learning organization requires learning to occur at the time when it is most meaningful, just at the right moment. The learning is incremental, to help ensure that the established goals of the organization are met, and transformational (culture-changing), to encourage continual reexamination of the values, methods, and policies of the organization. Each organization must identify the learning needed to meet the organizational goals, to develop support for learning at all levels of the organization, to implement the learning plan over the long term, to utilize the experiences of the employees, and to decide on the best methods for delivery of learning opportunities. There must be freedom to ask questions and challenge belief systems that can be a threatening process for those accustomed to having power as well as for those who assumed more passive roles in the past. The range of learning activities range from formal to informal, from formal degree programs to self-initiated and self-planned experiences to unanticipated experiences and encounters at work or in one's personal life.

The Learning Organization as a Controlling Organization

While much of the language of the learning organization mirrors the ideas and concepts of post-formal thinking, in practice the concepts of empowerment, teams, and participation are used by most corporations and institutions to regain control of the workplace while taking advantage of increased input from workers. The concept of a learning organization is a social construct based on unspoken androcentric privilege. The civil rights and feminist gains of the 1960s along with the collapse of Fordism, standardized production based on fragmentation of work, and higher wages for workers created a threat to the structural norm of the white patriarchal organizational culture. The single-minded focus of corporate management is on the organization's ability to survive and profit within the global market while ignoring the increasing levels of poverty and suffering at the one extreme and the massive accumulation of wealth by the few at the other extreme. People become "human resources," another economic commodity to be combined with capital and other forms of material resources to produce increased wealth for the providers of the capital. Social and ethical issues are rarely a part of the discourse. The commitment to social responsibility, freedom, and human dignity, a key element of post-formal thinking, and the development of a post-formal educational psychology are largely ignored.

The concept of a learning organization is in danger of becoming a master narrative, another attempt to create a "totalizing" system based on instrumental rationality and the cult of efficiency. Many organizations have undergone extensive restructuring in an attempt to remain competitive in the fast-changing global market. These organizations utilize cheap labor provided by ethnic minorities and women, a segment of society long silenced by a dominant white patriarchal culture. Organizational learning uses a model of continuous self-directed learning at the individual, group, and organizational levels, an Eurocentric ideal based on individualism. Learning based on interdependence found outside the white-male dominated cultural perspective is not readily incorporated into organizational culture. Within a learning organization the lipservice given to collaboration and teamwork not only contradicts this norm of individualism, but fails to recognize the power differentials within self-directed workgroups. The dialogue required for a collaborative model of work organization is not possible within a socio-economic framework of inequality where those at the margins are silenced. Negotiated team consensus based on the core values of the dominant white male culture rationalizes work behaviors which become acceptable because they are created in the name of the team. Socio-economic exploitation and hardship are ignored while holding out the promise of participation, empowerment, and collaboration within a culture of trust and equity; issues of power and control are ignored.

Knowledge in the Control of Management
In *Building the Learning Organization* (Marquardt, 1996), copublished with the American Society for Training and Development, the author uses a cookbook approach to guide organizations in building a learning organization, thus putting the concepts of a learning organization back within the safer realm of technical rationality and the cult of efficiency while still allowing organizations to take advantage of worker knowledge and know-how. "The demands put on corporate America now require learning to be delivered faster, cheaper, and more effectively to a workplace and mobile workforce . . . "(Marquardt, 1996, p. xvi). The language reverts to the old behavioristic "banking" concept, learning as something that is passed from the teacher (trainer) to the student (worker). The author talks about "managing know-how . . . getting more from your intellectual asset" (Marquardt, 1996, p. 7).

Human Performance Technology (HPT), a field of practice developed over the past 25 years by behavioral psychologists, instructional technologists, and training designers among others, is also adapting to the perceived popularity of the learning organization concepts. HPT is a system to measure performance of humans through the use of procedures based on scientific research and practical experience (Stolovitch and Keeps, 1992, pp. 3-4). In an article entitled "Performance Technology: Blueprint for the Learning Organization?" (Gordon, 1992), the author sees human performance technology as the precursor to the learning organization, matching the various facets of performance technology to those of a learning organization. Human performance technology is seen as the tool needed to implement the concepts of a learning organization which are seen as too vague and esoteric to be practical. However, the literature on human performance technology clings to its behaviorist roots. Again we see control of knowledge and information within the hands of others, not the workers. "Suppose . . . there are many reasons why people don't behave the way their bosses want them to (or in the manner most likely to achieve the organization's goals . . .)" (Gordon, 1992, p. 27). Then human performance technology comes to the rescue, providing the solution by correcting a problem with the individual.

Learning Organization Concepts Used by Managers
The predominant emphasis in the literature concentrates on management's role, especially that of upper-level management, as a key element in building the learning organization. Marsick and Watkins (1990) identify generic skills needed by managers. Strategic thinking involves visioning and goal-setting, identifying ideas of others, understanding how decisions made in one area affect actions, results, and decisions made in other areas and understanding those factors that affect the company's plans. In carrying out these responsibilities they also must take care to listen and observe.

The learning organization supposedly depends on a commitment by everyone in the organization to learn on a continual basis. From the systems perspective, competitive advantage in the global market place requires that learning and action be linked (Senge, 1993). DeGeus (1988), formerly of Shell Oil, and Stata (1989), of Analog Devices, link learning to planning. Shell Oil was able to survive the escalating oil prices in the 1980s because the leaders of the organization used models to develop strategies for oil prices at all levels. For DeGeus the important learning is done by those with the power to act. Stata lead Analog Devices through a similar planning process as their management team examined their commitment to providing highly specialized products at high cost in limited numbers. Analog Devices eventually changed their strategy to a low-cost high-volume strategy to stay competitive in the global market place. The shared insights, knowledge, and mental models linked to past knowledge and experience provide a powerful tool in the hands of managers dealing with the rapidly changing environment. Managers in these corporations are in the position of power, controlling knowledge creation and utilization.

Vision and leadership are seen as coming from the top despite the language of participation. Senge uses the terminology commonly associated with teamwork and participatory management schemes, that of leader rather than manager. According to Senge (1990b), the leader in a learning organization must assume new roles in guiding the cultural change that is required. The leader as *designer* must guide the organization through three tasks: 1) establishing the governing purpose, vision, and core values by which the organization will live, 2) initiating the policies, strategies, and structures that translate guidelines into decisions, and 3) identifying the learning processes that will be used to ensure continual improvement. The leader as *teacher* uses coaching and facilitation to guide the organization toward gaining more insight into current reality, going beyond the superficial to the underlying causes and then to seeing new possibilities for the future. The leader as *steward* is a servant first with a commitment to the people in the organization and a commitment to the organization's larger mission. These new leadership roles require new leadership skills: 1) building a shared vision, 2) surfacing and challenging mental models and 3) engaging in systems thinking. Building a shared vision involves 1) encouraging personal vision, 2) communicating and asking for support, 3) visioning as an ongoing process, 4) blending extrinsic and intrinsic visions, and 5) distinguishing positive and negative visions. Surfacing and challenging mental models by testing assumptions without raising defensiveness requires reflection and inquiry skills. Defensive routines must first be recognized and then defused. Systems thinking focuses on underlying trends and the forces of change, seeing interrelationships, moving beyond blaming individuals to fixing poorly designed systems, and identifying root causes, not symptoms.

Hart (1992) provides a critique of Marsick's advocacy of liberal learning as the best response to the crisis in management and organizational theory and practice that results from rapid change and from the increased complexity of organizations. The paradigm shift proposed by Marsick is missing any ties to the larger social, economic, and political issues identified by Hart as important. Marsick uses the vocabulary of reflection, participation, and empowerment while actually remaining embedded in traditional forms of hierarchy. The focus is on upper-level management and learning to create a position of power with no consideration of jobs below the management level. Marsick does not question the concept of economic growth and productivity that governed the industrial era and that remains unquestioned during the post-industrial era. The prevailing socio-economic context is not questioned. Hart questions Marsick's use of paradigm shifts and organizational transformation while the economic, social, and political structures remain intact and unquestioned. Hart's critique of Marsick's position is also relevant for the rest of the literature reviewed.

Learning Organization as Management of Human Thought

Bensimon (1995) places total quality management (TQM) within the modernist discourses, a systemic modernism. In the analysis of the language of TQM, the concepts of customer, variation, and measure are shaped by those who control and, therefore, shape the discourse, those in positions of power. Bensimon notes that TQM's first postulate defines quality as customer satisfaction. However, quality is also a reflection of the interests, values, and beliefs of those with power (stockholders, customers, etc.). TQM does not always benefit the larger community. "Historically, subjectivity has been the privilege of those with the power to control institutionalized discourses, which for the most part have been white males. Thus, the subjectivity of women, as well as that of racial, ethnic, and sexual minorities, is recognized as long as it reflects the norm. The subordinate position of women and minority groups . . . deprives them of subject status in the discourses that structure the practices and processes to which they must conform in order to succeed" (Bensimon, 1995, p.599). Second, quality consists of the reduction of variation and elimination of defect. These concepts require shared beliefs about knowledge and fixed meanings. When applied to humans, the workforce is "manufactured" to meet the specifications of the customers and management. Third, quality is measurable. This implies that difference equals inferiority and reinforces the concept of social similarity. TQM is the total management of human thought and identity.

The control of thought and identity is found in the learning organization literature. Senge (1990a, 1990b) and Nonaka (1991) uses the metaphor of the system, a living organism, in contrast to a machine, to describe the learning organization. When describing the Japanese implementation of total quality initiatives the first step is the "fitness to standard," making reliable products within the set vision, plans and goals of the organization. The next step focuses on "fitness to need," understanding the customers' need before the customers realize the need (Senge, 1990b, p. 8). Nonaka (1991) attributes human qualities to the organization, for example, self-knowledge, shared understanding, and a sense of identity.

Leymann (1989) refers to organizational learning as a myth. The humanistic psychology of the 1960s that focused on group dynamics, sensitivity training and organizational development did not suggest use of these insights by individuals in the workplace. In Leymann's view, power structures prevent the use of the increased knowledge which individuals possess. Argyris was one of the first to identify faulty organizational learning. The conception of the organization as an organism separate from the individual is not tenable. Leymann's critique of the literature finds that organization refers variously to a leader in power or to patterns of communication among individuals. There is no empirical evidence of organizational learning. Only people learn, behave, and exhibit creativity. Through communication individuals with power form organizations. Those without power are often forced to join these organizations. Exploitation of power allows certain individuals to achieve their goals at the expense of others. In an attempt to equalize power relationships, Swedish legislation put trade unions on an equal standing with management. Because of this forced equality, both groups gain knowledge that then is utilized to the organization's benefit. Individuals gain the knowledge that is then applied in the workplace.

The Learning Organization and Post-formal Workers

The characteristics of the post-formal workplace include a vision based on democracy, recognition of power structures, a feminist ethic of caring, personal development viewed as important as profit, all employees considered as learners with untapped contributions to make, decision-making delegated to employees, and job security maintained through continual retraining. The post-formal workplace moves beyond the competiton of the capitalist marketplace to address issues of social justice and economic inequality. The workplace becomes a place for learning where workers see themselves as producers of knowledge which is valued and rewarded (Kincheloe, 1995, pp. 229-238).

According to Wells (1987), quality initiatives in the workplace define power in terms of personal conflict as social deviation. Solving these pockets of individual conflict and aberration will dissolve the barriers between labor and management. Empowerment and teams actually undermine working-class solidarity and increase the control managment has over workers. Like Kincheloe (1995), Wells (1987) sees these participatory initiatives as powerful weapons in the hands of management. But these initiatives also create possible sites of learning that can be turned in favor of workers (pp. 1-14). Shared power has the potential to increase worker control and true democracy. The ability of workers to increase their job skills builds confidence in their ability to take control of their lives and their work. In practice, however, workers too ofen underestimate the amount of control that is built into the formation of teams and the boundaries within which their work is done (Wells, pp. 117-121).

Using a qualitative case study, Brooks (1994) examined issues of power within four teams in a high-technology manufacturing corportation. The purpose of the study was "to propose an explicit link between the distribution of formal power of individual team members and the collective team-learning outcome of producing useful new knowledge" (p. 214). According to the author, the collective team-learning process was affected by power differences which inhibit contributions from individuals lower in the lower hierarchy. An atmosphere of fear and intimidation prevented problem identification. Technicians and operators did not have control over their time, movement, and work, limiting their attendance at meetings and their ability to complete assigned tasks. While the so-called "empowered" team, with members from all levels of the organization, involved every member in some way, it was the leader who defined and directed all participation. The "People's Team," composed of technicans and operators, created new structures to overcome their lack of control over time, movement, and work. Smaller teams of individuals within a work unit were created so that tasks could be assigned to groups. This increased the likelihood that at least one individual could accomplish the task and attend meetings. They also created a newsletter to ensure that communications would reach all team members. The "A Team" identified an expert to act as champion of each project to ensure the likelihood of success of the project. On both teams social learning was attributed 1) to teams composed of members of the same level of the hierarchy, 2) to each team member being viewed as making an important contribution, and 3) to a team focus on making a contribution to the organization. Brooks encourages the study of team learning in different contexts as a means to better understand how power differences influence collective team learning. Kincheloe (1995) reinforces these conclusions by encouraging post-formal workers to be active researchers 1) to provide a perspective of work from the margins, 2) to legitimize worker knowledge, 3) to empower workers, 4) to force reorganization in the workplace, 5) to service democratic goals, 6) to replace technical rationality with solutions based on expert worker knowledge, and 7) to recognize the workers' ability to learn from and teach each other. By naming and identifying power structures within the work organization, Brooks (1994), Wells (1987), and Kincheloe (1995) point out the spaces on the margins where post-formal workers can work to increase social justice and equality.

Conclusion

Organizational learning uses a model of continuous self-directed learning at the individual, group, and organizational levels, an Eurocentric ideal based on individualism. Learning based on interdependence found outside the white male-dominant cultural perspective is not readily incorporated into organizational culture. Within a learning organization the lipservice given to collaboration and teamwork not only contradicts this norm of individualism but fails to recognize the power differentials within self-directed work groups and organizations as a whole. Dialogue for a collaborative model is not possible within a socio-economic framework of inequality where those at the margins are silenced. Negotiated team consensus based on the core values of the dominant white male culture rationalizes work behaviors which become acceptable because they are created in the name of team. The concept of a learning organization takes advantage of the ideas underlying post-formal thinking when it is an advantgage, but control remains with those with power.

References

Argyris, C. and Schön, D.A. (1978). *Organizational learning: A theory of action perspective.* Reading, MA: Addison-Wesley.

Bensimon, E.M. (1995). Total quality management in the academy: A rebellious reading. *Harvard Educational Review, 65*(4), 593–611.

Brooks, A.K. (1994). Power and the production of knowledge: Collective team learning in work organizations. *Human Resource Development Quarterly, 5*(3), 213–235.

DeGeus, A.P. (1988). Planning as learning. *Harvard Business Review, 88*(2), 70–74.

Ellerington, D., Marsick, V.J. and Dechant, K. (1992). Capability development at Imperial Oil Resources Ltd. In H.K.M. Baskett and V.J. Marsick (Eds.), *Professionals' ways of knowing: New findings on how to improve professional education* (pp. 51–60). San Francisco: Jossey-Bass.

Fiol, C.M., and Lyles, M.A. (1985). Organizational learning. *Academy of Management Review, 10*(4), 803–813.

Gordon, J. (1992). Performance technology: Blueprint for the learning organization? *Training, 29*(5), 27–36.

Hart, M.U. (1992). *Working and educating for life: Feminist and international perspectives on adult education.* New York: Routledge.

Kincheloe, J.L. (1995). *Toil and trouble: Good work, smart workers, and the integration of academic and vocational education.* New York: Peter Lang.

Leymann, H. (1989). Towards a new paradigm of learning in organizations. In H. Leymann and H. Kornbluh (Eds.), *Socialization and learning at work: A new approach to the learning process in the workplace and society* (pp. 281–299). Brookfield, VT: Gower.

Marquardt, M.J. (1996). *Building the learning organization: A systems approach to quantum improvement and global success.* New York: McGraw-Hill.

Marsick, V.J. (1988a). A new era in staff development. In V.J. Marsick (Ed.), *Enhancing staff development in diverse settings* (pp. 9–22). San Francisco: Jossey-Bass.

Marsick, V.J. (1988b). Learning in the workplace: The case for reflectivity and critical reflectivity. *Adult Education Quarterly, 38*(4), 187–198.

Marsick, V.J. and Watkins, K.E. (1990). *Informal and incidental learning in the workplace.* New York: Routledge.

Morgan, G. and Ramirez, R. (1983). Action learning: A holographic metaphor for guiding social change. *Human Relations, 37*(1), 1–28.

Nonaka, I. (1991). The knowledge-creating company. *Harvard Business Review, 69*(6), 96–104.

Senge, P.M. (1990a). *The fifth discipline: The art and practice of the learning organization.* New York: Doubleday.

Senge, P.M. (1990b). The leader's new work: Building learning organizations. *Sloan Management Review, 32*(1), 7–23.

Senge, P.M. (1993). Transforming the practice of management. *Human Resource Development Quarterly, 4*(1), 5–31.

Stata, R. (1989). Organizational learning: The key to management innovation. *Sloan Management Review, 31*(3), 63–73.

Stolovitch, H.D. and Keeps, E.J. (1992). *Handbook of human performance technology: A comprehensive guide for analyzing and solving performance problems in organizations.* San Francisco: Jossey-Bass.

Watkins, K.E., and Marsick, V.J. (1993). *Sculpting the learning organization: Lessons in the art and science of systemic change.* San Francisco: Jossey-Bass.

Wells, D.M. (1987). *Empty promises: Quality of working life programs and the labor movement.* New York: Monthly Review Press.

CHAPTER NINE

Research
Remaking an Old Critical Tool:
Notes Towards the Formation of a
Post-formal Semiotics

David P. Pierson

According to Scholes, one of the most invaluable interpretive methodologies for studying literature as well as other texts is semiotics (Scholes, 1982). Semiotics, with its emphasis on breaking texts down into a multiplicity of interrelated signs, can be used to study a wide range of texts, from Shakespearean dramas to the latest in fashion wear. Although semiotics has immense interpretive strengths, as a methodology, it does have inherent weaknesses and limitations. One limitation is that, as a text-based methodology, it is primarily concerned with isolating and analyzing the text, and this critical practice often includes removing the text from its specific social context. For example, while a semiotic reading of Shakespeare's *Hamlet* will most likely investigate how this complex text communicates to its audience through a diverse, multi-layered arrangement of signs (major and minor characters, narrative, language, stage settings, etc.), this type of in-depth interpretation usually neglects to explore the intricate social contexts of Shakespeare's dramatic works, such as the assumption that they generally supported the traditional Tudor view of history and historical events.

Another limitation of semiotics involves the isolated sphere of the semiotician. Because the methodology is predicated on the skills of an individual analyst to determine the deeper levels of meaning within a text, there is often little chance to establish a consistency of agreement among analysts on what is found in the text. Also, with the time-intensive act of identifying the explicate and implicate meanings embedded within the texts, the semiotic researcher often fails to highlight specific patterns of meaning across a wide range of disparate texts and to connect them to historically-situated cultural struggles over the definition of such social discourses as gender, race, and social class.

One possible solution to these innate limitations of semiotics is to inform the methodology with the critical orientation of what Kincheloe and Steinberg call, "post-formal thinking." Primarily, post-formal cognition is "a post-Piagetian cognitive theory" that is informed by and extends the philosophical tenets of critical, feminist, and postmodernist thought. Although post-formal cognition has undeniable attributes as a progressive pedagogical theory, exposing many of the limitations and tyrannies associated with a traditional modernist educational system, it can also be used to enhance and expand the domain of existing modernist, critical methodologies such as semiotics (Kincheloe and Steinberg, 1993). Because post-formal thinking is concerned with questions of meaning along with the nature and function of social contexts, it provides ample pathways by which semiotic "text-based" interpretations can be effectively interconnected to historic social contexts and readers.

Furthermore, post-formalism's meta-theoretical approach to the production of knowledge and meaning making enables it to inform semiotics with a number of distinct theoretical insights. Post-formalism highlights the ways in which everyday signs from rap music to advertising messages can either reinforce or even challenge existing power relations within society. Invariably, post-formalism, with its own postmodernist awareness, carries on an on-going struggle with purpose, directing attention to issues of freedom, human dignity, power, authority, and social responsibility. As Kincheloe mentions in his introduction, post-formal thinking with its critical dimension of upholding such modernist concepts as freedom, democracy, and social justice, provides the seemingly objective, ahistorical (yet modernist) positionality of semiotics with a critical social purpose. Ultimately, post-formalism "grounds" semiotics within a progressive, critical theory that enables the researcher to not only detect implicate patterns of meaning across a range of texts but also to interconnect these meanings to specific, historically-determined social discourses.

Likewise, semiotics shares a symbiotic relationship with post-formal thinking. As Baudrillard has aptly pointed out, everyday life within modern western societies has become beset by the almost limitless, non-stop circulation of "signs" and media representations (Baudrillard, 1994). Many of these signs are not only perplexingly, contradictory in meaning, they have also become detached from any definite signified or implied meanings. Therefore, the individual, within this expanding postmodernistic realm of signs, becomes increasingly confused over the multifarious sources of these signs along with facing the seemingly, daunting task of searching for socially relevant, connective meanings among them. Postformalism argues that due to the escalating complexities associated within western modernist and post-modernist media-saturated cultures, one of its most critical goals should be helping educators, students, consumers, and the public to understand the production and circulation of knowledge within their societies. In this respect, one of the most accessible hermeneutical tools not only for academic researchers and educators but also for students and citizens is the methodology of semiotics. Post-formalism relies on semiotics along with other interpretive methodologies as ethnography, to formulate how individuals create meanings and identities through a diversity of cultural signs.

As one example of how post-formal thinking both informs and extends semiotics, this study will focus on advertising in general and, more specifically, print advertisements targeting adult male consumers. In order to further investigate the symbiotic relationship between semiotics and post-formal thinking, this essay will: first, outline the association between the study of advertising and semiotics; second, examine some of the inherent limitations of semiotics; third, define post-formal thinking and its symbiotic relationship with semiotics; and fourth, utilize semiotics informed by critical men's studies to conduct a close textual analysis of two print advertisements aimed at American men. Finally, it will suggest other ways in which semiotics and post-formalism synergize each other.

Semiotics and the Study of Advertising
One of the main methodologies in the study of advertising messages is semiology or semiotics. Semiotics as a methodology primarily designed for the close study of "texts" emerged from linguistics and literary studies rather than from social scientific research. Essentially, semiotics can be used to analyze every aspect of communication such as words, images, music, traffic signs, medical symptoms, and much more. On the whole, semiotics examines the way such signs communicate along with the rules that govern their use. The Swiss linguist Ferdinand De Saussure whose scholastic interests included the internal structures of linguistic systems, applied the term, "semiology" to what he described

as "the science of signs." Semiologists have focused their attentions on the interrelations among the parts of a message or within a communications system primarily because they contend that actual "meaning" is only formed through the interaction of a message's component parts. Roland Barthes, a French theorist, was one of the first to employ semiotics to analyze the deeper meanings embedded in advertising texts. He applied a semiotic analysis to a wide range of popular cultural forms, from published photographs and Citroens to toys and laundry detergent commercials. One of the central theoretical benefits of semiotic theory is that it is interdisciplinary in nature since its focus easily intersects the arbitrary divisions between academic fields of study while drawing liberally from a wide range of disciplines (literary theory, communications, education). This makes it particularly well suited to the study of culture and advertising (Seiter, 1987; Leiss et al., 1990).

In semiotics, the smallest unit of meaning is called a sign. Semiotic theory starts with the sign and constructs a series of internalized rules for the combination of signs along with the range of connotative meanings generally associated and produced from them. Saussure theorized that the sign is composed of two distinct parts: the signifier or the materialized sign (the image, object, or sound itself) and the signified, that is, the concept it represents. Although Saussure separated these two concepts into distinct parts it is important to recognize that they are inseparable in actual communications, and this distinction is made only at the theoretical level. In written language the sign "cat" is composed of three letters on this page (the signifier) and the definition of cat (signified), that is, a soft-furred, domesticated feline. Saussure also contends that the relationship between the signifier and the signified was conventional and completely arbitrary. In this respect, words or signs have no inherent meaning in and of themselves. He argued that a word's meaning derives exclusively from its "difference" from other words in the complete sign system of language. For instance, the signifier "cat" derives its meaning from its distinguishability from bat or rat or spat or mat or other similar words. Also the signified is meaningful because of its difference from a lion, a leopard, a cougar, or a tiger. Invariably, every language system designates a distinct set of meaningful differences for words. Although one may be able to imagine an almost limitless number of possibilities for signifiers and signifieds, each language makes only some differences important and detectable (Seiter, 1987).

Since semiotics recognizes the arbitrary relationship of the signifier to the signified, it can be used to examine a wide range of signs that are literally taken for granted or naturalized in everyday life. Eco defines a sign as "everything that, on the grounds of a previously established convention, can be taken as something standing for something else." Of course, Eco includes in this definition natural signs as well as cultural ones, relating that it is only through social convention that we have learned to associate billowing smoke as a probable sign of fire (Eco 1976, pp. 16-7).

One of the best examples of a semiological analyses of advertising messages is Judith Williamson's *Decoding Advertisements*. In her study, she analyzes print advertisements for the French perfume Chanel to illustrate how advertising messages communicate certain meanings to readers or viewers. For example, one simple Chanel print ad features the face of the famous French model and actress Catherine Deneuve along with the product, a bottle of Chanel No. 5 perfume, in the corner of the image. The ad's primary meaning connotates the message that Chanel No. 5 perfume is "chic, sophisticated, and elegant," that by wearing it one would be transferring the culturally associative qualities of "Frenchness," fashionable glamour, and beauty to one's own character (Williamson, 1978, p. 41).

Breaking this ad into semiological parts one can easily determine the signifier—the bottle of perfume and the signified—glamour, French fashion, sophistication and beauty as represented by Deneuve and their unified "sign"—Chanel No. 5 perfume, which equates with French glamour, sophistication, and beauty. This unified meaning is not made explicitly in any part of the ad but is comprised of the specific ways in which the ad's different signs are organized and interact with each other. This interaction between the signs in the ad not only takes place within the ad but also through external references to broader social belief systems. Williamson relates that in order for advertising to create meaning, the reader or viewer has to perform some specific cognitive "work" with the ad's different sign elements (Williamson, 1987).

Williamson traces the steps by which a viewer creates meaning from a print advertisement. In the first step, the meaning of one sign is literally transferred onto another sign. For instance, the glamourous French aura and style of "Catherine Deneuve" is transferred to the product—Chanel No. 5. It is important to acknowledge that this transference is not completed in the ad itself but, in fact, is made in the minds of the viewer. She also relates that a sign is only capable of being transferred to another if it has meaning in the first place for the reader or viewer. In this regard, in order for the sign "Catherine Deneuve" to have resonating meaning for the viewer/reader, he/she must already know what Catherine Deneuve stands for—what she means within the world of glamour—or there would be no significance to transfer. In essence, this act of transference is an active process that requires the viewer/reader to fill the unspoken "gap" or space where the implicit spokesperson for the advertiser and the product should be located (Williamson, 1987).

Furthermore, Williamson identifies these systems of meaning by which the reader/viewer draws cultural materials to complete the transfer process as "referent systems." These referent systems comprise a wide body of knowledge from which advertisers draw their inspiration for creating advertising messages. In order for the reader/viewer to appropriately "decode" their ad messages and, therefore, to complete the transfer of meaning, advertisers have to draw from the same pool of cultural and social knowledge as their audiences; then, they must transform this shared material into the advertising message, configuring it to enact a "cycle of communication" from the audience's experiences to the ad's contents and back again to complete the cycle (Williamson, 1987).

The Limitations of Semiotics

Despite the tremendous value of semiotics as a method for studying how advertising messages are encoded and resonate with certain meanings for readers/viewers, this methodology does suffer from a number of related weaknesses. First, since this methodology is predicated on the skills of an individual analyst to determine the deeper levels of meaning within a text, it often operates as though all meanings were translatable and predictable through the work of a gifted semiotician. In this respect, semiotics frequently speaks of a text as though it were understood in precisely the same way by everyone. Also within these individualized studies, there is often little chance to establish a consistency of agreement among analysts on what is found in a message. Second, with the time-intensive act of identifying the explicate and implicate meanings embedded within certain ads, the semiotician often fails to highlight specific patterns of meaning across a wide range of advertising texts. Third, often the semiotician's predominant interest in collective structures such as genres, discourses, codes, and the like will cause the uniqueness of the text to be lost (Leiss et al., 1990).

One of the central critiques of semiotics is that with its inherent interest in the structures of signs and their meanings, it frequently fails to consider the particular contexts (social, political, historical) within which these signs are embedded. Eco also points out that semiotics' penchant for categorizing sign-types (such as Peirce's symbolic, iconic, and indexical categories) tends to overlook the historical and social production of signs. Instead, Eco offers a definition that casts all signs in terms of this context: "Semiotics is in principle the discipline studying everything which can be used in order to lie. If something cannot be used to tell a lie, conversely it cannot be used to tell the truth: it cannot in fact be used 'to tell' at all" (Eco, 1976, pp. 18-20).

Similarly, John Stewart, in his critique of linguistic theories, argues that semiotics' tendency towards "decontextualized" interpretations is related to its rigid structure based on a "symbol model." Stewart points out that one of the fundamental assumptions of the semiotic symbol model is that there is a distinction between two realms or worlds, the world of the sign and the signified, symbol and symbolized, name and named, word and thought, linguistic and non-linguistic meanings. While he does acknowledge that some theorists have described significant differences between signs and symbols, he contends that these two phenomena are ontologically similar because they are both primarily semiotic units, which means that they are viewed as fundamentally different from whatever it is that they signify or symbolize (Stewart, 1995).

Furthermore, while Stewart readily admits that some theorists recognize the sign and signified are inseparable, nevertheless, he contends that once the semiotic assumption has been made, a basic reductive "structural a priori" is put into place, and even those who argue for inseparability must struggle to make their accounts of language coherent with what is often termed the "Janus-faced" character of language. One problem with this process is that it treats language as a formed or created product rather a major component of a dynamically fluid communicative process. Invariably, the semiotic structure literally takes an active communicative process (i.e., conversation), imports a modernist subject-object distinction, and transforms language into an objective "lived event." Although this procedure enables the linguistic scholar to approach his or her work more "scientifically," this objectivity tends to distort the phenomena of interest beyond recognition. Finally, Stewart also contends that the structuralist paradigm of semiotics necessarily ignores other significant factors in the active communicative process such as non-verbal communications and the situated context of oral communications or writing (Stewart, 1995).

Moreover, closely related to its rather rigid structure and tendencies towards decontextualized meanings, semiotics frequently fails to acknowledge that signs also have specific ideological functions. One of the earliest theorists to point out the ideological nature of signs in culture was V. N. Volosinov in *Marxism and the Philosophy of Language*. Volosinov relates the inseparability of ideology and language when he explains that, "Everything ideological possesses meaning: it represents, depicts, or stands for something lying outside itself. In other words, it is a sign. Without signs, there is no ideology." He also argues that beyond the realm of language, most everything else can be turned into a materialized ideological sign (food, clothing, human body). He also postulated that signs have a dual existence: they have a material existence within an external reality and another existence within the symbolic world since they also reflect or refract another reality—"the ideological." Put simply, the domain of ideology is intimately interconnected to the domain of signs. Or as Volosinov aptly explains, "Everything ideological possesses semiotic value" (Volosinov, 1973, pp. 9-10).

Perhaps Volosinov's most compelling concept is the significance of signs in the formation of individual consciousness. While conventional psychology has tended to overlook the concept that both thought and understanding are only possible within a domain of signs, it also neglects to comprehend that consciousness can only be formed within the material embodiment of signs. Volosinov points out that signs are mainly understood in relation to the comprehension of other existing signs and that this chain of ideological development and understanding leads to the formation of individual consciousness. Significantly, a much broader social link is formed when this ideological chain stretches from individual consciousness to individual consciousness, connecting them together. Signs are only transferred within the process of human interaction (language, images, sounds) between one individual consciousness to another. Finally, consciousness only becomes consciousness when it has been filled with semiotic or ideological content, which happens because of the process of social interaction between people (Volosinov, 1973).

One of the central problems with Volosinov's ideas is that he tends to conceptualize them within the same Cartesian dualism as structural semiotics, in that, not only does every sign have a material reality but also an opposite reflective or refractive reality as well. While he asserts that all signs are a material part of the external world, he fails to acknowledge the existence of such non-materialized "signs" as theories, concepts, and social myths. In many ways, these non-material signs (Lockean individualism, free market philosophy) are the most influential elements in the formation of both collective as well as individual consciousness. Although there are some definite problems with some of Volosinov's conceptualizations, nevertheless, his work has made an inestimable contribution to understanding the ideological nature and function of signs and language. Overall, his most valuable conception is the notion that signs can be "internalized" and therefore, serve a major role in the formation of individual consciousness.

While Volosinov's work illustrates the pervasive function of signs in the formation of individual consciousness, the French psychoanalyst Jacques Lacan explores the role of language in the complex formation of the unconscious. Lacan, drawing on the Saussurian notion of language as a system of signs, argues that the distinction between the signifier/signified does not refer to the objects themselves but rather to the "psychic representations" created by their interactions. From this traditional Saussurian perspective, there is no direct connection between a word and the materialized object with which one associates to this word. Lacan asserts that meaning is mainly created through linguistic differences and "through the play of signifiers." He also contends that it is only through the means of these linguistic differences that specific signified meanings can be established and maintained. As with Saussure, Lacan perceives that the relationship between the sign and its object is provisional and arbitrary, and its uses depend on specific historical and cultural situations (Elliot, 1994).

Primarily, Lacan's main interest in language is to examine the vital role it plays in the formation of the human unconscious. Lacan, with his theory informed by Freudian psychology, postulates that the human subject, once separated from the narcissistic wholeness of the "imaginary other," is placed into the symbolic realm of language. Within this realm, the subject uses language to represent itself. Under the domain of language, the subject creates a personal subjectivity within the perceived gaps and differences provided by language. Lacan contends that language as well as other communicative means serve the primary function of concealing the subject's repressed inner desires for unification with the imaginary other. He also theorizes that the unconscious can best be understood as not an individual space within the subject but rather an "intersubjective" one existing between people and within social conditions (Elliot, 1994).

Although Lacan's theory has been criticized for overstating the role of language in the formation of the unconscious realm (neglecting other facets such as the imagistic), nevertheless, his ideas have proven to be an invaluable tool for understanding the seductive nature of contemporary advertising and popular culture. For instance, Lacan's theory of the "imaginary other" illustrates the tremendous seductive power of various media images and glamourized commodities that rework and display a range of illusive psychic desires. As Elliot relates, the dominant realm of advertising, television, popular cultural images, and even media politics all serve a vital role in the psychic formation of identities, gender roles, and hidden desires in a society that consistently reproduces itself on an "imaginary plane" (Elliot, 1994).

Hyperreality, Semiotics, and Post-formal Thinking

Jean-Francois Lyotard defines the "postmodern condition" as the loss of belief in the historically legitimated "grand narratives" (including the historicizing explanation offered within the modernist Enlightenment tradition) of Western civilization. This loss of faith in the traditional historical narratives (including Marx's historical materialism), the rapid extension of non-legitimated science and technology, and the incredible proliferation of unabated narrative "language games," have all contributed greatly to the creation of a contemporary "hyperreality" (Lyotard, 1993). Hyperreality can best be defined as a kind of "social vertigo" associated with the decentering of the long-standing stability of modernism and caused by a disconnection with such traditional notions as "time, community, self, and history." Through the predominance of both older (television, music) as well as newer information technologies (computers, cellular phones), both public and private spheres are continuously bombarded with a non-stop deluge of electronic sounds and images from local, national, and international locations which shake the very foundation of one's "personal sense of place" (Kincheloe, 1995).

In addition, this decentering of a personal sense of place combined with the accelerated excess of new signs and images has led to the cultural creation of a definite "loss of meaning." Under this constant barrage of signs and images, the goal of culturally shared meaning becomes not only implausible but practically impossible. Disturbingly, much revered humanistic values like democracy or social justice become lost within the chaotic rush of signs. One characteristic of signs within this postmodern hyperreality is the predominance of what

Baudrillard has defined as the "simulacra" or signs that replace the real with the simulated real (Kincheloe, 1995).

Critical theorists like Frederic Jameson have determined that the economic engine driving the expansion of this postmodern condition is actually a purer, more dominating form of "late capitalism." In effect, this postmodern economy is dominated by the presence of multinational capitalism and its neo-colonialist exploitation of Third World resources (labor and material). Of course, within this form of late capitalism, advertising plays a dominant role in the incessant drive for the creation of new capitalist markets and its continued effort to invade (and capitalize) on practically every facet of human existence (Jameson, 1984). Advertising itself changes under the domain of hyperreality, as its pervasive appeals continue to have less to do with a "lived world" than a realm of unconscious desires for moral stability, sensorial stimulations, and the quest for rooted cultural identities. For critical and humanitarian scholars, one of the central goals of their work within the dislocated hyperreality of America and Western civilization is to begin to recover meaning as well as provide a necessary moral guideline through the confusing sphere of postmodernity. Invariably, semiotics with its centralized methodology of detecting patterns of meaning within seemingly disparate "signs," would appear to be an invaluable tool for mapping the perplexing terrain of this postmodern media landscape. Unfortunately, traditional semiotics, as previously mentioned, does have some associated weaknesses. Overall, what is really needed is an extremely elastic critical meta-theoretical approach that skillfully uses the method of semiotics to trace the multiple layers of unconscious desires and appeals found in contemporary advertising and popular culture.

As previously mentioned, one active solution to this pressing theoretical dilemma is to inform semiotics with the meta-theoretical domain of "post-formal thinking." Essentially, post-formalism involves a critical, postmodernist reconceptualization of the reductive assumptions of intelligence that underscore modernist cognitive development theories. Post-formal thinking's central project is the reformulation of a post-Piagetian cognitive theory that is informed through existing critical, feminist, ecological, and postmodernist thought. However, rather than calling for the eradication of all existing modernist conceptions, post-formal thinking retains most knowledges along with some centralized humanistic values (such as social justice, liberty) while at the same time exposing the tyranny of the hyperrationality of modernist grand narratives, the limitations of science and technology, and fostering the realignment of the power relations between the dominant and marginalized cultural groups (Kincheloe and Steinberg, 1993).

While this post-formal cognitive theory has immense pedagogical implications for the restructuring of school curriculums, its call for a more self-actualized, politicized cognition has tremendous ramifications for the study of culture in general. Since this cognitive theory is informed through a postmodernist perspective, it readily admits that post-formal thinking is itself only a historically situated, social construction designed to explain the prevailing social conditions of a still-dominant modernist society. This means that post-formal thinking has an innate elasticity to not only resist the impending rigidification of its theoretical assumptions but is also flexible enough to accommodate new perspectives and to eliminate the non-productive ones. Significantly, post-formal thinking's theoretical flexibility makes it ideally suited for the critical analysis of the meaning-slippery terrain associated with the hyperreal postmodern cultural landscape (Kincheloe and Steinberg, 1993).

According to Kincheloe's introduction in this text, because post-formal thinking is concerned with issues of "meaning, self-awareness, the nature and function of social context," it has a definite hermeneutic dimension. In essence, the post-formal psychological hermeneutic seeks to provide a socio-historical analysis in order to understand the contextualized situations under which knowledge and meaning are both produced (by scholars, mass media) and received (by students, consumers). Invariably, a psychological hermeneutics analyzes the multiplicity of ways in which a socio-psychological, "conscious-unconscious process" is enacted within specific activities and through symbolic forms. One of the central methodologies for the practice of psychological hermeneutics is semiotics since the approach explores the ways signs and symbols are employed by individuals to make meaning and to explain their own existence. In this regard, post-formal's psychological hermeneutics can be used to examine how the multiplicity of signs within contemporary advertising texts are employed by individuals to create meanings at both conscious/unconscious levels. In terms of advertising and other cultural messages, semiotics not only provides undeniable insights into the construction of consciousness but into the construction of the unconscious as well.

One of the main advantages of incorporating post-formal thinking's postmodernist psychological perspective with traditional semiotic theory is that it fosters semiotics to go beyond structured representational-ism (the domain of the signifier/signified) into the social and psychological nature of the communicative process. Through post-formal thinking, the critical social researcher becomes less involved with detailing meaning structures and more focused on how people create meanings through symbolic forms within specific social contexts. This proposed theoretical change involves a shift away from the modernist fixation with classifying and categorizing structures (signs, codes, genres, etc.) to studying how cultural forms are interpreted by diverse individuals and cultural groups. One of the central components of this postmodernist interpretive turn is the critical analysis of the political and power dynamics underlying every cultural form (music, clothes, language) in that some forms may either implicitly support the dominant political order or may provide a "space" for resistance. Post-formal cognition, rather than simply rejecting semiotics because of its structuralist inclinations, "recovers" it as an invaluable interpretive tool while at the same time informing with a critical postmodernist perspective.

Another central characteristic of post-formal thinking is its predominant interest in exploring the tacit forces, the deep patterns of meaning and hidden assumptions that shape human perceptions within the world (Kincheloe and Steinberg, 1993). Of course, these hidden patterns of meaning can be easily found within the domain of advertising messages and popular cultural forms. For instance, the psychoanalytical film critic Robin Wood (although not explicitly utilizing a post-formally informed perspective) has defined a wide range of seemingly disparate 1980s Hollywood films (*Raiders of the Lost Ark, The Great Santini, Friday the 13th*) as "Reaganite entertainment" primarily because these films employ a non-problematicized, classical film narrative as part of the implicate reaffirmation and recovery of the patriarchal social order. In effect, Wood utilizes a critical psychological hermeneutic to uncover the tacit, unconscious desires underlying these dominant Hollywood films (Wood, 1986). Another related post-formal characteristic evident within this example is that of metaphorical cognition. In this respect, Wood not only used deep pattern recognition to detect an identifiable pattern within these Hollywood films, he also used the explanatory power of metaphors (in this case, "Reaganite entertainment") to provide a cognitively accessible definition of these films. Since post-formal thinking recognizes the limitations and problematics (the tendency for some terms to support the dominant social order) of contemporary language, the post-formal scholar frequently has to turn to metaphorical expressions to properly identify these hidden patterns of meaning. Overall, the critical postmodernist perspective of post-formal cognition combined with the methodology of semiotics provides an invaluable heuristic tool for the crucial analysis of contemporary advertising messages and other cultural forms (Kincheloe and Steinberg, 1993).

Post-formalism, Advertising and Critical Men's Studies

In order to illustrate how semiotics informed by post-formalism can be effectively utilized to examine advertising texts, this study will conduct a close textual analysis of two print advertisements from 1995 issues of *Gentlemen's Quarterly*, a popular American men's magazine. While a typical, close semiotic reading of each advertisement will undoubtedly highlight how the ads' signs communicate with the individual reader's conscious and unconscious desires, a post-formal semiotic reading will connect these same meanings to existing power dynamics and ideological formations. In other words, a post-formal semiotics is not interested in merely unpacking the meanings embedded within signs, it also searches for patterns of meaning across other ads and texts (TV, film, fashion) which may either reinforce or challenge dominant ideological and discursive formations.

One of the main attributes of a post-formally informed semiotics is its innate meta-theoretical elasticity in that it enables the researcher to utilize theories appropriate to the subject matter. Since the objects of this study are advertisements targeting adult male consumers, post-formal semiotics will most likely draw from the theoretical domain of critical men's studies. Critical men's studies, itself informed by feminist theory, is not only concerned with the social construction of masculinity but also the advancement of equality and freedom between both genders.

A central objective of critical men's studies is to understand how men have experienced history as men and as "carriers of masculinity." Catherine Stimpson notes that in American culture to be "masculine" means to have a particular psychological identity, a social role, and a place in the labor force. In secular industrial culture, "real men" are defined by their ability to earn money in the public labor force and support their families through their wages. Men are also defined as having formal power over women and children. Stimpson perceives that post-industrial cultures have undercut such a definition of masculinity. These cultures have eliminated many of the industrial jobs that men have traditionally filled while generating lower-paying service jobs that women frequently occupy. Post-industrial cultures also tend to accept the values of egalitarianism within the family along with a greater diversity of sexual lifestyles (gay and lesbian) (Brod, 1987).

Nevertheless, the dominant image of the strong, aggressive provider male still persists since this image is inherently tied to capitalist patriarchy. Harry Brod insists that this dominant image is more closely associated with public male power rather than private men's lives. Brod explains that public male power is an outcome of the pre-capitalist industrial era when power, "was transferred from the hands of individual patriarchs to the institutions of capitalist patriarchy." But Brod explains that this system is flexible enough to tolerate certain changes in male personality traits such as a shift from authoritarian to nurturing traits, because interpersonal relations are no longer the site of male power and these changes concern men as fathers rather than bosses. On the other hand, there are strong incentives for men to retain certain dominant traits of masculinity insofar as they interact with the dynamics of capitalist patriarchy in ways functional to the system (Brod, 1987).

There has been only limited use of a critical men's studies perspective in analyzing the changing social construction of masculinity within various advertising texts. For example, Kervin analyzed the representation of males in *Esquire* men's magazine from its earliest advertisements in the mid-to-late-1930s as compared with advertising from the 1980s, pointing to how representations of masculinity have both changed and remained the same over time. One of Kervin's most invaluable contributions to the study of the men's advertising is the central idea of social compensation embedded within the advertisement. While the specter of the dominant patriarchal image (typified by the "sturdy Oak" image from the thirties) appeared to diminish in 1980s men's advertising in *Esquire*, Kervin reminds us that this image has been compensated with a more self-absorbed, consumerist male ethos. This concept of social compensation for the public and private reconfiguration of the attributes of Western patriarchy is implicit in contemporary advertising images aimed at adult males. In order to explore this concept as well as others, in 90s men's advertising, I will conduct a post-formally-informed semiotic reading of two recent print advertisements (Kervin, 1990).

In the print advertisement for Gant men's clothes, the ad's primary visual represents an elevated wooden fishing (note the fly-fishing basket) cabin nestled in the piney woods. Various clothing (sweaters, shirts, pants) has been placed and displayed in a carefree manner along the wooden railings surrounding the cabin. In the upper right-hand corner of the ad, a visual of a Gant clothes' label is imposed over the primary visual of the cabin. This label combined with the clothes featured in the visual connotates to the reader that the ad features the latest in Gant menswear.

Furthermore, in the upper left-hand corner of the visual is the ad's main copy area, which reads, "This time it's pasta instead of peanut butter. Plumbing. Girls definitely allowed." These phrases, combined with the ad's primary visual of an elevated outdoor cabin, tie this imagery to the American folk myth of the boyhood backyard treehouse. The backyard treehouse has been customarily representative of a boyhood safe haven, a youthful fantasy of escape from the world of adult authority and restrictions. The treehouse has also been linked with the concept of boyhood male-bonding activities such as membership in a secret club. In this respect, this ad represents a modernized adult version of a treehouse, the man has added several new necessities such as gourmet cuisine ("pasta instead of peanut butter"), indoor plumbing, and, of course, girls. Drawing on post-formalism's central concern with detecting patterns of meaning, the ad's particular conception of an adult male treehouse taps into the underlying male desire to escape from the complex social and cultural binds associated with modernity. In other words, the ad appears to offer men a return to the uncomplicated world of childhood, when gender roles were more clearly defined. Unlike contemporary family households in which wage-earning couples must continuously balance their own priorities, the boyhood treehouse offers men a domain or terrain controlled exclusively by males.

Moreover, the ad's implicit offer of an escape into a fantasized, adult male boyhood runs directly counter to the dominant, mature male provider image. Barbara Ehrenreich (1983) argues that in terms of the American cultural definition of masculinity, the concept of maturity is irrevocably linked with the underlying assumption of male adulthood, that every man is expected to grow up, get married, and obtain a good-paying job in order to support a family. In contrast, being "one of the boys" implies being irresponsible or, at least, temporarily rejecting the inevitability of assuming the dominant male provider role (Barbeau, 1982).

One of the central requirements of this dominant image is that men retain the role of the provider of what Ehrenreich has defined as the "breadwinner ethic." She describes this "breadwinner ethic" as the product of industrialization, when the concept of the family wage was

Copyright (1994) Gant Corporation. Used by permission.

firmly established. The central principle of the family wage system, that the male worker should be paid enough to support a family, can easily be distinguished from social reality. Throughout most of the this century, only the most privileged male workers—those employed by powerful unions or in highly-paid, skilled professions—were actually able to earn enough to support a family. Yet this principle applied to everyone: as a goal for personal upward mobility and as a social ideal (pp. 1-13). Historian Heidi Hartmann (1981) has explained that the fight for the family wage helped establish our present gender-based occupational hierarchy. Women were squeezed out of higher-paying craft jobs and professions and were pushed down to the bottom of the labor market. As it turned out, the other side of the concept that a man should earn enough to support a family has been that a woman does not need enough to support even herself (p. 1).

Therefore, the emergence of the family wage system created a serious structural instability within the social institution of marriage. Certainly, this is not to discount that other factors such as love, sexual desire, and emotional dependency are integral to the perpetuation of marriage as an institution. However, on a purely economic basis, marriages under the auspices of the early twentieth-century family wage system effectively make the wife dependent on the wages of her husband (Ehrenreich, 1983).

Ehrenreich further contends that in direct contravention to the socially-sanctioned pervasiveness and oppressive nature of this dominant provider image, over the past four decades various movements have emerged (largely generated by men), each defining a certain flight from commitment to this image. For instance, in the 1950s, there were attacks on social conformity and "the Gray Flannel Suit mentality"; the *Playboy* celebratory and consumeristic bachelor male; and the beatniks, who outwardly rejected both work and marriage. Additionally, other common drifts include the counterculture of the sixties and the psychological re-evaluation of masculinity in the seventies. Ehrenreich notes that by the late 1970s and early 1980s, the automatic expectation of men to adhere to the provider image has greatly lessened although the image itself still persists. In a rather skeptical assessment of the men's movement of the seventies, she fears that its only repercussion has been to legitimate a consumerist personality for men (Ehrenreich, 1983).

In terms of the Gant advertisement, the wilderness locale of the treehouse represents the popular "nature-as-escape" motif found in contemporary men's advertisements. In this regard, Roszak points out that this whole-scale resuscitation of nature as the repressed "other" of an urbanized, industrial environment is directly related to the "anti-technocratic" side of the 1960s counter-culture movement. While ecologism and health campaigns have been its most evident political expressions, the cultural reaction has also had an aesthetic side —in food and decor, a preference for natural materials over plastic—for the new middle class. In keeping with such changed sensibilities, personal items such as clothes began to be tied to leisure-related fantasies of rural escape (Roszak, 1969).

In this particular advertisement, nature provides a fantasy arena, a place where man can once again assume his rightful role as master but without any of the burdensome responsibilities normally associated with this role in a modern, urbanized society. The ad's lower copy, "Clothes for the man comfortable in his own skin," coupled with its wilderness imagery reinforces the conception that masculinity is a "natural" rather than a social construct. Also, through its copy and imagery, the advertisement associates its product (Gant men's clothes) with the essence of this back-to-nature or natural man. In other words, this specific Gant ad assures the average male that it recognizes this perceived ideal of the natural man and that Gant designs clothes "for the man comfortable in his own skin." Also, the visual display of women's underwear amongst the exhibition of men's clothes interjects a note of adolescent sexual naughtiness. Combined with the treehouse imagery, the ad undeniably invokes a primitive "Tarzan and Jane" mythology.

Through conducting a close post-formal semiotic reading of this Gant advertisement, one is faced with a number of contradictory meanings. On the one hand, the ad clearly supports the patriarchal assumptions that masculinity is natural (and not a social construct) and that men naturally hold formal power over women (granting them admission to the treehouse) and children. On the other hand, following Ehrenreich's (1983) conception of a male "flight from commitment," the ad's boyhood treehouse scheme reveals a hidden desire to escape from the tenets of the dominant male provider image.

Beyond the ad's symbolic construction of unconscious male desires and fantasized gender relations, a post-formal analysis also tells us that this ad effectively codes itself within the parameters of the white, middleclass lifestyle. Since the traditional boyhood backyard treehouse is a cultural image from predominantly white, middle-class suburbia, the ad appears to address white adult males who desire to recapture this nostalgic image from the past. It is important to point out that the nostalgic

Before

There's something you should do before life hits you in the knees with ten bags of

the spouse,

groceries and the need for a garden hose. You should know how it feels to have the

the house,

sun on your head and a growl at your back as you flick through five gears with

the kids,

no more baggage than a friend. This has been known since the beginning of cars.

you get

Which is why roadsters were invented. The Mazda Miata. The roadster returned.

one chance.

mazda
IT JUST FEELS RIGHT.®

element in this ad is a nostalgia for the protected domain of a white, middle-class childhood in America's suburban past. While the ad does not explicitly exclude other racial and social classes from its marketing designs (i.e., selling men's clothes), nevertheless the ad's visual imagery is prescribed and taken from the symbolic imagination of white, middle-class males. Also, the ad's intertextual referencing to the "Tarzan and Jane" mythology is a cultural image that resonates within the imaginary terrain of Western colonialism (Green, 1993). While the ad's particular usage of images from white, middle-class suburbia and colonialism may seem relatively insignificant, post-formalism reminds us that one of the most potent forces of a dominant social hegemony is the colonization of human imagination.

In the print advertisement for the Mazda Miata, the primary visual features a white male driving a Miata across a rural, hillside stretch of country road with a white picket fence bordering the roadside, and a traditional white farmhouse in the far background. Invariably, many of the visual's elements (the white picket fence, farmhouse, rural countryside) resonate with the nostalgia for an earlier, sentimentalized, simplified, and unfettered lifestyle. Like that of the Gant ad, the Mazda ad's rural imagery is undoubtedly anti-modernistic in its validation of a simplified lifestyle. Although the ad's bucolic background imagery seems to promote an agrarian way of life, its main product, the automobile, is itself emblematic of the reigning technocratic dimension of modernity. Ultimately, as with most planned advertising images, the implied values of these visual background elements is magically transferred onto the advertised product, the Mazda Miata.

Directly above the ad's primary visual is centered bold copy exclaiming, "Before the spouse, the house, the kids, you get one chance." Invariably, the ad's visuals and copy effectively tie the idea of adult male freedom to their product, the Mazda Miata. The particular brand of freedom offered is "one last chance" to enjoy his carefree bachelor status before the inevitable crushing burden of a family and a thirty-year mortgage—in other words, before he assumes the male provider role. Embedded within this bold declaration of a "last chance" is a small-type copy written in a verbose, aggressive manner that men who agree with the bolder statement are intended to identify with. With phrasing such as "before life hits you in the knees with ten bags of groceries," rarely has domesticity been reviled with such verbal wrath.

As with the Gant ad, this advertisement implicitly offers the adult male a temporary escape or flight from commitment to the traditional male breadwinner role. Significantly, despite the immense economic, cultural, and social compensations of the male provider image, these advertisements as well as others represent an implicit contradiction embedded within the image. With the emerging specter of flexible, on-demand employment, late capitalism, and a competitive global economy, the older patriarchal breadwinner role appears like an anachronism from an earlier industrial era. However, as Ehrenreich (1983) contends, the dominant male provider role still persists, primarily because the image continues to be intimately tied to the social formations of patriarchy and capitalism.

The copy also alludes to the nostalgic tradition of the "roadster," and since the automobile has always been associated with the ideal of male freedom within American culture, it reminds us that "the roadster has returned." The automobile as a product of industrialized mass production was initially associated with and symbolic of technological progress. Andrew Wernick reminds us that besides serving as a "self-promoting, commodity-sign," the modern automobile has always been a gendered object. In the first instance, and from the viewpoint of the male driver, the car has been projected as Woman— whether as a flashy possession, mistress, or wife. In this respect, the visual presentation of the male driver and his car is that of the male-led couple—the perfect representation of patriarchy (Wernick, 1991).

The automobile and the image of the vast open road have been closely associated with the ideals of adult male freedom. Todd Gitlin, in his essay on 1980s television car commercials, relates that the car is advertised not as a means of transportation but as a "carrier of popular feeling." In this respect, he argues that one irrefutable aspect of these commercials is the desire to take flight accompanied by a fear that around us everyone else has taken flight too. He also associates this feeling with other expressions that include, "the longing for open space, innocence, the sense of infinite possibility, and the distance one has to go to recapture the plenitude of the wild frontier." Although these commercials clearly manipulate the romance of freedom to sell automobiles, Gitlin argues that they also share other features of contemporary American culture including the desire to break free from the social bonds of society along with the worship of the lone individual stripped of any imposing social preconditions—"indeed, we see something of the prevailing American ethos, its promises and evasions and secret fears" (Gitlin, 1986, p. 140).

In this essay, through utilizing the methodology of semiotics informed by the psychological hermeneutics of post-formal cognition, I have been able to detect the underlying conscious and unconscious desires of a pervasive male revolt against the dominant male provider image. It is important to remember that just as some men have struggled against the family wage system, women, too, have fought against it. For if the family wage system has confined men to the provider role, it has relegated women either to domesticity or, on average, low-paid employment.

This research study has also illustrated the tremendous interpretive strengths of incorporating the methodology of semiotics within the critical postmodernist perspective of post-formal thinking. One of the central merits of post-formal thinking's meta-theoretical perspective is that it allows the researchers to inform their studies with critical, feminist, men's studies, ecological, and postmodernist thought. Although this research has focused its study on advertising messages primarily directed at men, this post-formal interpretive approach, with its focus on signs and their meanings, is versatile enough to be applied to a wide range of existing cultural forms (language, human interaction, institutions, etc.).

References

Barbeau, C. (1982). *Delivering the male.* Minneapolis, MN: Winston Press.

Baudrillard, J. (1994) *Simulacra and simulation.* Trans. Sheila Faria Glaser. Ann Arbor, MI: University of Michigan.

Betcher, W. R. and W. S. (1993). *In a time of fallen heroes: The re-creation of masculinity.* New York: Atheneum.

Brod, H. (1987) *The making of masculinities.* Boston: Allen and Unwin.

Eco, U. (1976). *A Theory of semiotics.* Bloomington, IN: Indiana University.

Ehrenreich, B. (1983). *The hearts of men: American dreams and the flight from commitment.* Garden City, NY: Anchor Press/Doubleday.

Elliot, A. (1994). *Psychoanalytic theory: An introduction.* Oxford, U.K.: Blackwell.

Gitlin, T. (1986). Car commercials and *Miami Vice*: We build excitement. In T. Gitlin (Ed.) *Watching Television* (pp. 136–161). New York: Pantheon.

Green, M. (1993). *The adventurous male: Chapters in the history of the white male mind.* University Park, PA: Penn State University.

Hartmann, H. (1981). The unhappy marriage of marxism and feminism: Toward a more progressive union. In Lydia Sargent (Ed.), *Woman and Revolution* (pp. 1–15). Boston: South End Press.

Jameson, F. (1984, July-Aug.). Postmodernism, or the cultural logic of late capitalism. *New Left Review, 146*, 53–92.

Kervin, D. (1990). Advertising masculinity: The representation of males in *Esquire. Journal of Communication Inquiry.* 14(1), 51–70.

Kincheloe, J. (1995). *Toil and trouble: Good work, smart workers, and the integration of academic and vocational education.* New York: Peter Lang.

Kincheloe, J. and Steinberg, S. (1993). A tentative description of post-formal thinking: The critical confrontation with cognitive theory. *Harvard Educational Review,* 63(3), 296–320.

Leiss, W., Kline, S. and Jhally, S. (1990). *Social communication in advertising,* second edition. Toronto: Nelson Canada.

Lyotard, J. (1993). *The postmodern condition: A report on knowledge.* Trans. G. Bennington and B. Massumi. Minneapolis, MN: University of Minnesota.

Roszak, T. (1969). *The making of a counter-culture: Reflections on the technocratic society and its youthful opposition.* Garden City, NY: Doubleday.

Scholes, R. (1982). *Semiotics and interpretation.* New Haven, CT: Yale University.

Seiter, E. (1987). Semiotics and television. In Robert C. Allen (Ed.), *Channels of discourse: Television and contemporary criticism* (pp. 17–24). Chapel Hill, NC: University of North Carolina.

Stewart, J. (1995). *Language as articulate contact: Toward a post-semiotic philosophy of communication.* Albany, NY: SUNY Press.

Volosinov, V. (1973). *Marxism and the philosophy of language.* Trans. L. Matejka and I.R. Titunik. New York: Seminar Press..

Wernick, A. (1991). *Promotional culture: Advertising, ideology, and symbolic expression.* Newbury Park, CA: Sage.

Williamson, J. (1978). *Decoding advertisements: Ideology and meaning in advertising.* London: Marion Boyars.

Wood, R. (1986). *Hollywood from Vietnam to Reagan.* New York: Columbia University.

CHAPTER TEN

Multiculturalism
Post-formal Thinking and Critical Multiculturalism

Marcia Middleswarth Magill

Post-formal Thinking and Critical Multiculturalism

As the make-up of our classrooms has rapidly changed to reflect the growing percentage of different racial and ethnic groups in our country, much educational discussion and debate have centered around the learning styles, abilities, and preparedness of these seemingly disparate groups of students and how public education can best meet their collective and individual needs. Such professional dialogue and musings inevitably lead to discussion of multicultural education: what it is or should be; its purported positive effect on student self-esteem and the correlative desire to learn; and, indeed, whether it is even desirable or necessary for public schools to introduce such curricula into their programs. Query into the nature and purpose of multicultural education, rather than illuminating the most desirable course of action, has led, rather, to much heated debate and contestation, for it lays bare the inequities of some of our most historically ingrained educational ideologies.

Although education is beset—and stymied—by political and ideological factions often in bitter opposition, it seems unlikely that any of the disparate panoply of educational philosophers and theorists would fail to concur that education is, or should be, a process of human betterment through the actualization of human potential. If we accept this, then, as an ultimate aim, we are left to formulate as best we can our programs of education in ways that will promote and enhance the realization of such potential—both individual and collective—regardless of ethnicity, race, gender, or class. It is at this present confluence of critical need and firm resolve that we turn to the application of post-formal thinking.

Post-formal Thinking as Critical Hermeneutic

Most useful to an investigation of how transformative critical inquiry informs pedagogy and curricula is Kincheloe and Steinberg's (1993) theory of post-formal thinking. Having sifted through the argot of post-modernists' critical theory and addressed some of its fundamental, intraphilosophic contradictions, they have developed a means of approaching education and teachers' work that preserves the intent and tenor of a reconstructive critical theory. What Kincheloe and Steinberg have done is to provide educators with practical tools for creating a radical classroom within the presently stultifying and moribund context of our public schools: Post-formal thinking becomes the hermeneutic through which we explore knowledge production and make meaning of our world. As delineated by Kincheloe and Steinberg, there are four aspects of post-formal thinking: etymology, pattern, process, and contextualization. Although in practice there is a fluid interplay among and between these, such an imposed breakdown is useful for a discussion of how post-formal thinking can be used to create a curricula and pedagogy that is innately multicultural.

Etymology

Attention to *etymology* in the critical classroom encourages and facilitates a questioning of "what we know, how we come to know it, why we believe or reject it, and how we evaluate the credibility of the evidence" (Kincheloe and Steinberg, 1993, p. 302). Our knowledge not only shapes our perceptions and understanding of the past and present but what we know and how we come to know it are also inextricably intertwined with who we are and our personal sense of worth and agency. Knowledge, in that it is a "social construction that reflects the social, political, and cultural context in which it is formulated" (Banks, 1991, p. 126), is, therefore, power. If this power is to be used to liberate, not subjugate, both educators and students must attend closely to epistemological concerns and to the highly political, market-driven nature of the purveyor of that knowledge—the school.

Rather than facilitating the enlightenment of students and promoting inquiry that could ultimately empower rather than repress, the school is, ironically, one of the institutions implicated in both effectuating and perpetuating the marginalization of people. Cherryholmes (1988) contends that schools, as structural and hierarchical institutions, are both normative and coercive in that their "exercise of power negatively sanctions some discourses and inquiry and provides opportunity for others" (p. 73). Similarly, Giroux (1992a) refers to schools as "cultures which legitimize certain forms of knowledge and disclaim others" (p. 14). Such a pronouncement of the normative power of public education also comes from others than the postmodern theorists; indeed, even the more moderate Hunter cites the school as "the central institution in modern life through which the larger social order is reproduced" (1991, p. 174).

To what purpose and for whose benefit we educate our citizenry has long shaped both the composition and content of American education, and even a brief retrospection reveals that our schools, despite our perhaps naive and provincial desire to see them otherwise, have historically had little to do with those egalitarian ideals that quicken the pulse of the patriot.

Although democratic ideology played a large part in the conceptualization of the public common school of pre-Civil War days, its progenitors were "largely British-American in ethnic origin, bourgeois in economic outlook and status, and evangelically Protestant in religious orientation" (Kirst, 1984, p. 28). Understandably, therefore, the program of the common school both embodied and taught the ideologies of this founding group. Later, in the early 1900s, in response to vast numbers of immigrants and growing expectations of efficiency and functionalism that were the result of increased modernization and industrialization, schools, as the primary vehicles of socialization, were assigned the task of graduating good citizens and productive workers who would move smoothly into the mainstream of society without disrupting the status quo. It was at this point in our nation's history that the concept of the "melting pot" was born and had, at least on the surface, broad-based appeal; semantically, it struck a chord and resonated with democratic ideals.

The metaphor of the "melting pot" was, however, somewhat inaccurate for, historically, an amalgamation of peoples (wherein the distinct cultures of all would be transformed into a unique cultural group) was never the intent. Clearly, the dominant culture, steeped in its lineage and possessing the power of influence, was to remain the standard by which all others were to be judged and referenced; it was the "Others" who were to do the "melting," and the vehicle for assuring this cultural indoctrination that would lead to cultural assimilation was the school. Both the overt and hidden curricula of American schools strove inexorably to this assimilationist end of cultural reproduction, stripping many cultures of what was uniquely their own. Assimilationist theory is unquestionably one of Anglo-conformity: Over time, ethnic minority groups will presumably become more and more like the dominant majority until finally "all are part of one culture patterned after the dominant group" (Appleton, 1983, p. 29). And what was the composition of this dominant culture in which these ethnic groups were subsumed? It was, and so continues to be, European American, upper-middle class, English-speaking, and male (Nieto, 1992, p. 21).

In the intervening decades since the beginning of this century, schools and government have continued to join forces to neutralize those socio-cultural situations perceived as threats to national stability: first in management of the work force—through enacting compulsory schooling laws and laws prohibiting child labor; then in the "life adjustment training" of post-World War II—by "dumbing down" curricula for those students deemed ill-equipped for more rigorous learning by their poor cultural environment at home; and, finally, in squaring off to regain a competitive edge in global economics—by centralizing control of curriculum and monitoring success through standards and measurements.

Throughout all of our nation's history, the myriad initiatives recorded and reforms enacted have changed little, however, with regard to the fundamental nature and intent of our system of education. Despite much superficial reorganization, what has remained unchanged is that our schools have always disseminated a knowledge of the world that is told through the voice of the traditional canon, and, as such, the culture, viewpoint, and history taught and legitimized have been essentially "white."

A grounding in the traditional canon has been for many decades both the hallmark and distinguishing feature of what is deemed a "quality education," one purpose of which is to mold a diverse citizenry into a cohesive whole. Indeed, the economic and political security of the country is, to an alarming degree, still believed to rest in large part on a polity that operates from a collective ethos and ideology. This philosophy, which reflects a Cartesian-Newtonian way of organizing individual psyche as well as the world, has "analytically steamrolled the diverse pasts of the non-West, collapsing them into a single ideal . . . in an effort to make manageable the world's non-Western pasts by incorporating them into a more familiar Western past" (Nandy, 1992, p. 267).

Advocates of preserving the sanctity of this canon argue that it has stood the test of time because it embodies a corpus of knowledge that communicates universal truths. Postmodernists, however, eschew this Aristotelian belief espoused by the more traditional theorists and practitioners that there are absolute truths and values that are knowable. To the postmodernist, such a metanarrative is inimical to the tenets of true democracy; to presuppose a reality to which all must subscribe is to exercise a power of domination that subjugates and silences entire groups of people. Knowledge and meaning, they assert, are unknown terrains that must be continually mapped and remapped since, as Cherryholmes claims, they "cannot be grounded on something stable and fixed beyond the sign system in which [they] occur" (1988, p. 61).

To counter such curricular hegemony, the perhaps well-meaning but sometimes myopic and frequently misguided, attempts by liberal educators to honor our larger racial and ethnic groups have resulted in a fashioning of a multicultural education in the cultural pluralist mode. Such an "add on" approach allows local districts and individual teachers to bask in the "good feelings" engendered by their seemingly more egalitarian, inclusive approach. Indeed, this perspective holds for many much allure: Most of us, particularly dominant-group members, choose to believe that we are all working, with equal access and opportunity, toward universally shared goals and affluence and, further, that we all reap the same rewards for equal effort.

It is, however, this very smugness in a multicultural job well done, this plan to know and then respect one another so that, in the end, we may all be one, that sets on edge the philosophic teeth of those in the more transformative of camps. Representative of one oppositional perspective are Gollnick and Chinn (1994), who contend that these multicultural approaches of addition or infusion are of most advantage to students of the dominant group, those whose horizons have been broadened, presumably, but whose behaviors have undergone little or no adjusting. There is also the legitimate concern that infusion and cultural awareness strategies place the burden of enlightening majority group members squarely and exclusively on the shoulders of those who have been disadvantaged by the ignorance and bias the programs seek to ameliorate. The tacit implication in such an arrangement is that minorities must defend their culture in a successful enough way that dominant group members will be convinced of its value. However, although this concern is valid, the fundamental weakness and inadequacy of such an ameliorative approach runs much deeper. Banks (1991) reflects the view iterated by many theorists when he explains that multicultural education along such lines leaves unchallenged and substantially unchanged "the basic assumptions, perspectives, paradigms and values" of the dominant culture as reflected in the curriculum (p. 130). There is often and unfortunately in the cultural pluralist approach the defense of cultural expression coupled with a paradoxical disregard for the lack of structural access.

Giroux asserts that such curricular attempts to acknowledge these minority groups (the Others) via curricular "add ons" have served only to perpetuate their separateness and subjugation:

> Diversity is not ignored in the dominant cultural apparatus, but promoted in order to be narrowly and reductively defined through dominant stereotypes. Representation does not merely exclude, it also defines cultural difference by *actively* constructing the identity of the Other for dominant and subordinate groups (1992a, p. 58).

Specifically, then, a common criticism of the popular, pluralist attempts at "diversity awareness" is that they "enable, even encourage, both pupils and teachers to minimize, compartmentalize or sidestep issues relating to racism" (Nixon, 1985, p. 40), and that "to aim at mutual tolerance . . . without also aiming at an increased understanding and firm rejection of the existing state of inequality is an attempt at ideological control" (Nixon, 1985, p. 24). Under the guise of inclusive tolerance and understanding, therefore, many feel that cultural pluralism, in its lack of critical inquiry aimed at substantive change, serves only to reproduce social and economic inequities.

Through etymological inquiry, we are able to uncover irrefutable evidence that our system of education has always sought to serve political and economic ends, and the tacit understanding is that the political and economic interests of some have been addressed while those of others have been trivialized, ignored, or prescibed. However, such illuminated insight does not make easier an attempt to develop a truly multicultural curricula, for, despite their theoretical bases and espoused intents, neither content nor methodology is ever apolitical. As much as we may attempt to design curricula that is value-free and antiseptic, curricula that would neither offend nor excite anyone, close inspection will always reveal that attempt to have failed; it will without exception either be drafted and/or presented in ways that are very much value laden. Further, we must acknowledge that just as telling as what we choose to include in our curricula is that which we choose to exclude. It is here that perhaps our most silent "sin" is committed and perpetuated, for, historically, students have entrusted schools to teach a representative sample of essential knowledge. Therefore, if there are entire areas, groups, and traditions absent from what schools teach, it is only logical for students to infer that there was not much of import in those areas; "it follows that students' academic experiences can support misconceptions or even prejudice by default, if not by design" (Diaz, 1992, p. 202).

However, critical theory, as applied via the hermeneutic of post-formal thinking, can profoundly illume even curricular content that enshrines the canon. Specifically, when viewed through the lens of critical pedagogy, the traditional canon can become a vehicle through which students confront and question the gap between the academic distillation of human experience and the world they perceive around them (Diaz, 1992, p. 202). Both the "Great Books" and the contextual reasons why they and not others were so labeled are telling statements of operant power and domination and, as such, can become the springboards for a rigorous classroom dialectic that is recursive, synthetical, and, ultimately, transformational. Additionally, there is much in the canon that is valuable and of intrinsic merit: literature that is beautifully crafted and philosophy that depicts the original insightfulness and brilliance of humans trying to make meaning of the universe in which they find themselves. To dispense entirely of this is to dispense with much that is good. Further, if we were to expunge literature from our curricula solely because it was written by European males, what, then, would we have accomplished in our egalitarian pursuit?

Examination, therefore, of these sometimes very divergent views leads us to borrow and incorporate that which is most compelling from the postmodernists: the need for critical inquiry and for a continual rethinking and remapping of what is qualitatively significant and relevant. Using the very practical tools of post-formal thinking, one can teach the canon *critically*, i.e., in a way that will arouse and invite debate and questioning of the relations of power that existed at the time and place the particular stories of the canon (fiction or nonfiction) were written and why they continue to be the cornerstone of education in the United States. Etymological questions would be probed: What structured the choices, actions, and utterances of the historical canon? For whose benefit and why have these "traditional works" continued to be taught in our schools? Such inquiry and reflective dialectic can be liberating and enlightening. Indeed, Cherryholmes (1988) has noted that this pedagogical stance "offers opportunities to expose the benevolent and constructive operations of power as well as those that are malevolent and destructive" (p. 186).

The etymological facet of post-formal thinking, therefore, makes possible both an individual and collective discovery of *how* we have come to the knowledge we possess and, perhaps more importantly, *why* and *for whose benefit*. Contrasted with the modernist emphasis on totality, mastery, and metaphysics, post-formal thinking and pedagogy seek to liberate meaning and truth from that which is defined solely by the referent position and exclusive possession of the privileged.

Pattern

The second element of post-formal thinking, *pattern*, seeks to differentiate between the explicate and implicate orders of society and our world. The explicate, or what Kincheloe refers to as the "unfolded order" (1995, p. 205) is that part of experience to which Enlightenment thought has brought its tools and scientific methodology to bear in order to quantify, verify, and control; it is the world readily apparent to us as reflected in our institutions, mores, culture, and social positionings. Post-formal thinking hearkens, instead, to an exploration of the implicate, to that which is tacit or hidden, for it is here that "ostensible separateness vanishes and all things seem to become a part of a larger, unified structure" (Kincheloe and Steinberg, 1993, p. 208). Attention to pattern in the implicate structure, therefore, seeks to cut beneath the fragmented surface of our highly technological modern society to reveal connections we have not yet observed or destroyed. In the classroom, such attempt to uncover pattern is characterized by continual exploration and excavation, an unearthing of the pattern embedded in chaos—social or physical.

Surely, as we acknowledge that our world's growing ecological ills and social pathologies can be rectified only through a keen sense of the interplay of their underlying issues and structure, such "intunement" as post-formal thinking affords becomes imperative. In this excavation of the implicate, the post-formal thinker becomes conversant with a cognition that is intuitive, metaphoric—a way of knowing that is quintessentially original, creative thought. Further, this more fluid, less quantifiable and reductionist mode affords an awareness of the fragility and oftentimes *imaginary* nature of that which our schools frequently package in curricula and pedagogy as unassailable truth—a faux reality that ultimately controverts any espoused intent of an education that is to liberate or empower. We must not be seduced into believing that simply because we talk about something it actually exists. Post-formal thinking illuminates that much that we consider to be an accurate reflection of the "natural order" of the world around us is, in fact, merely a human construct that mirrors nothing.

In amplification of Foucault's (1972) contention that discourse forms as much as refers to that of which it speaks, Vygotsky's (1986) more generative theory sees discourse in an equally reciprocal relationship with thought itself, whereby words form as much as articulate thought. Further, as part of his work with regard to mediated action, Vygotsky holds that words, as linguistic signs, are "tools" used to move (to action or to response) both others and ourselves. Following Vygotsky's reasoning, actions, as a physical articulation both shaping and shaped by thought, are also tools by and through which we shape one another.

Harré (1983) would move slightly beyond this to address the critically pivotal issue of how actions and speech, in their power to form as much as respond to a reality, can alter the distribution of status positions and the consequent conversational rights attributed thereto. That is to say, if power relations in a society or classroom exist in such a way as to silence or qualify the actions or speech of a person or group, the agency of that person or group—their opportunity to become creators of their own and mutual reality—is robbed.

Close attention to how we create our reality by and through our speech and actions is essential, therefore, if we acknowledge Harré's claim (cited in Shotter, 1993, p. 94) that the personal psychology of the individual is created by his/her appropriation of the conversational forms of the public. The power, then, of an articulation/representation of what we perceive as knowledge or truth is, indeed, awesome—one that carries with it, Shotter (1993) would argue, a moral responsibility. There is a fluid interplay, a continual recreating, between individual psyche and perception on one hand and our discourse and actions on the other. Herein, in fact, lies the power of rhetoric: that what we perceive ourselves and others to be (e.g., desirable/repellent, intelligent/stupid, articulate/inarticulate, lovable/abhorrent) will inform our actions, and such actions will, in turn, continually redefine/recreate one's perceived socio-cultural reality—a reality that may, in fact, be imaginary. Further, as Bartlett explains in his 1932 work on remembering (cited in Shotter, 1993, p. 84), in our acts of living and making meaning in the present we construct facts, detail, and "truth"—a perceived reality—that will substantiate and justify an attitude or impression we hold (of a person, a situation, an institution) and wish to remember, to retain, and perpetuate.

Within the context of our schools, then, in our various classes and curricula, we are not just disseminating facts that exist a priori. These "facts and truth," as we come to believe them to be over the years, are always contextual and contentious. Further, it is misleading and erroneous for educators to convey all knowledge as the correct representation of an independent reality. There is, therefore, both a moral and political aspect to be considered in the approach and sharing of these so-called facts. Curricula that take such a moral and political stance with regard to classroom dialectic and attend closely to the implicate under-structure are exciting and electric, creative and promising. It is the nature of the implicate to defy quantification and measurement, to possess an illusiveness that pushes students to explore intellectual, spiritual, and physical terrain on levels impossible from the vantage point of traditional pedagogy. As Wertsch (1995) explains, existing mediated action can be transformed by the introduction of new mediational means (p. 67), and it is nothing less than transformation that the excavation of deep structures seeks to effectuate. Once again, through post-formal thinking, diversity in our classrooms becomes a natural and necessary part of the curricula, a "cognitive window" from which to expand our vision of ourselves and our world (Kincheloe, 1995, p. 209).

Process

With regard to *process*, Kincheloe and Steinberg (1993) define post-formal thinkers as those who see the world as a text to be read, a process in which, as in any act of reading, encoded meaning is deconstructed. Exploring the world from this proactive position reveals that what is absent is often more telling and more important than what is left in (p. 311). We want our students and our children to apply this process of decoding hidden or contradictory meaning when they are confronted with persons or social situations we find troublesome or dangerous, and as teachers and parents we become exasperated and frightened by their frequent inability to do so. Such deconstruction is a level of inquiry that needs to inform the very essence of pedagogy in our schools. If we wish our students to be critical thinkers in social arenas, we must help them to discover how to be critical thinkers in *all* arenas. Postmodernists would suggest that an imperative first step is to see the task of education reform and the restyling of pedagogy and curricula in particular as being essentially "value laden, and to adopt a correspondingly critical stance to one's own efforts in this arena" (Nixon, 1985, p. 35).

With regard to such positioning and inquiry, Kincheloe (1995) notes that one of the best ways to glimpse the implicate and uncover relationships is to confront oneself with diversity, of seeing through the eyes of the Other in order to gain new perspective and knowledge (pp. 08-209). Similarly, Giroux (1988) proposes the implementation of what he terms a "border pedagogy of postmodern resistance." He labels this new methodology *border* because it presumably both enables and encourages those whom he calls the Others to traverse the borders of their respective groups and intellectually position themselves where critical inquiry of individual and collective histories is possible. It is the paramount function and importance of this pedagogy to "address the important question of how representations and practices that name, marginalize, and define difference as the devalued Other are actively learned, interiorized, challenged, or transformed" (Giroux, 1988, p. 174). In Giroux's vision of emancipatory education, this border pedagogy is assigned the dual task of "not only creating new objects of knowledge but also addressing how inequalities, power, and human suffering are rooted in basic institutional practices" (Giroux, 1992a, p. 29).

Just as with Bakhtin's contention (cited in Shotter, 1993) that the importance and efficacy of dialogue is negotiated and constructed on the *boundaries* of speech, so, too, are our perceptions and knowledge formulated on the boundaries, the borders, between action and response. Our inner knowing, perceptions of ourselves vis-á-vis the world around us, is formulated in a way quite external to what we would usually perceive as being private, autonomous thought. Such a perspective sheds dimensional light on Giroux's advocacy of traversing borders: Having positioned ourselves outside the intellectual bounds of our particular enclave or identifying group, not only will we be able, as Giroux suggests, to more critically and objectively explore respective histories and power relations, we will also be poised on the very borders where our thought, action, and voice take form. Having so traversed beyond the haven of what we presume to be the sanctity and autonomy of our mental life and inner being, we are more likely able to recognize the extent to which we have constructed an external reality that in large measure serves to corroborate our personal desires and perceptions.

In application, Giroux's "border pedagogy" as it plays out in the educational milieu necessitates both a new use for and a reading of the popular disseminator of truth: the text. Specifically, since texts are written, produced, and marketed in a way, whether explicit or tacit, that both illustrates and promotes the dominant culture, we must begin to transform canon by reading it critically, both from the students' particular lived cultures as well as from the culture and context of the authorship. We must analyze the absences of text, which often speak more eloquently than its insertions and interpret, criticize, and rewrite the past, present and future from this newly broadened perspective (Giroux, 1988, p. 173).

To accomplish this reconstruction, the post-formal classroom is, therefore, one much more *transformational* in its potential, one that will, as Banks (1992) explains, "change the canon, paradigms, and basic assumptions of the curriculum and enable students to view concepts, issues, themes, and problems from different perspectives" (p. 33). Echoing this view, Lynch (1992) calls for an education that will enable students to make decisions on rational grounds, identify alternatives, consider and take on the perspectives of others, and hypothesize about consequences across time and space (p. 73). As delineated by postmodernists, this would be a much more challenging, radically revitalizing paradigm of multicultural education that is both emancipatory and rational, what Nixon (1985) calls the *permeation process* (p. 41).

Engaging and challenging, this process is one of critical inquiry whereby diverse cultures and experiences are analyzed to see how they have been organized and constructed historically and socially, enabling or disabling. In order to introduce such post-formal inquiry into our schools, the curricula must include, in addition to the canonical texts, works of note outside the Western tradition. Of course, one must state the obvious: What to include and what to exclude from other cultures as well as our own, regardless of who does the choosing, leads circularly back to our original problem. Reading a particular text by an Hispanic author, for example, would necessitate, from this pedagogical stance of critical inquiry, examining the power relations and struggles in that culture that allowed this particular voice to speak and silenced others. Notwithstanding these admitted difficulties (for one should not abandon a worthwhile tact simply because it may be difficult), Etzioni claims that "educated people—whatever their origins—ought to be conversant with the main works and seminal ideas of other civilizations, especially those many of his or her fellow Americans consider part of their heritage" (1993, p. 151). Searle would presumably agree; he states, in a defense of Stanford University's making available to students an alternative course to its more traditional "Culture, Ideas, and Values," "One of the most liberating effects of 'liberal education' is in coming to see one's own culture as one possible form of life and sensibility among others" (1990, p. 39).

It would seem, then, that our aim as educators to better the human condition necessitates social practices that break rather than continue existing forms of social and psychological domination (Giroux, 1983,

p. 32). We have seen that critical, post-formal thinking and inquiry with an eye to social reform and lasting reparation of injustices is essential as is an education equal for *all* in *all* respects. So, too, we need to enrich our curricula with readings from diverse cultures. In addition, as has been discussed, social transformation of any scope or kind would be impossible were we to limit reality and our notions of what is imperative simply to that which is known to our own experience. Broad change necessitates collective effort, effort by all toward a goal that speaks to the commonalities of all its constituents.

Contextualization

Finally, Kincheloe and Steinberg (1993) speak to the necessity of "attending to the setting" and understanding the "role of power in the way the world is represented," both elements of post-formal thinking's *contextualization*. Educators have long known that learning takes place more readily when material is placed in a context relevant to students' lives. However, whether through fear or neglect, educators seldom apply such contextualization to a broader corpus of knowledge and lived experience. In his introduction to this text, Kincheloe speaks extensively to the social ills caused by such rampant decontextualization in our hyperreal world. Action and experience, removed from the context that infuses them with meaning, become simply affect, empty shadow. Such bifurcation of context and human experience is at the root of what Kincheloe calls socio-psychological schizophrenia, a cognitive illness that threatens the very existence of humanity. Attention to context is essential for the success of post-formal thinking, for only when reading the world through a contextual lens can we hope to recognize the etymology and process that inform the praxis of critical inquiry and transformation.

If multiculturalism as it is commonly applied in our schools "lacks an historical dimension and thereby ignores the dynamic nature of culture, of forms of resistance and struggle within cultures" (Bonnett, 1993, p. 35), it is exactly that which should be instilled in any new fashioning of multicultural education. Only within an historical context, it is claimed, can transformation take place. Tierney (1989) refers to this historical analysis of pedagogical practices as an "excavation" (p. 86), an apt metaphor that expresses the layers of meaning and struggles for power, from which our curricula are built, that must be stripped away to reveal the true relationship between knowledge and power. In application, Giroux (1992b) explains that this process would manifest itself as "a shift[ing] away from an exclusive focus on subordinate groups . . . to one [a focus] which examines how racism in its various forms is produced historically and institutionally in various levels of dominant, white culture" (p. 10).

Postmodernism, as applied via the tools of post-formal thinking, rejects that which is ethnocentric and hegemonic and hearkens, instead, to both the lure and imperatives of a critical analysis of how we, each and all of us, are "constituted as subjects within a rapidly changing set of political, social, and cultural conditions" (Giroux, 1988, p. 164). As we have seen (Shotter, 1993; Vygotsky, 1986; Wertsch, 1995), we are both actors and acted upon in this drama of life, both created by and creating our perceived reality and the meaning we make of it. Therefore, how we are "constituted," our setting and positioning within that sociocultural reality, begs inquiry and careful exploration if we are to hope for a citizenry that is "educated" in the truest sense of the word.

If the relation of word and thought to action is not a static thing but a negotiated process within a temporal context (Vygotsky, 1986), we cannot overlook that context, historical or contemporary, if we are to make meaning and become an educated people. Attention to contextualization, although with radical potential, is not a new concept to education, for, as early as 1916, Dewey defined the sophisticated thinker as one who was able to see events and occurrences not as isolated incidents but, rather, as threads in the tapestry of collective human experience (p. 343). Anything less, therefore, than a frank reading of how multiple contexts have and do inform our thought, speech, and actions is, by design or inadvertence, a dangerous deception. Such narrow, censored introspection and retrospection perpetuate stereotypes and cripple personal efficacy, thereby limiting possibilities for our future—individual and collective. Humanity can only be diminished by such contextual neglect.

Once seen contextually, the imperative of acknowledging moral and ethical responsibility for our actions and speech stands in bas relief. However, it is this—an assertion that there exists a collective, interwoven experience that should be guided by ethic—that excites unsettled debate as well as occasional accusations of veiled, supremacist tyranny.

As Beyer (1992) explains, many postmodernists maintain that there is no unified representation of the world and that any attempt to do so is, as he quotes Giroux, "totalitarian and terroristic" (p. 374). Meta-narratives that speak to a universal truth are felt to be innately oppressive, responding to only one reading of the lived world. However, a vision of reality defined solely from the perspective and experience of each individual is particularistic—and relativistic—to a point of absurdity. If a driving purpose of postmodernist philosophy is transformational, namely, to alter oppressive relations of power as they exist in all arenas and institutions of the Western world, any effectuation of change would necessitate a perception beyond the individual of what reality and democracy *should* be. Beyer is articulate in his explanation of this point:

> Local efforts frequently require insight attainable only through the examination and critique of non-local sources of exploitation and oppression, and necessitate directions that are ascertainable through cultural and moral visions that may transcend the immediate situation (1992, p. 375).

As an example of this intraphilosophic contradiction noted by Beyer, Giroux would appear to veer at times off the strict postmodernist course and speak from a terrain decidedly more moderate: "Ethics . . . is not a matter of individual choice or relativism but a social discourse that refuses to accept needless human suffering and exploitation. Ethics becomes a practice that broadly connotes one's personal and social sense of responsibility to the Other" (1992a, p. 74). Such a prescriptive for behavior and social response resounds with all the attributes of the "grand narratives" that the postmodernists, including Giroux himself, so vehemently eschew.

Critics, (some of whom are postmodernists tracing their philosophic roots to deconstructionists Derrida or Foucault) would contend that this transcendent moral vision to which Beyer hearkens, as well as the application of the social ethic Giroux expounds, are, once again, attempts by those in "power" to impose a universal vision of what is moral and good upon those who have been stripped of voice. The clarity of these oppositional stances becomes further obscured when one notes that, paradoxically, even a relativist perspective of the world can itself be viewed as a vehicle for perpetuating the tyranny of totalitarianism, of rationalizing political and social inaction, complacency, and even oppression (Appleton, 1983, p. 59). Indeed, when relativism is unchecked, "all that remains are competing interests, the power to promote those interests, and the ideological constructions to legitimate those interests" (Hunter, 1991, p. 313).

There are, therefore, among the many theorists and philosophers who would denote themselves as postmodernists, diverse perspectives as to the possibility—or even the advisability—of establishing and affirming among peoples a common ground that transcends differences.

However, to adhere to such criticism and discount as invalid and totalitarian any but a particularistic perception of reality and our place in it leads to unrestrained moral relativism, a situation which would render impotent *any* attempt at social transformation, postmodernist or otherwise. If, as these oppositional voices contend, there is no extracultural meta-language, then the standards of right conduct become culture bound. Without a language or understanding beyond that which is particular to an individual's experience and culture, there exist no means to "describe and analyze the concepts, beliefs, and social practices rooted in culture" (Strivens, 1992, p. 213). Where there are no shared commitments, lives have no meaning because the world has no meaning; all would have retreated, each into the silence of his or her private experiences. "When all our concerns have . . . been stripped to the common denominator of 'experience' we will have reached the last stage of nihilism" (Dreyfus, 1981, p. 136). In such a world, therefore, discussion about multicultural education becomes moot; indeed, any attempts at meaningful communication between and among individuals or groups would be considered not only pointless but impossible.

If we refuse to accept the systemic impoverishment of our schools and its subjugation of human spirit and allow ourselves to yield to the lure of what could be—if we truly desire to achieve the ideals of social justice, equality of access, and the defense of human dignity—we must turn from the nihilistic and seek to restore and promote human agency. It appears, then, that to uphold the rights and value of the individual, as one would envision in a democracy, necessitates "an elementary and somewhat universal agreement in the public realm about the criteria for distinguishing the social good from the socially destructive or about the rules of reason for making equitable public policy" (Hunter, 1991, p. 314).

We must find, therefore, broader and more relational contexts—a basic ethic which we can apply as an acceptable standard to our admittedly fallible human endeavors, however noble in intent. Carter, in his *The Culture of Disbelief* (1993), asserts that there are some broad values on which vast majorities of Americans tend to agree (p. 203); Etzioni (1993) illuminates these in an expansive way:

> That the dignity of all persons ought to be respected, that tolerance is a virtue and discrimination abhorrent, that peaceful resolution of conflicts is superior to violence, that generally truth telling is morally superior to lying, that democratic government is morally superior to totalitarianism and authoritarianism, that one ought to give a day's work for a day's pay, that saving for one's own and one's country's

future is better than squandering one's income and relying on others to attend to one's future needs (p. 259).

So it is that one initial step in our post-formal quest for contextualization is to return to a sense of community but not in a way that either tacitly or overtly coerces assimilation and necessitates subjugation and loss of cultural and personal historicity. Rather, we must fashion a community of humankind in which its diverse parts define themselves not just by the particularities of culture or social positionings but also over a range of common concerns and interests (Beyer, 1989; Carter, 1993; Dewey, 1916; Etzioni, 1993; Kincheloe, 1995). With our modernist emphasis on individualism, autonomy, and personal fulfillment, our nation has forsaken the affiliative, the collaborative, indeed the knowledge and awareness of context, that make possible the betterment of humankind on levels both collective and individual. Kincheloe (1995) characterizes this "social vertigo," endemic to postmodern hyperreality, as consequent to the separation of emotion from intellect, the substitution of affect for meaning, and the denigration of indigenous knowledge in the veneration of reason. Human experience, the production of knowledge, and the making of meaning are relational, not relative; so, therefore, must be any serious attempt to create an education in our schools that is liberating and empowering position itself and its inquiry in a relational, contextual framework. When all is seen and explored as part of a larger, interwoven tapestry, it may then be possible to reconnect with a sense of personal tradition and affiliative community now lost.

Through the hermeneutic of critical, post-formal thinking and dedication to the betterment of humankind, our individual and collective histories can become contextual and, once seen in the framework of being both fashioned by and subsumed in this admittedly dominant culture, take on a denotation and connotation much larger, richer, and more potentially transformational than when viewed exclusively as unique experiences of individuals.

Although helpful, and probably necessary, for our understanding and present discussion, so labeling these four aspects of post-formal thinking is reductionism that diminishes their collective, transformative power. Post-formal thinking is a process that is dynamic and recursive: Each of the four elements can exist only in the exercise of the others, and all—etymology, pattern, process, and contextualization—are a fluid hermeneutic through which we can rethink experience and the production of knowledge.

Resistance to Change

Having arrived at a direction for the reconstruction of educational experience, we must acknowledge that to presume unchallenged acceptance and immediate success of any change to the curricular and pedagogical status quo is naive. Indeed, the very diversity of the nation that our education strives to serve assures both challenge and debate. Multiple constituencies, the boundaries among which are fluid and oftentimes contextual, vie for control of our schools in order to assure redress as well as adoption of future curricula that is ideologically supportive of their particular interests. Since education in the United States is funded largely by the people, and since we would, presumably, strive for it to serve the people, it stands to reason that, at least in certain areas and on certain levels, our education should be responsive to the needs and desires of the people. However, the marginal success of the various waves of education reform over the years is due in no small part to the extreme reactive nature of our institutions of learning. What are seen as "low priority" groups or minority factions of discontent are either ignored or given token voice, while curricula and pedagogy are driven by larger, more organized, and more monied constituencies. However, history has shown that, over time, as the external context becomes more favorable to their interests, these "low-status" groups mobilize and the priorities of education are shifted once again. As Kirst (1984) explains, these "cycles of education policy leave lasting deposits as structural accretions" (p. 9), and it is this lack of substantive, meaningful change that has perpetuated a system of education that is bureaucratized and monolithic.

Therefore, if we are to positively refocus educational objectives in any lasting way, it seems both necessary and advisable to position our public schools such that they can be sensitive to, but not controlled by, the ephemeral desires, and sometimes spurious whims, of various interest groups. Of course this position, too, is paradoxical, for as we have seen *no* curricula or pedagogy, indeed no ideological approach to education, is value neutral or interest free. What, then, is "just" about establishing a philosophical base and moral framework for public education? Whose criteria will be used and whose ignored in order to fashion such a fundament?

Critics of a reconstructive, transformative postmodernist theory hasten to point out that there is implicit in the belief of a radical egalitarianism and non-marginalization of peoples a metanarrative that resounds with universalism and is profoundly normative (Dickman, 1993; Kimball, 1990). Although accurate, such criticism sidesteps, in its artful simplicity, the larger challenge facing education today. As has been previously discussed, our institutions of learning have always been and will always be reflective of a particular value system and political ideology. What remains, then, is to arrive at and establish a moral framework against which the merit of decisions pertaining to education in our democratic state will be judged. These moral principles should be, as much as any can be, universal, democratic, and reflective of both the tenor and intent of our Constitution and statute; as such, therefore, they will be defensible in both public and private arenas as well as in our courts of law.

These moral principles are more easily recognized and understood when contrasted with principles of self-interest or social advantage (Beyer and Wood, 1986, p. 5), and it is here the application of transformative critical theory via post-formal thinking seeks to take the higher ground. We must attend to the imperative of breaking with the historical reality of an American education that is driven by Capital and personal greed, is unequal in qualitative as well as quantitative terms, and is in countless ways perpetuating the economic, spiritual, and social repression of various groups of peoples. We must seek to embrace a moral perspective that will both formulate and inform a court of arbitration for the inevitable conflicts of interest and plays of power (Beyer and Wood, 1986, p. 5). It is for these reasons that a truly transformative theory of education will hold fast to principles of equality, social justice, and the defense of human dignity.

However noble this intent, conflict will inevitably arise *within* these attempts to fashion education in ways that hearken to principles moral and egalitarian, for the balance of assuring distributive justice, leveling playing fields, and creating equality of access is hard to achieve, harder to maintain, and frequently pits against one another desires and values equally worthwhile and "moral." To further complicate transformative intent is the issue of who presumes to speak for the marginzalized when we fashion an education that gives them voice. As Martin (1993) points out, "groups, oppressed and otherwise, are not monolithic" and, consequently, do not necessarily, or even probably, have a single set of interests (p. 224). Martin's argument on this point, succinct and well founded, is given further weight by the fact that most individuals find themselves to be members of "multiple and often contradictory social positionings" (Ellsworth, 1989, p. 316). Not much imagination is required to project how such multiple positionings would create value conflicts that transect group boundaries. Ellsworth applied a radical, critical discourse and dialectic based on students' personal experience and subjective knowing to a course she taught at the University of Wisconsin, Madison; her experience in those months highlighted how such intra- and inter-group conflicts can surface and inform the levels of trust, risk, fear, and desire in the classroom (Ellsworth, 1989).

Where, then, are we left in this conundrum of fashioning an education for the twenty-first century that is morally responsive and liberating without becoming, as critics fear, as repressive and culturally normative as the system it seeks to displace? Potential conflicts cannot be explained away, for they are both real and inevitable, but to not strive to dismantle oppressive institutions of power and to not work concertedly toward attainment of equality, social justice, and the defense of human dignity, however ideal, is to perpetuate a situation that is ultimately self-destructive and nihilist in its passivity. Post-formal thinking provides educators with the pedagogical tools to work toward and ultimately achieve a fundamental recreation of our education.

Conclusion

Through a pedagogy of post-formal thinking, the need for a multicultural education added to curricula would become redundant, for a post-formal approach would render any curricula as many-faceted, diverse, and multicultural as the students they serve. Our concern may begin with ourselves and our families, "but it rises inexorably to the long-imagined community of mankind" (Etzioni, 1993, p. 266). As educators, our vision *must* be more synoptic; we must strive to build for a collective future as shareholders in this planet without forsaking our personal heritage, histories, and potential for individual purpose.

References

Appleton, N. (1983). *Cultural pluralism in education: Theoretical foundations*. New York: Longman.

Banks, J.A. (1991). A curriculum for empowerment, action, and change. In C.E. Sleeter (Ed.), *Empowerment through multicultural education* (pp. 125–141). Albany: SUNY Press.

Banks, J.A. (1992). Multicultural education: Nature, challenges, and opportunities. In C. Diaz (Ed.), *Multicultural education for the 21st century* (pp. 23–37). Washington, DC: National Education Association.

Beyer, L.E. (1989). Perspectives and imperatives: The social and educational conditions for democracy. *Journal of Curriculum and Supervision, 4*, 178–186.

Beyer, L.E. (1992). Discourse or moral action? A critique of postmodernism. *Educational Theory, 42,* 371–393.

Beyer, L. and Wood, G. (1986). Critical inquiry and moral action in education. *Educational Theory, 36,* 1–14.

Bonnett, A. (1993). *Radicalism, anti-racism, and representation.* New York: Routledge.

Carter, S.L. (1993). *The culture of disbelief: How American law and politics trivialize religious devotion.* New York: HarperCollins.

Cherryholmes, C.H. (1988). *Power and criticism: Poststructural investigations in education.* New York: Teachers College Press.

Dewey, J. (1916). *Democracy and education.* New York: Macmillan.

Diaz, C.F. (1992). Resistance to multicultural education: Concerns and responses. In C.F. Diaz (Ed.), *Multicultural education for the 21st century* (pp. 201–217). Washington DC: National Education Association.

Dickman, H. (1993). *The imperiled academy.* New Brunswick: Transaction Publishers.

Dreyfus, H.L. (1981). Knowledge and human values. In D. Sloan (Ed.), *Toward the recovery of wholeness: Knowledge, education, and human values* (pp. 135–148). New York: Teachers College Press.

Ellsworth, E. (1989). Why doesn't this feel empowering? Working through the repressive myths of critical pedagogy. *Harvard Educational Review, 59,* pp. 297–324.

Etzioni, A. (1993). *The spirit of community.* New York: Crown Publishers.

Foucault, M. (1972). *The archaeology of knowledge* (A. M. Sheridan, Trans.). London: Tavistock.

Giroux, H.A. (1983). *Critical theory and educational practice.* Victoria, Australia: Deakin University Press.

Giroux, H.A. (1988). Border pedagogy in the age of postmodernism. *Journal of Education, 170,* 162–180.

Giroux, H.A. (1992a). *Border crossings: Cultural workers and the politics of education.* New York: Routledge.

Giroux, H.A. (1992b). Curriculum, multiculturalism, and the politics of identity. *NASSP Bulletin, 76*(548), 1–11.

Gollnick, D.M., and Chinn, P. C. (1994). *Multicultural education in a pluralistic society.* New York: Macmillan College Publishing.

Harré, R. (1983). *Personal being: A theory for individual psychology.* Oxford: Blackwell.

Hunter, J.D. (1991). *Culture wars: The struggle to define America.* New York: HarperCollins.

Kimball, R. (1990). *Tenured radicals.* New York: Harper and Row.

Kincheloe, J.L. (1995). *Toil and trouble.* New York: Peter Lang.

Kincheloe J. and Steinberg, S. (1993). A tentative description of post-formal thinking. *Harvard Educational Review* 63, 296–320.

Kirst, M.W. (1984). *Who controls our schools: American values in conflict.* New York: W.H. Freeman.

Lynch, J. (1992). *Education for citizenship in a multicultural society.* New York: Cassell.

Martin, J. (1993). The university as agent of social transformation. In H. Dickman (Ed.), *The imperiled academy* (pp. 203–237). New Brunswick: Transaction Publishers.

Nandy, A. (1992). State. In W. Sachs (Ed.), *The development dictionary* (pp. 264–274). London: Zed Books Ltd.

Nieto, S. (1992). *Affirming diversity: The sociopolitical context of multicultural education.* White Plains, NY: Longman.

Nixon, J. (1985). *Multicultural education.* New York: Basil Blackwell.

Rich, J.M. (1988). *Innovations in education: Reformers and their critics.* Boston: Allyn and Bacon.

Searle, J. (1990, December 6). The storm over the university. *The New York Review*, 34–42.

Shotter, J. (1993). *Cultural politics of everyday life.* Toronto: University of Toronto Press.

Strivens, J. (1992). The morally educated person in a multicultural society. In J. Lynch, C.

Modgil and S. Modgil (Eds.), *Cultural diversity and the schools: Education for cultural diversity* (pp. 211–231). London: Falmer Press.

Tierney, W.G. (1989). Cultural politics and the curriculum in postsecondary education. *Journal of Education, 171*, 72–88.

Vygotsky, L.S. (1986). *Thought and language.* Cambridge, MA: MIT Press.

Wertsch, J. V. (1995). The need for action in sociocultural research. In J. V. Wertsch, P. Del Rio, and A. Alvarez (Eds.), *Sociocultural studies of mind* (pp. 56–74). Cambridge: Cambridge University.

CHAPTER ELEVEN

Instructional Systems
Peeking Under the Fig Leaf: Are There Post-formal Parts in Instructional Systems?

Vicki K. Carter

Introduction

> Guard me from those thoughts men think
> In the mind alone
> He that sings a lasting song
> Thinks in a marrow bone.
> —William Butler Yeats

There is a collection of multi-media educational software called ADAM. Major components of the ADAM product include diagrams, illustrations, and other supporting materials for studying human anatomy and physiology. When using the software there are some display alternatives. For example, a male or a female body may be chosen and certain skin tones are selectable. And yes, a fig leaf is also an option in order to hide genitals and breasts from view. The person using ADAM elects this "feature" to be either on or off. When configuring the ADAM system a teacher has the option to lock (FICUS = TRUE or FALSE is the command) the fig leaves in place so that it is impossible for students to completely unclothe either Adam or Eve.

Why introduce a chapter about instructional design and post-formal thinking with a fig leaf? First, there is the idea of the fig leaf in its literal and traditional role, that of concealing parts of the human body often considered to be offensive, provocative, or "too advanced" for certain viewers' age or experience. I do not wish to explore here the moral or value-laden issues associated with public display of the unclothed human body, real or pictorial. Instead, consider the leaves symbolically.

How, as a leaf hides parts of the body, might it also prevent acceptance, understanding, and full participation of that same body as integral to the way learners come to know and understand their world? This symbolic covering may eliminate, as well, potential insights into feelings, pain, and emotions embedded in experiencing the body *and* the process of thinking as a totality, a whole. Even in its symbolic or metaphoric sense, the fig leaf conceals, camouflages, and inhibits.

In terms of post-formal thinking, metaphorical fig leaves applied to educational theories and structures, such as those underlying instructional systems and design, cover and restrict exploration, critique, and accommodation of postmodern pedagogical forms. Because the subtle influences of modernist masculine logocentric thought have been well hidden behind modern cognitive theory, its assumptions and inadequacies have remained largely unexposed and unexamined in most academic disciplines. Given their decidedly traditional roots, how well do instructional systems facilitate and enhance teaching and learning in a postmodern world? Can the formalism of instructional systems sustain learners who are increasingly defined by globalization, electronic isolation, and the socio-psychological maladies described in Kincheloe's explanation of post-formal thinking in this book? Increasingly, the theoretical inertia and ongoing maintenance of educational homeostasis obstruct consideration and adaptation of alternative ways of thinking.

True to its modernist roots, instructional design (and its historical parent, educational psychology) promotes rational analytical linear thinking; it is comprised of Eurocentric canonical thinking which adheres to standards and can be measured. Instructional systems and technologies very often connect people via wires to machines and to each other but seldom connect them in an emotional or human sense. And so orthodox education and traditional instructional design, both based upon educational psychology, sever head from sensation and knowing from feeling. Consciousness or the mind, in formal Piagetian thinking, is viewed as separate from physical acts and enjoyment of the senses. Except as input/output devices, the physical and sensual come to be seen as intrusive and irrelevant elements in a learning process which is theorized to be purely cognitive and completely abstract.

In any case a fig leaf does have the effect of creating curiosity about what might be found underneath; surely there must be something very interesting associated with that which is hidden from us. Accordingly, underneath this metaphorical fig leaf lies a means to explore whether or not instructional technologies can accommodate any or all of the four features of post-formal thought. This chapter will peek under the fig leaf in order to compare and contrast the field of instructional systems and its closely associated partner educational technologies with the tenets of post-formal thought. Are there parts of instructional systems to be discovered that can support and contribute to post-formal ways of thinking? How strong or tenuous are the connections between the features of post-formal thinking, instructional design and educational technologies? Which, if any, of post-formal thinking's attributes might benefit from, or be enhanced by instructional design processes, and which ones would be better accommodated by other forms of teaching and learning?

Understanding the Foundations of Instructional Systems
The field of instructional systems is based on the theory and practice of cognitive science, educational psychology, and communications theory, with its roots in military and weaponry applications. To obviate this relationship, a perusal of educational psychology texts turns up references to judging student performance only by clear measurable standards, adding up the amount learned and the number of errors, and discussing vital higher-order intellectual abilities which, although elusive, must be pinned down in concrete terms to be considered valid desirable outcomes (Anderson and Faust, 1974; Klausmeier and Ripple, 1971; Woolfolk, 1993). Similarly, instructional design texts demand precise goals and objectives and refer to educational aims as 1) what to provide for or *do to* the learner (emphasis added), 2) what the learner should develop in the way of internal capacities, and 3) what the learner should be able to do as a result of learning. Instructional design theory is described as comprehensive and generalizable to a wide range of situations. Additionally, some of the instructional design literature suggests that systematic design methodology will be increasingly important because of contemporary movements toward more educational accountability. (Jonassen, 1988; Roblyer, 1988; Romiszowski, 1981).

In most contemporary design of instructional systems, educational technologies play a major role. Increasingly in education, learning via technology has become a powerful center for communication of information, representation, and image as well as an emerging source of present-day teaching and learning processes. In many ways, machines, not human beings, have become models for construction of values and attitudes. Heinich (1970) has defined instructional technology as a "complex, integrated process involving people, procedures, ideas, devices, and organization, for analyzing problems and devising, implementing, evaluating, and managing solutions to those problems in situations in which learning is purposive and controlled" (1985, p. 439). Without question, instructional technologies are methods for structuring the experience of education, concerned not just with controlling it on a conscious level but in their very forms tending to bound how education is thought about. The learner (and thinker and knower) is governed and processed as an object, an object "with no history, no future, no self. Educational technology has turned the subject into the object" (Muffoletto, 1994, p. 26). In many ways, instead of pedagogy and pedagogues, education involves cybernetics and "cybergogues," reason enough for forward-thinking educators and cultural workers to become critically aware of the growing role of instructional systems in the educational milieu.

The discipline of instructional systems is characterized and delineated by formalism. Traditionally, mainstream instructional design practice is scientifically grounded in the ideals of modernist thinking— in other words within the core hubris of the empirical, positivist, objective, and observable. The view within the field is that thinking, learning and instruction are constituted by behaviors that can be seen and cognitive skills that are identified, planned, and regulated. The practice of instructional design is based on very specific assumptions and scientific principles framed by verifiable, empirical data. In this discipline, its "fundamentalists" avow that educators who suggest knowledge is founded on collaboration or that truth is relative cannot even be called instructional designers (Merrill, 1996). Although perhaps not this extreme, many of the field's theorists and practitioners come from an elemental technical rationalist perspective, one which separates and distinguishes process, content, and medium.

The process of creating an instructional system involves the breaking down of learning into sequences and discrete models and modules. It is, for the most part, prearranged and linear. The jargon in the field involves terminology such as yardsticks, instructional interventions, definitions of discrepancies, prompting, and outcome criteria. The learning process is mapped, charted, plotted, and blueprinted. In terms of context, it is most often the context of the instructional designer and educational technologist whose language, backgrounds, experiences, ideological groundings, and theoretical underpinnings are embedded in the designs. Philosophically, the discipline is grounded in scientific process and progress and by a belief in a material reality. The inclusion of emotion, for example, would not be understood as a mode of perception within its methods and techniques for building instruction (Muffoletto, 1994; Reeves, 1996; Romiszowski, 1981; Yeaman, 1994). With this in mind, Glendinning's (1990) admonition that education must question technologies that undergird rationality as the cornerstone of human potential and technical progress as the overwhelming measure of social progress is timely and germane to this topic, which is awash in technological accessories.

Post-formal thinking, in its attempt to move beyond Piagetian stage theory and form a substantive body of literature which valorizes other ways of thinking and knowing, will necessarily have to contend with a world incrementally defined by technology and the hyperreal. Technologies, including educational technologies, are put into place by large societal institutions and tend to benefit privileged sectors of society. Educational technologies, in particular, are often viewed as the apex of human consciousness and a symbol of how humans and human thinking can be perfected. Ironically, computers, reflective of a mechanistic paradigm and an assumption that human psychology is reducible to rules and elements, have come to be viewed as a mythological invention innately and automatically capable of being liberating, democratizing, and revolutionary. Given the abstract, detached, and totalizing "nature" of instructional design and its powerful technological partners, it is important to understand how the systems it constructs coincide and collide with the ideas cultivated by post-formal thought. In what ways can post-formal thinking benefit from or co-exist with the discipline of instructional design and likewise take advantage, when appropriate, of educational technologies? Alternatively, how does the instructional design process inhibit, suppress, or devalue ways of thinking that move beyond the modernist techno-rational paradigm?

A Real-life Example

Perhaps a recent experience of the author will provide real-world context to a discussion of these foundational concepts. As a member of a recently formed instructional design team, I was meeting with my group for the purpose of presenting, reflecting upon, and coming to an agreement about our individual philosophical points of view on the design process. We hoped to arrive at an approach to teaching and learning on which we would base future design efforts and select and use educational technologies. To that end, we had all been charged with "sketching out a personal instructional design model." I put this in quotes because I took the task quite literally and spent several hours over a weekend fabricating a comprehensive and notably unartistic attempt at a model complete with circles, colors, and three dimensions.

In my representation, I placed the learner in the center along with the interface to the course or module and associated learning activities. In a web-like fashion I connected the learner with both a personal "world" and an educational "world." The learner's personal world included her private or inside world, surrounded by her environment and learning context including time, space, institution, and location. The personal world was encircled by social, public, and outside contexts along with the learner's socio-historical and socio-political positionality. The corresponding educational world was constituted by conventional components of the instructional design process such as learning activities, outcomes, needs analysis, assessment, and authoring of the courseware presented non-linearly and overlapping. These activities were rooted or embedded in the customary systems development paradigm of analysis, design, development/programming, implementation, and evaluation. I drew these constructs as iterative in nature and each was continually being revisited as the course or module evolved. Surrounding the design process was a critical analysis of the teaching/learning context including the examination of power, privilege, culture, stakeholders, freedom, equality, and social justice.

Not being particularly enamored of models and charts, I was rather proud of my attempt and looked forward to the philosophical and theoretical discussion with an experienced staff of instructional design professionals. When individual efforts were laid out on the conference room table, all of them were linear, flowchart-like depictions. Steps were numbered and arrows pointed from one step to the next. Mine, of course, was very different from the others and upon inspection by my peers it was accompanied by expressions such as "hmmm" "that's unusual," and "I like the colors." Eventually, when my creation came up for discussion, I was asked why power and privilege would be considered a part of an educational design project. I mounted my best explanation as to why these factors were of substantial importance, but my co-workers appeared to be increasingly bewildered and unwilling to pursue an ongoing dialogue. The final comment I received about the model was that it just wasn't clear *in what order* the design steps were to be done.

What this experience illuminates is the formal, hyper-rational and non-critical view of developing instruction permeating most of the field of instructional systems and the design of educational and training materials for public schools, higher education, and the workplace. Although the resulting course materials may be extraordinarily attractive, incorporating multimedia resources and including facilities such as video, the World Wide Web, graphics and sound, underneath the fig leaf lies a firmly structured approach to thinking about the design of education and extremely formalized perspectives on meta-cognition or "thinking about thinking." This example paints a self-portrait of instructional systems professionals immersed in lockstep reductionist processes, methodologies, and techniques in pursuit of clearly defined goals and outcomes. It is a significant mental stretch to imagine most instructional systems professionals as cultural workers or emancipatory educators who understand or acknowledge the role of power and privilege or who are aware of the ill-effects of contemporary obsessions with details, measurements, and fact-based rule-following schooling. Instructional systems can be very much embodiments of such absurd reductionism as learning how to start a car by following the Vehicle Starting Inventory Checklist (VSIC) described in Joe Kincheloe's introduction.

Beyond Figs and Formalism?
In previous work, Kincheloe and Steinberg (1993) and Kincheloe (1995) outlined four features of post-formal thinking including etymology, pattern, process, and contextualization. These attributes of post-formal thought form the basis for the following comparison with corresponding theoretical, philosophical and practical characteristics of instructional design. This kind of extra-paradigmatic critique is helpful in understanding how cultural studies can function as an interdisciplinary and counter-disciplinary way of seeing that reveals, integrates, and complements modernist disciplinary discourses.

Etymology: To Babelize or De-Babelize?
The best-established and most-often-applied instructional design paradigm rests upon the scientific process, the quantitative and "separate, material reality that exists apart from the beliefs of individuals, groups, or societies" (Reeves, 1996). Subscribers to objectivist approaches to designing instruction believe education is currently fluttering in unscientific breezes, that "people are anxious for answers," and when answers are not instantaneous, "the void is filled with wild speculation and philosophical extremism." In fact, "persons who claim that

knowledge is founded on collaboration rather than empirical science, or who claim that all truth is relative, are not instructional designers. They have disassociated themselves from the discipline of instructional design" (Merrill, 1996, lines 9-12, 30-31).

Although Merrill expressed the standpoint of many instructional systems professionals, he was partially reacting to subjective philosophies cropping up in the field. For example, some professionals adopt a pragmatic and eclectic stance, mixing and matching methods according to the tasks at hand and the tools available. Others follow almost religiously their favorite recipe, outline, or model. In contrast, the constructivist contingent believes people shape their reality individually and collectively; they see curricula as value filled and contextual, affected by culture and influenced through multiple perspectives (Reeves, 1996). This more qualitative approach to research and design has been dubbed by Merrill as helping the structure of educational technology slide "toward the sea of constructo-babble" (Merrill, 1996, lines 152-153). Underpinning Merrill's statement is an unhappy awareness of the current ebb, flow, and changeable nature of bodies of knowledge (Kincheloe and Steinberg, 1993). Between traditional instructional systems professionals and the constructivists exists a fundamental etymological gap about what instructional design theory is and whether approaches such as those embraced by constructivists are even part of the field's theoretical base. (Bednar, Cunningham, Duffy and Perry; 1992; Carroll, 1990; Dick, 1991; Reigeluth, 1989)

Most radical and even rarer in the field of instructional systems are the critical theorists and postmodernists whose presence, if not their influence, is slowly being acknowledged. Proponents of critically-oriented design philosophies attempt to deconstruct the multiple texts hidden within learning materials developed by instructional designers while at the same time adhering to the notion that truths are not grand narratives but instead are small and situational (Reeves, 1996). In a critical philosophical and conceptual frame of reference, instructional technology can never be seen as neutral or as a way to guarantee progress or outcomes (Yeaman, 1994).

Given Merrill's point of view and Reeves' and Yeaman's interpretations of the foundational beliefs of instructional systems, understanding the etymology of the field is critical to understanding its practice in contemporary learning environments. Being versed in the origins of a discipline and how they may insidiously restrict the vision of its practitioners (Kincheloe and Steinberg, 1993) is crucial if instructional design is to grapple with its own limitations and move toward a point of view such as the critical accommodation described in Kincheloe's introductory essay. Forward-looking instructional systems specialists must confront advocates of a rigorous and entrenched set of theories evolved from military-industrial weapons development and deeply embedded in cognitive science. Post-formal instructional designers clearly would need to become aware of how that inheritance connects to current and future educational practice. Educational technology, and its link to the history of education in general, is joined philosophically and economically with positivism, progress, reductionism and empirical science. And so these genealogical roots do not legitimize or easily facilitate intuitive, emotional, or indigenous ways of thinking (Feenberg, 1991; Merrill; 1996; Muffoletto, 1994).

In addition to ADAM, and speaking of techno-babble, another piece of currently available software is called the De-Babelizer. Its function, not surprisingly, is to translate a variety of languages and protocols and homogenize them. The De-Babelizer converts a technically diverse world into a standard and easily understood meta-language. It turns sundry conversations into a monologue. De-Babelizing software is a suitable analogy for understanding etymology and the instructional design process because instruction designed for several, hundreds, perhaps thousands of students is necessarily a process of standardization. For postmodernists such as Lyotard (1984), however, there could be no universal meta-language; rules of language "games" were not able to be reduced from one to another. Lyotard's postmodern argument, although critiqued by Shotter (1993) as continuing to explain knowledge as part of a rules-based orderly system, was nevertheless in stark contrast to the notion of the universal truth of science and reason. The universal meta-narrative is symbolized by this software which attempts to make language rules and language itself transferable and generalizable. Much of the ability to market and distribute software designs hinges upon the elimination of difference along with an expectation of overall outcomes that can be generalized and measured. This very process imposes conformity, eliminates variability, and is etymologically consistent with its military-industrial inheritance. The De-Babelizer program with its mission to eliminate myriad protocols and rampant techno-babble effectively represents these unitotalitarian principles. Designing weapons and, apparently, designing instruction are both much easier to invent, map out, deliver, and monitor if everyone speaks and understands the same language. This basic functionality, that of building general and standard products inherent in software design and distribution, is in stark contrast to the multi-vocal, contextualized, and flexible features of post-formal thinking.

Correspondingly, the conventions of instructional design are very much problem-solving versus problem-detecting. Its very language delineates the mission of seeking solutions by asking designers to artic-ulate the instructional problem. This paradigm does not necessarily eliminate the capacity to ask unique questions, but it does make it con-siderably more difficult by espousing a formalized and procedural step-by-step formula for defining instructional goals, objectives and sequencing. Furthermore, because instructional designs are typically intended to be accessed by large audiences, even if unique questions are asked, it is not easy to incorporate the possibility of uncommon ways to confront these questions or innovative ways to explore alternatives. Within the field, were it to embrace post-formal thinking, an etymolog-ical and self-critical stance would always consider unforeseen possibil-ities and ingrained limitations. Given its etymology educators must question when, where, and under what circumstances are systems of instruction most beneficial to learners and similarly when must this form of education be supplemented, enhanced, or omitted entirely from consideration?

Leafy Patterns

Kincheloe (1995) illustrated the post-formal feature of pattern by describing implicate and explicate orders. He pointed to the special learning experiences that result when various levels of connections are revealed between mind and life forces. In a similar vein, Briggs and Peat (1989) in their explanation of chaos theory felt the idea of nuance was significant for thinking about different ways of knowing and under-standing the world. They believed by searching for the simple and fun-damental, all kinds of complexities and different dimensions could be uncovered. In this very act of seeking, the interweaving of life and learning could be grasped. Post-formal ways of thinking would recog-nize and augment these moments of extreme sensitivity and flashes of insight "long enough to permit something new to bloom there" (p. 195) while formal ways of knowing would dismiss or even suppress such thoughts because they could disrupt the theoretical base and threaten the rational and customary.

On the surface, it would appear that instructional systems and tech-nologies would restrict pattern recognition to that of the explicate order.

In analyzing educational opportunities, patterns and categories usually emerge upon which instruction is based and sequenced. Critical paths through these patterns are constructed. Content is framed according to parts, kinds, and categories. Hierarchical levels and degrees of complexity are identified. Learning is classified by domains, structures, and paths; although they may branch off occasionally, all routes converge in order to guarantee the desired performance outcomes (Jonassen, 1988; Romiszowski, 1981). However, in the act of analyzing how to create instruction, in that very search for explicate patterns, may lie revelation of implicate orders. Ironically, the concept of pattern, explicate and implicate, deep and large, could be the feature of post-formal thinking best supported by a counter-cultural instructional design. In the analysis and the thought processes associated with designing instruction many patterns are recognized and connected, similarities and differences are revealed. Hidden patterns emerge and can be included in designs. Modern technologically-mediated resources such as Gopher services and the World Wide Web, when incorporated with designs permitting branching out from the confines of conventional tutorials and structures, allow learners to discover and blend other places, spaces, and locations into their study. Incorporating a means of escape, a way of unearthing routes to diverse people and places, gives access to non-hegemonic points of view and voices speaking against a dominant culture. This kind of possibility is diametrically opposed to the inclusivity and insularity of many classrooms and instructional "texts." An instructional design of this sort could, arguably, play a major role in support of post-formal thinking initiatives.

Computers, networks, and instructional designs are not good at nuance or sensitivity to disruptions in pattern. On the other hand, given an open versus a closed system, one able to extend the classroom beyond the institution and help learners make connections, the possibility of recognizing deeper patterns and hidden structures is made more accessible and achievable. In the process of branching out, learners and teachers can search for connections among seemingly disparate topics and experiences. The straightforward quantitative technique of search algorithms and hypertext links support both connected and discovery kinds of learning which may juxtapose locations, spaces, and people in unexpected and revealing ways. The potential is to trigger subjective modalities of perceiving and knowing the world, opening up discourses currently impossible within places of school and work, and contradicting the closely held assumptions of mainstream thought. The coming together of a diverse group of learners, via educational MOOs and MUDs for example, creates opportunities for environments to be built and challenged, discourses examined and changed, and personas to be examined and modified. Learners can step out of bodies and transcend time and space. Accordingly, patterns change, disappear, and emerge; links are broken and built. As Kincheloe and Steinberg (1993) pointed out, the nature of interconnections shapes the web of reality and its form, and the implications of recognizing the reflexivity between self and positionality are revolutionary. Integrating resources such as the Internet and other active collaborative forums into instructional designs can be a place of embarkation on a robust pattern-seeking journey.

On the other hand, the features and potentialities of virtual realities, hypertext and hypermedia incorporated within a critical approach to instructional design are not without caveats. If disengagement, low affect, and alienation from modern life are symptomatic of cognitive illness and socio-psychological schizophrenia, virtual selves and lives consumed by electronic presences may exacerbate these circumstances. If life becomes increasingly virtual, does this alter the meaning of implicate and explicate? Or, as Baudrillard (Bayard and Knight, 1995) asked, what is the meaning of history, what is historical reality, in a world which has become increasingly virtual? If "human beings cannot be simply separated from the context that have produced them" (Kincheloe and Steinberg, 1993, p. 310), then conditions such as virtual reality, virtual history, and copies without originals introduce contradiction, creating proclivities for disengagement and living a prosthetic life, especially in terms of understanding the nature of imitation, difference, self, and other. Therefore a serious and ongoing questioning of the influence of a virtual life upon context must take place in sites of teaching and learning if mediated lesson designs and technologically supported decontextualized environments are not to create, reproduce, and magnify cognitive maladies such as alienation, destruction of community, and confounding of identity.

Process: Coloring Inside the Leaf

In contrast to that of pattern, the idea of process as a feature of post-formal thinking is, more than likely, the least accommodated by instructional systems. In the same way as traditional reading materials are texts, instructional designs, especially those supported by multi-media, are also texts to be read by teachers and learners. Designs are full of hidden assumptions, embedded codes, sedimented meanings and values.

Moreover, educational software itself accesses a bounded body of knowledge—a serious shortcoming compounded by the limitations it subsequently passes on to its audience (Bracey, 1990). Unfortunately, teachers seldom read instructional designs as texts, and because of the situated and individuated nature of instructional technologies, the reactions and dilemmas of the learners are hardly ever "read" either. Simplistic, narrow, and poorly designed mediated instruction can sometimes trap learners within a design where students cannot extricate themselves without providing a correct response. "Success" is predefined for learners; goals are set according to deviations from norms; expected outcomes are measured and recorded. Unexpected learning outcomes or insights are difficult if not impossible to recognize or reward. Creativity and imagination are almost "built out" rather than built into processes which are, for the most part, sequential accumulations of detail and reactions, many times without comprehensive and substantive thought acting as an impediment to an essentially constipated process (Kincheloe and Steinberg, 1993; Reeves, 1996; Romiszowski, 1981; Yeaman, 1994).

Good pre-deployment testing of instructional design finds some of these procedural inadequacies, but the scientific mind set and psychological basis for designing instruction preclude much of what is inherently good in post-formal thinking's orientation toward creative and insightful processes. When instructional technologies are used, good teachers will take the strength of the content and critique its "text" using deconstructive methods to look for missing voices and absences, for silencing of under-represented groups, or for language which would express violence or oppression toward women, Afro-Americans or other non-mainstream student populations. For instance, the research of Belenky, Clinchy, Goldberger and Tarule (1986) found that women, who preferred and valued intuitive and subjective knowledge, always had to pay personal and social costs in a world which emphasized scientific, rational ways of thinking. As students, these women were at a disadvantage in today's learning environments and in the modern workplace. Unfortunately for women, indigenous people, and other marginalized populations, instruction in general and instructional design in particular often objectify and quantify people. As they define process they also process people and, in doing so, dehumanize them. When people begin to feel dehumanized they may, according to Elliott, be "caught within a global, computational network of random signifiers and cultural representations which seduce and tantalize, but ultimately fail to make sense" (1994, p. 157). Given the etymology of the field, it is understood and intended that proceduralizing and systemizing of instruction, valuing of business and military practices in management of human behavior, and computer-like models of thinking are desirable objectives for human beings. Thinking and learning in these kinds of instructional venues can therefore become painting, or rather thinking and learning, by the numbers. Perpetuating these formal ways of thinking has significant repercussions for understanding, appreciating, and promoting post-formal thought. (Bowers, 1988; Wells, 1986; Yeaman, 1994).

Peters (1995) studied knowledge and the legitimation of science in a postmodern and computerized era, particularly with regard to the thinking of Lyotard. Peters felt knowledge that cannot be exteriorized, translated, and processed into quantities of information—in other words, transformed into computer language—"will be abandoned" (p. 28). He expressed concern about technology's adherence to maximizing output, minimizing input (optimal performance), and using criteria of "efficiency rather than truth . . . or justice" (p. 34). From an economic and political perspective, Peters questioned whether production of knowledge for the purpose of selling and exchanging it was even legitimate or valid. If knowledge is outside of the knower, connecting thinking to the spiritual, empathetic, or emotional will become increasingly difficult as reproduction of technical ways of knowing, commodification of knowledge, and the subordination of thinking to sales and investment are progressively intertwined. Instructional systems best support these procedural ways of knowing and commodification of knowledge by privileging logical abstractions and systematic inquiry.

In contrast, instructional designs can assist and support "passions for knowing" (Belenky et al., 1986) through interfaces with and access to worldwide libraries, resources and databases. On the other hand these design processes, based on breaking the whole down into analyzable bits, do not promote a unified way of viewing one's lifeworld or connecting mind and body, spiritual and material, logic and feeling, or individual and nature. Educators concerned about technology and systematic ways of thinking would say these factors serve to further disconnect mind and body, magnifying rational, procedural, and scientific aspects of learning and knowing. This perspective was supported by the views of Gilligan who said "development itself comes to be identified with separation, and attachments appear to be developmental impediments, as is repeatedly the case in the assessment of women" (1982, p. 16). For the most part, processes within instructional systems contradict the goals and hopes of post-formal ways of thinking.

The Power of Context, But Whose?

Educational technologies and instructional systems research acknowledge that the field's greater strengths are in delivery and presentation of content (Bracey, 1990; Reeves, 1996). If, as Kincheloe and Steinberg have suggested, context is more important than content, how does the artificial context created by educational technologies affect educative processes? What threads are woven into the "fabric of relevance" (1993, p. 314)? For example, proponents of situated learning base their efforts upon learners carrying out tasks and solving realistic "authentic" problems which are often contextualized within artificial computer-based environments. Tasks are sequenced to guide students through the knowledge acquisition process toward a successful conclusion. In this baffling scenario there is a confounding and paradoxical contradiction in the juxtaposition of authentic problems inside simulated environments.

Ken Wilber's (1993) study of consciousness as pluridimensional is helpful when considering context in terms of systems of instruction. Comparing consciousness to a spectrum, Wilber used the analogy of a range of electromagnetic radiation made up of many forms such as infrared and ultraviolet; the spectrum was constituted by various bands or levels. In this view, a multi-layered range of consciousness coalesced into an integrated continuum, thereby uniting disparate Eastern and Western thought about the nature of consciousness and knowledge. Wilber focused on Western dualistic knowledge characterized by the symbolic, objective, verifiable, and quantifiable, contrasting it to non-dualistic Eastern approaches which sought transcendence of self. The West's overwhelming valuing of symbolic and inferential modes of knowing was an inherently dualistic concept, preventing knowledge and consciousness from being enriched by the intimate, direct, non-dualistic forms of Eastern thought. In order to reconcile the opposites of the dual and non-dual, Wilber suggested viewing consciousness as a single spectrum able to be perceived and experienced at different levels or positions on the spectrum.

Wilbur (1993) described at length how Western consciousness confused its map, or heuristic, with the actual territory or terrain, a concept easily applied to a critique of systems thinking. The tool, the heuristic, the model, and the procedures became reality; thinking became the tool, and these artificial constructions became naturalized and reified. For learners, the essence of their consciousness was at the mercy of heuristics. In Wilbur's view, the map determined what was discovered.

In instructional systems the map or symbolic representation functions as a learner's reality, but clearly it is not. Worse, as the cleverness of innovative technologies is continuously glorified, and their supporting doctrines and modularized development techniques are brought into the classroom and extended classroom more frequently, educators consciously and unconsciously promote and defend these mind-body, reality-illusive dualisms. As Wilbur (1993) pointed out, the world is then understood as broken and fragmented, "sliced to bits" and afterwards presented as though it had always been that way. Consequently, as Wilbur remarked, "social conceptions have become individual perceptions" and Western thought has "thoroughly overstepped the usefulness of the map by almost totally confusing it with the actual territory" (p. 218). This phenomenon caused a paradox, a contradiction, because maps inherently represented dualisms and pointed in different directions, thereby governing action because of "the manner in which we divide and delineate reality" (p. 222). Therefore when systems or models of instruction were applied to learning the process of abstracting necessarily addressed only what was observable, erasing all other forms of knowing. Consequently the practical and useful act of making maps must be complemented by non-dualistic schools of thought in order to access more levels of the spectrum and reduce the risk of the maps owning both their cartographers and the traveling public.

If one of the purposes of education is transformation as well as adaptation and understanding, instructional systems must become more attuned to the atomization, attenuated relationships, and disengagement of learners which its orthodox models now assume and reproduce. In learning environments there are always crucial contextual, spacial, and temporal variables generally unaccounted for in mediated instructional systems and its rubric of efficiency and instrumental rationality. In essence, the product of instructional design is a model based on designers' constructions and assumptions about what knowledge is. Unless designers also serve as pseudo-anthropologists, their products are restricted to their own disciplinary culture and socio-cultural positionality. Instructional systems and educational technologies, particularly through their use of multi-media affordances, colonize in ways other than through traditional educational text. Instructional design "texts" colonize representation, experience, and imagination, creating what Horkheimer described as a "technological veil" that is powerfully exploitive and indoctrinating. If people learn by mimicking, what is learned by mimesis of an imaginary, non-existent Other created by a multi-media producer? What are the implications of imitating the fictive, the non-real, and what kind of consciousness is formed as a result? What sorts of differences between self and Other exist within worlds created by instructional design? (Hess, 1995; Taussig, 1993).

Instructional designers create contexts within contexts, but the contexts they create are their own and are not necessarily comprehensible to every learner. For example, one instructional design strategy using multi-media technologies is to create microworlds and locate the learner within them in a way similar to video games where Mario is manipulated and put through his paces, faced with increasingly more difficult obstacles and situations. Whose worlds are these? Do they translate to real life? Does solving a problem in a microworld necessarily translate to solving a similar problem at work? It may, and sometimes does for students who are adept at formal ways of thinking and are able to abstract, connect, and transfer their understanding from one situation to another. But for students whose ways of thinking differ from the standards set by educational psychology and logocentric formats, coping with microworlds can be an unrewarding task at best, debilitating and alienating at worst. This pseudo-context can leave learning and thinking without an intimate personal framework while inducing and perpetuating the robot-like understanding of institutional gamesmanship required to survive in school and at work. It is this disconnected passionless gamesmanship that is so often bemoaned by faculty at all levels of education and by many supervisors in the workplace.

Damarin's perspective on ethics in instructional design was that "at its most extreme, instructional design is clearly anti-ethical in that it denies the voice of 'the learner' in the determination of the learner's need" (1994, p. 37). Damarin believed the needs of the designer were imposed upon the learner and that the work of designers (who are by and large white, male, and of European descent) was often far too remote from people the designs were intended to instruct. Moreover, ethical links to learners were unlikely to arise from standard instructional design models. This author's viewpoint resonated with that of Carol Gilligan (1982), whose studies indicated that connectedness among women was more hospitable (and therefore more ethical) than systems founded on just rules and laws. Mechthild Hart (1992) also expressed concern about forms of consciousness shaped outside a Western male instrumentally rational paradigm. Given the disconnected situations, facts, and fragments to which marginalized people were exposed, Hart wondered if linking fragments together or producing true knowledge or self-knowledge under these circumstances was even possible, "a situation which should be of prime concern to education" (p. 171). As Shotter warned, designs based on analytical formats created a "monological, ahistorical, detached, theoretical account that can specify ahead of time the order of things" (1993, p. 45). Accordingly, technologically mediated instruction can be seen as overly explanatory, disconnected, fixated on immediacy, the literal, and the visual, not facilitating thinking and learning that is self-representational or internal.

New dimensions of contextual issues are illuminated by Shotter's (1993) challenge to mainstream psychology, his reconsideration of the nature of setting, and his notion of the intersubjectivity and tacit knowledge characterized by a different kind of "knowing." Shotter's formulation of a "third kind of knowing" or "knowing from within" blurred the boundaries between self and social. This third way of knowing involved ontological connections and relationships which understood that people lived inside a culture as well as existing as natural beings. For modern psychology, knowing from within meant that cognition was not self-contained. Rather, knowledge and learning were created at the moment, at the time of the discursive occasion and the making of meaning was a transaction negotiated among two or more parties involved in the process. According to Shotter, the security of systemic relationships and the assumptions of sharing a common discourse community as components of modernity's master systems of certainty had to be reconsidered and be based on the positionality of the participants. Because knowledge was generated within the moment, rule-based systems, mechanistic and behavioristic and cognitive psychological theories became partial and incomplete, creating significant barriers for recognizing and appreciating the chaotic disorderly nature of agency and socio-historical conditions.

For instructional systems, distance education and workforce training, and development, the implications of Shotter's (1993) work were overarchingly significant because it disposed of the notion of the abstract "self." In this view, designers of instruction must understand more than traditional psychological cognitive theory. Cultural workers must seek to understand the moral, political, and ethical issues inherent within discursive circumstances. Shotter's "knowing from within" connoted the developer of the instruction and the learner using the product do not necessarily share the occasion and may not even be a part of the same community of discourse. In fact, the "texts" generated within the standpoint of a closed instructional system may be completely unintelligible or meaningless for those who are genuine "others" and whose ways of knowing live outside the assumptions and boundaries of the schools of thought inhabited and accessed by instructional designers. In Shotter's view, outcomes were based on the joint action of the parties involved, not predetermined by the mechanistic or systematic cognitive processes a developer expected learners to follow when interacting with a structured learning process. People were not shaped just by mental or systematic cognitive process and "habits of thought" (p. 28) but instead shaped the moment by contributing their voice to a fluid, flexible, idiosyncratic context. As Shotter pointed out, knowing and understanding were rationally invisible. He expressed dismay that knowing from within, a foundational form of common sense, was often dismissed by academics in favor of representational-referential theories or methods which inflated "monologic, systematic, theoretical, surveyable 'realities' of the individual mind—realities which can be thought, but in which people cannot live" (p. 143).

If education is viewed in terms of personal and public interconnection, understanding, knowledge and skills are then configured by a unity of mind and body. In crafts and skilled labor elements of distance promote critical awareness and the abilities to make judgments. Aspects of mimetic nearness which engender a sense of the material and its qualities are also involved. Mimetic elements draw upon what is real and tangible while the creative individual is trying to understand the processes involved and fabricate an intimate form of knowledge. The dialectical nature of nearness and distance, control and mimesis, touch and thought create a tangible reality which a mediated learning atmosphere is incapable of simulating. In one case knowledge and reality come together, in the other the interaction between the objectified learner and object of learning is unreal, severed, and frozen (Hart, 1992; Taussig, 1993; Zuboff, 1988). As Dewey (1966) described, bringing the educative potential to fruition required involving concrete actuality with a learner's thinking as well as sensuous capacities. Can such educative moments as this be captured in mediated learning and instructional designs?

In his review of the Rodney King trial, Macedo (1994) discussed how fragmentation of skills and bodies of knowledge deadened the senses, disturbing the ability to make linkages and resulting in a form of "not seeing." Design of instruction can accomplish this by blinding learners to the intent of the system and creating a wholly contained artificial social construction. Instructional systems can also create such perfect isolation from real world contexts that the learner becomes just another object, another representation along with the collection of virtual images, icons, graphics, and avatars. In these constructed worlds there is seldom subjective particularity or unique learner experience. The social forces shaping these worlds are not learner centered but designer centered. It is the designer's autobiography that is prominent. For the most part, the power to construct lies with the designer and with the tools of construction provided by the designer which make up and define what is valuable, important, and assumed.

Tools are another critical problematic and computers themselves are cultural tools. As Wertsch, del Río, and Alvarez said, tools were being "harnessed for a purpose other than the one that shaped its evolution" (1995, p. 27). This borrowing may very likely have consequences in terms of shaping actions "in ways that are not helpful or are even antithetical to our expressed intentions and assumptions about the design of the tools we employ" (p. 28). Specifically addressing the dilemma of the computer, del Río and Alvarez pointed out that although abstraction and decontextualization of meaning can be positive, the cultural control of action by mechanisms and tools were negative influences "in the form of the social and affective decontextualization of sense" or the psychological management of sense and emotion (1995, p. 228). Similarly, Mander (1992) argued that artifacts have immanent qualities stemming from, for instance, the effects of the political environment within which they originated. The intrinsic aspects of technologies determined how they were used and, it followed, the consequences of their use. The texts they gave birth to were not just educationally outcome driven but also circumscribed by the political and social. From this standpoint, Macedo strongly argued that preparation of future teachers as leaders and change agents will be unsuccessful if colleges of education "continue to advocate the use of neatly packaged instructional programs that are presented as the panacea for difficulties students face in the acquisition of prepackaged knowledge" (1994, p. 152).

Mander has also expressed concern that as linear objective knowledge grows even more dominant, other more subtle forms of knowing would recede and "many ways of thinking will also disappear" (1992, p. 62). Similarly Hart (1992) poignantly described the risks of decontextualizing and over-valuing certain ways of thinking when she wrote:

> In many ways, the glorification of knowledge work, and the one-sided description of a certain kind of intelligence with generally higher rea-

soning and problem-solving skills must be looked at from the perspective of a tremendous loss. Lost are those skills, knowledges, and abilities which have been shaped by, and which can only survive through active involvement in and productive transformation of material reality. These skills are lost not only because they are no longer practiced, but also because they are socially devalued. (p. 161)

Educators must understand that instructional designs also have to be read and acknowledged as texts which, because of their existence within artificial contexts within real contexts, are conceivably hazardous to learners' and society's educational health and future.

Conclusion

Post-formal ways of thinking celebrate both order and disorder. Thinking and learning are not just products of systems of order and purity but are instead messy, swirling and volatile, i.e., sans fig leaf. In instructional systems, thinking and learning are seen in fragments via domains, measured outcomes, atomized elements, and separation of tasks. These assumptions predict learning progresses linearly, and interpretation proceeds from separate parts into a whole. Learning and intelligence are regarded as fixed, unidimensional, univocal, and normative by mainstream educational psychology and instructional designers. At the very least, alternative paths to the same outcome for individual learners—a place where Piagetian theory is seriously inadequate—must be acknowledged. Nichols pointed out that problems with educational technology are "inextricably bound to a too rational-technical way of life, where rational-technical indicates an over-extended reason that is distant from affective, tacit, intuitive, contextualized and discourse- or conversation-based processes and forms" (1994, p. 40). Therefore, as more and more designs implemented through instructional and educational technologies become situated in public, higher and workplace education, the following words of Mary Daly (1978) serve as a reminders to continually value and seek other ways of thinking along with the formal, scientific and rational:

The mindbenders and those who remain mindbound do not see the patterns of the cosmic tapestries, nor do they hear the labyrinthine symphony. For their thinking has been crippled and tied to linear tracks. Spiraling/Spinning is visible/audible to them only where it crosses the straight lines of what they call thinking. Hence the integrity of Spinning thought eludes them, and what they perceive is mere-

ly a series of fragmented breaks/crosses, which might appear like an
irregular series of dots and dashes. (p. 412)

In looking under ADAM's symbolic fig leaf many contradictions
have emerged. Too often educational technologies are not critiqued outside of testing and assessment processes and are implemented as unconsidered solutions for what are thought to be educational problems.
There are many reasons for a lack of critique including techno-phobic
teachers and faculty, a desire for simple cost-effective training plans in
business and industry, and America's love affair with anything that
appears to be high-tech. Mediated instruction is often efficient and
effective (a debatable objective) when it supports teaching and learning
processes for canonical, formal ways of thinking. But instructional systems, especially in the arts, humanities, and social sciences, are best
used in conjunction with more subjective holistic forms of teaching,
learning, and knowing.

As yet, the idea of post-formal thinking has not arrived in the educational mainstream. How instructional systems could be used with
ways of knowing that go beyond the Cartesian-Newtonian paradigm is
currently unknown, untested, and unconsidered. Nevertheless, with the
explosion of mediated and distance education instructional formats, the
technological implications for post-formal thinking and its project of
critically transformative education must be kept in mind and incorporated in future research and practice. Likewise, the disciplines of
instructional systems, educational technologies and distance education
should look to each other, to other disciplines and to cultural studies for
a less insular view of their worlds. There appears to be some accommodation, possibly even critical accommodation, of post-formal thinking within instructional systems. A critical, post-formal discipline of
instructional systems would continue to remove the metaphorical fig
leaves of rationality, the idealized and abstracted individual and the separation of mind from body. In doing so, instructional systems would
begin to facilitate and support as much as possible additional ways of
thinking that are intuitive, affective, historical, and cognizant of context
in a re-union of mind-body-spirit.

References

Anderson, R. and Faust, G. (1974). *Educational psychology: The science of instruction and learning.* New York: Dodd, Mead and
Company.

Bayard, C. and Knight, G. (1995). Vivisecting the 90's: An interview with Jean Baudrillard. CTHEORY [online]. Available: http://www.ctheory.com/a24-vivisecting_90s.html.

Bednar, A., Cunningham, T., Duffy, T. and Perry, J. (1992). Theory into practice: How do we link? In T. Duffy and D. Jonassen (Eds.), *Constructivism and the technology of Instruction: A conversation* (pp.17–34). Hillsdale, NJ: Lawrence Erlbaum.

Belenky, M., Clinchy, B., Goldberger, N. and Tarule, J. (1986). *Women's ways of knowing: The development of self, voice, and mind.* New York: Basic Books.

Bowers, C. (1988). *The cultural dimensions of educational computing: Understanding the non-neutrality of technology.* New York: Teachers College Press.

Bracey, G. (1990, January). Results of cognition research could help improve educational software. *Electric Learning,* 18–19.

Briggs, J. and Peat, F. (1989). *Turbulent mirror.* New York: Harper & Row.

Carroll, J. (1990). *The Nurnberg Funnel: Designing minimalist instruction for practical computer skill.* Cambridge, MA: MIT Press.

Daly, M. (1978). *Gyn/Ecology.* Boston: Beacon.

Damarin, S. (1994). Equity, caring, and beyond: Can feminist ethics inform educational technology? *Educational Technology, 34*(2), 34–39.

del Río, P. and Alvarez, A. (1995). Tossing, praying, and thinking: the changing architectures of mind and agency. In J. Wertsch, P. del Río and A. Alvarez (Eds.), *Sociocultural studies of the mind* (pp. 215–247). Cambridge, UK: Cambridge University Press.

Dewey, J. (1961). *Democracy and education: An introduction to the philosophy of education.* New York: Macmillan.

Dick, W. (1991). An instructional designer's view of constructivism. *Educational Technology, (31)*5, 41–44.

Elliott, A. (1994). *Psychoanalytic theory: An introduction.* Cambridge, MA: Blackwell.

Feenberg, A. (1991). *Critical theory of technology.* New York: Oxford University Press.

Gilligan, C. (1982). *In a different voice.* Cambridge, MA: Harvard University Press.

Glendinning, C. (1990, March). Notes toward a neo-Luddite manifesto. *Utne Reader,* 50–53.

Hart, M. (1992). *Working and educating for life.* London: Routledge.

Heinich, R. (1970). *Technology and the management of instruction.* Washington, DC: Association for Educational Communications and Technology.

Hess, D. (1995). *Science and technology in a multicultural world.* New York: Columbia University Press.

Jonassen, D. (1988). Preface. In D. Jonassen (Ed.), *Instructional designs for microcomputer courseware* (pp. xi–xxi). Hillsdale, NJ: Lawrence Erlbaum and Associates.

Kincheloe, J. (1995). *Toil and trouble.* New York: Peter Lang.

Kincheloe, J. and Steinberg, S. (1993). A tentative description of post-formal thinking: The critical confrontation with cognitive theory. *Harvard Educational Review, 63*(3), 296–320.

Klausmeier, H. and Ripple, R. (1971). *Learning and human abilities: Educational psychology.* New York: Harper and Row.

Lyotard, J. (1984). *The postmodern condition: A report on knowledge.* Minneapolis, MN: University of Minnesota Press.

Macedo, D. (1994). *Literacies of power: What Americans are not allowed to know.* Boulder, CO: Westview Press.

Mander, J. (1992). *In the absence of the sacred.* San Francisco: Sierra Club Books.

Merrill, D. (1996, February 20). Reclaiming the discipline of instructional design. *ITFORUM Listserv,* 166 lines. Available: ITFORUM@uga.cc.uga.edu.

Muffoletto, R. (1994). Technology and restructuring education: Constructing a context. *Educational Technology, 34*(2), 24–28.

Nichols, R. (1994). Searching for moral guidance about educational technology. *Educational Technology, 34*(2), 40–48.

Peters, M. (1995). Legitimation problems: Knowledge and education in the postmodern condition. In M. Peters (Ed.), *Education and the postmodern condition* (pp. 21–40). Westport, CT: Bergin and Garvey.

Reeves, T. (1996, February, 21). A hopefully humble paradigm review. *ITFORUM Listserv,* 245 lines. Available: ITFORUM@uga.cc.uga.edu.

Reigeluth, C. (1989). Educational technology at the crossroads: New mindsets and new directions. *Educational Technology Research and Development, 37*(1), pp. 67–80.

Roblyer, D. (1988). Fundamental problems and principles of designing effective courseware. In D. Jonassen (Ed.), *Instructional designs for microcomputer courseware* (pp. 7–33). Hillsdale, NJ: Lawrence Erlbaum.

Romiszowski. A. J. (1981). *Designing instructional systems.* New York: Kogan Page.

Shotter, J. (1993). *Cultural politics of everyday life.* Toronto: University of Toronto Press.

Taussig, M. (1993). *Mimesis and alterity.* New York: Routledge

Wells, S. (1986). Jurgen Habermas, communicative competence, and the teaching of technical discourse. In C. Nelson (Ed.), *Theory in the classroom* (pp. 245–269). Urbana, IL: University of Illinois Press.

Wertsch, J., del Río, P., and Alvarez, A. (1995). Sociocultural studies: history, action, and mediation. In J. Wertsch, P. Del Río, and A. Alvarez (Eds.), *Sociocultural studies of the mind* (pp. 1–34). Cambridge, UK: Cambridge University Press.

Wilber, K. (1993). *The spectrum of consciousness.* Wheaton, IL: Quest Books.

Woolfolk, A. (1993). *Educational psychology.* Boston: Allyn and Bacon.

Yeaman, A. (1994). Deconstructing modern educational technology. *Educational Technology, 34*(2), 15–24.

Zuboff, S. (1988). *In the age of the smart machine.* New York: Basic Books.

CHAPTER TWELVE

Evaluation
The Dangers of Standardized Testing of Young Children: A Post-formal Alternative

Marianne Exum Lopez

School readiness is the first of six national education goals for the United States. "By the year 2000, all children in America will start school ready to learn" (U.S. Department of Education, 1990). Both President Bush and the nation's governors endorsed this goal in the National Education Goals, emphasizing the tremendous importance of preparing U.S. schools (and their students) to be the very best as we enter the twenty-first century. One of the dangers of meeting such a goal has been in the administration of readiness and screening tests to locate preschool children who are *not* ready to learn at the start of school. In an effort to identify and serve the children having the greatest preschool needs, readiness and screening tests have, paradoxically, served to prematurely label the nation's poorest and most disadvantaged. Where standardized testing has historically been reserved for the more fully developed student, it has, driven by an insatiable desire for profit from testing companies, discovered a surprisingly lucrative market in the testing of young children. How these tests are used can have severe consequences for children who score poorly—particularly non-mainstream children whose home environments are so different from the traditional school environment. These concerns become increasingly important in light of the President's emphasis on the value of school readiness for all children today. This paper will examine critical issues of school readiness assessments in regard to special populations based on the principles of post-formal thinking.

Why Post-formal Thinking?

Piaget's stages of development have directed primary educators for the past 20-30 years based on the notion that learning occurs in stages. According to Piaget, a child must develop in a particular stage before he/she can progress to the next stage. It is not my desire to discredit Piaget but rather to extend intellectual thinking beyond one man's quantitative prognosis of child development that has kept primary education mired in a currently ineffective paradigm for today's children and their manifold needs. As Kincheloe mentioned in the introductory essay, Piaget decontextualized his studies of children, failing to consider the social and cultural dynamics that made them respond as they did. Kincheloe's question cannot be neglected: "Did children in non-European cultures develop in the same way?" (p. 4). When one considers the diversity of children in America's schools today, is it appropriate to limit our understandings of their psychological development to the work of Piaget?

Post-formal thinking is one way of pushing the edge of education to new levels—levels that recognize the debilitating effects of culture bias and mainstream assessments for non-mainstream children. Post-formal thinking confirms different ways of knowing as well as different measures of assessing such knowledge. It is not limited to standardized assessment; rather, it goes far beyond such basic recall to explore deeper understandings about the world and illuminate relationships among seemingly unrelated matters. Post-formal thinking doesn't demand that learning be a top-down condition where the teacher is the sole knowledge bearer. Post-formal educators are keenly aware of the academic potential among their students, particularly those students who are not of the mainstream, whose learning styles may be different, and whose home language may not be English.

Post-formal assessments are a crucial link to identifying early signs of giftedness and intelligence among all school children but particularly among those who do not fit the mold in traditional schooling. It is imperative that the most disadvantaged children be given the greatest opportunity to succeed in school, according to their needs, and this cannot be done by the current readiness and screening tests used throughout the country today. First, I will examine some current tests for readiness and then, after a brief discussion of why they are not acceptable, will look at some alternative methods to evaluate a child's progress in the early years of school based on post-formal thinking.

A Look at Readiness and Screening Tests

Readiness tests are "measures of achievement and their purpose should be to provide instructional information for educational planning" (Bagnato and Neisworth, 1991, p. 154). Screening tests, on the other hand, are used for early identification and intervention of children who seem to have special needs for their age (Taylor, 1993; Bagnato and Neisworth, 1991). Screening tests are not used for diagnostic or prescriptive purposes. Bagnato and Neisworth give two cautions:

> 1. *Readiness and achievement format tests should not be used in the screening stage of assessment.* (p. 154)
> 2. *In no way should screening tests be used for the exclusion, classification, or placement of children.* (Italics in original, p. 155)

A great deal of confusion surrounds these terms. Often, they are used interchangeably among school professionals and even among test publishers. The Educational Testing Service has literally hundreds of readiness tests in their *Test Collection* (1985) from scores of test publishers, whose purposes vary widely, despite the cautious warnings above. Some readiness tests are considered preliminary screening devices, while others are used to predict future academic performance, while still others are for diagnostic assessment of skills (*Test Collection, Reading*, 1985). Isn't it interesting that test publishers themselves do not agree on the purposes and functions of readiness and screening tests? Therefore, schools must have their own policies when it comes to using these tests on young children. Bagnato and Neisworth (1991) argue that tests are misused when they diagnose needs, deficiencies, and give premature labels to children. Screening tests have often been used to keep children out of kindergarten who appear to be "not ready." Clearly, this type of misuse is more concerned with a child's ability to adapt to school than the school's willingness to meet the needs of the child.

A closer look at some of the more commonly used readiness tests gives the reader a better picture of what these tests measure. The Lollipop Test is a criterion-referenced "diagnostic screening test of school readiness" (Chew and Morris, 1989, p. 462). It is used for diagnostic purposes even though Bagnato and Neisworth argue that screening tests are not to be used in such a way. The Lollipop Test contains four subtests which are administered individually: 1) identification of colors and shapes and copying shapes; 2) picture description, position, and spatial recognition; 3) identification of numbers and counting; and 4) identification of letters and writing (Chew and Morris, 1989). This particular test is administered in kindergarten to predict school success in first grade.

The Metropolitan Readiness Test is also designed to measure readiness for first grade. It is a much longer test (80 minutes compared to 15 to 20 minutes for the Lollipop Test) with six subtests: auditory memory, rhyming, letter recognition, visual matching, school language and listening, and qualitative language. It is considered to be a good predictor of first-grade achievement (Chew and Morris, 1989). In fact, Chew and Morris, in a recent study (1989), use this test to predict later academic achievement and find it to be a significant predictor up to the fourth grade.

A more critical look at their study reveals a weaker correlation between the test scores and teacher grades, implying that teachers may see more potential in their students than what the tests revealed. Further, this study is a good example of the notion that those who test well (i.e., meet the criteria which fits a select population) will continue to test well. The corollary is that those who do not test well will continue to do poorly in school. In the current modernist discourse, that translates to a perpetuation of the misguided assumption that those who do not test well, i.e., poor minorities, inferior intellectually in comparison to their white, middle-class counterparts. Again, as stressed by Kincheloe in the introduction to this book, lack of opportunity is confused with intellectual ability. Note also that the tests themselves focus their attention on matters of recall and trivia. Letter and number recognition, rhyming sounds, identification of colors and shapes are all learned facts that have little to do with actual thinking. In this sense, the readiness tests formerly discussed do not measure intelligence as much as they measure a child's ability to recite bits and pieces of rote-learned facts.

Many have criticized readiness tests for a number of reasons (NAEYC, 1988; Kamii, 1990; Schweinhart et al., 1993; American Academy of Pediatrics, 1995). Early childhood staff have a big responsibility in the testing of young children and, more importantly, in evaluating the tests. It is easy to make incorrect interpretations about a child's development as a result of minimal formal training (American Academy of Pediatrics, 1995). Staff who wrongly identify children with special needs may jeopardize their educational future. Further, the tests themselves are looking for one right answer without assistance. Children may tire or reject this method of assessment. Children are simply not good test takers (NAEYC, 1988). At such a young age, children change and grow rapidly in their development, and a test taken at a particular time does not reflect ongoing growth. Tests focus too strongly on academic and physical responses while ignoring broader domains of child initiative, social skills, background influences, and general logical skills (Schweinhart et al., 1993).

An alternative assessment that has become increasingly popular is the method of systematic observation of children in their day-to-day educational settings. The High/Scope Child Observation Record is an example of this type of alternative instrument, used to measure developmental status of children two and a half to six years old. To score accurately, the High/Scope does require a certain amount of training. The rationale of an observation assessment is based on the assumption that young children learn best in developmentally appropriate practice. The National Association for the Education of Young Children (NAEYC) affirms that young children learn by doing and teaching should involve guidance and facilitation (Schweinhart et al., 1993). High/Scope looks at six areas of development: 1)initiative; 2) social relations; 3) creative representation; 4) music and movement; 5) language and literacy; and 6) logic and mathematics. In order to score well on the observation record, a child must be able to express him/herself. Thus, scoring high depends on a child's ability to express thoughts, feelings, and choices clearly. One advantage of the High/Scope is that it can be administered at different times during a child's development, optimally in the fall and spring of each school year, to recognize a child's progress (although this may not be the case in schools that use the High/Scope). By following a child through periods of growth, the observation has the potential of becoming longitudinal, more reflective, and, in the long run, a much more accurate summary of the child's progress.

It appears that all children can be assessed equally and fairly from such an instrument. But let us think for a minute about the children who would benefit from this type of test and, much more importantly, those who would not benefit. All tests have underlying values and assumptions about the subjects being tested. Beliefs about what students should know, whose knowledge is important, what it means to be ready for first grade, etc., imply basic unspoken values within every readiness test. The High/Scope is no exception. Children who would score high on this type of test are the children who have been well socialized into the expectations of public schooling. Relating to adults, relating to children, solving social problems, and cooperating are items on the observation that show evidence of what the test perceives to be development. A child who is shy or timid might score poorly in areas requiring detailed verbal descriptions, even though there is no correlation between shyness and intelligence.

Imagine, if you will, the child who comes from a family where English is not spoken in the home. When the child arrives in school, his/her English development will naturally be quite poor, regardless of his/her academic ability. Taking a readiness test that requires English fluency would be the equivalent of a high school student taking the Scholastic Aptitude Test (SAT) blindfolded! Validity is totally disregarded. Yet, time and again school systems are using such testing instruments to place such children unfairly, ignoring language differences between the test and the student. Inaccurate and inequitable assessments are made when schools fail to consider their special populations who do not speak English proficiently.

A Word about Reliability and Validity

All norm-referenced tests have information regarding the test's reliability and validity. Reliability refers to the consistency of a test. It is an "assurance" that scores will be similar if the same test is taken by the same person on different occasions or if it is scored by different people. Validity refers to the test's ability to measure exactly what it is supposed to measure. In developmental tests, validity can also be proven by showing a relationship between performance and chronological age. If a child's performance on a test increases as age increases, then a type of construct validity is proven (Taylor, 1993). The greatest problem concerning validity of readiness tests (and most norm-referenced tests) is that they do not consider English Language Learners (ELLs) as a population different from the normed group. "Assessing diverse groups of students . . . with instruments written in English and normed on monolingual English-speaking students inevitably yields data of unknown validity that cannot be meaningfully aggregated. . . . [P]olicymakers must bear in mind that the validity of any given standardized test is not absolute" (LaCelle-Peterson and Rivera, p. 66). To assume that ELLs can be placed appropriately based on such tests is an egregious and discriminatory presumption.

Tests that Consider both Languages

Educational Testing Service (*Test Collection*, 1985) also provides information on scores of tests designed for students learning English as a second language. Again, the purposes of the tests vary, but most instruments measure either oral language ability or language dominance of

Spanish/English bilingual students. In many cases, the directions may be given in Spanish or English. There are also a number of readiness tests in Spanish which measure more than just language proficiency. However, many of them, like the Brigance Diagnostic Assessment of Basic Skills, are direct translations of a test in English (*Test Collection*, Spanish Speakers, 1985). Scholars have agreed that a translated test is an inaccurate and unacceptable performance instrument. Some tests, such as the Escala de Intelegencia Wechsler para Niños, are Spanish adaptations of the WISC-R Intelligence Test. ETS does not elaborate on the term "adaptation" (*Test Collection*, Spanish Speakers, 1985). Another test, the S-D Primary ESL Inventory, is designed to measure English proficiency of non-native speakers, and the publisher invites schools to use the test "as a tool for class placement" (*Test Collection*, Reading, 1985, p. 36). The warnings of Bagnato and Neisworth regarding readiness tests and placement for all children clearly show that those who publish test instruments do not have a minority student's best interests in mind.

Who Are the ELLs?

English Language Learners (ELLs) refers to students whose first language is not English. It includes students who are non-English speaking as well as those who have become nearly proficient. Traditionally, the US Government has labeled these students as Limited English Proficient (LEP). This type of labeling exposes an ethnocentric view that something is wrong with these students, that they have a deficit (Freeman and Goodman, 1993). LaCelle-Peterson and Rivera (1994) explain why LEP is a derogatory label for these children. The term ELLs focuses on what students are accomplishing rather than on their limitations, "just as we refer to advanced teacher candidates as 'student teachers' rather than 'limited teaching proficient individuals,' and to college students who concentrate their studies in physics as 'physics majors' rather than as 'students with limited physics proficiency'" (p. 55). Throughout this paper, ELL will replace the traditionally negative label, LEP.

The number of ELLs in this nation is amazingly large and growing. The 1990 census reports that over 6.3 million people between ages five and seventeen speak a language other than English in the home, 13.9% of all the school-aged children in the nation (Wagoner, as cited in LaCelle-Peterson and Rivera, 1994). The U.S. Department of Education cites that approximately 2.26 million students, K-12, have "limited

English proficiency, or, more than one in every twenty students enrolled in US schools is learning English as a second language (LaCelle-Peterson and Rivera, 1994). Even these figures are low because of the migratory patterns of many of these students and their families. Quite a large number of students may not be counted for that reason. Further, the number of ELLs in the United States has grown by 51.3% between 1985 and 1991 (Olsen, as cited in LaCelle-Peterson and Rivera, 1994). Based on population predictions, the numbers will continue to rise at a progressively faster rate.

The Inequities of Assessing English-Language Learners

One need not search far to find strong criticism against assessment instruments that are used to measure academic performance of ELLs alongside their monolingual peers (Grosjean, 1985; Farrell, 1987; Jackson, 1994; García, 1993; LaCelle-Peterson and Rivera, 1994; Hudelson, 1984; and Cummins, 1992). "The implicit guiding assumption appears to be that whatever curricular revisions and/or assessment innovations contribute to the success of monolingual students will also work for ELLs—that once the ELLs know a little English, the new and improved assessments will fit them too" (LaCelle-Peterson and Rivera, 1994, p. 56). The problem with this line of thinking is that when ELLs test poorly, they are assigned to lower tracks and even special education classes. Inappropriate placement is justified by a low test score. Language needs are not considered to have any relevance, when, in fact, they are the only relevant issue.

Pre-literate, non-English speaking children already have tremendous exposure to English in their environment. They are surrounded by English in their day-to-day interactions. Words like *Crest, McDonalds, Wonder Woman* and *Cheerios* are all a part of the child's literate world (Hudelson, 1984). These children come to school with a great awareness of English which readiness tests do not measure, because the child's pre-existing knowledge is so far removed from the knowledge that schools expect of children.

A similar concern is that the tests do not recognize the knowledge bilingual children have about reading and writing in their native language, which could be easily transferred to reading and writing in the second language, i.e., English (García, 1993). This becomes a more serious issue if the child is older and has achieved literacy in his/her first language in addition to a great deal of knowledge in content areas. Even though the student may be very bright in science, for example, an

English test will most likely be an inaccurate assessment of that student's knowledge of science, for no other reason than that the test would be in the student's second language. "Every test will inevitably measure both what the learner knows about the particular subject matter and the learner's proficiency in the particular language" (LaCelle-Peterson and Rivera, 1994).

Culture is another factor which can have a negative influence on the testing of ELLs. "We simply cannot assume that the educational practices which have been demonstrated to be 'successful' among learners in one culture automatically will 'work' with learners from a different culture, even if they are living in our own nation-state" (Farrell, 1987, p. 4). Francesina Jackson (1994) speaks of preferred learning styles of students, which tend to be culturally specific. That U.S. schools remain entrenched in a Eurocentric middle-class style of learning is damaging to ELLs because not all ELLs learn well in such a typically Western mode.

The cultural bias in U.S. tests is ubiquitous; there is no way of escaping it. The most egregious examples of bias come in the form of vocabulary and picture tests, where a non-native student would have no way of identifying certain items that are representative of the traditional middle-class, mainstream forms of knowing in this country. A classic example is to show a newly arrived Puerto Rican child a picture of a snowman and ask him/her to identify it. As silly as this may seem, it happens all the time. But there are more subtle forms of bias against ELLs. Take for example the High/Scope Child Observation Record, which looks for language-rich interaction among children as a sign of high development. Would it be fair to assume that a non-native student had poor developmental qualities because he/she could not express thoughts, choices in English clearly? Is any allowance given to the ELLs for their language needs?

The entire concept of readiness tests generates controversy. If children are legally entitled to education at a certain age, then why should a readiness test be necessary at all? Children's differences will naturally arise through the course of the school year, and a critical, informed teacher has the wherewithal to embrace differences and look for signs of thinking and development among her/his students. Disturbing ideologies emerge in an insistence upon school readiness. Are we more concerned with a child's adaptation to the socialization of school or a school's responsibility to teach that child from where he or she is?

Recommendations

After examining screening and readiness tests thoroughly, I return to the initial concern of this study: How does standardized testing of preschool children help in meeting their educational needs? If the objective is to provide disadvantaged children with access to high-quality preschool programs (U.S. Dept. of Education, 1990), then I strongly support Goal 1 of the National Education Goals. However, if the Goal leads to inappropriate assessment of children at an early age, then the educational system is putting our children at risk before they can even begin school. I feel that President Bush's emphasis on school readiness puts too much pressure on the identification of those who are not ready. Readiness tests which highlight deficiencies in the learner cannot be positive in light of the way many test instruments are being used. Furthermore, for ELLs to be assessed like their monolingual peers is intolerable and indefensible. Readiness tests and screening tests are only the beginning of a student's life-long journey through public schooling which insists upon labels and lower tracks for those who do not fit into the mainstream. The Southern Association on Children Under Six recommended "*a ban of the routine, mass use of standardized, intelligence, achievement readiness and developmental screening tests for young children through the age of eight* " (National Education Goals Panel, 1991, italics added). I concur wholeheartedly.

An Alternative Evaluation Based on Post-formal Thinking

I would argue that there must be alternate ways to evaluate development in preschool, kindergarten, and the primary grades, and that readiness tests and screening tests are culturally biased, trivial, and unnecessary. Assuming that standardized testing instruments will no longer be tolerated by enlightened professionals who work with young children, I propose that the evaluation of young children's progress be compared to the art of research. Just as a good researcher examines multiple sources of data before making preliminary assertions, so must an early childhood professional consider manifold examples of a child's knowledge at work in a school setting before making an evaluation of that child's progress. I would caution, however, that examples of knowledge not be confined to more traditional ways of thinking and learning. True and fair evaluations of all children cannot depend on matters of recall or success at workbook pages. Indeed, dissatisfaction with traditionally structured "learning" tasks might be the first indication that students are quite smart. Evaluations that extend beyond modernist understandings of knowledge must look for examples of post-formal thinking in a child's development.

What if school personnel had an intrinsic belief that each and every child had a talent that was altogether unique and exemplary? What if the focus of each observation rested on the premise that all children were gifted, and it was the responsibility of the trained staff to recognize the "gift" of each child? I believe that standardized tests, under this umbrella of purpose, would be defunct. When schools can focus on the talent of the learner rather than the deficiencies, then schooling will be revolutionized. Post-formal thinking is based on the generative model of cognition, as Joe Kincheloe alluded to in the Introduction. The generative model, a culturally-fair style of learning, focuses on developing the knowledge that a child already has rather than looking for weaknesses based on standardized test scores. It respects all styles of learning and all types of knowledge. "Therefore, the challenge for public schools is to recognize alternative, culturally relevant indicators of outstanding talent that will be translated into effective assessment strategies and programming models for children not from the dominant culture" (Callahan and McIntire, 1994, p. 7).

The U.S. Department of Education has identified four areas where a gifted/talented child will excel: intellectual ability, creative or artistic areas, unusual leadership capacity, and excellence in specific academic fields (Callahan and McIntire. 1994). However, each culture has its own opinions of what constitutes giftedness within that culture. I would argue that the four guidelines provided by the US Department of Education are culturally specific to giftedness among Anglo-Saxons, and they do not necessarily represent giftedness within all cultures. For example, a study of selected Pueblo Indian tribes in New Mexico yielded the following areas for identifying giftedness: special abilities in speech and song, ability to create with the hands, abilities in acquiring and knowing when to apply knowledge, and ability to empathize and give to others (Romero and Schultz, as cited in Callahan and McIntire, 1994). Cultural behaviors, values, and beliefs have a strong impact on one's understanding of giftedness. Further, a subordinate culture's strengths (such as the visual-spatial abilities of American Indian children) may not be manifested in a test of verbal skills that is produced by the dominant culture and may result in misleading data.

Conflicts among the Discourse Communities

Many researchers have argued that the discourse community of the school is incompatible with the discourse community of homes which are not a part of the dominant culture (Heath, 1983; Delgado-Gaitán, 1991; Fillmore and Meyer, 1992). The home, the home language, and the social environment of the child's community are basic to the child's development. Heath (1983) recognized a tremendous mismatch between home environments of working-class black and white communities and the school environment where these children studied. The children had different ways of learning, talking, and interacting, and these ways were not embraced by the school community. In fact, they were rejected and often misunderstood in negative contexts, contributing to school failure. Crago (1992) found a similar incongruity among Inuit children and the discourse features in their classrooms taught by non-Inuit second language teachers. Crago emphasizes the importance of sociocultural aspects of communication, and how "all cultures do not have the same patterns of communicative interaction" (p. 499). In a related study, Michaels (1983) found that ethnic differences in discourse styles between the teacher and the student had an important influence on classroom interaction and learning. In her comparative study of the discourse styles of black and white students, she noted that differences in discourse styles between teacher and student "decrease[d] the *quality* of interaction in key classroom activities, such as Sharing Time, which then interfere[d] with [a child's] development of a prose-like oral discourse style" (p. 84, italics in original). How well a child understands the discourse community of the public school has everything to do with the child's success in school. The unspoken assumptions that often underlie a school's discourse are built upon one particular society's understandings of academic excellence. As was previously clarified by Kincheloe, those understandings are socially constructed, subjective, and ideologically hegemonic.

Effective Multicultural, Post-formal Teaching

One of the greatest challenges to teachers who come from the mainstream (or those who have been immersed in Western knowledge all their lives) is to consider the ideology of Whiteness and its effects on subordinate cultures in the classroom. Even without realizing it, teachers can be acting on racial presumptions that discount the education a minority child brings to school. Stereotypes are embedded within our ethnocentric culture. The way a classroom is conducted and the expectations teachers have of their students are elements of a social, historical culture called school. The problem for very young children is that they do not distinguish the differences between their home culture and the school culture. Ann Haas Dyson (1993) describes it well:

> The boundaries of the cultural bridge inevitably blur inside the children's worlds, because, from their points of view, school is not *one* social sphere. The issue thus becomes not how children make a transition from the home world to "the" school world, but how they find themselves— how they compose a place for themselves— amidst the diverse, potentially contradiction-ridden worlds of the classroom. (p. 18, italics in original)

Thus, the teacher's task is to create a place in the classroom for each student that is safe, respected, and openly aware of the contradictions—even confronting the contradictions—as a pedagogical site for learning.

A multicultural classroom is exactly the type of place necessary for all children but especially those who do not come from the dominant culture. A multicultural classroom, as a pedagogical site, is critical for the development of post-formal thinking. Margaret Pusch and her colleagues (as cited in Acheson and Gall, 1992) identified 10 effective multicultural teaching practices to effectively teach ethnically and racially diverse students. Effective teachers:

1. are open-minded to new ideas and experiences
2. have empathy for people from other cultures
3. accurately perceive similarities and differences between a student's culture and their own
4. describe a student's behavior without judging it
5. are free from ethnocentrism
6. express respect and positive regard for all students through eye contact, body posture, voice tone, and pitch
7. are knowledgeable about the contributions of minority groups to America and to the world
8. use multicultural materials in the classroom
9. recognize and accept both the language spoken in the home and the standard language
10. help student develop pride in and identification with their native culture. (p. 34)

If we take these suggestions seriously, then the child's learning environment will be transformed. Portfolio assessment, as a type of post-formal evaluation, requires a different perspective on a child's progress. It affirms the NAEYC position of developmentally appropriate practice, that children learn by doing, and that teaching should involve guidance and facilitation. A colleague commented recently that, in the course of her portfolio class, one of her students remarked, "Gosh! I've got to change my whole way of teaching!" To extend this even further, one must realize that developmentalism is not the only way to view intelligence. To stop there misses "the rather obvious point that individuals operate simultaneously at divergent cognitive stages," (Kincheloe and Steinberg, 1993, p. 299). The post-formal classroom must be a place where learning is shared, where teachers can recognize elements of giftedness in all students, and where evaluation is an art of observation. The way we evaluate students has everything to do with the way we choose to teach them. If one actually believes in the principles of post-formal thinking, then, out of necessity, the class dynamics will change. Kincheloe and Steinberg (1993) give us a lucid description of what post-formal classrooms might be like:

> A school guided by empowered post-formal thinkers would no longer privilege White male experience as the standard by which all other experiences are measured. Such realizations would point out a guiding concern with social justice and the way unequal power relations in school and society destroy the promise of democratic life. Post-formal teachers would no longer passively accept the pronouncements of standardized-test and curriculum makers without examining the social contexts in which their students live and the ways those concepts help shape student performance. (p.301)

As a tool, I have designed a framework for evaluation based on Kincheloe's theory of post-formal thinking. Naturally, this is a tentative framework, based on the principles of post-formal thinking. Post-formal thinking focuses on thinking, or intelligence, if you will, and early childhood development must consider other critical areas of growth: the social, emotional, physical, and spiritual. Yet, I would argue that post-formal thinking supports development in all these areas; indeed, from a postmodern perspective, such vital areas of growth cannot be separated from the individual (Wilbur, 1993). Hence, physical development is critical to the intellectual development of every person—not just young children. Likewise, social, emotional, and spiritual growth are essential to the overall progress of anyone's mental capacities to learn. Further, postmodernism denies the existence of any individual outside of a sociocultural, historical context. A child cannot be observed in a vacuum, and the qualities that a child possesses come from a sociocultural background that must be considered when evaluating that child. Using some of the elements of the High/Scope Observation Record (Schweinhart et al., 1993) and some of the principles of post-formal thinking, I have devised an evaluation instrument that more appropriately considers the learning styles of diverse learners, including those whose first language is not English. Unlike the High/Scope, this instrument is not quantitative; it is a narrative summary. Through the trained eye of a teacher as researcher, ethnographic reports can successfully record a child's progress well into the primary grades far more successfully than any quantitative measure.

A POST-FORMAL OBSERVATION INSTRUMENT

A. POST-FORMAL ETYMOLOGY

1. How is the student integrating ideas, detecting problems, asking unique questions? Provide examples.
2. How does the student show an awareness of the way society works? The significance of race? Class? Gender?
3. Does the student question the "ironic contradictions" in the origins of knowledge?

B. FORMING PATTERNS

1. Is the child conscious of an implicate order of things? If so, how? What has the child verbalized or conceptualized that reveals this understanding?
2. Cite examples of how the student connects with his/her environment.
3. How does the student connect experience with knowledge in ways that are fundamentally new?
4. Has the student recognized patterns of exclusion, hidden assumptions, etc. that determine the way school works?

C. PROCESS

1. In what ways is the child's creativity and imagination free of boundaries?
2. What are some expressions of creativity that the child displays?

    a. Intricateness of free-style drawings and paintings (not color-ing)?
    b. Ability to make complex 3-dimensional structures?
    c. Ways a child mimics others or shows a refusal to mimic?
3. How does the learner express his/her feelings in social situations?
4. How do emotions influence thinking?
5. What behaviors is the child exhibiting and why?
6. Does the child get along with others? Who are some of his/her best friends and why?

D. CONTEXTUALIZING LEARNING (For the teacher—Are the educational experiences meaningful to *all* the students?)
1. How is the child responding to the school environment?
2. How does the student show a pride in his/her background knowledge, experiences, and home language?

E. LEARNING IN THE CONTENT AREAS
1. In what ways does the child show an interest in reading and the literate world?
2. Give an example of how the child makes connections between mathematical concepts.

F. PHYSICAL DEVELOPMENT
1. Consider body coordination, fine motor skills, the ability to keep rhythm. How is the child progressing?

G. FOR ENGLISH LANGUAGE LEARNERS (ELLs)
1. What is the dominant language of the child?
2. What are some specific ways the child is adjusting/adapting to learning the English language?
3. How does the child creatively overcompensate for his/her inability to be understood?

Conclusion

It is important to remember that this framework for evaluation is nothing but a tool, and a tentative tool at that. It can be changed and adapted to one's needs, always keeping in mind the important task of culture fair, unbiased evaluations of students. As an evaluator, the teacher has a tremendous responsibility, both to herself and to her students. Yet, who else but the teacher should be given such a responsibility? In this way, teachers reclaim the authority and power they deserve as they take on the role of researcher, always looking for ways their students can break out of the mold and exhibit various aspects of post-formal thinking. Teachers themselves break out of the mold in their efforts to critically evaluate and interact with their students. Imagine the freedom of no longer living according to the dictates of standardized tests. School readiness for all children would be a given, not because they have been tested or screened, but because they have had the privilege of high quality Head Start and kindergarten programs, and the knowledge they bring to class would be accepted as the basis for their curriculum. I will end with the following suggestions for making early childhood programs exemplary:

- Children should enter school based on their chronological age, which is their legal right, and no test should mar their eligibility (NAEYC, 1988).
- Children should be exempt from standardized readiness, screening, or diagnostic tests until the age of eight.
- Children's development should be assessed through ongoing and systematic observations (NAEYC, 1988).
- Minority parents should be involved in the process of identifying giftedness among minority children.
- Children should be evaluated for what they know instead of what they don't know.

References

Acheson, K.A. and Gall, M.D. (1992). *Techniques in the clinical supervision of teachers.* New York: Longman.

American Academy of Pediatrics (1995). The inappropriate use of school "readiness" tests. *Pediatrics.* 95(3), 437–438.

Bagnato, S.J. and Neisworth, J.T. (1991). *Assessment for early intervention.* London: Guilford Press.

Callahan, C.M. and McIntire, J.A. (1994). *Identifying outstanding talent in American Indian and Alaska Native students.* Washington, DC: U.S. Dept. of Education.

Chew, A.L., and Morris, J.D. (1989). Predicting later academic achievement from kindergarten scores on the Metropolitan Readiness Tests and the Lollipop Test. *Educational and Psychological Measurement.* 49, 461–465.

Crago, M.B. (1992). Communicative interaction and second language acquisition: An Inuit example. *TESOL Quarterly* . 26(3), 487–505.

Cummins, J. (1992). Bilingual education and English immersion: The Ramirez report. *Bilingual Research Journal*. 16(1 and 2), 91–104.

Delgado-Gaitán, C. (1991). Relating experience and text: Socially constituted reading activity. In M. McGroarty and C. Faltis (Eds.), *Languages in school and society: Policy and pedagogy*. New York: Mouton de Gruyter.

Dyson, A.H. (1993). *Social worlds of children learning to write in an urban primary school*. New York: Teachers College Press.

Farrell, J. (1987). Cultural differences and curriculum inquiry. *Curriculum Inquiry*. 17(Spring),. 1–8.

Fillmore, L.W. and Meyer, L.M. (1992). The curriculum in linguistic minorities. In P.W. Jackson (Ed.), *Handbook of research on curriculum*. New York: Macmillan.

Freeman, Y. and Goodman, Y. (1993). Revaluing the bilingual learner through a literature reading program. *Reading and Writing Quarterly*, 9(2), 163–182.

García, G.E. (1993). Assessing the literacy development of second-language students: A focus on authentic assessment. In IRA (Ed.), *Children come in all languages: How to teach ESL children* (pp. 180–203). Newark, DE: IRA.

Grosjean, F. (1985). The bilingual as a competent but specific speaker-hearer. *Journal of Multilingual and Multicultural Development*. 6(6), 467–477.

Heath, S.B. (1983). *Ways with words*. New York: Cambridge Univ. Press.

Hudelson, S. (1984). Kan yu ret an rayt en Ingles: Children become literate in English as a second language. *TESOL Quarterly*. 18(2), 221–238.

Jackson, F.R. (1993). Seven strategies to support a culturally responsive pedagogy. *Journal of Reading*. 37(4), 298–303.

Kamii, C. (Ed.). (1990). *Achievement testing in the early grades: The games grown-ups play*. Washington, DC: NAEYC.

Kincheloe, J.L. and Steinberg, S. (1993). A tentative description of post-formal thinking: The critical confrontation with cognitive theory. *Harvard Educational Review*. 63 (3), 296–320.

LaCelle-Peterson, M.W. and Rivera, C. (1994). Is it real for all kids? A framework for equitable assessment policies for English language learners. *Harvard Educational Review*. 64(1), 55–75.

McLaren, P. (1993). *Schooling as a ritual performance.* London: Routledge.

Michaels, S. (1983). The role of adult assistance in children's acquisition of literate discourse strategies. *Volta Review*, 85(5), 72–86.

National Association for the Education of Young Children (1988). *Testing of young children: Concerns and cautions.* Washington, DC: NAEYC.

National Education Goals Panel (1991). *Measuring progress toward the National Education Goals: Public testimony.* Volume 3, August 26.

Popkewitz, T. S. (1981). The social contexts of schooling, change, and educational research. *Journal of Curriculum Studies.* 13(3), 189–206.

Ramey, C. T., and Ramey, S. L. (1994). Which children benefit the most from early intervention? *Pediatrics.* 94(6),1064–1066.

Schweinhart, L. J., McNair, S., Barnes, H., and Larner, M. (1993). Observing young children in action to assess their development: The High/Scope child observation record study. *Education and Psychological Measurement.* 53, 445–455.

Taylor, R. L. (1993). Instruments for the screening, evaluation, and assessment of infants and toddlers. In D. M. Bryant and M. A. Graham, (Eds.), *Implementing early intervention: From research to effective practice.* New York: Guliford Press.

Test collection, Educational Testing Service, reading readiness, PK-3 (1985). Princeton, NJ: Educational Testing Service.

Test collection, Educational Testing Service, Spanish speakers, PK-3. (1985). Princeton, NJ: Educational Testing Service.

U. S. Department of Education (1990). *National Goals for Education.* Washington, DC.

Wilbur, K. (1993). *The spectrum of consciousness.* Wheaton, IL: Quest Books.

CHAPTER THIRTEEN

Multiple Intelligences
Cultivating Post-formal Intra/Interpersonal Intelligence: Cooperative Learning Critically Considered

Joe L. Kincheloe

Little doubt exists in mainstream research about the value of "cooperative" learning or "cooperative" education. Typical findings involve claims that students learn more, interact more positively with their peers, gain better self images, and harbor more productive feelings about their schools. While problems undoubtedly exist, mainstream literature touts cooperative learning as a good way to modify the role of teacher as dispenser of information to sponge-like students. Student dialogue becomes as important as teacher monologue, and classroom situations where students share information and creative abilities take the place of individualized competition (Grossman and Grossman, 1994; Tozer, Violas, and Senese, 1993). With these modifications cooperative education begins to subvert the traditional social relations of the classroom.

In addition mainstream researchers claim major benefits for cooperative learning in affective areas of the curriculum, particularly in the attempt to promote racial, socio-economic, and cultural integration of students. Students in cooperative settings tend to manifest an increase in collaboration skills and seem to develop a more differentiated and realistic appreciation of their peers. As their stereotypes of students with different racial, ethnic and socio-economic backgrounds begin to fade, the problems with the individually-grounded competitive curriculum become more and more apparent.

Several researchers have pointed out the problems of cooperative models, focusing on race, class, and gender dynamics that often undermine the goals of cooperative instructional strategies. Evidence points to the fact that females are often the losers in mixed-gender groups. Even though females tend to nurture and provide assistance, males reject female students' request for help. Girls often revert to passive behaviors in cooperative groups and frequently allow males to dominate them. The experiences of some African American students in mixed-ethnic cooperative groups may be similar to the problems experienced by some females. Such dynamics create instructional challenges for teachers who must understand the nuances of interaction between different groups. For example, when some females fall into stereotypical behavior that avoids open disagreement on the grounds it's not "lady-like," teachers must be ready to explain why such actions are self-defeating or be prepared to model a more desirable behavior (Grossman and Grossman, 1994; Tozer, Violas, and Senese, 1993).

Such problems do not, of course, subtract from the benefits of a cooperative education. Indeed, I have little problem with most of the principles of cooperative education. My difficulty with the movement involves not as much what it is, but what it is not. Too often cooperative education fails to transcend the moral blinders of mainstream empirical science and the assumptions of the cult of the expert with its manipulative personnel management (Oakes and Lipton, 1990). Justifications for cooperative curricula often come from industrial leaders who argue that cooperation and team membership skills are necessary for the new, flexibly dynamic businesses of the post-Fordist future. While team membership skills are important, a democratic cooperative education program cannot neglect the examination of the nature of the work for which students are learning to cooperate. Do workers have a voice in workplace decision making? Are products being produced socially and ecologically beneficial? Are workers rewarded for developing their talents? Is the workplace a learning place?

One of the most important questions that is sometimes neglected in cooperative curriculum development involves the issue of meaning making. Are student improvements simply measured by standardized tests that emphasize the acquisition of isolated and often unconnected bits of data—factoids? Or is there something more at work here? Meaning is made in application-based high level math and science. Meaningful education often synthesizes vocations and scholarship, bringing together the realms of the hands and the head. In social studies it means engaging students in social and cultural themes that help them make sense of the way the world works and where they fit in the process. In meaningful cooperative pedagogy, students understand what they're doing and why; they are so much in control of what they learn that they transcend traditional rule following and rote memorization (Tobin and Jakubowski, 1992). In addition to these examples, one form of meaning making particularly stands out in our discussion of cooperative education. I am fascinated by the mysterious notion of intrapersonal and interpersonal intelligence and the attempt to make meaning in the context it creates. If one of the central purposes of cooperative education involves learning to work with others and learning to be a team player, shouldn't it stand to reason that we should investigate this entity Howard Gardner has labeled interpersonal/intrapersonal intelligence?

Cooperative learning researchers speak at length about student's ability to work in a group to complete a task, communicate in a group, lead a team, or manage conflict. Employers complain that their workers don't possess such skills—IBM managers claim that nine out of ten of the employees they fire don't possess such skills (Pasch, et al., 1991). Teachers in cooperative programs are urged to take notes on what interpersonal skills students lack or possess, so such skills can be taught in the context they are needed. While teachers are urged to directly explain social skills, model them, use discovery or role playing to teach them, little analysis of what constitutes a higher-order expression of their skills exists. It seems to me that a central feature of cooperative education should involve the exploration of higher order intrapersonal and interpersonal intelligence, its role in democratic and moral education, and strategies for cultivating it in cooperative learning.

Howard Gardner (1983) writes of personal intelligence which includes what he calls intrapersonal and interpersonal intelligence. Intrapersonal and interpersonal intelligence are both aspects of human nature and ultimately cannot be separated from one another. Intrapersonal intelligence involves the development of the *internal* aspects of a person, especially access to the way one feels, the continuum of his or her affects or emotions. The intrapersonally intelligent individual exhibits the ability to discriminate among these feelings, to isolate and define them, and to employ them as a means of comprehending and shaping one's behavior. At its most basic expression intrapersonal intelligence consists of little more than the ability to distinguish pleasure and pain and, on that basis, to react to a situation. At a higher level of expression, this intra/interpersonal ability empowers an individual to uncover and describe symbolically ambiguous and highly diverse forms of feelings. Novelists such as Alice Walker or James Joyce who write with introspective insight about feelings, the wise therapist who attains dramatic insight into his or her inner feelings, or the sagacious tribal leader who uses his or her own lifetime of experiences to counsel members of the community all display intrapersonal intelligence.

Interpersonal intelligence faces outward toward one's associates and friends. This form of intelligence involves the ability to analyze and make distinctions among the moods, epistemologies, motivations, self-interests, and intentions of other people. At its most basic level, interpersonal intelligence involves the ability of a child to identify and distinguish between individuals around him or her and to determine their different moods. Its advanced expression allows an adult to deconstruct intentions and motivations, even when they have been hidden, and to operate effectively on the basis of such analysis. Effective politicians such as Mahatma Gandhi or Nelson Mandela, moral leaders such Martin Luther King, skilled parents and teachers, or social workers may exhibit high levels of interpersonal intelligence. While both intrapersonal and interpersonal intelligence concern specific forms of knowing, ability in one domain facilitates competence in the other. Neither form of intelligence can develop independent of the other.

The need for these personal intelligences in everyday life, academic life, and vocational life is great. The absence of personal knowledge may hold greater consequences than an absence of other forms of knowing. We sometimes refer to absences as pathological, bizarre, immoral, or even criminal. The consequences of retarded development in personal knowledge may hold dramatic repercussions for the individuals themselves or for those people with whom they come into contact. Nevertheless, Westerners have rarely placed much emphasis on the analysis or cultivation of personal knowledges, focusing their efforts instead on logical-mathematical and linguistic intelligences. Conversely, cultures outside the West, such as Japan, have placed significant emphasis on the development of intrapersonal and interpersonal intelligences. Given the problems resulting from the arrested growth of personal intelligences including, violence, murder, rape, hate crimes, racism, and the like, one is tempted to argue that more emphasis on such intelligences is needed in the late twentieth-century education (Gardner, 1983).

Given the tremendous need for personal intelligences and the consequences of their neglect, it is interesting to note the indifference, or better, the disdain cognitive scientists have shown the topic. Because of such neglect, I would argue that the Western view of the intellect is incomplete. No one has laid out just how instruction for personal intelligence should take place or how we might determine the success of such instruction. Nevertheless, the convenient removal of such intelligence from the cognitive domain is ill advised. When an individual feels paranoid, elated, or threatened, he or she has interpreted a situation in a particular way—that is a cognitive act. There are significant differences between an accurate assessment of an interpersonal situation and a fundamental misinterpretation. When humans misconstrue their own feelings, it becomes more likely that they will be consumed by them. The less humans understand the feelings and behavior of others, the greater the possibility that they will not act appropriately with them.

I want to share with you my thinking about the study of intrapersonal/interpersonal intelligences in a way that extends concerns of cooperative learning—a way that views it in the context of post-formal thinking. As described in this book, Piagetian formal thinking implies an acceptance of a Cartesian-Newtonian mechanistic worldview that is caught in a cause-effect, hypothetical-deductive system of reasoning. Unconcerned with moral questions, power relations, and the way they structure our consciousness, formal operational thinkers accept an objectified, unpoliticized way of knowing that breaks a social or educational system down into its basic parts in order to understand how it works. Emphasizing certainty and production, formal thinking organizes verified facts into a theory. The facts that do not fit into the theory are eliminated, and the theory developed is the one best suited to limit the contradictions in knowledge. Thus, formal thought operates on the assumption that resolution must be found for all contradictions. Schools and standardized test-makers, assuming that formal operational thought represents the highest level of human cognition, focus their efforts on its cultivation and measurement. Students and teachers who move beyond formality are often unrewarded and sometimes even punished in educational contexts (Kincheloe and Steinberg, 1993).

Post-formal Thinking

Post-formalism defines the kind of thinking that might occur when students *and* teachers move beyond the boundaries of Piagetian formalism. Though Piaget exerted a dramatic impact on our understanding of cognitive development, he never understood the confines on thinking imposed by the abstract rationality of the formal stage. The emphasis of formalism was not engaged with the particulars of everyday life but with disengagement, a focus on distanced, disinterested, and abstract contemplation. The move to post-formality politicizes cognition as post-formal thinkers liberate themselves from interpersonal norms and ideological expectations. The post-formal concern with questions of meaning, moral and ethical conflict, new insight via ideological disembedding, and attention to the process of identity formation moves beyond formal thought and its affair with the scientific method. In such a context formalism becomes obsessed with proper procedure, i.e., the scientific method. Post-formalism grapples with purpose, devoting attention to issues of human dignity, ethical behavior , freedom, authority, and social responsibility (Lave, 1988; Walkerdine, 1984, 1988; Kincheloe and Steinberg, 1993).

Before proceeding any farther, a brief review of the four main features of post-formal thinking, as Shirley Steinberg and I have theorized in Chapter Two of this text, will be useful:

1. ETYMOLOGY—THE EXPLORATION OF THE FORCES THAT PRODUCE WHAT THE CULTURE VALIDATES AS KNOWLEDGE An individual who thinks etymologically pays close attention to the source of her or his intuitions and "gut feelings," aware that we rarely develop such feelings independently and draw them instead from a cultural kitty of approved perceptions. Without such awareness, the ability for reflection and analysis is seriously undermined. It is not an exaggeration to maintain that the capacity for critical thought is grounded upon the post-formal concern with etymology.

2 PATTERN—THE UNDERSTANDING OF THE CONNECTING PATTERNS AND THE RELATIONSHIPS THAT UNDERGIRD THE LIVED WORLD Like hurricanes shaped by interactive pressure systems and winds, schools, student lives, economic systems, and social systems are constructed by interlocking activities that create invisible patterns—patterns extremely difficult to identify when one is standing in the system's center. Modernist science and education have typically focused on separate components, like declining SAT scores, oblivious to the long-term cultural systems, like language, that affect the parts. As a result, mainstream "experts" fail to solve serious problems because of their narrow focus.

3 PROCESS—THE CULTIVATION OF NEW WAYS OF READING THE WORLD THAT ATTEMPT TO MAKE SENSE OF BOTH OURSELVES AND CONTEMPORARY SOCIETY All human beings hold the potential for creative thinking processes, but through acculturation and education in a Cartesian-Newtonian world, many have lost such a capacity. Many analysts argue that prehistoric peoples, who devised not only tools and useful objects but also ornamental and spiritual objects, lived a more creative existence than many of today's workers and students who daily follow a mechanical routine. The post-formal process attempts to devise new and

creative ways to perceive the world, ways to rethink thinking in order to reposition students as active producers, not passive receivers of knowledge (Bohm and Edwards, 1991).

4 CONTEXTUALIZATION—THE APPRECIATION THAT KNOWLEDGE CAN NEVER STAND ALONE OR BE COMPLETE IN AND OF ITSELF To abstract is to take something away from its context. Abstraction is necessary in everyday life because there is too much information for the mind to process. The post-formal thinker is certainly capable of abstraction but at the same time refuses to lose sight of the conceptual field, the context that provides separate entities meaning (Raizen and Colvin, 1991). For example, abstract academic knowledge may best be learned in a vocational context, like an apprenticeship. Novices need academics as well as familiarity with specific social, symbolic, encoded, technical, and other types of workplace resources—i.e., the context of the workplace (Raizen, 1989). With these frames in mind, the construction of a post-formal notion of intrapersonal/interpersonal intelligence can be considered.

Post-formal Intrapersonal Intelligence
META-CONSCIOUSNESS—EXPANDING THE CAPACITY FOR SELF-REFLECTION Meta-consciousness opens the long-locked door of the primal as it moves individuals to transcend the boundaries of instinct. Post-formal self-reflection asks why we are the way we are, i.e., the etymology of self. As individuals explore personal meanings, the origins of their actions, they gain an awareness of alterations, of possibilities in their lives. Meta-conscious individuals refuse to accept or reject validity claims of any body of information without considering its discursive nature, that is, where the information comes from, what can be officially transmitted and what cannot, and who translates it and who listens. Without such reflection, individuals travel through life imprisoned by the prejudices derived from everyday existence or by what is often labeled common sense. The habitual beliefs of an individual's historical age become tyrants to a mind unable to reflect on its genesis. We often emerge from sixteen to twenty years of schooling without having been asked to think about our thinking. Such a formal education too often ignores the effects of the emergence of a social climate of deceit with its marketing strategies, political image making, discursive practices, and its decontextualized and allegedly disinterested science.

The concept of post-formal intrapersonal intelligence can be extended by William Pinar's (1994) notion of *currere* (the Latin root of the word "curriculum" meaning the investigation of the nature of the individual experience of the public) that moves us to a consciousness of our own inner world of psychological experience. The effort involves our ability to bring to conscious view our culturally created and therefore limited concept of both self and reality, thus revealing portions of ourselves previously hidden. Post-formal interpersonal intelligence involves understanding the way our consciousness is constructed, appreciating the forces that facilitate or impede our accommodations. Post-formal thinking about thinking involves our ability to engage in ideological disembedding, the ability to remove ourselves from sociointerpersonal norms and expectations. This post-formal concern with questions of meaning and attention to the process of self-production rises above the formal level of thought and its concern with proper procedure. Our conception of post-formal thinking about thinking never allows us to be content with our intrapersonal understandings. Never certain of the appropriateness of our ways of seeing and always concerned with the expansion of self-awareness and consciousness, postformal thinkers engage in a running meta-dialogue, a constant conversation with self (Codd, 1984; Kegan, 1982).

Teachers as post-formal intrapersonal thinkers in cooperative learning situations generate strategies to promote such self-reflective thinking among themselves and their students. In addition to journal-writing assignments that explore "how I felt when . . . ," post-formal teachers conceptualize techniques to encourage such dialogical situations in ways that promote self-reflection. Such introspection demands a critical meta-perspective on the nature of classroom conversations (how do we talk to one another?), the nature of the classroom learning (what do we call knowledge?), curriculum decisions (what do we need to know?), and assessment (is what we're doing working?). When thinking advances and the dialogues grow in sophistication, students come to reflect about the sociopolitical nature of their school experience, asking whose interest it serves for them to see the world in the way they do.

TRANSCENDENCE OF EGOCENTRISM—THE DIFFICULT JOURNEY OUTWARD
The social climate created by the postmodern hyperreality with its constant commercial inducements to consume, to gratify the self contributes to an egocentric culture. In the context of personal intelligence this cultural egocentrism holds serious consequences. Egocentrism (as opposed to connectedness) reduces our awareness of anything outside our own immediate experience. In our self-centeredness we tend to reduce everything to an individual perspective that causes us to miss

meanings of significance. Many would argue that this self-absorption leads the way to an introspective self-knowledge that will move us to higher levels of experience, new dimensions of cognition. Post-formal intrapersonal intelligence does not buy into such analysis. While self-knowledge is extremely important, egocentrism tends to reduce our ability to critique the construction of our own consciousness—we cannot gain the meta-consciousness to recognize the social forces that have shaped us. Unless we learn to confront our egocentrism, the possibility of gaining critical perspectives in regard to ourselves and the world around us is limited. In other words, we will fail to develop post-formal intrapersonal intelligence. While post-formal teachers must make sure that students have confidence in their own perceptions and interpretations, they must concurrently work to help students overcome the tendency to see the world only in terms of self. Such self-centeredness lays the foundation for ethnocentrism, racism , homophobia, and sexism. In a way post-formal thinkers must learn to cope with a lifetime struggle between the tendency for self-confidence and the tendency for humility. We do not seek resolution, just a healthy dynamic between the impulses (Greene, 1988).

THE CREATION OF KNOWLEDGE—UNDERSTANDING OURSELVES AS WE MAKE SENSE OF THE WORLD Post-formal thinkers manifest their intrapersonal intelligence at the level of knowledge seeking and knowledge production. Such individuals no longer see themselves as passive receivers of expert produced information. The act of knowledge creation not only teaches us to think and make meaning, but it allows us to understand ourselves. At the intrapersonal level, post-formal thinkers demonstrate the ability to use knowledge they've created about the world to make personal meaning. Knowledge, they understand, is never independent of human knowers. The frontier where information about the world collides with personal experience is the point where knowledge is created. In other words, to be considered knowledge, information must be incorporated into one's own life. Teachers in cooperative learning situations must constantly emphasize and act upon this understanding—the process of knowledge production changes who we are. Thus, post-formal intrapersonal intelligence knows no precise boundaries —it is elastic. Such intelligence expands in relation to what men and women make of themselves, what they can produce in new understandings.

Post-formal Interpersonal Intelligence

COGNITIVE CUBISM—UNDERSTANDING THE WORLD AND ITS PEOPLE FROM DIFFERENT PERSPECTIVES Post-formality values a spatial distancing which allows an observer diverse frames of reference. The distancing may range from the extremely distant such as astronauts looking at the Earth from the Moon, to the extremely close like Georgia O'Keefe viewing a flower. At the same time, post-formality values the emotional intimacy of feminist connectedness which allows interpersonal passion to draw knower and known together. Post-formal interpersonal intelligence understands that different observers stand in different places in the web of reality and thus see the world from different angles. The acuteness or obliqueness of these different angles shapes not only what they see but their consciousness as well. Post-formal interpersonal observers understand how an individual gains his or her particular consciousness and as a result gain unique and revealing interpersonal insight.

William Carlos Williams illustrated such post-formal qualities in the early twentieth century as he depicted multiple, simultaneous images and frames of reference in a verbal manner. Williams attempted to poetically interpret Marcel Duchamp's *Nude Descending a Staircase* with its simultaneism serving as a model for what post-formality might label "cognitive cubism." Post-formal teachers use such ideas to extend the holographic nature of their own and their students' memory, as they create situations where students come to view reality from as many frames of reference as is possible. The single angle of the traditional photograph is replaced by the multiple angles of the holographic photograph (Dobrin 1987; Mandell 1987; Talbot 1986, 1991).

EMPATHY—THE ABILITY TO PLACE ONESELF INSIDE THE CONSCIOUSNESS OF SPECIFIC OTHER INDIVIDUALS Western modernism has encouraged a competitive impulse that has moved humans to experience themselves and their consciousnesses as separate from one another. Such an orientation is an important aspect of a Western cognitive illness that holds destructive and socially pathological implications. Our social imagination is restricted, as we are bound to simple personal desires. With the emphasis on ethnocentric family values and the accompanying impoverishment of the public space, our affections and empathy are limited to the family unit and a few individuals close to us. Part of our therapy, our emancipation from the cognitive illness involves expanding our realm of concern to the public space, to the larger society in its interrelated complexity. Our private experience of empathy must be transferred not only into cooperative education but to public policy in general.

Acting on this empathetic aspect of post-formal interpersonal intelligence, teachers in cooperative programs engage students in the exploration of the consciousness of other people. The ability to understand others' joys and their pains, their dreams and motivations becomes a central feature of a democratic education for the violent late twentieth century. Special attention is focused on empathy for the poor and the dispossessed—a perspective often ignored in schools and the mainstream media. Critical empathy involves understanding an institution from the perspectives of those who have suffered as a result of its existence. Such an empathy provides a sophisticated appreciation for the nature of justice and the invisibility and, thus, power of oppression. In such a cognitive context, teachers of cooperative learning utilize such understandings to push students to higher levels of interpersonal thinking. Post-formal teachers can lead students to study patterns of conduct in friendships, through experiments involving possible interactions with different individuals. A curriculum of interpersonal relations can be developed in a classical Deweyan motif. Such a curriculum would center around the problems of interpersonal relations in an age of violence and the enhancement of interpersonal intelligence. Examples from literature, music, art, theater, science, and social studies could be woven around this core.

CONNECTED CONSCIOUSNESS—ONE'S SELF IS OTHER PEOPLE Cartesian-Newtonian separate knowing has been a prime target of feminist theory. Connected knowing values intimacy and understanding instead of distance and proof. Even some versions of critical theoretical emancipation privilege autonomous self-direction based on an understanding of how the influences of one's past shape and mold consciousness. A feminist reconceptualization of emancipation grounded on connected knowing uses this understanding of one's past not only to free oneself from its repressive characteristics but to facilitate connection with other people around visions of community. Thus connected consciousness experiences self essentially in relationship to others. Separateness, from this perspective, couches democratic principles only in the negative. For example, freedom *from* interference, not freedom *to* connect, self-dependence rather than an interrelationship with the community, and liberty as the right to do as we please not as the right to engage in socially beneficent activities (Greene, 1988; Belenky, Clinchy, Goldberger,

and Tarule, 1986). Post-formal connected consciousness no longer glo-
rifies, as Kohlberg did, the early Clint Eastwood in his role as the man
with no name. The high plains drifter asked nothing from nobody and
had no need for interpersonal intelligence. To hell with other people—
he didn't need to establish connections with a core of friends.

Howard Gardner (1983) provides insight into the social relations of
interpersonal intelligence in his distinction between a *particle* society
and *field* society. Contemporary America is the quintessential example
of a particle society with its focus on the specific individual, his or her
autonomy and alleged control of personal fate. The social environment
serves only as a movie backdrop with little interaction with the individual. Continuing his physics metaphor, Gardner contrasts the particle
society with the field society. In the field culture an individual's locus of
control resides with other people or with society as a whole. De-empha-
sizing the individual's agency, the surrounding context is viewed as the
force that shapes an individual's life. Obviously, a healthy integration of
the two models is more desirable than one extreme or the other. In postmodern America, the individualist ethic of the particle society holds
devastating consequences for students taught that their failure is always
their own fault. Post-formal interpersonal thinking does not seek to simply excuse an individual from personal responsibility, but it does help
individuals understand the interaction of social and personal forces that
impede or facilitate our efforts.

Post-formal Integrated Intrapersonal
and Interpersonal Intelligence

RECOGNITION OF NON-HIERARCHICAL DIFFERENCE Modernist scholars
have long contended the foundation of political and ethical thinking has
rested on a close-knit community with a common set of precepts.
Sharon Welch challenges such a perception, arguing from a postmodern
perspective that heterogeneous communities with differing principles
may better contribute to the cultivation of critical thinking and moral
reasoning. A homogeneous community often is unable to criticize the
injustice and exclusionary practices that afflict a social system.

Criticism and reform of cultural pathology often come from the
recognition of difference from interaction with individuals or communities who do not suffer from the same injustices or who have dealt with
them in different ways. We always profit in some way from a confrontation with another system of defining that which is important—
indeed, our interpersonal intelligence is enhanced through such experi-

ences. Consciousness itself, or intrapersonal intelligence, is spurred by difference in that we gain our first awareness of who we are when we are aware that we are different from another or another's ways.

Welch maintains that the concept of solidarity is more inclusive and transformative than the concept of consensus. Even if we perceive consensus to involve a common recognition of cultural pathology and the belief that we must work together to find a cure, we first have to accept the value of interpersonal solidarity. Welch claims that the ethic of solidarity has two main aspects: (1) It grants social groups enough respect to listen to their ideas and to use them to consider existing social values, and (2) it realizes that the lives of individuals in differing groups are interconnected to the point that everyone is accountable to everyone else. No assumption of uniformity exists here—just the commitment to work together to bring about mutually beneficial social change (Welch, 1991). In the classroom, this valuing of difference and its political and cognitive benefits exhibits itself in a dialogical sharing of perspective. In this process, students slowly come to see their own points of view as one particular sociohistorically constructed way of perceiving. As the classroom develops, students are exposed to more and more diverse voices in various texts and discussions, a process that engages them in other ways of seeing and knowing. Thus, their epistemological circle is widened, as difference expands their social imagination, their vision of what could be. Students are liberated from the blinders of dominant culture, the purgatory of only liberal or conservative alternatives.

OVERCOMING AUTHORITY DEPENDENCE—CONFRONTING THE CULTURE OF MORAL/POLITICAL PASSIVITY In modernist teacher education and modernist schools both teachers and students are encultured into a culture of passivity. In the worst modernist, technicist teacher education programs, teachers are taught to tame their pedagogical imagination. They are barred from discussions of educational purpose of the social or economic context of teaching. Such teachers lose their autonomy and become accustomed to an academic culture of passivity, which teaches both teachers and students to conform, to adjust to their inequality and to their particular rung of the status ladder, and to submit to authority. Teachers and students are induced to develop an authority dependence, a view of citizenship that is passive, a view of learning that means listening. The predisposition to question the authority structure of the school and the curriculum it teaches or to reject the image of the future that the structure presents to teachers and students is out of bounds. The politics of authoritarianism rub democratic impulses the wrong way (Shor, 1992).

Post-formal teachers and students have much-too-well-developed personal intelligence to stand for this passivity. Post-formal teachers of cooperative learning help students learn to become researchers. Depending upon their students' developmental level, teachers engage students in ethnographic, semiotic, phenomenological, and historiographical research. In the process students learn to deconstruct their lives. In such a context, students explore their place in the social hierarchy of their peer group, their romantic relationships, their vocational aspirations, their relationships with teachers, and their definitions of success. They become researchers, in other words, of their intrapersonal and interpersonal lives, in the process gaining a post-formal meta-consciousness of who they are.

Armed with a meta-consciousness of their relationship to the culture of passivity, teachers and students begin to question the nature of ethical interpersonal relations and democratic forms of administration. In this frame of mind they begin to challenge conceptually the administrative structure of schools and other institutions. Such students and teachers find it interesting that administration is taught only to people who serve at the head of administrative structures and not to people who are to be administered. Post-formal cooperative learning thus begins to expand into various curriculums, exploring reconceptualized notions of interpersonal power relations and the intrapersonal effects of such relations. Post-formal thinkers, thus, reexamine the nature of human management in democratic societies and its effects on classroom interpersonal relations, interpersonal relations between genders, principal-teacher interpersonal relations, husband-wife interpersonal relations, and so on. There are many ways to extend the concept of cooperative learning

If cooperative education is to transcend the faddish comings and goings of far too many education reforms, it has to be tied to larger social and cognitive ideas. There are profound contemporary social justifications for an emphasis on those abilities that help us get along with one another. When I lived in Miami, I watched a city plagued by violence, schools overwhelmed by conflict, and students traumatized by constant exposure to such circumstances. Such a context creates a compelling need for the cultivation of the personal intelligences. In no way do I want to be misunderstood on this particular point: analysis of intrapersonal and interpersonal intelligence is not an attempt to socially decontextualize or psychologize the notion of personal relations.

Indeed, it is just the opposite, as one of the central features of post-formal thinking involves social contextualization and the recognition of the effect of power on the personal. The post-formal interpretation of cooperative education and post-formal personal intelligence maintains that only when cognition is socially contextualized will we get beyond the trivialization of both educational reform and the public conversation about education in general.

References

Belenky, M., Clinchy, B., Goldberger, N., and Tarule, J. (1986). *Women's ways of knowing: The development of self, voice, and mind.* NY: Basic Books.

Bohm, D. and Edwards, M. (1991). *Changing consciousness.* San Francisco: Harper.

Bozik, M. (1987). Critical thinking through creative thinking. Paper presented to the Speech Communication Association, Boston.

Codd, J. (1984). Introduction. In J. Codd (Ed.), *Philosophy, common sense, and action in educational administration.* Victoria, Australia: Deakin University Press.

Dobrin, R. (1987). The nature of causality and reality: A reconciliation of the ideas of Einstein and Bohr in the light of Eastern thought. In D. Ryan (Ed.), *Einstein and the humanities.* NY: Greenwood Press.

Gardner, H. (1983). *Frames of mind: A theory of multiple intelligences.* NY: Basic Books.

Gardner, H. (1991). *The unschooled mind: How children think and how schools should teach.* NY: Basic Books.

Greene, M. (1988). *The dialectic of freedom.* NY: Teachers College Press.

Grossman, H. and Grossman, S. (1994). *Gender issues in education.* Boston: Allyn and Bacon.

Kegan, R. (1982). *The evolving self: problem and process in human development.* Cambridge, MA: Harvard University Press.

Kincheloe, J. and Steinberg, S. (1993). A tentative description of post-formal thinking: The critical confrontation of cognitive theory. *Harvard Educational Review, 63*(3), 296–320.

Lave, J. (1988). *Cognition in practice.* Cambridge, MA: Cambridge University Press.

Lawler, J. (1975). Dialectical philosophy and developmental psychology: Hegel and Piaget on contradiction. *Human Development, 18,*. 1–17.

Maher, F. and Rathbone, C. (1986). Teacher education and feminist theory: Some implications for practice. *American Journal of Education, 94*, 2, 214–35.

Mandell, S. (1987). A search for form: Einstein and the poetry of Louis Zukofsky and William Carlos Williams. In Ryan (Ed.). *Einstein and the Humanities.* New York: Greenwood Press.

Oakes, J. and Lipton, M. (1990). *Making the best of schools: A handbook for parents, teachers, and policymakers.* New Haven, CT: Yale University Press.

Pasch, M. et al. (1991). *Teaching as decision-making: Instructional practices for the successful teacher.* White Plains, NY: Longman.

Pinar, W. (1991). *Autobiography, politics, and sexuality: Essays in curriculum theory, 1972-1992.* New York: Peter Lang.

Raizen, S. (1989). *Reforming education for work: A cognitive science perspective.* Berkeley, CA: NCRVE.

Raizen, S. and Colvin, R. (1991). Apprenticeships: A cognitive-science view. *Education Week.* December 11, p. 26.

Senge, P. (1990). *The fifth discipline: The art and practice of the learning organization.* New York: Doubleday.

Shor, I. (1992). *Empowering education: Critical teaching for social change.* Chicago: University of Chicago Press.

Talbot, M. (1986). *Beyond the quantum.* New York: Bantam Books.

Talbot, M. (1991). *The holographic universe.* New York: HarperCollins.

Tobin, K. and Jakubowski, E. (1992). The cognitive requisites for improving the performance of elementary mathematics and science teaching. In E. Ross, J. Cornett, and G. McCutcheon (Eds.), *Teacher personal theorizing: Connecting curriculum practice, theory, and research.* Albany, NY: SUNY Press.

Tozer, S., Violas, P., and Senese, G. (1993). *School and society: Educational practice as social explanation.* New York: McGraw-Hill.

Walkerdine, V. (1984). Developmental psychology and the child-centered pedagogy: The insertion of Piaget into early education. In J. Henriques, W. Hollway, C. Urwin, C. Venn, and V. Walkerdine (Eds.), *Changing the subject.* New York: Methuen.

Walkerdine, V. (1988). *The mastery of reason: Cognitive development and the production of rationality.* London: Routledge.

Welch, S. (1991). An ethic of solidarity and difference. In H. Giroux (Ed.), *Postmodernism, feminism, and cultural politics: Redrawing educational boundaries.* Albany, NY: SUNY Press.

PART THREE
INFORMED PRACTICE

CHAPTER FOURTEEN

Pedagogical Theory
Destabilizing Educational Thought and Practice: Post-formal Pedagogy

Kathleen Berry

Recognizing Formalism

If John von Neumann and Alan Turing had used a modern day public school classroom as a base, their study of complex systems theory, the prototype for digital technology, might not have evolved so rapidly or at all. Immersed in a formalist culture, education is not the best site for the study of complexity or the development of the theory of chaos. Modern education is entrenched in simplicity and order, a product of Eurocentric philosophy, scientific method, positivism, objectivity, and the "logos" of rationalism. Curricula, administrative and pedagogical structures, relationships of teaching and learning, and the entire range of content and organization are directed by these reductionist theories. In turn, certain discourse and elements determine the theories and practices of a vast educational realm which fall under the rubric of formalism. The "grand narratives" of formalism offer structures and methodologies that are problematic in the context of a post-formalist world. In this chapter, I challenge the status of formalism in education and explore the potential of post-formalist pedagogy, not as an agent of change, shift, or additional information but as a means of destabilizing the present dominance of formalism in education. To do so, I borrow from the discourse and principles of several major contemporary theories to assist in the discussion, theories that both question the stability, structures, and methodologies of formalism and provide discourse to rethink educational theories and practices.

Cultural studies and criticism, postmodernism, poststructuralism, postcolonialism, postfeminism, deconstructionism, and phenomenology are all employed in the humanities. Theories of complexity and chaos hail from the current flow of thought in science and technology (see Hayles' 1991 book for the border crossings between these disciplines and their discourses). Each one of these domains challenges the totalizing narratives and practices of formalist theories and methodologies with the clear intent to destabilize, shake up, and fracture the foundations of modern thought and institutions, including those of education.

Initially, formalism imposes order on our world, including the landscape of education and pedagogy. I use education to refer to the organization of a range of theories and practices which structure areas such as imagination, administration, curriculum documents and structures, classroom relationships, materials, politics, and economics. By pedagogy, I am referring to the phenomenological relationship of all these elements which indeed carry different notions of what it means to be in an educational context. The former construct has designated powers gained by the historical and hegemonic dictates and validity of formalism. The latter is powered by its philosophical purpose to destabilize the dominance of the scientific method and Cartesian dualism (where the known and the knower can be separated as objects). Whereas I see modern education ruled by content and form, I see pedagogy as a responsibility to the "other" governed by a sensitivity to context and lived experience. A post-formalist world, that is, a world quite different in imagination and practice, favors a pedagogical orientation more than a modernist approach to education.

There are several factors at play that are challenges to modern culture. Similarities and differences exist among these contemporary theories, each in their own way challenging modern modes of thought, structures, institutions, history, knowledge, values, curriculum, and pedagogy. The winds of change tumble one theory against or into the other. The major areas of thought that have determined each element of life (its constructions, discourse, actions, and practices in all disciplines) are subject to the influence of a post-formalist way of thinking. Education and pedagogy are dominoes that stand to be influenced, tumbled, and capsized.

Modern pedagogy, like all other areas of life, is constructed mainly through an emphasis on method. Method has dominated Western culture for several centuries with the major claim that, by following a particular "formalized" method, the knowing subject can impose a systemized, so-called, objective reality on the world. In other words, educators develop a priori methods/theories removed from the phenomenological experience and presence of their students and impose, through methodology or theory, a system of order that lies outside the students. This dominant imposition of order upon not only the behavior of classrooms but on the very thinking of our students must be addressed. Any thoughts that this should be otherwise creates pedagogical angst and political backlash. Without a different discourse or challenge to formalist pedagogy, teachers continue to work without any movement forward and, I would argue quite passionately, without any hope for revitalized or creative energy.

In modern pedagogy, with its emphasis on formalism, teachers and students work in a relationship that is opposed to insights gained through the metaphysics of presence or, as Barb Laws (1972) claims, "you eventually have to go with your intuition and gut feelings. Not only that, there is no one way [method], but the students also need to be encouraged to have *guts*." Perhaps Barb is not expressing the sentiment very formally, but she is expressing the reality or the lived experience of how creative, non-formalistic, and grounded in the presence of the other is what good teachers have been doing without noticing, i.e., responding to the presence of the other in a manner that does not occur in a formalist pedagogy. In Barb's example lies a discourse and practice—a local narrative—as resistance to the grand narratives of formalism that represents the end of an epistemologically-centered philosophy. Discourse provides a ground for destabilizing the dominance of formalism in pedagogy.

Many teachers, myself included, believe that we work as individuals and are sensitive to the needs, abilities, and desires of our students. We have, in fact, been conditioned otherwise. Or perhaps the hegemonic world in which we have worked, so comfortably, and so successfully, has made us fear the dismantling or dissolving of the modernist approach and see it as a threat to our continued success and comfort. In the introduction to this book, Kincheloe examines how the demise of formalist thinking is influencing many traditions and fields, with teaching and learning, in particular, and educational psychology not the least affected. I propose that as educators we forego our comfort and complacency with the dominance of formalism, which appears mainly in the disguise of educational psychology, and turn to what might have been happening in classrooms. A different picture of what is masked by a formalist infrastructure offers creative interpretations, pedagogical possibilities, and dismantling discourse to teachers, students, teacher education, administrators, parents, and others. To do so, as mentioned before, I will borrow heavily from contemporary theories and practices.

Hegemonic Status of Formalist Thought and Methods

More than any other formalist discipline, educational psychology attempts to impose order on the world—so much so that it infiltrates, directs, and governs the consciousness and structures of how we think and act especially in relation to students. Through the categorization of human existence, it has framed how we teach, learn, organize, plan, develop, and evaluate human beings within an educational context. The drive of educational psychology to purify its knowledge and legitimize its place has reduced education, including knowledge and value, to a empirical, positivistic, objective, and, in several matters, decontextual-ized, ahistorical, and clinical control of the world. More importantly, as a dominant discipline and discourse, it has reduced human beings to sci-entific categories and methodologies which order and control educa-tional thought and pedagogical relationships. The power given to edu-cational psychology, especially in the last four to five decades of the twentieth century, has imposed order upon and limited the capacity of the institution, and subsequently, its members.

Formalism comes in many guises. It is, however, dressed mostly in categorical discourse and scientific, empirical methods. The plethora of prefabricated methods readily offered—in areas ranging from " how to," or "what to do Monday morning," or "what teachers/students must know," or "what teachers or students must do when" to the evaluation and determination of people within those frameworks—seems to be a major application of formalism. Readers may note the lack of regard I have for the field, not only as a totalizing discourse but also as a disci-pline racked with theories that advocate imposing order on my peda-gogical thoughts, actions, and relationships. This diatribe does not indi-cate lack of respect for the authority and contributions that educational psychology has made to the field of pedagogy but a challenge to its long-term hegemonic status. It seems that in my thirty years of teach-ing, each year is inundated by another category of labeling and limita-tion emitted by the formalist discourse and thinking of psychology. It seems that in the late 90's, students are brought to order (as by a judge's gavel) by, for example, the decree of ADD (Attention Deficit Disorder) or ADS (Attention Deficit Syndrome).

Formalist thinking and methods provide several elements upon which individuals (sometimes consciously) and institutional systems become dependent. The discourse of formalism organizes and orders the world mainly through categorization; it is a cycle that exists through methods which direct the subjects, knowledge, and values into ordered, status quo categories. Once a subject or other element is moved into a category by the discourse, for example, ADD or ADS, the subject is both reduced to a category and subjected to methods which manipulate and control his/her behavior and thoughts. Although such subjects are not included as mainstream and tend to carry the label for a lifetime, they are at least seen as being brought to order. ADD/ADS is only one example, yet it is representative of the multiple over-categorization that occurs within formalistic discourse and structures of educational psychology. Other areas are governed by formalism; however, since educational psychology is the dominant discipline which governs education, it becomes the best example of hegemony to dismantle.

Why is it that the formalism of educational psychology and other areas has been left unchallenged for so many decades? In other words, why have these areas been able to maintain their hegemonic status to which educational circles have consented? Most formalist constructs are based on scientific method, and therefore perceived as legitimized and validated, containing the truths, knowledge, and values of reality. The problem here is that reality has been constructed in such a manner that the discourse and constructs of the discipline are privileged. Teachers don't risk challenging psychology's constructions of reality, because they would be seen to be either oppositional, outside the mainstream, or not knowledgeable about the world. In addition, how do we "cooperate" or get along with colleagues? How do we test? How do we expect standards? How do we organize and implement curriculum that is inclusive of individuals? With this in mind, individuals and groups accept mainstream constructions that, over a long period of time, have become accepted truths and knowledge about the educational world. Challenges to the discourse, categories, and methods of formalism are soon delegated to the margins, isolated from the mainstream, and in many cases, rejected as radical or impossible.

The hegemonic status of any field can be dissolved or dismantled by individuals, groups, and by new theories, discourses, and metaphors or by force and coercion. Obviously, the former means of toppling the hegemonic status of formalism is cogently peaceful but disruptive.

Counter-hegemonic Education

In the past, the classroom and all that determines its context, from teachers and students to administrators and curriculum planners, from public politics to theoretical influences, have order imposed by dominant formula-izations (methods). This empiricism has ruled for too long, producing stagnant thoughts and thus stagnant pools of organization and inactivity. What is assumed is that order is imposed upon the world, including, for example, knowledge, values, behaviors, institutions, history, law, and for our purposes, pedagogy. Furthermore, as all these facets of the world become objectively ordered through methods, the world is formalized. Anything or anyone who does not fit into or agree with the formalist world either lies outside as resistant to categorization or impossible to control (ADD/ADS?). What falls outside the formalistic world is considered non-existent, invalid, false, or illegitimate. This includes knowledge, values, concepts, behaviors, thoughts, and so forth. Education and pedagogy are two areas which continue to embrace the formalist vision.

The shift away from formalism in all realms from science to literature to pedagogy is to post-formalism. In a manner of speaking, the move is away from seeing the world as ordered to destabilizing thoughts and methods, thus creating a world of chaos. The world is not viewed as disordered or lacking in order but is conceptualized as extremely complex information, unstable meanings, and multiple readings. Teachers who work outside the boundaries of formalism, like scientists working in physics and other natural sciences, challenge the reductionist view presented by the constructs and discourse of areas such as psychology and conceptualize systems of chaos as complex systems rich in information rather than viewing them as disorder or misbehavior. The application of chaos is not a change to an entirely different world but merely a new way of viewing the world, in our case, the world of pedagogy. Within this world of chaos one would find neither a reduction to simplicity nor the kind of control, manipulation, and prediction that is seen in formalism. There is, rather, a complexity that engages the teacher as an observer of emergent phenomena.

As observers and employers of destabilized formalism, chaos becomes creative and productive information. Teachers shift their center of pedagogical discourse and practice. Complexity, unexpected conclusions, spontaneity, self-organization, fragmentation, importance of scale, sensitivity to momentum, destabilized theories and discourse, deep structures of order, noise, inconsistencies, instabilities, play (ludic postmodernism), local sites and knowledge, discontinuity, heterogeneity, and the locale of reality are only a part of the qualities of chaos. This presents inconsistences in teachers' views and discourse about the world in which they stand. Destabilizing principles, such as those of chaos theory, don't ask teachers to change their practices per se. One might ask, however, how chaotic energy causes teachers to shift their gaze from the ordered *center* of the classroom to the chaotic *margins* (McLaughlin, 1997)?

Discourses that Destabilize Modern Education

In formalism, chaos is seen as the opposite of order. However, in the new ways of thinking, chaos is considered as a site for new information about phenomena (Hayles, 1991, p. 6). For our purposes, phenomena are all things that exist within our educational context, including ways of thinking about and practicing administration, curriculum, teaching, learning, materials, evaluation, and so forth. These phenomena become locations for observation and construction of chaos. Whereas modern education has expended dollars and labor to extract order from chaos as a means of control and manipulation, postmodern education shifts monies and energy to chaos as a means of developing, organizing, and evaluating systems of education.

Even the discourse shifts.

Words such as "systems" take on an entirely different meaning in a theory or science of chaos. This radical shift in thinking about the world of pedagogy is seen as less threatening than the formalistic curriculum that has been imposed on teachers for the past century.

An immediate response might be that chaos is the very state that teachers want to avoid. I would, however, like to argue that chaos is more representative of the reality of education than that of decades of modern formalistic education. The task now is to clarify how chaos is a more productive and realistic way of living in a pedagogical world, as perhaps it is in many other situations or institutional structures traditionally constructed along formalistic lines. In this case, it is important to provide some initial understanding of how a state of chaos is more beneficial to teachers and the educational field in general.

Chaos is not disorder. Chaos is complexity. It is a field that, when read differently, becomes an information source that can be reorganized at a higher level of complexity. This, I argue, is a powerful alternative to the traditional simplistic reductionism of formalism. Post-formalist pedagogy would recognize the inherent complexity of the student in a pedagogical context and raise his or her thinking, acting, and being to a different level. In a formalist process, complexity is reduced to a state of simplicity in which the teacher controls the student.

One might argue, from a formalist perspective, that order needs to be maintained and preserved (a good hegemonic argument) when one teacher is responsible for some thirty students at the same time. In short, the formalist views "learning" and "chaos" as incompatible. If indeed teachers read chaos as a state of disorder, not just of behavior but of the organization of knowledge, values, consciousness, imagination, and so forth, then formalist pedagogy would seem to place order on the text (in this case, reading the classroom as a text). A shift in thinking about chaos as disorder to thinking of chaos as a text of complexity destabilizes many elements of pedagogy.

To read chaos as an entity of complexity is to read, for example, a student as a site that embodies information that is hard to get at (e.g., has no clear meaning, categorization, or definition that allows the teacher to reduce a student to some simplistic state of being). Most, if not all, of the contemporary theories and practices in the sciences, arts, and humanities are harmonious with the notion of chaos as a state of complexity that would raise the disciplines, knowledge, and so forth to a higher state instead of the static complicity of reductionism. In deconstructionism, a text is seen as a site of complexity in which the interaction between signs, symbols, and meanings provides a range of complexity. In other words, minute detail cannot exist without its relationship to other details of text. In fact, Derrida, the major guru of deconstructionism, argues that a text cannot be reduced to minute detail but can only generate complexity or, in his words, a text of multiple meanings. Each reading is self-generating as the reader uses the complexity of the text as new information. As the reader reads the excess noise as information, and, in so doing, challenges the cultural constructions of gender, class, race, sexuality, knowledge, values, history, politics, and so forth, the text is deconstructed for its contingency, multiple meanings, and contradictions.

The readers and authors of texts in a poststructuralist, postmodern, postcolonial, and post-formalist world are self-conscious about the position from which they read and write in terms of their own autobiography (for example, gender, race, sexuality, history, values). This self-consciousness renders a text complex, creating chaos that does not reduce to the formalism of traditional literary analysis. Not only do the purposes for reading and writing change in deconstructionism, but there is never a traditional closure. It appears that this just adds to the chaos of a text. From the chaos and multiple meanings and structures, new information becomes the location for multiple readings and provides a spurt of intellectual and political energy to the evolving consciousness of the reader and writer.

Incorporation of the discourse of contemporary theories borrowed from the sciences, arts, allows us to view classroom life as a text of chaos and complexity, including students as entities of complexity (entities, here, refers to living, dynamic, complex organisms not to objects upon which theories and practices are imposed). As Ruelle (1991) states, an entity is complex if it embodies information that is hard to get at—that has no sharp meaning—and depends on self-organization and deep structures of order to handle the information (p. 136). Unlike formalism that reads information as noise to be ignored or eliminated, students and other educational texts are the entities of complexity where pedagogical intervention takes place. Teachers, without the limitations and discourse of traditional formalist methods, move beyond the categories and control of formalism. Transformation and transgression are pedagogical departures from the confines of formalism, never arrivals.

Complexity, as Coveney and Highfield (1995) state, is both intrinsic to nature and seeks self-organization. Given this point of view, teachers are assured that reading and incorporating complexity into their field of practice, materials, and evaluation is a better and fairer description of their world than formalists' reduction to simplicity. Whereas formalism has provided only highly idealized representations of the world, complexity is intrinsic, more natural, and perhaps a more truthful representation of pedagogy. Truthful in a manner similar to Levinas' notion:

> the search for truth has to be drawn out of appearance . . . every manifestation is partial . . . consequently truth is a progression and exposed in several moments, remaining problematic in each (Levinas, 1981, p. 24).

The task is to illuminate chaos, bringing it to the center of consciousness of educational participants and practitioners. In other words, complexity becomes the idealization of pedagogical reality.

An immediate response to the foregrounding of complexity as pedagogical thought and practice might be either "but students need to have order in which to work" or "bless our pedagogical hearts, we have been living in a state of chaos all along." Guarantees that this is how reality really works or how the world is naturally have implications for teacher intervention in the process of moving from complexity to self-organization. It seems logical that in the theory of complexity in which chaos is foregrounded, teachers as postmodernists and post-formalists are the major loci of reality with the goal to move the participants from simplicity to complexity. In other words, a teacher or method cannot impose order nor organization upon the consciousness of a system in the process of moving to an emphasis on complexity. On the one hand, left to their own devices, students, knowledge, values, and so forth have a tendency to wind up in a more disordered state. Required to read a student in the process of learning, knowledge in the process of being organized as a discipline, and other cultural instructions, post-formalism, like deconstructionism and complexity, are ways that destabilize the elements of pedagogical arenas and yield unexpected conclusions. On the other hand, teachers and students are engaged in spontaneous self-organization, whether in regard to knowledge, history, behaviors, gender, or whatever. The pedagogical environment becomes one in which everyone and everything is exposed to and interacts with the complexity of a rich and varied environment. As Coveney and Highfield (1995) state

> [the] edge of chaos is a good place to be in a constantly changing world because from there you can always explore the patterns of order that are available and try them out for their appropriateness to the current situation. What you don't want to do is to get stuck in one state of order, which is bound to become obsolete sooner or later . . . complex systems poised for that creative step into emergent novelty (p. 273).

The postmodernist, post-formalist, poststructuralist, postcolonialist, and deconstructed modern world are asking, if not demanding, that a world of plurality become the sites where challenge to the formalism of the modern world and discourse, including pedagogy, and a context-sensitive dependence on chaos-as-creativity can take place. Some examples of sites in which complexity is the frontier of post-formalism and other contemporary locations, both in theory and practice, need to be described to show how processes produce structure at the same time providing a unity in diversity and illustrating how order can emerge from a mass of complexity. "Our present educational system hardly prepares us for such an approach," claim Coveney and Highfield (1995, p. 8).

Pedagogical Sites as Complexity
If the classroom is seen as a text to be read, it follows that there are multiple possibilities for reading the content of a classroom. In addition to the visible texts of the classroom, such as the teacher, students, materials, discourse, textbooks, and knowledge, deeper, less visible structures

lend themselves to deconstructionism and the observation of complexity. These elements, along with the deep structures of curriculum philosophy, design, reason and means of evaluation, values, attitudes, gender, race, interest, needs, desires, physical and mental bodies, and a host of other cultural constructions are only a few of the dimensions that create a very complex text. We are redirected from a system of simplicity and order to a field of chaos, not as disordered world but as a field in which the dynamic interaction and the celebration of noise as information is considered as a forthcoming post-formalist, pedagogical sensitivity.

Once a world of complexity is accepted, post-formalism requires an understanding of the various principles that direct us to value the classroom text, including the teachers and students, as partners in chaos—as a source of information for post-formalist pedagogy and as a site of creativity that prepares us and changes us as we meander to the future. Let me return to the student as one of the major texts and as an entity in the classroom and apply the implications of complexity and chaos for pedagogy. The example I previously introduced was of a student who is labeled by psychological discourse as ADD/ADS and seen to have a physical, mental, chemical, or biological deficiency or abundance that creates hyperactive attention deficit disorder. In other words, the student cannot order the world (e.g., knowledge, learning, behavior, values) according to the mainstream order of a formalist text such as the classroom. Likewise, the teacher can not impose order upon an individual who is seen to have a part missing or interfering with the "order of the classroom." A switch to viewing the student as a text of complexity and chaos destabilizes not only how the student is read but how he/she is labeled by the discourse. If students with the label ADD are viewed as, for example, not fitting the mainstream and are renamed or reviewed as creative, they are repositioned amid a world of possibilities. So, too, are our pedagogical thoughts and practices if we conclude that the student has *not* a "deficit" but differences (in the plural, please note).

To read a student as a text of complexity threatens the power and discourse of formalism, for example, the field of educational psychology, as a major constructor of classroom texts. Van Manen (1991), writes intensely and passionately from the position of the phenomenology of pedagogy, which "offers a (self)-reflective approach to teaching children. However, pedagogical thoughtfulness and tact are unlearnable as mere behavioral principles, techniques, or methods. . . . Neither a science nor a technology" (p. 9). While the phenomenology of pedagogy describes the moments of fascination with the growth of the other from a practical and lived experience and there are no behavioral principles or methods to impose upon or direct, phenomenology still works from a complexity that depends on contingency as well as self-organization—that is, on creativity (Coveney and Highfield, 1995, p. 284). With this in mind, a teacher is required to read a student, not in the manner of formalistic reductionism and positivistic objectivity but in a way that reads the reality and experience of a student as a text of "change, complexity, plurality, fragmentation, conflict, and contradiction of beliefs, values, faiths, living conditions, aspirations, and lifestyles that makes the lives of young people today an experience in contingency" (van Manen). This is where the phenomenology of pedagogy and the principles of complexity and chaos can meet. Each acts as a complement to one another as well as a check on either becoming just another world of formalism. I am not claiming a state of either/or or a state of both but a contingency that incorporates multiple contemporary discourses and practices as a means to foreground educational texts, such as students, in manner that avoids and rejects formalist pedagogy, even hints of it.

Phenomenology moves us into reading educational texts as sites for "the meaning of pedagogical thoughtfulness and tact." Although phenomenology rejects formalism and reductionism, there appears some discourse that might make the reader think phenomenology of pedagogy is just another empirical scientism disguised as a theory or methodology. Phenomenology of pedagogy uses descriptions of lived experience, in other words, the world of the teacher and the student and how they are living the moment as "thoughtful and tactful." The description of the experience, which is intended to reveal the experience as lived, provides information from which the teacher as pedagogue can act thoughtfully and tactfully. If a teacher rereads and rewrites, for example, the student who has been labeled as ADD/ADS and treated accordingly by the application of psychological discourse or clinical methods (formalism) as a text of complexity, a different action and discourse are used with different intentions. Different information is pulled out of the noise of complexity and chaos. The student's actions, thoughts, attitudes, and behaviors become foregrounded as different information, not as a person who is hyperactive or disruptive or disorderly but as a student living in a state of chaos with no room for self-organization. The teacher had imposed the dictates of formalism by naming the text as ADD, thus reducing the student to a simplistic unit of disorder, when in fact, he/she should be read as a person unable to live in a state of chaos and equally unable to self-organize the complexity of the surrounding world.

From a phenomenological perspective, the student, in a state of chaos, becomes a site of momentum which informs the teacher on how to act with thoughtfulness and tactfulness. Intervention by the teacher is not based on some methodological information or textbook-driven information from teacher education days or the "teach-as-we-were-taught" method. Tactfulness is based on a sensitivity to the context and informed by information selected from the noise—how do I act at this moment, for this person—a present and presence that contains the past and the future. Pedagogical tactfulness happens as a spontaneous, ludic locale, a heterogenous, destabilizing decision. What appears as a field of chaos is, in fact, a gaze that uses the multiple complexity of information and decides on action/intervention. The traditional dependence on objectivity, order, subjectivity, and methods as formalist standbys is blurred, not lost, in the action of pedagogical tact-full-ness (Gadamer, 1982). The teacher gathers the information; destabilizes the order, unity, discourse, and the homogeneity of the field; reads elements of the experience, describes and reflects on how that moment is being lived; uses the information to act tactfully, thoughtfully and with a fascination for the multiple "epiphanies of the face" (Levinas, 1981). The next moment is unpredictable, unexpected, and energized by the previous reading. No reading is the same. No decision is fixed unless it acts as a momentum for the next pedagogical action. Thus, post-formalist pedagogy, like other contemporary theories and practices, informs, educates, guides, sensitizes, and places education in a state of complexity. The work of teaching, learning, organizing, evaluating, knowing, and behaving becomes "play," that is, ludic postmodernism. No longer can we label students, design curriculum, or test within the constraints of formalism. We can only create sites for possibilities.

Responsibility as Post-formalist Practice

In a post-formalist pedagogy, the borders of objectivity and subjectivity disappear and are collapsed into responsibility. No longer do the categories, discourse, and methods of formalism drive the pedagogical decisions and actions, but complexity as responsibility does. Levinas (1981) speaks of reductionism as a determinative structure of subjectivity. In this way, responsibility precedes and makes possible the theoretical will. But responsibility is not some esoteric or ephemeral notion without a ground in the practicalities of pedagogy. Levinas talks about responsible subjectivity which contains certain elements compatible with the notions of complexity and chaos as challenges to formalism.

Levinas (1981) provides us with discourse that acts as both a challenge and an alternative to the conceptualization and the scientific methodologies that are products and processes of formalism. His notion of responsible subjectivity grounds pedagogy into a concrete world, in large part because of its phenomenological roots. For him, and for pedagogy, responsible subjectivity contains the following:

1. Responsibility is a fact prior to the facts assembled by coherent formalist discourse and methods.
2. Responsibility is a bond that not only determines that we act responsibly, but determines that we are, as pedagogues, responsible to the other.
3. Responsibility is the response to the imperative addressed in a concrete act of facing the other in his or her alterity [*complexity, differences, possibilities*, my italics].
4. Responsibility is a form of recognition . . . a summons to arise, to be and to present one's self . . . not a cognitive act, but concretely the acts by which one recognizes the other as acts of exposing, giving, of one's very substance to another [the act of parenting].
5. Responsibilities increase in the measure that they are taken up. They take form in an unendingly opening horizon, and infinition [can not be "reduced," only increased, in complexity and chaos].
6. Responsibility makes us not only answerable for what we initiated in a project or commitment of will, but responsible for the situations in which we find ourselves and for the existence in which we find ourselves [context is important, e.g., socially, historically, and so forth].
7. Responsibility is a bond between our present and what came to pass before.
8. Serious responsibility recognizes itself to be responsible for the course of things beyond one's own death (pp. xiii-xiv).

Privileging Imagination

Another area of consideration is the construction of the imagination, not as a mental act as defined by formalism but as an experience that "arises constantly in the midst of concrete actions and events" (Casey, 1976, p. 4). In formalism, the imagining is reduced to an inferior position as a mental act, and, in fact, psychological theories of imagining reduce imagination to causal explanation. In the theories of complexity and phenomenology discussed previously, imagining is distinguished from other mental acts and, although not raised as a hierarchical level in comparison to other mental acts, is a state that "remains open to what can be called the multiplicity of the mental. Within this multiplicity there is . . . only a proliferation of unforecloseable possibilities" (Casey, p. 19).

Similar to the elements of complexity, the phenomenology of imagining provides additional discourse and ways of thinking about the classroom as a text. The student's unfolding consciousness is no longer seen as a location of mental acts in which imagining is an act of associationist psychology (behaviorism), an act of wish fulfilment (Freud), an act of pseudo-knowing (Plato), a mediation between perception and intellect (Aristotle), or, what has become the dominant theory of imagining in modern education, the developmental psychologist's (Piagetian) notion of imagining as a single ingredient of the symbolizing stage of cognitive growth, one which is no longer needed at later stages (Casey, 1976, p. 10).

The phenomenology of imagining returns us to reading the educational text, such as the student, in a manner that is complementary to complexity, chaos, and post-formalist pedagogy. To read the educational text as a "proliferation of unforecloseable possibilities" requires the elements of spontaneity, self-containedness, self-evidence, indeterminacy and pure possibility (bringing with it a sense of endlessness of open development). The openness of the teacher to receive the complexity and spontaneous imaginings of a student requires a resistance to psychic hegemony and a release to pedagogy of the possible.

There is also a shift in power, both in the concrete act and abstracted act of reading the text. With the elimination of method and without recourse to a preestablished hierarchy of discourse with which to read the text (e.g., a student) the power and seduction of a formalist pedagogy is lost to the foregrounding of complexity, chaos, spontaneity, indeterminacy and so forth. Not only do the classroom texts become read in a particular way that avoids the reductionism of psychological discourse and scientific formalism, but the entire field of education and all its players, curriculum documents, administration, curriculum thinking, instructional technology, in fact the politics, economics, constructions, institutional structures are influenced and required to move towards a post-formalist world that joins with postmodernism, poststructuralism, postcolonialism, complexity and chaos, and the phenomenological descriptions of responsible subjectivity as creative engagement with the field of educational and pedagogical texts.

The Post-formalist Subject

Because the subjects of pedagogy are in a continuous process of construction, we could also argue that students live in a state of crisis, not in psychological confusion but as an opportunity for the players to select out from the noise that information which they self-organize and provide for a change within the constructs of subjectivity. Unlike the discourse of educational psychology, where subjectivity is constructed and contained within a single unified and well-adjusted self, the postmodern subject is constructed along the lines of complexity, responsibility, and self-organization as a struggle that is fragmented, discontinuous, disjunctive, and a dislocation of a formalist construction. Whereas educational psychology attempts to explain deviations from a hegemonic social "norm," post-formalist pedagogy serves as a ground "for the conflict of self between what is submissive to the inherited and hegemonic, discursive practices of society [in this case, the practices of educational psychology] and a self that is not synonymous with the subject of that discourse" (Thompson, 1992, p. 9).

The possibility of transformation within the complexity, chaos, and fragmentation of post-formalist pedagogy demands that the subjects are involved in a conscious selection of subjectivity that is useful and meaningful in a particular context and allows counter-hegemonic selections from the noise instead of the selection from outside the constructs imposed by formalism. This openness as provided by the ground of post-formalist pedagogy becomes a site for multiple actions and thoughts.

We can appropriate and approximate the elderly formalist and the youthful post-formalist (intellectually speaking, not chronologically) as a move towards pedagogy as an act of responsibility and thus a response to the "other," that is, the ability to respond to plurality, complexity, chaos, differences not only as individuals with free will and independence but also as a "subject" influenced by cultural constructions. Whereas formalism encourages and protects the autonomy of the individual, the "poststructuralist pedagogical practice displaces the notion of the individual in favor of the concept of the subject and sees the individual as the effect of the signification" (Zavarzadeh and Morton, 1994, p. 29). This statement returns the construction of the subject by history, discourse, theory, and practice into the realm of the political, which, in turn, adds another dimension to the classroom text and requires a reading of complexity from the multiple sites of curriculum, including teaching and learning. In addition, Zavarzadeh and Morton call for a pedagogy which produces "a critical subject who knows that knowledge is a social product with political consequences who will be willing to intervene in the way knowledge is produced [circulated, maintained] not only in the classroom, but in all other sites of culture . . . [and] is a result of his/her situatedness in a complex network of gender, class, and other cultural relationships" (p. 19).

Educational psychology, in its rush to label the individual as part of a larger subjective construction such as ADD/ADS, groups individuals into a neutral construction that ignores two factors. The first factor is that the label suggests there is some standard normalization of the individuals within that category. In other words, all people with ADD/ADS have the same qualities, behaviors, difficulties, bodies, intellectual capacities, and pedagogical histories. In addition, all those within this category are neutralized in terms of economic, political, and cultural and social backgrounds. The second factor is that all the individuals in this category are reduced to objects upon which methods of treatment and application of pedagogical strategies are applied in order to "normalize" the individuals to some hegemonic state. Teachers claim that the lack of recognition of these students means their special needs are ignored. However, what is really ignored in a formalist reduction of individuals with special needs is the complexity of the individual living in a culturally constructed world such as education while at the same time being constructed by that world. As Donald Crimp (in Grossberg et al., 1992) suggests, the practice of reducing people with AIDS to a category in order to treat a person with AIDS both perpetuates the social conditions that make AIDS a crisis and keeps people with AIDS safely within the boundaries of their private tragedies. No one ever utters a word about AIDS politics . . . (p. 120).

But What About Monday Morning?

The resistance to post-formalist pedagogy and other postcontemporary theories is a reality, not understandably so from my point of view. However, for teachers and other people involved in educational arenas, it is very problematic to entertain any notions of destabilizing discourse and practices to mainstream and status quo thinking. No other field seems as burdened by formalism and its accompanying theories, discourse, structures, and methods as education. To overcome decades of hegemonic status with limited to nil challenge to the status quo seems ludicrous in the context of my argument. In a graduate class, I recently experienced resistance to change even at the intellectual level. After discussing a rough draft of this chapter, the graduate students claimed that teachers (of course, not themselves?) would not be able to cope without the structures, materials, tests, dictates, and methods that are now in place. In other words, what do we do Monday morning if indeed we accept the principles, premises, and practices of post-formalist pedagogy? As a teacher-educator of both undergraduate and graduate students and as a person who is constantly working with professionals and in the classrooms with teachers, I find this statement resonates with resistance to and apprehension of working towards a post-formalist, postmodern millennium.

All of us involved in the educational field and in pedagogical circles/circus (parents, teachers, daycare, medical, and legal aspects of adult-child relationships) have perhaps in many ways reached a limit. Faced with creative voids and pedagogical apathy, what is needed is, not change, but a new source of educational energy. This is not a plea to throw out the bath water or the baby but a shake-up of consciousness which reads the world of education and pedagogy as an organism of complexity. A space for pedagogical passion in which no one area can be reduced to formalism, methodologies, or Monday morning hegemonic consent. Furthermore, hegemony is a status that is well entrenched through history, politics, public influence, and teacher security. No real philosophical or practical changes have been made since the days of John Dewey and other American pragmatists.

Over the decades, educational psychology has made contributions to the fields of education and pedagogy, and in many ways these contributions have moved us beyond the authoritarian and dominant approach of a church-based education of the late 1800s and most of the 1900s. But when limits are reached, as the argument is stated by the post-formalists, a redrawing of the map of curriculum and pedagogy requires a transdisciplinary border crossing, which opens up a new space for rising radical and revolutionary constructions of education and subjects (Zavarzedeh, 1994, p. 19). Zavarzedeh suggests a pedagogy of priorities, Graff a pedagogy of conflict, Barthe a pedagogy of fantasy, and Lacan a pedagogy of desire. While some seek a pedagogy of pleasure/fancy in which the memory is emancipated from [imposed] order, humanism denies the institutionality of pedagogy. I feel that Ebert's notion of ludic postmoderninity as pedagogy would encompass an entire range of contemporary thoughts, including complexity, chaos, phenomenology, and the other positions of a post-formalist pedagogy.

Where does this leave us Monday morning? We need political power, as we destabilize the entrenchment of formalism in educational and pedagogy consciousness and practices. Learn to dance to the music of chaos, complexity, unexpected conclusions, multiple readings, and be sensitive to the different discourse, beats, and rhythms as subjects self-organize the world including themselves with the presence of a responsible pedagogue enchanted by the other's alterities.

References

Casey, E.S. (1976). *Imagining: A phenomenological study.* Bloomington: Indiana University Press.

Coveney, P. and Highfield, R. (1995). *Frontiers of complexity: The search for order in a chaotic world.* New York: Fawcett Columbine.

Gadamer, H.G. (1982). *Truth and method.* New York: The Crossroad Publishing Company.

Grossberg, L., Nelson, C., and Treichler, P. (Eds). (1992) *Cultural studies.* New York: Routledge.

Hayles, N. K. (1991). *Chaos and order: Complex dynamics in literature and science.* Chicago: University of Chicago Press.

Laws, B. (1972). Personal Communication. London, Ontario.

Levinas, E. (1969). *Totality and infinity: An essay on exteriority.* Pittsburgh: Duquesne University Press.

Levinas, E. (translated by A. Lingis). (1981). *Otherwise than being or beyond essence.* The Hague: Martinus Nijhoff Publishers.

McLaughlin, J. (1997). Personal quotes. EDCI 6314, *Curriculum as Literacy.* University of New Brunswick, Fredericton, Canada.

Ruelle, D. (1991). *Chance and chaos.* New York: Penguin.

Thompson, J. (1992). *Lion in the streets.* Toronto: Coach House Press.

van Manen, M. (1991). *The tact of teaching: The meaning of pedagogical thoughfulness.* London, Ontario: Althouse Press.

Zavarzadeh,M. and Morton, D. (1994). *Theory as resistance: Politics and culture after (post)structuralism.* New York: Guilford Press.

CHAPTER FIFTEEN

The Dissociative Nature of Educational Change

Raymond A. Horn, Jr.

The Multiple Personality of Education

In observing the past and present behavior of the educational community when engaged in reform, one could conclude that educators are afflicted with Dissociative Identity Disorder (formerly Multiple Personality Disorder). The definition of this disorder in the fourth edition of the *Diagnostic and Statistical Manual of Mental Disorders* (DSM-IV) of the American Psychiatric Association (1994) provides a compelling description of educational behavior when engaged in change or reform.

> Confusion about personal identity or assumption of a new identity (partial or complete); . . . inability to recall one's past; . . . distress or impairment in social, occupational, or other important areas of functioning; . . . failure to integrate various aspects of identity, memory, and consciousness; a primary identity . . . (that) is passive, dependent, guilty, and depressed; alternate identities are experienced as taking control in sequence, one at the expense of the other, and may deny knowledge of one another, or appear to be in open conflict"; . . . frequent gaps in memory for personal history, both remote and recent; . . . an overall loss of biographical memory for some extended period (p. 484).

These diagnostic features are certainly evident in all levels of education. On an ideological level, educational history and current trends are rife with examples of education's identity crisis. In one instance the scientific management of education has produced educators who emulate the techniques and strategies of business managers, scientists, and

efficiency experts. In contrast, the beliefs espoused by the social melior-
ists and critical theorists conflict with the business and scientific roles
expected of teachers in that educators must facilitate social progress by
correcting social evils (i.e., health issues, family issues, psychological
issues) and promoting social justice (i.e., sexism, racism, ethnocentrism, classism, and exceptionality).

The critical theorists, who promote educators as critical peda-
gogists, would transform society into a more democratic community.
This school of thought requires educators to become adept in critically
reflecting on their own personal and professional lives as well as the
oppressive action of the dominant culture on the marginalized. The critical consciousness that arises from this reflection is to be promoted in
their students, who, in, turn critically challenge the social realities transmitted and imposed by the dominant culture. The problem for the educator is how to reconcile this viewpoint with those that require educators to be transmitters of traditional practices and values. How do
educators integrate these varied and diverse requirements in their educational identity?

A great deal of a teacher's or administrator's professional life is
determined by these dueling ideologies (Beyer and Liston, 1996;
Kliebard, 1995; Cremin, 1964). The momentary ascendancy of an ideology is marked by the passing from one fad to another. The result is the
development of a curriculum that is a deleteriously eclectic hodgepodge
of pedagogy. Current public schools rarely exhibit a vibrant ideological
continuity except in their extracurricular program and their hidden curriculum. Their written and taught curriculum is a melange of politically
expedient decisions that satisfy the various interest groups within and
outside the school. The dilemma for the educator is how to accommodate
the demands of this dissociative environment. Unfortunately, the traditional educational system does not empower the educator, and seldom do
educators appropriate power beyond their immediate circumstance.
Therefore educator's professional lives mirror the dissociation inherent
in their environment. Is it any wonder why some may lack a primary
identity, fail to remember important germane learnings from their past
experiences, and appear to be different people in different situations.

On a personal level, educators were at one time students themselves, and as students they learned valuable lessons about education.
They experienced the gamut of emotions that arose from their success
and failure in school. They could tell a "good" teacher from a "bad"
one. They knew the fallaciousness of certain instructional and assess-

ment techniques. The irony is that many teachers forget or repress this valuable data and teach as they were taught, perpetuating the illogical, inefficient, and oppressive curricular and instructional strategies that they grew to dislike. They deny their hard-earned intuition and follow the often inauthentic and irrelevant strategies gotten from booksellers and consultants. This "overall loss of biographical memory" (APA, 1994, p. 484) contributes to the development of dissociation by denying the process of critical reflection that is necessary to discern the deeper patterns and contexts that affect our reality.

The teacher and administrator are often required to be creative, imaginative individuals in making educational decisions within a tightly defined context; and in other contexts passive recipients and transmitters of edicts from above. They are exhorted and driven to achieve educational goals in their classroom but are denied accessibility to the debates in which the crucial decisions are made that determine their classroom success and failure. They are directed to promote creativity and critical thinking in their students while at the same time ranking and sorting them through assessments geared only to linguistic and logical-mathematical intelligences (Gardner, 1983). Educators are expected to be different people in different situations. In one situation they must be compassionate, empathic, and personal. Yet in the next they are required to be objective, neutral implementers of standardized mandates and procedures. Is it any wonder why some teachers are passive (burned out?), dependent (on textbooks, administrators, outside experts), guilty, and depressed?

Metaphorically, the teacher's professional life becomes a cacophony with no discernible themes or continuities; a random eclectic mix of adversarial psychological strategies and tactics. In coping with these diverse demands, some teachers frenetically attempt to comply with these dueling psychologies and ideologies, while others withdraw or regress to the security of the old modernistic methods that were used on them. In either case the all-too-common result is the cognitive disability, emotional pathology, and social alienation previously identified by Joe L. Kincheloe. This erosion of the identifiable self is caused by the "plurality of voices vying for the right to reality—to be accepted as legitimate expressions of the true and the good" (Gergen, 1991, p. 7). Plagued by this plurality of voices and bereft of a biographical memory, educators become uncentered—neither centered autonomous selves nor decentered individuals who critically recognize the influence of the social and historical on their thoughts and actions.

These educators are lost in the borderland between what was certain and reliable. They are not Henry Giroux's (1994; 1992) border crossers who, by their movement in these spaces of uncertainty, recognize the multiple nature of their identity. These educators drift in this borderland as fragmented ghosts of past certitudes. These marginalized people are trapped in the interplay between the postmodern condition and the modernistic psychology and pedagogy of which they are a part. This interplay has decentered educators to the point where their behavior toward change is metaphorically dissociative. For change to be successful, the professional personalities and world views of educators must be reintegrated. Instead of being centered on a set of pedagogical principles, methods, or universals, they must be centered on the need to phenomenologically and hermeneutically engage reality, recognizing the systemic and holistic nature of reality.

These inordinate demands of the dissociative educational system at best attenuate the educator's capabilities, often resulting in piecemeal and fragmented pedagogy. The result is that teaching becomes more like the application of triage in an emergency room than the implementation of a well-thought-out curriculum.

Public Response to Education's Disorder

The public is aware of the negative effects of this educational dissociative disorder. The somewhat acrimonious debates within the educational community are not perceived by the public as esoteric debates within the realm of academia, but as "distress or impairment in . . . functioning" (APA, 1994, p. 484). This perception is a high-profile politicized concern of the general public. Presidential candidates try to enhance their electability by promising to be an "educational President"; the implication being that since educators can't effectively run education, that politicians and government can. Candidates wouldn't use this kind of tactic if the polls didn't indicate a significant dissatisfaction with the current operation of education.

From a political and public context, educational reform does not have a good track record (Smith, 1995; Branson, 1987). Critics paint bleak pictures of the effectiveness of American education. Perceptions are that reform is generally ineffective or at best episodic and local in its successes. After the Education Summit at Palisades, New York, *Newsweek* columnist Jonathan Alter (1996) rejoiced in the fact that, with a few exceptions, educators were left out of the conference. Alter continued his commentary on education, as a "sea of mediocrity," by proclaiming that "whatever their individual talents, teachers unions and educrats have failed as a group to save the public schools. It's time to let someone else try" (Alter, p. 40). The educational establishment's handling of change was characterized in this manner. "It's not really a wall—they always talk about change—but rather more like quicksand, or a tar pit where ideas sink slowly out of sight, leaving everything just as it had been" (Alter, p. 40). The conclusions of the Summit were that instead of the "usual educational fads," deep structural change must occur in standards, assessment, and accountability. One might criticize Alter's writing as an attempt to sensationalize a complex issue, however, these opinions are apt to be read by the general public rather than the reasoned debate in educational journals.

Newsweek (Kantrowitz, 1996) and *U.S. News & World Report* (Toch and Daniel, 1996) reported on two very different views concerning educational reform as represented by Theodore R. Sizer and E. D. Hirsch, Jr. The fact that these two educators were profiled in two major news magazines significantly indicates the public's concern. The *Newsweek* article was entitled "The Jargon Jungle" and Kantrowitz's greatest praise was for Hirsch and Sizer's attempt to help parents "through the pedagogical wilderness" and "work past the muddle" (Kantrowitz, p. 86).

This perception that education is in a state of distress and impaired in its functioning is critically important in relation to the continuation of large-scale public education administered by educators. As society struggles with the postmodern condition the educational community must be perceived as the solution instead of as part of the problem. Being perceived as the solution will negate the insidious efforts of those who wish to minimize education or control it for purposes of self-interest. The task of the educational community is to determine why this situation of perceived failure exists and how it can be remedied.

The generally negative public reaction to educational change is exacerbated by a situation created by the postmodern condition. Postmodernity allows the creation of spaces where political and commercial interests can utilize media and popular culture to promote their own agendas at the expense of education (Giroux, 1994). This opportunism further denigrates the mission and effectiveness of education which adds to the public and professional criticism of education. The mechanism that can restore public and professional confidence by fostering successful educational change is the process of integration in a post-formal context.

Healing Through Integration:
Postmodern Solutions for Postmodern Problems

Integration as the Solution for Multiple Personality

The solution for dissociative disorders such as multiple personality is the reintegration of the personality. The goal of the therapy is to reestablish a primary personality that can cope with the past traumas that induced the condition as well as the future stress and trauma that will be encountered. The individual's fragmented self must be replaced with a self that is an integrated whole through various means that may involve drug therapy, talk therapy, or other procedures and techniques as deemed relevant. One unique aspect of this disorder is that it is a relational one as the personality is often shattered or was never integrated due to abuse (Kluft, 1985). Therefore the affected individual must engage these past traumas in an autobiographical frame, draining the psychic energy that maintains the various personalities. And then, through self-reflection and reinterpretation of past experience, new meanings can be constructed that will form the basis of an integrated, healthy personality.

Integration as the Springboard for Effective Educational Change

Like those afflicted with multiple personalities, education suffers from a fragmentation of its personality and must integrate. The trauma that creates the disorder occurs when the essentialized beliefs and grand narratives of modernistic solutions are applied to postmodern conditions. The modernistic principles of educational and social psychology are not relevant to the hyperchange that characterizes the technologically driven information society. In Piagetian terms the chaos and indeterminacy of postmodernity cannot be assimilated through modernistic strategies. Education must seek accommodation by turning to postmodern strategies. The postmodern condition exacerbates the dissociation of education but also provides opportunities to move in new directions that will facilitate the development of educational strategies relevant to the twenty-first century.

The Piagetian analogy is incomplete in that if educational psychology is to extend its relevancy to the postmodern, then it must also move from the formal thinking of Piaget to a post-formal thinking. Joe L. Kincheloe and Shirley R. Steinberg propose a socio-cognitive theory that moves beyond the essentialism and grand narratives that exemplify modernistic thinking (1996). Two post-formal concepts fundamental to educational reintegration are: (1) a reflective dialogue "that is always concerned with the expansion of self-awareness and consciousness, never certain of emancipation's definition, and perpetually reconceptualizing the system of meaning" (Kincheloe and Steinberg, 1996, p. 170); and, (2) "post-formal thinking and post-formal teaching become whatever an individual, a student, or a teacher can produce in the realm of new understandings and knowledge within the confines of a critical system of meaning" (p. 173). The previously described dissociation mainly occurs because of the lack of reflective dialogue, the belief that essential meanings can be discovered that will remain stable over time, the resistance to the participant's (teachers and students) construction of knowledge, and the refusal to incorporate critical components (i.e., race, gender, class, ethnicity) in discussions about educational change.

A critical psychology predicated upon post-formal thinking is necessary to create an umbrella of integration over the ability to authenticate and validate local and individual educational experience, as well as to provide a forum that allows for professional dialogue that can lead to compatible discourses that complement each other in the creation of effective education. This integration would include the aspects of current educational and social psychology that are relevant to the postmodern condition. However, the key would be the inclusion of the critical educational psychology which provides postmodern strategies for a postmodern world.

The postmodern world is a relational, probabilistic quantum world of indeterminacy. Our children experience this quantum reality, not the reality of Newton, Bacon, or Descartes. If education is to earn the public's confidence, it can only do so through the effective education of the public's children. The time has come to cast off the ineffective modernistic solutions and move ahead into postmodernity.

Educational Change in a Postmodern World

Teachers are the central agents in educational change. When the classroom doors close and the teachers engage their students, this is the time when the status quo is maintained or change occurs. This is when all else becomes extraneous and the teacher defines curriculum and instruction. At this point all of the consultants, outcomes, standards, supervision, and any other initiatives or mandates become external to the classroom reality and contingent upon the teacher's construction of meaning. Mandated values that are to be inculcated in the students are filtered and transformed consciously or unconsciously by the teachers. If an innovation like cooperative learning or portfolio assessment is mandated, teachers have the power to bring it to life, or to assimilate it into their existing practice. Their ability to contextualize the innovation and to translate its intent are the determining agents in the quality of the implementation. The power and motivation of teachers are the significant factors in understanding the mechanism of educational change.

The crucial location for an understanding of the centrality of teachers in the change process is the point at which conversation takes place. Meaning and motivation are constructed when one teacher talks to another. This moment, whether in a hall, lunchroom, or in-service, is a highly contextualized socio-historical setting and, because of its relational and linguistic nature, is the point that must be studied to understand why change succeeds or fails—in actuality, why *teachers decide* whether the change will succeed or fail. Therefore the essential elements in understanding change are the context of the conversation as well as the types of conversation that occur.

In relation to the context of change, the dynamic of this model is that conversation and discourse trigger powerful forces that determine the outcome of a change initiative. Where these forces and conversation intersect, a change process occurs that attempts to influence those participating in the change. This process affects the individual and collective pedagogy of those involved. The results of this process are the dialectical reconstitution of the original forces and their representative discourses that were originally triggered by the conversation. In a sense, education is the battleground upon which powerful forces marshaled by rival discourses attempt to win the prize, control over the pedagogy.

Forces that Affect Educational Change
Modernistic and critical pedagogical paradigms attempt to control and reconstruct the forces of power, culture, praxis, and spirituality. Current educational theory and practice are constituted by this dialectic. The psychological and pedagogical research of modernistic and critical education is a manifestation of these dialectical positions. These adversarial positions utilize the integrated and dynamic forces of educational change to give structure to their ideas and to advance their agendas.

POWER Power is ubiquitous; it permeates all of education. Administrators, teachers, students, parents, and school boards are all power brokers. Some inherit power because they are part of the dominant culture and can overtly and publicly exercise that power. Others have limited power; delegated and controlled. Some are marginalized and have little power, even at times ironically defending and sustaining the power of the dominant group. Many appropriate power from others who fail to maintain their own agency. Power is exercised by some through resistance and non-compliance. Power can be obtained and wielded through the commodification and objectification of people. Also, power can manifest itself as passivity. As many ways as there are to interact with others, there are manifestations of power. Power can be centralized or decentralized, vertically structured (top-down or hierarchical), or in the form of a flatter structure (consensual), and these structures organize and affect gender, race, ethnicity, age, and class.

Traditional, modernistic perceptions of power in education mirror the characteristics of modernism. Power is bureaucratically compartmentalized, located in centralized structures with interventionist tendencies (Hargreaves, 1994). The bureaucratic exercise of power is to promote efficiency, productivity, and maintenance of the dominant culture. Flexibility to respond to change is limited by this hierarchical arrangement. Individualism, the balkanization of the faculty, and contrived empowerment (power when shared is limited and controlled) are the results of this authoritarian, hegemonic structure. Some school districts resemble a feudal system with each school's principal, to some degree, the lord of the manor. These modernistic power brokers maintain their control by separating logic and emotion, decontextualizing situations and experience, and suppressing diversity (Kincheloe and Steinberg, 1996). Essentializing grand narratives provide the necessary justifications for the promotion of the dominant culture.

A critical perspective on power could be summarized by the words shared ownership, voice, equity, and system-wide empowerment. This perspective recognizes and emphasizes the relational consequences of power. Power can be discussed openly by all, not restricted to the furtive conversations of the hallway, faculty room, or boardroom. Framing power in a systemic, critical context, implies the sharing of power by all members of the system. Necessary conditions for a critical construction of power are the opportunity and ability to deconstruct one's environment and experience in a quest to understand the construction and restriction of one's knowledge, placing one's self and one's experience in a socio-historical context, and, the recognition of the holistic and integrated nature of human activity as opposed to the reductionism of modernity.

PRAXIS The relationship between theory and practice is a determining factor in the success of reform. Paulo Freire defines praxis "as a dialectical movement that goes from action to reflection and from reflection upon action to a new action" (Leistyna, Woodrum, and Sherblom, 1996, p. 342). Freire sees a relationship between theory, transformative action, and reflection on the action (Leistyna et al., 1996).

The importance of praxis as a force in education is especially evident when viewed as part of the endemic frame of reference problem. Public school educators lack a frame of reference for the postmodern condition, the postmodern critique of modernism, and the use of theory. In most cases the reform that is packaged for quick implementation deals exclusively with teacher practice. The theoretical foundations of the packaged reform are determined by others. Rarely do reform projects start either from teacher action research (Kincheloe, 1991) or from teachers' perusal of their experiential knowledge.

Teachers are trapped in practice. Rarely do they work with theory or inform their practice with theory. Without theory as a referent the necessary dialectical reflection on practice cannot effectively take place. Instead of becoming transformative intellectuals (Giroux, 1993) who work "to ensure the development of a socially responsible citizenry and a critical, multicultural, democracy" (Leistyna et al., 1996, p. 335), teachers without the engagement of theory become mere technicians— "uncritical, objective, and efficient distributors of information" (Carlson, 1996, p. 277).

CULTURE Culture is about difference and the human attempt to deal with this difference through the development of relationships. In education difference occurs in such essentialized forms as gender, age, class, ethnicity, race, sexual orientation, and ability. This short list of difference is utilized by traditional discourse to essentialize the people who represent these characteristics. Research is replete with examples of the negative consequences of this essentializing, especially concerning gender, class, and ability. Also, traditional psychological discourse exacerbates the negative aspects of difference by focusing exclusively on the individual and not including the effects of society and culture on the individual. If an individual is in some way deficient compared to others, it is because of the individual's failure to negotiate a stage, or the individual's low intelligence, or the individual's poor self-esteem; or a deficiency in the chemical, physiological, and genetic mechanisms of the individual's cognitive function. The two most oppressive results are

(1) manufactured consent of the marginalized in which they accept "their exploitation and subordination, and become uncritical tools" (Leistyna et al., 1996, p. 337) of the dominant culture; and, (2) the creation of the teacher and administrator as technicians who unwittingly support this oppression.

Critical psychology deconstructs the operation of these stereotypes with the intent to unmask their deleterious effects and, in turn, to foster the development of egalitarian relationships between those in the mainstream and those who are marginalized by this essentialization. This ideological disembedding (Kincheloe and Steinberg, 1996) of the stereotypes is done through the inclusion of a critical analysis of the effects of culture and power on the social construction of the individual and the group. "Critical pedagogy focuses on the idea that cultures are always produced within particular social and historical conditions, and that any understanding of their production, reproduction, and representation is inherently subjective—that is, determined by one's own experiences, beliefs, values, and interests" (Leistyna et al., 1996, p. 334). Therefore, a traditional belief about gender would be characterized as masculine, framed within a justice paradigm; a critical perspective would entertain a gender framework that includes feminization, caring, and nurturing.

Also, the critical psychologist is a cultural worker who recognizes the importance of language in relationship building. Language is both the emancipatory and enslaving mechanism within the cultural context. Individuals must learn how certain types of language intrude on their meaning making and how to use language to withstand the discriminatory effects of this intrusion. The inclusion of critical pedagogy in educational psychology provides an opportunity for the marginalized to acquire the cultural capital (Bourdieu and Passeron, 1992) and rediscover the subjugated knowledge (Kincheloe and Steinberg, 1996) necessary to compete with the dominant culture.

SPIRITUALITY David Griffin provides this definition of spirituality: "to refer to the ultimate values and meanings in terms of which we live, whether they be otherworldly or very worldly ones, and whether or not we consciously try to increase our commitment to those values and meanings. The term does have religious connotations, in that one's ultimate values and meanings reflect some presupposition as to what is holy, that is, of ultimate importance. But the presupposed holy can be something very worldly, such as power, sexual energy, or success"

(1988, p. 1). In the postmodern age spirituality is used as an umbrella term relating to morality and ethics, not in the context of the denominational and political debates about religion in American schools. Spirituality is included as a force affecting educational change because of its motivating potential. A tentative hypothesis would be that in schools where change does not occur and reform fails, spirituality is either not evident to a large degree or contrived and controlled by the dominant culture.

The inclusion of spirituality in the reform formula is essential if the virtues of duty, reverence, and personal participation are to be realized. The phenomenological component is that to achieve virtuous commitment requires the participants to construct meaning through an interpretive inquiry of their experience and condition. William Pinar's (1994) process of *currere* would be an appropriate personal and collective discourse model that would lead to spiritual commitment.

The exclusion of spirituality in education is a product of the modernistic bifurcation of intellect and emotion. The resultant secularization and objectification of educational reform has contributed to the failures of that reform. The spiritual commitment and purpose that are essential components of effective reform are evident in those who debate the virtues of their visions; however, it is sadly lacking and often not even allowed on the level of implementation where the teacher resides.

Philip Wexler (1992) conducted an ethnographic study of three high schools, and his reporting of teacher "burn out," "ritualized job performance," and "regimented attitudes" is indicative of the lack of spiritual commitment by teachers, administrators, and districts to the educational process. The joyless schools, the indifferent attitudes, and the desperate longing for retirement are indictments of the despiritualized modernization of our schools. The imposed spiritual neutrality is a modernistic artifice that breeds passivity and apathy.

Conversation as the Catalyst

Conversation is what brings these forces to life. All change, reform, or progress must start with conversation. The status quo can be changed when conversation occurs. Metaphorically, the moment of conversation is like the moment of measurement for Schrödinger's cat (Gribbin, 1995). This is the point when reality becomes tangible or defined. When conversation occurs, the forces affecting change are activated, and become agents attempting to influence the outcomes of the conversation. Modern and postmodern discourses marshall these forces in an attempt to affect the outcome.

Conversation can range from an informal exchange of ideas and opinions to a structured dialectical engagement of discourses, from a casual communication between two people to a system-wide discussion or dialogue. The important consideration is that without written or oral conversation, nothing happens. Change of any kind is predicated on communication. This communication can be a faculty room exchange, an idea presented at a faculty meeting, a new method imposed by an expert, commentary in a newsletter, hidden hallway complaints about the status quo, or discussion about ideas learned in a graduate course. When communication occurs, the forces of change are immediately activated. Using David Bohm's idea of holographic representation (Bohm, 1992; 1980), the forces become immediately activated because we carry all of them in one form or another within us. As more people become involved in the conversation, the strength of the representation of these forces increases exponentially because the threat to or change opportunity for existing ideologies proportionally increases.

As communication, conversation is frequently cited as an essential element or necessary condition if the prescribed reform method is to be implemented or the desired outcome achieved. This ubiquitous reference to conversation indicates the agreement that the most basic skill or activity for change or reform is conversation. Yet conversational skills are rarely taught, much less practiced. It is assumed that if dialogue is an integral part of the implementation of an educational idea, the participants are capable and willing to engage in dialogue. In addition, a modernistic view assumes that the outcomes of the conversation can be predicted. A postmodern view reveals that often this prediction is accurate because of the manipulation of the conversation by those who hold power.

Forms of Conversation

Peter Jenlink and Alison Carr (1996) review and expand David Bohm's (1992; 1980) ideas about thought and dialogue. This framework presents a continuum of four types of conversation ranging from dialectic to discussion through dialogue culminating in design.

DIALECTIC AND DISCUSSION Probably the most frequently occurring types are dialectic and discussion. Dialectical conversation is characterized by logical, disciplined argument used to promote ideologies and beliefs (Jenlink and Carr, 1996). This is considered closed conversation in that "participants are often rigid in their beliefs and debate for what they perceive as truths" and "are unwilling to suspend their assumptions or their judgment of others' beliefs" (Jenlink and Carr, 1996, p. 32). The result of dialectical conversation is debate and logical argument leading to "factionalization or breaking apart of individuals into different camps" (Jenlink and Carr, 1996, p. 32). Dialectical conversations usually occur when administration or outside experts wish to convince a faculty to engage in change. Strong logical arguments are presented with predetermined answers to any possible objections. The logic may seem irrefutable because of the lack of knowledge on the part of the faculty. In the face of research selected by the expert to support the change, faculty inability or lack of desire to research the change removes the possibility of an intellectual challenge by the faculty, thus allowing only an emotional response. This seemingly scientific (unbiased and objective), logical and pedantic approach may often "win" the conversation but alienate the faculty.

Discussions are similar to dialectics in that the participants are closed to other viewpoints and arguments. The difference is that "discussion is more subjectively influenced by opinion and supposition" (Jenlink and Carr, 1996, p. 32). Jenlink and Carr see this type as perhaps the most common when school change is the issue. Also, due to the competitiveness among the participants, the outcome is again fragmentation and divisiveness. Jenlink and Carr report that "historically, discussion and dialectic have both been oriented toward political transactions" and "coalesce like-minded people into organized political movements" (1996, p. 32).

DIALOGUE In David Bohm's conception (1992; 1980), *dialogue* is characterized by the suspension of mindsets, which allows participants to uncover hidden intentions. Unrecognized and unacknowledged, such "incoherent intentions" perpetuate stagnation by creating unconscious resistance to a change in behavior. Thus, dialogue facilitates the development of a "oneness" and shared culture between the participants. Bohm also conceptualized *thought* as a participatory system in which idea and feeling interpenetrate one another. Moreover, *thought* is an active agent shaping how people interact with others and influencing how others reciprocate another's behavior (Senge, 1990).

Thought processes that result in confusion or incoherence are counterproductive to the successful implementation of change. Incoherence is characterized as inconsistency, conflict, contradiction, and stress

(Bohm, 1992). "You want to do something but it doesn't come out as you intend" (Bohm, 1992, p. 10). Teachers who are unaware of the hidden consequences of their practice are experiencing incoherence. For example, teachers who are egalitarian by nature may be unaware that their use of traditional grading practices results in sorting, ranking, and promotion of competition, which in turn reinforces classism, sexism, and racism. Dialectic and discussion conversation prompts defensive incoherence, which is an unconscious resistance preventing us from performing the change behavior (Bohm, 1992).

In Bohm's theory, dialogue is the process that reveals the incoherence. To create coherent perceptions of problems and solutions, people must learn to engage in these individual and collective actions: describe what is happening in their thinking, see the source of their thinking, engage in self-perception, and start dialogue without consideration of specific questions.

How people think is reflected in their conversation. If people are defensive about implementing a change, they will engage in dialectics or discussion, not dialogue. Second, thoughts are collective in nature due to the shared meaning that exists through culture. When engaging in dialogue, relationships are the most important considerations. When dialogue is working, a "oneness" arises between people, and the developing shared culture is held together by the system of thought created by its members (Bohm, 1992).

DESIGN Incoherent thinking as it emerges in conversation is problematic in many ways. Besides a general unawareness of how the individual and group thoughts are affecting the change, there is the condition of systemic fault (Bohm, 1992). The fault that enervates the change effort is not in an isolated part, but ubiquitous throughout the entire system.

Peter Jenlink and Alison A. Carr (1996) address systemic fault in their proposal of design as a form of conversation. Here the focus is on the process of change in a systemic context, not the content of specific changes (i.e., portfolios, block scheduling, learning styles).

Critical strategies in creating change through design conversation are: (1) "commitment to change *of* the system rather than change *within* the system," (2) the identification of diverse voices whose inclusion will "impart the value of democracy," (3) the facilitation of the construction of a common language by the participants, and, (4) the "focus on building a conscious collective mindfulness of community through dialogue that creates a common sense of purpose and shared vision" (Jenlink and Carr, 1996, p. 35).

A distinction between design conversation and modernistic responses to the exigencies of the postmodern world lies in the contextualization of responsibility. In the design process, responsibility for the outcomes of the conversation are shared by the whole group. However, the primary distinction is that "we must begin to see that we are not responsible for other people's development or actions, but instead that we are responsible to them as fellow human beings. We are also responsible with them as a collective for the future of our children's learning, and our own" (Jenlink and Carr, 1996, p. 37).

Post-formal Conversation

Post-formal conversation is central to postmodern professional development because it embodies dialogue and design conversation, and provides a mechanism to transcend reflexive thought. William Doll's characterization of postmodern curriculum as "rich, recursive, relational, and rigorous" (Pinar, Reynolds, Slattery, and Taubman, 1995, p. 501) is an apt description of what conversation would be like if performed in the context of post-formal thinking. This kind of conversation can be characterized as collective post-formal thinking. Just as Kincheloe (1993) sees post-formal thinking about thinking as "a running meta-dialogue, a constant conversation with self" (p. 146); so would post-formal conversation be a constant conversation among educators about the etymology, patterns, process, and contextualization of educational issues and experiences. As post-formal thinking is an "expansion of self-awareness and consciousness" (Kincheloe, 1993, p. 146); post-formal conversation includes an expansion of the awareness of self in relation to others, and a critical awareness of the communication process in relation to how it emancipates or constrains our relations with others. Additionally, post-formal conversation expands our awareness of: the origins of knowledge, the deep hidden patterns that shape our construction of reality, the need to deconstruct the texts that limit our potential, and the "fabric of relevance" (Kincheloe and Steinberg, 1996, p. 189) that has to be constructed for an effective understanding of the issue or experience. Post-formal conversation is a dynamic investigation of our selves, our relations with others, and the political implications of the type of conversation in which we are engaged. Since the political implications affect gender, class, age, race, and ethnicity; post-formal conversation includes a crucial ethical component.

Embedded in post-formal conversation are facilitative mechanisms reminiscent of the principles of Lev Vygotsky. The techniques and understandings that prove useful in the instruction of children would be just as effective with adults. As in Vygotsky's zone of proximal development where a child benefits from the collaboration with a more advanced peer (Wertsch, 1985), dialogic and design conversation allows teachers to facilitate each others' understanding and development. Vygotsky's belief in the importance of social interaction in cognitive function applies to learners in group situations regardless of age. The use of language in cooperative contexts enhances the social and ethical as well as cognitive functioning of the participants.

CHARACTERISTICS OF POST-FORMAL CONVERSATION Post-formal conversation is a dialogue about power. All conversation has a political or power component, but post-formal conversation in education is about teachers spiritually exercising that power, about teachers exploring theory and practice with a sense of moral rightness and passion. Kincheloe describes this as a connection of logic and emotion. "Teachers as post-formal thinkers are emotionally committed to their thoughts, tapping into a passion for knowing that motivates, that extends, that leads them to a union with that which is to be known" (1993, p. 153)

This is not the contrived empowerment that is currently so endemic to reform but a critical exploration of issues with a certitude of control and efficacy. Contrived empowerment is when administrators mandate a change, set faculty committees, and "empower" the faculty to carry out the mandate within the guidelines established by the administration. Power, as created through post-formal conversation and wielded in post-formal conversation, is when faculty initiate a conversation about change and critically engage the change through post-formal thinking.

The conversation does not focus on superficial manifestations of reform such as portfolios, intensive block scheduling, or community projects; it focuses on the critical pedagogical issues that are framed in a post-formal context. In a critical pedagogical context conversation about portfolios would be replaced by conversations about assessment and its effects on children. Intensive block scheduling would be replaced by conversation about the purpose of schooling and how to best achieve that purpose, and community projects would be replaced by conversation about democratic values and how to teach them without violating the rights of students.

Each of these post-formal conversations would be characterized by critical explorations of the etymology, the patterns, the process, and the contextualization of the issues (Kincheloe and Steinberg, 1996). These features of post-formal thinking are the mechanisms that emancipate and truly empower the teacher. As the perceived reality of the situation is post-formally explored, power shifts from the modern essentialized structures that oppress the teachers, to the teacher's culture, which with each shift incrementally becomes more collegially empowered.

In a sense faculty engaged in a post-formal conversation would be in a state of flow (Csikszentmihalyi, 1993; 1990)—excited, energized, focused, sharply attuned to every nuance of the conversation and issue. A sense of moral purpose would pervade the room. As indicated by Jenlink and Carr, elements of dialectical and discussion conversation would occasionally emerge but as mechanisms to unveil mindsets and clear the mind of those worn-out narratives that blind us to opportunities for effective emancipatory and egalitarian action. This altered state of consciousness facilitates a holistic awareness of the need to grasp "the overall structure of a set of relationships" (Kincheloe, 1993, p. 168), which is in sharp contrast to the reductionist tunnel-vision approach of traditional engagements of change.

William Pinar's four stages of *currere* (Pinar, 1994) provide a model for individual and collective post-formal conversation as well as a framework for the reconceptualization of curriculum. As an individual or collective endeavor educators could use this model to engage in a conversation that would contextualize, authenticate, and justify their action.

Pinar's four stages are:

- REGRESSIVE—a return to the past; an exploring, reliving of the past; an analysis of how the past affects the present; the goal is freedom from the past.
- PROGRESSIVE—an exploration of the future; a free association of what the future will bring; a realization that "the future is present in the same sense that the past is present" (Pinar, 1994, p. 24).
- ANALYTICAL—a description of the "biographic present, exclusive of the past and future, but inclusive of responses to them" (Pinar, 1994, p. 24).
- SYNTHETICAL—a look at the whole as representation of the integrated past, present and future; a visible "conceptual gestalt"; a "conceptualization of the present situation."

In an empirical reductionist context, this process would appear to be an extravagant, complicated waste of time. However, the individual or collective utilization of this technique results in the expansion of consciousness. Along with this expansion of consciousness is an expansion of complexity that introduces a plethora of variables that would overwhelm traditional research and conversation. Ironically, through the technique of *currere*, by seeing the whole and experiencing the synthetical, the answer or meaning becomes simple and clear.

Another characteristic of post-formal conversation is an explicit awareness of place. Joe L. Kincheloe and William F. Pinar propose the use of social psychoanalysis and the study of place as the means to analyze one's life history to offset the myths created by "social distortion and repression" (1991, p. 2). The foundations for this analysis of the historical antecedents of our current reality are beliefs in human agency and the primacy of language in the interpretation of human experience. Place has a unique position in this process in that the study of the "local, present, unspectacular day-to-day human experience" (Kincheloe and Pinar, 1991, p. 4) facilitates our understanding of our social world. Our understanding is authenticated through the study of "the concrete, the named, the identified" (Kincheloe and Pinar, 1991, p. 5). The relationship of history and place creates a larger context from which to evaluate current situations and reconstruct our essential meanings. This social psychoanalytic process is appropriate as an individual or group "therapy" in relation to the disorders found in education.

Many schools undertake reforms without reflecting on the pedagogical and educational psychological history of their collective and individual experience. They fail to situate the intended reform in the context of their place. This denial of history and the local results in the disconnection of the reform from any relevant and authentic aspects of the situation. The ensuing disconnection guarantees a half-hearted attempt or outright failure. As a central feature of post-formal conversation, place facilitates the sense of spirituality or moral rightness and reinforces the growing sense of power. In tandem, a sense of power and moral action are the motivators for democratic change and the safeguards against the specter of relativism.

HOW POST-FORMAL CONVERSATION AFFECTS THE CHANGE PROCESS One of the most crucial aspects of the change process is detection of the problem. What is the problem? Who decides it is a problem? Is the problem a symptom of a larger, hidden situation that needs correction? Educators who are bound to modernistic-problem solving techniques fail to penetrate the superficiality of the problem and engage it on a significant level because they cannot engage the problem in a holistic context with an emotional component fostered by the problem's relation to a place. The comprehensive nature of a problem cannot be detected without the scrutiny of the knowledge related to the problem, without a recognition and acceptance of the emotional or spiritual component of the problem, and without the willingness to systemically contextualize the problem. Kincheloe (1993) reports that school problems "are constructed by social conditions, cognitive assumptions, and power relations and are uncovered by insightful educators who possess the ability to ask questions never before asked; questions that lead to innovations that promote student insight, sophisticated thinking, and social justice" (pp. 150-151).

Contemporary educational problem detection is ineffective due to the politicization of every problem. The needs of the interest groups become the focus of the problem-solving process, thus limiting the change process to this narrow perspective. Conversation becomes dialectical and discursive as each interest tries to gain advantage. The bureaucratization of education exacerbates this focus on interest groups. The administrative imperative is to always seek compromise, not to thoroughly and critically understand and address the larger nature of the problem. This very real need to control the change process restricts the degree of empowerment of teachers. Post-formal thinking and conversation oppose this imperative.

One common control strategy is to create an artificial scarcity of time. Action must be taken now. "We can't waste time arguing about it." This strategy serves two purposes: (1) conversation can be controlled, and (2) power remains with the groups representing the dominant culture or interests. The result is that significant change doesn't occur, either because the negotiated compromise has caused the change to be assimilated or because disenchanted teachers resist the change.

In a Piagetian context post-formal conversation is a catalyst and an accommodating mechanism of disequilibrium. When change creates a cognitive dissonance, traditional conversation works to assimilate the change within the present structure whereas the process of post-formal conversation critically accommodates the change. In both cases, conversation is the key process in dealing with the change. In one case conversation is controlled and directed to resolve the change within the person's or school's existing cognitive structures. However in a post-formal context, conversation critically accommodates the change and at the same time empowers and emancipates the critically reflective conversant.

To return to our metaphor of multiple personality, the aspects of post-formal conversation are the integrative techniques that allow a fragmented educational community to reestablish its focus and unified direction. Post-formal conversation has therapeutic power because of its ability to facilitate these outcomes: recognition of the systemic or holistic nature of contexts and meanings, the development of history that offsets the deleterious effects of the postmodern condition, the emancipatory power that is unleashed by awareness, the recognition that change is an ongoing and dynamic process, and the development of ethical referents beyond self-interest and efficiency. When used conjointly, post-formal conversational techniques represent a powerful, synergetic process that can not only transform change but also the people within the educational community.

The Process of Change

When the forces of change are activated by conversation, a process begins in which competing discourses attempt to influence or control the conversation. This process is best understood in a socio-psychological context in which modernistic and postmodernistic discourses exist in a dialectical relationship, adversarially pursuing their ideological agendas and pedagogical philosophies. This process for control occurs within multiple texts with both discourses trying to make sense of the forces of change by interpreting them within the context of their discourse and then utilizing these forces to promote their position.

An important point that more realistically frames this competition for control of the change process is that, in most cases, change has been and is now controlled by the modernistic paradigms. Seldom are large-scale critical or radical change initiatives promoted or engaged in by educators. The entrenchment of modernistic psychology and pedagogy in educational thinking and media allows them to control the multiple texts which convey information essential to the development of change initiatives. Therefore the change process should not be construed as two equally powerful points of view vying for control on an equal playing field.

Multiple Texts

As the discourses grounded in modernistic and postmodernistic thinking attempt to control the change process, text becomes a critical battleground. The broader meaning of text provides a framework for a more systemic view of the change process. Besides the more traditional and obvious manifestations of text such as written or spoken discourse, viewing text in the context of its root *texere* ("to weave") extends our perception of text to include vehicles and formats that weave our meanings and intentions into non-traditional communications. These additional sources of information range from media representations of popular culture to the messages sent by school board budgets and state and federal appropriations.

Also, inherent in all texts is an implicit sense of authority. To be represented in text automatically creates the perception of validation by some authority. If it is published, on television, or decreed, then it must be true. Obviously, in academia the scrutiny to which text is subjected establishes the degree of rigor behind the text and its contextual veracity. However, most of the communication that affects those involved in change occurs through text that is not subjected to academic scrutiny. Significantly, most of the educational practitioners and almost all of the general public rely on texts other than academic writing for the information that constitutes their conclusions about education. Parents form their conclusions about education from their own experience as students, what they see in the media, what their children share with them, and their interactions with the school. Teachers, administrators, and parents entertain the results of government studies, think tank findings, such topical information as school violence and SAT score fluctuations as messages filtered through the lenses of the media.

During times of change, modern discourse exemplified by educational bureaucracy and administration seeks epistemological and pedagogical support. This need opens the door for the further commodification of the educational community by providing an opportunity for experts to sell "pedagogical packages" that allegedly facilitate the change. These packages are centered on specific philosophies or strategies that are mostly traditional in nature. When the need for change arises either out of public perception, state mandate, or educator-generated initiatives, professional development relies on traditional educational psychology as espoused by the consultants for the answers. Each pedagogical subspeciality motivated by profit vies for influence over the educators.

The effect of popular culture as experienced in the classroom and through the representations of the media is central to an understanding of the success and failure of reform. Television and film provide important texts in the construction of educational identity. Films like *The Substitute, Dead Poet's Society, Mr. Holland's Opus, Teachers, Stand and Deliver* and *Dangerous Minds* are texts that provide powerful messages about the efficacy of education and educators and what constitutes the problems and solutions of education. Television sitcoms and dramas contribute to this representation of education by non-educators. Media appropriates the problems of education and reconstructs them into superficial, simplistic representations that pander to media's self-interest.

Professional development as manifested in in-service training provides an additional text in the context of the change process. Who makes the decisions about in-service, who teaches the sessions, and the courses or workshops that are offered communicate important messages to the teachers about their own power, professional esteem, and efficacy. How professional development needs are generated and the manner in which they are resolved are direct indicators of which discourse controls the educational system. Modernistic systems pay lip service to teacher empowerment by allowing teacher decision making in controlled and regulated situations. Systems with a postmodern orientation allow the in-service needs to be generated by the teachers, organized by the teachers, and taught by the teachers. Teachers as action researchers gather data, evaluate it in relation to their experiential knowledge, and take action. Cognizant of the fact that this is an ongoing process, they will need to reflect on their action and make necessary changes. When professional development needs are generated by the teachers, professional development is transformed into an authentic, relevant activity that has direct and positive benefits for the whole school community.

Teachers and the Change Process

Teachers fail to assert themselves in pedagogical matters as they assert themselves in economic matters. This failure indicates a lack of confidence in their understanding of pedagogical theory. Teachers are confident that they can deliver curriculum but not in their ability to create theory. One reason for this lack of confidence is the deskilling of the teacher that occurred in the twentieth century (Bennett and LeCompte, 1990). Larry Cuban (1984) details how teachers have been limited in their decision-making capacity, essentially limited to management concerns. Their exclusion from the decision-making process negates their need to entertain theory in any manner. The development and critique of educational theory are left to the academics, politicians, consultants, and (somewhat) to the administrators.

This disenfranchisement from educational theory and the accompanying deleterious attitudes are reinforced by the messages found in the multiple texts of educational discourse. The messages of these texts foster the debilitating attitudes that effectively alienate the teacher from policy and theoretical debates. This alienation has an enervating effect on the teacher's sense of efficacy in dealing with policy and theory. Bennett and LeCompte report that when teachers are allowed to work with external reformers, they feel that they are a part of the solution and assiduously work towards a successful resolution of the initiative. However, "their efforts may be illusory, because the ultimate effect of centralized curriculum management is to remove control from the jurisdiction of teachers" (1990, p. 142) as the theoretical underpinnings of the change and the consequent implementation policy are decided by other people. Once again the message is clear that theory is not in the realm of teachers.

How do teachers move into the realm of theory? How do teachers become skilled in the formation of theory and the consequent critical evaluation of theory? The answer is simple: by engaging in post-formal thinking and conversation. The dictates of an external authority will never bear the scrutiny of a post-formal examination because they will be universal, standardized, canned ideas that have limited relevance to the unique reality of the local place. By dissecting and eviscerating these ineffectual palliatives teachers regain a sense of power and personal effectiveness. Once the artificial program of the expert has been disposed of, teachers can post-formally deconstruct their own current situation, history, experience, place, and future. This examination of their practice will generate authentic theory which, in combination with best practice theory, can be developed into innovation that can be implemented with confidence and passion. At this point, the teacher truly becomes a powerful agent of change.

The Change Process: Two Scenarios

Much if not all of the change occurs in public schools occurs in a traditional, systematic manner. Tradition requires that the important strategic and tactical decisions are made by the administration, staff development is expert oriented, and precise implementation time plans are developed and followed. Faculty committees may be formed which allow faculty involvement in secondary decision-making and provide opportunities for faculty to "buy into" the change. Many times, the result is haphazard or "paper" implementation where significant change appears on paper, but in the classrooms the same old curriculum, instruction, and attitudes prevail. Even if change is implemented, members of the school wonder whether it was the best change for that time and in that place.

The result of this teacher and student skepticism is faddism. Faddism is an outgrowth of the lack of meaningful commitment to a change project. Ideas do not become fads if they can be justified through experience which validates the theory and practice.

The effects of change are a text which can be read in different ways. For example, schools that attempt to implement portfolio assessment in a traditional manner will end up with portfolios. However, the outcome will have different interpretations depending on how the text is read. A state auditor may find the change satisfactory according to state requirements. Administration may tout the change as a tremendous success. Some teachers may see the change as another ineffective fad that will soon fade. A critic might deconstruct the effort and see that in actuality there is no substantial difference in how students are assessed. Dutifully with some grumbling, students stuff their portfolios with paper, complain that it is a waste of time, wonder why they must do it, and worry about accumulating percentage points and letter grades. Another state mandate is fulfilled; the faculty is still jaded and suspicious; and the students are still ranked and sorted.

Change in a post-formal context would be different in its development, implementation, and outcomes. Assuming that teachers know how to post-formally think and converse, the change process would involve the dynamic and constant interplay of teacher research, critical reflection, and decision-making. Change could be initiated in many ways, from a state mandate to the faculty viewing of a segment of the evening news reporting more failures of the American educational community. Either example would be followed by conversation that would contextualize and deconstruct the report and the current local situation. The outcome of post-formal change is unpredictable because it more closely approximates the real chaotic complexity of life. However, one guarantee is that attached to the outcomes of this process will be the spiritual commitment to the outcomes that comes naturally from the sincere belief that what you did is right. Of all the variables that affect the change process, the most important in improving the quality of education is commitment.

The main obstacles to the use of post-formalism in the change process are the scarcity of time, the educational bureaucracy, and the teachers themselves. Whether this process is time-consuming remains to be seen. However, the resistance to this approach is not about time but about control—more succinctly, the fear of losing control. The self-perpetuating nature of bureaucracies is as well documented as their resistance to substantive change. Educational bureaucracies have a greater stranglehold on their profession than business bureaucracies because there is no measurable, easily discernible product. The problem with teachers is their willingness to perpetuate this system, their refusal to include students in significant, large-scale decision-making, and, their resistance to the unlearning that is a necessary condition for their empowerment and for quality changes in education.

To discern the effects of any change or reform we need to look to the forces of change. Who has power? Are the participants spiritually motivated? Are they passionate about their work? Are theory and practice mutually grounded in each other? Are all the members of the community aware of the theory behind their practice? Does the change or reform accommodate difference in an equitable manner? Is there a critical attitude and a will to continuously reflect upon the status quo? And finally, is the environment more nurturing, caring, and democratic than before?

Conclusion

If education is to escape its dissociative malady, then post-formalism must be integrated within the change process. In order for this to happen, the principles and processes of post-formalism must guide the professional development of teachers and administrators. Paramount to the epistemological aspects of professional development is discussion among administrators, teachers, students, parents, and school boards that engages the issues raised by post-formalism. Central to this dialogue is the commitment to an emancipatory philosophy related to all members of the school community.

On the university level, teacher preparation must provide spaces in which the student can deal with the critical issues of power, culture, praxis, and spirituality in the context of their future teaching. Experiences must be provided in which these students can unlearn their exclusively modernistic pedagogy that was inculcated in them by their pre-college experience. Educational administration certification programs must include these integrative processes if future administrators are to maintain the continuity of these critical efforts. Success and failure of educational change are systemic outcomes, and administrators cannot be isolated or neutral entities in a critical change effort.

Finally, a public dialogue must be initiated. A dialogue about systemic critical change cannot be relegated solely to an academic venue but must engage the general public. Physics is an exceptional model for this suggestion. In an era proliferate with science illiterates, physics has created an astonishing public interest in quantum mechanics as evidenced by the plethora of books presented for public consumption (Capra, 1991; Gribbin, 1995; Jones, 1992; Kaku, 1994; Lindley, 1996; Wheatley, 1994). Despite such an incredibly complex subject lay people read, talk, and integrate these ideas in their lives. For example, connections are made between quantum principles and all the aspects of wellness. With the inclusion of Eastern philosophy in the discussions about a quantum universe science, philosophy, and spirituality become reunited (Capra, 1991)—as must psychology, education, and spirituality. Even though these writings about quantum mechanics are generally metaphorical, they lay the groundwork for renewed interest in science and an understanding of one's own reality in a quantum universe. More importantly, science is once again relevant to people's lives. The same can happen to education if the post-formal dialogue can be extended to the general public.

How can the dissociative disorder of education be overcome? Thomas Jefferson shows us the way. "I know no safe depository of the ultimate powers of the society but the people themselves and if we think them not enlightened enough to exercise their control with a wholesome discretion, the remedy is not to take it from them but to inform their descension by education." The resolution of education's disorder lies in empowering the teachers and in facilitating their use of post-formalism to meet the unpredictable requirements of the postmodern world.

References

Alter, J. (1996). Busting the big blob. *Newsweek*, April 8, p. 40.

American Psychiatric Association. (1994). *Diagnostic and statistical manual of mental disorders* (4th ed). Washington, DC: American Psychiatric Association.

Bennett, K. P. and LeCompte, M. D. (1990). *The way schools work: A sociological analysis of education.* New York: Longman.

Beyer, L. E. and Liston, D. P. (1996). *Curriculum in conflict: Social visions, educational agendas, and progressive school reform.* New York: Teachers College.

Bohm, D. (1980). *Wholeness and the implicate order.* New York: Routledge

Bohm, D. (1992). *Thought as a system.* New York: Routledge.

Bourdieu, P. and Passeron, J. (1992). *Reproduction in education, society and culture.* London: Sage.

Branson, R. K. (1987). Why the schools can't improve: The upper limit hypothesis. *Journal of Instructional Development, 10* (4), 15–26.

Capra, F. (1991). *The Tao of physics.* Boston, MA: Shambhala.

Carlson, D. (1996). Teachers as political actors: From reproductive theory to the crisis of schooling. In Leistyna, P. , Woodrum, A., and Sherblom, S. A.(Eds.), *Breaking free: The transformative power of critical pedagogy* (pp. 273–300). Cambridge, MA: Harvard Educational Review.

Cremin, L. A. (1964). *The transformation of the school: Progressivism in American education 1876-1957.* New York: Vintage Books.

Csikszentmihalyi, M. (1990). *Flow: The psychology of optimal experience.* New York: Harper Perennial.

Csikszentmihalyi, M. (1993). *A psychology for the third millennium: The evolving self.* New York: Harper Perennial.

Cuban, L. (1984). *How teachers taught: Constancy and change in American classrooms, 1890-1980.* New York: Longman.

Gardner, H. (1983). *Frames of mind: The theory of multiple intelligences.* New York: Basic Books.

Gergen, K. J. (1991). *The saturated self: Dilemmas of identity in contemporary life.* New York: Basic Books.

Giroux, H. (1992). *Border crossings: Cultural workers and the politics of education.* New York: Routledge.

Giroux, H. (1993). Teachers as a transformative intellectuals. In Shapiro, H. S. and Purpel, D. E. (Eds.), *Critical social issues in American education* (pp. 273–277). New York: Longman.

Giroux, H. (1994). *Disturbing pleasures: Learning about popular culture.* New York: Routledge.

Gribbin, J. (1995). *Schrodinger's kittens and the search for reality.* New York: Little and Brown.

Griffin, D. R. (1988). *Spirituality and society: Postmodern visions.* Albany: SUNY.

Hargreaves, A. (1994). *Changing teachers, changing times.* New York: Teachers College Press.

Jenlink, P. and Carr, A. A. (1996). Conversation as a medium for change in education. *Educational Technology, 36* (1), 31–38.

Jones, R. S. (1992). *Physics for the rest of us.* Chicago, Illinois: Contemporary Books.

Kaku, M. (1994). *Hyperspace.* New York: Oxford University Press.

Kantrowitz, B. (1996). The jargon jungle. *Newsweek, October 7,* p. 86.

Kincheloe, J. L. (1991). *Teachers as researchers: Qualitative inquiry as a path to empowerment.* Philadelphia, PA: The Falmer Press.

Kincheloe, J. L. (1993). *Toward a critical politics of teacher thinking: Mapping the postmodern.* Westport, CT: Bergin and Garvey.

Kincheloe, J. L. and Pinar, W. F. (Eds.). (1991). *Curriculum as social psychoanalysis: The significance of place.* New York: SUNY.

Kincheloe, J. L. and Steinberg, S. R. (1996). A tentative description of post-formal thinking: The critical confrontation with cognitive theory. In Leistyna, P. , Woodrum, A., and Sherblom, S. A.(Eds.), *Breaking free: The transformative power of critical pedagogy* (pp. 167–198). Cambridge, MA: Harvard Educational Review.

Kliebard, H. M. (Ed.). (1995). *The struggle for the American curriculum 1893-1958* (2nd ed.). New York: Routledge.

Kluft, R. P. (Ed.) (1985). *Childhood antecedents of multiple personality.* Washington, DC: American Psychiatric Press, Inc.

Leistyna, P. , Woodrum, A., and Sherblom, S. A. (Eds). (1996). *Breaking free: The transformative power of critical pedagogy.* Cambridge, MA: Harvard Educational Review.

Lindley, D. (1996). *Where does the weirdness go? Why quantum mechanics is strange, but not as strange as you think.* New York: Basic Books.

Pinar, W. F. (1994). *Autobiography, politics and sexuality: Essays in curriculum theory 1972-1992.* New York: Peter Lang.

Pinar, W., Reynolds, W., Slattery, P. and Taubman, P. (1995). *Understanding curriculum.* New York: Peter Lang.

Senge, P. M. (1990). *The fifth discipline: The art and practice of the learning organization.* New York: Doubleday/Currency.

Smith, F. (1995). Let's declare education a disaster and get on with our lives. *Phi Delta Kappan. 76*(8), 584–590.

Toch, T. and Daniel, M. (1996). Schools that work. *U.S. News & World Report, 121* (14), 58–64.

Wertsch, J. V. (1985). *Vygotsky and the social formation of mind.* Cambridge, MA: Harvard University Press.

Wexler, P. (1992). *Becoming somebody: Toward a social psychology of school.* Washington, DC: The Falmer Press.

Wheatley, M. J. (1994). *Leadership and the new science.* San Francisco, CA: Berrett-Koehler.

CHAPTER SIXTEEN

Children's Lives
A Radical Assessment of a Given Reality:
Post-formal Thinking in the 'Hood

Elise L. Youth

In America, as white children leave the home and move on through the educational system and then into the work world, the development of cognitive and learning styles follows a linear and self-reinforcing course. Never are they asked to be bicultural, bidialectic, or bicognitive. On the other hand, for non-European-American children biculturality is not a free choice, but a prerequisite for successful participation and eventual success. These children are generally expected to be bicultural, bidialectic, bicognitive; to measure their performance against a middle-class European yardstick; and to maintain a psychic energy to maintain this orientation. At the same time, they are being castigated whenever they attempt to express and validate their indigenous cultural and cognitive styles. Under such conditions conflict becomes the norm rather than the exception.
　　—James A. Anderson, 1988

The Eurocentric character of school curriculum functions not only to deny role models to non-European-American students; it denies self understanding to white students as well.
　　—Castenell, 1990

As a public school educator of Latino and African American children for the past fourteen years, I have struggled with the task of facilitating a curriculum for my students which is based upon the indigenous knowledge they bring to the classroom in an attempt to move beyond "formal thinking." The modernist conception of "formal" intelligence is an exclusionary system based on the premise that some people are intelligent and others are not (Case, 1985; Klahr and Wallace, 1976). Post-formal knowledge, that which moves beyond the exclusionary aspect of formality, celebrates the knowledge that multiple races, classes, religions, and sexualities bring to schools, which is not represented in the curriculum.

Critical educators who employ the post-formal paradigm understand that cultural difference within a classroom provides an opportunity for cognitive growth as well as development of an emancipatory, democratic environment. Education, in such a classroom, becomes more than raising test scores and programming students to conform to prearranged curricular goals and objectives. A post-formal pedagogy moves beyond rote memorization, recall, and eventual preparation for corporate robotization. Intelligence is no longer the sacred ground of the Eurocentric privileged few. The layers of sophistication involved in previously labeled "unconventional and unintelligent" ways of knowing are uncovered. Multiple knowledges exhibited by culturally diverse students are valued, encouraged, celebrated and assimilated into a "student-friendly" curriculum. Most importantly, a post-formal theory of cognition enables schools to become meaningful, democratic and empowering collaborative junctures between all relevant aspects of students' lives—including, but not limited to—family, peers, spirituality, pop culture and indigenous tradition, heritage and knowledge.

> We are not, in fact, "other."
> —Toni Morrison, 1989

American classrooms are populated by people from diverse backgrounds. The schooling system is the major point of entry into mainstream society, and that experience is a major factor in later success. Unfortunately, this educational system is based solely on a Eurocentric worldview which negates multiple, indigenous knowledge bases and perspectives. Certain populations will be "fairly" well served by the system; "others" will not. My major concern deals with the creation of a category called "other" in that I would argue that "other" merely exists only as a biased separation created by the dominant Eurocentric mentality. What happens to these so-called "others" as they participate in the culture of schooling and how to ameliorate these inequalities form the material of this chapter as well as of my professional career.

At the risk of being "confessional," I will admit that my professional teaching career did not always have this focus. I began with quite "noble" intentions of imparting my concept of knowledge upon my "culturally deprived" students (of course, we all know about the paths paved with good intentions). I was extremely motivated, self-confident and, unbeknownst to me, close minded and egotistical. I had so much to teach; they had so much to learn. The knowledge I attempted to "transmit" to my students was a cacophony of rehearsed behavioral objectives formulated by teacher education courses—scope and sequence skills derived from teaching guides, goals mandated by my principal and standards espoused by the school district—interspersed with my personal concept of truth, values, and vision. I very quickly realized (thankfully so) that "my" knowledge, so well cultivated and nurtured throughout the years, may not be the "univocal Truth." However proud I felt about "my" knowledge, it did not seem to be relevant to my students. I had equated truth with facts and logic established and perpetuated by educational authorities. Furthermore, my carefully planned, highly creative and stimulating lessons were not fitting into the neat little blocks of my required and weekly evaluated lesson plans. Six hours a day were not long enough to transmit "my" knowledge and attend to the needs of my students. Was it more important to make sure that my lessons were taught and that test scores were improving or to foster an honest, unintimidating classroom community where my students could freely reveal the homelessness, violence, gang terror, drug and alcohol addiction, physical and sexual abuse, hunger, and so many more realities of their young lives? Their daily personal stories, filled with pain, struggle, fear, disillusionment, as well as joy, suddenly became so much more important than achieving "my" predetermined goals for "them." Thus, I began my search for more meaningful, relevant instruction, built upon student dialogue, interest and choice. The next section of this chapter will focus on "critical classroom incidents" which guided and strengthened my journey into post-formal thinking.

Tony: The Wild Boy
"Tony is uncontrollable and uneducable. He has never had any 'formal' education; eats with his hands; throws books, desks, whatever he gets his hands on. Even the male NTA has difficulty restraining him." Those were some of the phrases used to describe Tony, one of my African American students. Upon my determined research, I found that at a very young age he had witnessed his mother jump to her death from a bedroom window, was sent to live with an elderly grandmother, who had also died in his presence, and finally went to live with a poverty-stricken uncle who did not believe in "formal" schooling, Yes, Tony had

tantrums, threw books, desks, etc., until I realized that he had absolutely no idea why he was in school and what difference the isolated facts
he was being made to memorize would make in his life. At the same
time, I discovered Tony's ingenious artistic ability—this was something
I could encourage. Eventually, I incorporated his artistry into every
aspect of the classroom learning environment. He illustrated classroom
books written by the students, designed bulletin boards, and mentored
other students in art classes. His instruction became meaningful and was
designed around the fact that it could be applied to a possible future in
graphic design. Tony felt secure enough to illustrate the death of his
mother and his recurring fear of separation and loss. Although his uncle
may not have believed in formal schooling, he had taught Tony to draw
and appreciate indigenous southern African American artwork and
crafts. The "uneducable" had fostered compassion, empathy and humility within his "educated" teacher. After fourteen years, Tony visits me
regularly, always proud and eager to share his latest accomplishment:
"Miss Youth, I'm in the Navy; Miss Youth I'm studying architecture;
Miss Youth , I want you to meet my girl . . . ."

Darrin: Pedagogy of Hope

Darrin came to my classroom after being "schooled" within a cult in
Florida to which his teenage mother had run away. When Darrin would
not behave, the cult leaders would beat him with electrical cords—the
tell-tale scars visibly haunted his young body. His great-grandmother,
over eighty years of age, finally convinced DHS to grant her custody of
Darrin. He rarely spoke and made no attempt at peer relationships within my classroom. His big brown eyes longed for an explanation for his
past suffering and pain. During this time, I was doing classroom
research for my masters thesis. The topic, "individualized instruction
for a language-delayed (note, not deficient) student" had been developed before Darrin joined my class. Thus, I chose Darrin as my research
subject. At that time, the school district had not cut classroom assistants;
therefore, I could devote extra time to Darrin. Progress was slow (of
course, this is my Eurocentric anal fixation with time), and trust took a
long time to develop. One day Darrin sheepishly brought his bookbag
over to my desk and cautiously removed some books so that no one else
could see. They were children's Christian Bible storybooks which he
proceeded to read to me without difficulty. This child couldn't read; he
could barely communicate verbally! Had he merely memorized these
books in order to parrot them back? I decided to investigate by bringing

in children's Bible storybooks from my church that were written at his level. Darrin could read them easily and comprehensively. During the first report card conference, his great-grandmother unlocked the mystery. She had been allowed brief visits to Darrin when he was in the cult, at which time she snuck these storybooks in to him. With the minimal and censored schooling Darrin received in the cult, he feverishly struggled to learn each word in the books, without being discovered, for fear of being beaten. These books and the visits by his great-grandmother gave him the only hope, joy, and peace he knew. This learning had been relevant and vital to him as well as to his survival—much more so than the reading activities developed as a part of my masters thesis.

Jose: One Man's Trash

My students had been taunting Jose for several weeks: "Your father is a trash picker. He's always picking up dirty junk. You were born in a garbage can. I make more money ripping-off people. You couldn't even rent a video with the money your father makes!" All of these Latino students in my classroom were extremely poverty-stricken: most lived in condemned, boarded-up buildings. They could not go outside for recess during the colder weather due to inadequate clothing (flip-flops). Their parents spoke very little, if any, English. Jose also came from a large, poor family; however, his father was one of the only actual birth fathers in my classroom, and he also had a job as a junk collector. Every morning Jose would rise very early before school to help his father collect cans and scrap metal. Jose never missed a day of school, no matter how hard and long he and his father worked. The other students had no fathers in the home and were being raised by jobless, often illegally residing female caregivers. Today their vicious taunting finally drove Jose to tears. I decided, if possible, that it was time for a class visitor and field trip. I walked to Jose's home after school and asked if his father would visit our class and take us on one of his scrap metal rounds. I primed my class on the morning of his visit and our "excursion," both of which went relatively smoothly. The students, in fact, were rather amazed at the money which could be accrued from such a venture. A classroom project evolved from this experience which grew into a community clean-up effort to supply monetary funds for much-needed playground repairs and supplies. As I became closer to Jose's father, I discovered that his ingenuity and business sense were paving the way for his family to move out of that neighborhood as well as for the provision of proper nutrition, clothing, and medical care.

Before concluding this scenario, it is important to reflect upon the taunting statements made by Jose's classmates. Once again, the cultural incompatibility between Eurocentric values and perceptions and those of the culture of the students, in this case Latino, had reared its ugly head. These children were slowly being molded into Eurocentric robots without being the recipients of white, middle-class societal privileges. They were judging the work done by Jose's father as demeaning and actually worse than stealing. An individualistic, competitive, materialistic orientation, prevalent in Eurocentric society was being valued over a collective family and classroom community. Peer cohesiveness, interdependence, and respect were being traded in for the "each man for himself" mentality. Unfortunately, our schools continue to foster and reward these characteristics, further deculturalizing and alienating the very children we are morally, ethically, and humanly responsible for nurturing.

Georgia and Annie: A Mother's Love

The most marked turning point in the development of my personal appreciation for and validation of post-formal thinking came about during the past academic year when Annie became one of my students. Annie is a vivacious seven-year-old African American who has been diagnosed by the psychological "intelligentsia" as "a mildly learning disabled youngster with Attention Deficit Disorder who is in need of a self-contained learning support program." Upon entering my classroom, Annie was already receiving two daily doses of Ritalin as well as psychological counseling and language therapy due to a delayed speech pattern.

On Annie's first day in my classroom community, I was met by her seemingly mistrustful, uncommunicative, single, young mother, Georgia. Her eyes communicated her feelings more adequately than any words. I was viewed as yet another white upper-middle-class stranger who would be with her daughter from 8:45 to 2:45. That was all. Nothing was different except for my face. Each day Georgia would bring Annie to school, and, each day, I made certain to tell her something sincere and positive about her daughter's achievement. Gradually, I felt a bond being established—many times wordless but full of facial expression and gesture—until one day Georgia asked if she could talk with me during my lunch period. During this time, Georgia revealed her loneliness, depression, and suicidal tendencies. She spoke poignantly of her childhood as the daughter of sharecroppers, the death of her mother from cancer when she was eight years old, the sexual abuse by her stepfather, her older brother's continued incarceration for various crimes, leaving home at thirteen years of age with little "formal" schooling— homeless and hopeless—and her eventual drug and alcohol addiction and criminal record. She felt "uneducated" and inadequate as a mother and the nightmare of the brutality, loss, and pain of her childhood and already three times victimized by race, class, and gender oppression, she felt as if she had nothing to offer her daughter. She also feared Annie would succumb to the routine frustrations, anger, and hopelessness brought about by society's economic and cultural battles against minorities.

The week after my conversation with Georgia, I had arranged for a field trip to a farm outside of the city. There would be numerous animals to pet, feed, and discuss, swimming, and a barbecue—only chaperones were needed. I asked Georgia. She had never done anything like this before, and, even though Annie had previously attended other schools, Georgia had never been asked to be a part of her daughter's education-al experiences prior to this. She hesitantly agreed, and I gave her the responsibility for not only Annie but also two other students as well. I sensed her apprehension and that very little interaction was occurring between her and the other students until we went on a nature walk. There wasn't a bird or wildflower that Georgia couldn't identify. She then began explaining which plants could be used for food or medicine and how to prepare them. She related how "growing up poor meant hav-ing to know all of these things." I told her that I observed that same ten-derness in her toward Annie as well as with the other students and that the dignity and strength she possessed could never have been taught "formally" in school. By the end of the school year, Annie, the "speech delayed, learning disabled, Attention Deficit Disordered child," was speaking fluently and proudly of her accomplishments and was com-pletely free of Ritalin. Her mother, Georgia, was a permanent fixture in my classroom, deeply appreciated by me, my students, and, most importantly, her daughter.

> One of the most injurious factors contributing to poor academic per-formance of African American children, and the one that seems to have the most damaging impact, is the continuous deculturalization of the African American child, and the neglect of the African American cultural values in the curriculum.
> —Boateng, 1990

"I will not speak Spanish at school," wrote the young Mexican American boy. The words increasingly covered the chalkboard as he

repeated and repeated the teacher-imposed penance. The punishment: to write that sentence 50 times after school. The crime: having been caught speaking Spanish with his Latino classmates during recess.
—Cortes, 1986

The four "critical classroom incidents" described in the previous section comprise my modest, abbreviated attempt to portray post-formal thinking and indigenous ways of knowing shared with me by my students and their families. These turning points were crucial for me as an educator, in that they provided an emancipatory classroom discourse which makes connections between what students already know, how this knowledge has been created, and how it has been influenced by factors of race, gender, and social class. Once these exclusionary layers had been uncovered and exposed to critical analysis, I was able to disengage myself from socio-interpersonal norms and ideological expectations for my students, becoming attuned and sensitive to their cultural identities and personal perspectives. My classroom had developed a democratic, emancipatory purpose, far removed from that imposed upon it by the authoritative constraints of exclusionary, reductionist formalism. With this new direction, I then began to question how the educational system had become trapped in a modernist, formal discourse which negates post-formal thinking and indigenous knowledge by defining it in terms of cultural deprivation rather than cultural appreciation and sensitivity.

The burden of change, in a system that truly cares about its students, should not be placed on the individual child, but on the system.
—Cushner, McClelland and Safford, 1992

The American identity is being reshaped, as groups on the margins of society begin to participate in the mainstream and demand that their visions be reflected in a transformed America.
—Banks, 1993

All children who enter school possess a wealth of language and cultural experiences as well as a diversity of early life experiences rooted in their socialization by the home, neighborhood, church, gangs, athletic teams and fostered by families, caregivers, neighbors, friends as well as the media. However, the school itself also encompasses its own customs, values, language, and required "rites of passage" which are traditionally Eurocentric. An immediate cultural conflict emerges between the child's environmental experiences and classroom expectations.

Clearly, those children of different cultural backgrounds are automatically hindered in their adaptation to the demands of school, resulting in underachievement as measured by standardized tests, placement in stigmatized lower-tracked classes, and, most crucially, personal frustration and self-doubt.

Rather than addressing the need for appreciation and inclusion of the attributes, contributions and indigenous knowledge of the various cultures represented by student populations, educational and psychological experts term these students "culturally deprived." They argue that the cultural backgrounds in which these students are raised deprives them of the cognitive skills and values necessary for school success. I argue, however, that the assertion that some children are "culturally deprived" is simply an ethnocentric response by the dominant Euro-American culture. All people have cultural knowledge, rich and elaborate language and communication styles, organized behavior patterns, and value systems. Cultural deprivation is, therefore, an oxymoron.

Our nation has historically forced all children into a monocultural school culture which favors white, middle-class language patterns, values, behavior and, most importantly to this chapter, thinking skills. The experiences, perceptions, and motivational styles of many minority students are merely different that those required and validated by the schools. Anderson (1988) cites two issues which are of major concern with respect to "cultural deprivation" explanations of difference in school achievement. One is the assumption that Anglo-European notions about cognitive functioning, learning, and achievement are unquestionably the best and should be used as models of schooling. The second is an extremely ethnocentric assumption on the part of whites that minorities do not have substantive, valid cognitive framework which may be somewhat different but equally effective. Moreover, Baratz and Baratz (1970) argued that school programs based on the cultural deprivation model were examples of institutional racism and have, thus, violated the cultural integrity of students from diverse income and cultural groups. I would further argue that these premises seem to indicate the glaring fact that the culture of the schools needs to be substantially modified, not the cultural expression of minority students. The basic flaw is that "we" should not attempt to define culture at all!

The last critical classroom incident I will present drives home the harsh reality of the failure of our present modernist, ethnocentric, judgmental educational system in addressing the needs of one of my African American students.

Kareem: There Is No Safety

"What's wrong with his hands?" This question was asked by students and teachers alike when Kareem joined my classroom. Kareem had a severely malformed right hand with only two complete fingers. His left hand was also badly scarred. When Kareem was a baby, his mother—a crack addict—would put his hand on the hot stove in order to punish him or to stop his crying. After repeated skin grafts and reconstructive surgery, he at least had partial mobility in both hands; however, manual tasks were still extremely difficult for him. DHS repeatedly removed him from and returned him to his mother despite the pleas of other family members until she was eventually incarcerated (his father was also in prison). I don't know if she has ever received proper treatment or care. After several foster homes Kareem finally came to live with an older African American couple who lived in the neighborhood of my school. By this time in his few seven years of life, Kareem had already built up a wall of mistrust, fear, and severe psychological problems. He demonstrated no peer socialization skills and was abusive to younger, smaller children. He was embarrassed by his hands as well as his manual difficulties, had frequent tantrums, and would physically attack without warning.

Upon admittance to my program, I immediately questioned the extreme amount and variety of medications he was receiving as well as the fact that adaptive hand devices had not been experimented with in order to increase manual dexterity (i.e., pencil grips, adaptive utensils, etc.). After seemingly endless, dead-end phone calls, I was able to convince his doctors that due to the fact that his drug prescriptions were being given by different agencies who, incidentally, never attempted to contact each other, the medications were producing negative reactions when used in combination. I also demanded that Kareem be evaluated for physical therapy on a regular basis. Rather than subjecting him to the pain and humiliation of writing activities until he was properly fitted with adaptive equipment, I concentrated on verbalization skills, tape-recorded activities, and, in order to facilitate peer interaction, assigned fellow students as recorders for his narratives, reflections, and responses. Promised deadlines passed; weeks turned into months and even with my persistent letters, phone calls, and personal meetings, Kareem was not receiving any additional services. Remarkably, due to his own stubborn determination, he had learned to hold large crayons and then large pencils. He could write his name, a few numbers, but most importantly, he no longer hid his hands from view. I held and stroked those beautiful little hands as often as I could until he finally felt secure enough to actually tell the painful story of their damage.

Christmas was only three weeks away, and my students had excitedly chosen Pollyannas and decorated the classroom and our Christmas tree. No one was more excited however, than Kareem. This would be the first Christmas he had ever celebrated. One week before our party and gift exchange, I received an abrupt phone call that Kareem was being transferred to a more restrictive institutional setting. This was not the treatment and care I had requested! Besides, at this point, the longest period of time that he had spent at one school, he was forming friendships and developing self-confidence through personal accomplishment. Another upheaval in his life could again begin the vicious cycle of mistrust and fear that this little boy had worked so hard to overcome. Again, I spoke and met with everyone possible. Couldn't the transfer at least wait until after Christmas so that I could have time to talk with and prepare him? Needless to say, the answer was "no." I did however, demand to accompany him to his new treatment facility and diligently visited him and spoke with his therapists, who I requested to call me on a regular basis. Abruptly, the calls stopped and upon my next visit I found that Kareem had been transferred again, would no longer have the same therapists, and, to make matters worse, was being placed in another foster home.

I have deep admiration for and belief in the resiliency and strength of the African American people. One has only to look through the "unwritten" pages of history to experience this. And I am in no way trying to set myself up as a sort of "white savior" à la *Dangerous Minds*. However, when human beings, in this case a beaten and bruised young child, are repeatedly oppressed and damaged by our society, how often can they be expected to even care about trying again? How can one pull himself up by his bootstraps when he has no boots? As James Baldwin wrote in 1955, "There is not a Negro alive who does not have this rage in his blood—one has the choice, merely, of living with it consciously or surrendering to it."

Most sadly of all, will this child ever be given the chance to feel and express cultural pride; to come to grips with, and possibly even understand, that his mother was also indeed a victim of society; to develop and apply his indigenous knowledge, post-formal thinking and Afrocentrism? How many children must be beaten down before we realize the ineffectiveness, arrogance, and institutional racism of our educational system—of society? We must no longer ignore, deplore, or despise the culture, life experiences and knowledge that children bring with them to school. Again I quote James Baldwin: "There is no safety; we cannot hide from ourselves, cannot hide from our individual and collective histories, and cannot hide from the truth. We have denied who we are as a nation." We are an African, European, Latino, Asian and Indigenous Peoples nation. Our continued denial of this complex cultural identity and its wealth of subjugated and repudiated, multiple knowledges will further serve to erase the "Pluribus" from "E Pluribus Unum."

> . . . to provide a radical assessment of a given reality is to create, among other things, another reality. . . any criticism of society is, definitionally, a criticism of the ruling ideology. As the critic, I am always seeking to create a new world, to find an escape, to liberate those who see only a part of reality.
>   —Asante, 1987

The names used are the inventions of the author to protect and respect the privacy of my students and their families.

References

Anderson, J.A. (1988). Cognitive styles and multicultural populations. *Journal of Teacher Education 39* (1): 2–9.

Asante, M. (1987). *The Afrocentric idea*. Philadelphia, PA: Temple University Press.

Baldwin, J. (1955). *Notes of a native son*. Boston, MA: Beacon Press.

Baldwin, J. (1985). The fire next time. In James Baldwin, *Price of the ticket*. New York: St. Martin's.

Banks, J. (1993). The canon debate, knowledge construction, and multicultural education. *Educational Researcher, 22* (5): 4–14.

Baratz, S. and Baratz, J. (1970). Early childhood intervention: The social science base of institutional racism. *Harvard Educational Review 40*(1): 29–50.

Boateng, F. (1990). Combating deculturalization of the African American child in the public school system: A multicultural approach. In K. Lotomey (Ed.) *Going to school: The African American experience* (pp. 73–84). Albany, NY: SUNY.

Case, R. (1985). *Intellectual development: Birth to adulthood*. New York: Academic Press.

Castenell, Jr., L. (1990). The new south as curriculum: Implications for understanding southern race relations. In J. Kincheloe and W. Pinar

(Eds.), *Curriculum as social psychoanalysis: The significance of place* (pp. 155–166). Albany, NY: SUNY.

Cortes, C. (1986). The education of language minority students: A contextual interaction model. In California State Department of Education (Ed.), *Beyond language: Social and cultural factors in schooling language minority students* (pp. 3–33). Los Angeles, CA: California State University, Evaluation, Dissemination, and Assessment Center.

Cushner, K., McClelland, A., and Safford, p. (1992). *Human diversity in education: An integrative approach.* New York: McGraw-Hill.

Kincheloe, J. (1991). *Teachers as researchers: Qualitative inquiry as a path to empowerment.* New York: Falmer Press.

Kincheloe, J. (1993). *Toward a critical politics of teacher thinking: Mapping the postmodern.* Westport, CT: Bergin and Garvey.

Kincheloe, J. and Steinberg, S. (1993). A tentative description of post–formal thinking: The critical confrontation with cognitive theory. *Harvard Educational Review 63*(3): 296–320.

Kincheloe, J., Steinberg, S. and Gresson, A. (Eds.). (1996). *Measured lies.* New York: St. Martin's.

King, J. E. and Mitchell, C.A. (1995). *Black mothers to sons.* New York: Peter Lang.

Klahr, D. and Wallace, J. (1976). *Cognitive development: An information processing view.* Hillsdale, NJ: Erlbaum.

Morrison, T. (1989). Unspeakable things unspoken: The Afro-American presence in American literature. *Michigan Quarterly Review 28*(1): 1–34.

Pinar, W., Reynolds, W., Slattery, p. and Taubman, p. (1995). *Understanding curriculum.* New York: Peter Lang.

Slattery, P. (1995). *Curriculum development in the postmodern era.* New York: Garland Publishing.

CHAPTER SEVENTEEN

Special Education
Intelligence, Special Education, and Post-formal Thinking: Constructing an Alternative to Educational Psychology

Encarna Rodriguez

Approaching intelligence is always a challenging task. In many senses, it is like talking about a deity that pervades our understanding of the world in which we live but that escapes any attempt to make visible the nature of this understanding. Indeed, as in the case of a deity, the general belief in western countries that intelligence exists locates the study of this existence as trespassing the invisible limits of what can, and can not, be the subject of social inquiry. Aware of the difficulties of trespassing these limits, i.e., of making cultural assumptions susceptible to social criticism, I intend to de-sacrelize the widespread notion of intelligence. Particularly, I intend to critically explore the connections between this notion and certain dynamics of social exclusion that, ultimately, will make this notion not only visible but also accountable for important inequalities in our lives.

If we ask about the relationship between intelligence and citizenship, many people would probably think that we are just proposing an intellectual exercise for its own sake. When we start speculating about this relationship, however, things appear very differently. In "Citizens and Citizenship," Stuart Hall and David Held (1990) argue that "from the ancient world to the present day, citizenship has entailed a discussion of, and a struggle over, the meaning and scope of membership of the community in which one lives" (p. 175). Looking back at the 1920's in the USA, we can see that intelligence played an important role in this discussion of membership by legitimizing racist policies that advocated social exclusion through sterilization programs and restrictive laws of immigration (1976-77). The massive administration of IQ tests during World War I brought the USA a new vision that suited America's self-perception as the economic and political leader of the world. Discovering itself to be "intelligent," the country started discussing and implementing policies that would exclude those who represented a threat to this new national identity.

The "feebleminded" were among the first to be considered a "menace" to society. Associated with crime, depravation, and poverty, people diagnosed as such were often placed in separate institutions. Even more, advocates of more radical measures exercised their influence to approve sterilization programs that targeted the undesirables, namely, the foreign born and the black population. In the case of immigration, exclusion was enforced by the 1924 Immigration Act. The outcomes of tests showed that the "old" Americans of Nordic stock were intellectually superior to the new immigrants coming from the southeastern Europe. Thus, such scientific insights were deployed as a rationale for stopping immigration from this area. The 1924 Act echoed this argument and approved an immigration quota system that tried to keep the immigration figures as they were in the 1890 census—a census that favored Nordic immigration since it was taken before the massive immigration of southern and southeastern Europeans (Marks, 1976-77; Kamin, 1976).

The issues of membership, of who does and who does not belong, are, as Stuart Hall and David Held point out, just the place where the politics of citizenship begins. With all the changes involved in the disappearance of the nation-state as the primary referent to the modern notion of citizenship,[1] they suggest rethinking this notion in light of what belonging, or not belonging, means *in practice*, in light of whether rights are only individual entitlement or are practically enacted and realized. Here again we encounter the notion of intelligence. In the present decade, racist theories, such as the one enunciated in *The Bell Curve* proclaiming the existence of a cognitive elite, provide new rationales to exclude those who do not belong to this elite. This time the argument does not gravitate around whether blacks and Latinos belong or not to the USA, but asks what rights are involved in this membership and how these rights are enacted. Arguments against Affirmative Action, welfare or bilingual education programs clearly illustrate the strength of these theories and the difficulty of entering the debate of citizenship without exposing the dynamics of intelligence behind them. If superiority is embodied in racial identifiers such as the ones Herrnstein and Murray present, then these programs are no longer needed to achieve equality and, thus, constitute a misuse of public resources since racial equality is impossible.

This brief historical note should not lead us to think that intelligence follows the patterns of historical discontinuity. Much on the contrary, we should look at it as a permanent construct that has been very significant in the construction of particular discriminatory structures. Marks (1976-77) and Karier (1976), for example, illustrate how IQ testing in the early twentieth century served to stratify manpower (sic) in order to reinforce the mass production industrial system. According to Marks, testing created the myth that individual differences are the most important differences among individuals, a myth that served "to identify and classify efficient productive members as defined by the norms of an urban, industrial, hierarchical, competitive, meritocratic society" (p. 4). The unequal distribution of wealth based on merit in American society, his argument goes, became very difficult to maintain under the new system of mass production that required from workers the same task within the same setting and that did not demand great differences in talent but in production. In this context, intelligence tests came as a useful justification for hierarchical arrangements within the mass production system.

All the above inevitably raises one important question: if intelligence is such a relevant construct, why has it escaped social criticism for so long? Looking back at how this notion originated and developed will help answer this question. Since its "creation" at the beginning of the century, intelligence has been a very popular notion. However, from the beginning, there was an obsession to measure it rather than to define it. Very soon testing became a staple of psychologists, and the definition of intelligence became circular: intelligence is what intelligence tests measure (Owen, 1985). Two particular circumstances contributed to this identification of intelligence with measurement. First, testing became popular before psychology could seriously undertake the construction of a theory of intelligence. World War I gave testing the opportunity to be used on a mass scale in order to separate people according to skills. The success of this operation greatly contributed to both the popularization of intelligence as something that can be easily measured and to IQ tests as the proper instrument to assess it. Indeed, it popularized psychology as the discipline that created this notion. As a young discipline that was also involved in introspection and the study of the mind, psychology entered the scientific establishment during World War I. Modeled after a positivist paradigm of natural science, psychology rushed to prove its knowledge base by employing the rigor of the scientific method: it defined an empirical field of study, human behavior, and created the instrument to measure it, the intelligence test (Marks, 1976-77). As did natural scientists, psychologists assumed that since the "reality" under study (intelligence) was an obvious objective entity, there was no need to define it. All they needed to do, psychologists reasoned, was to develop an adequate instrument to measure it.

Intelligence tests also came to fulfil the American need to justify a particular understanding of democracy. Fundamental to the notion of democracy was the principle that while material rewards need not be distributed equally among citizens, the context in which these rewards are earned needs to be fair. Psychology, specifically intelligence tests, soon became the "impartial" referee to guarantee the fairness of the context. As a scientific discipline, psychology assumed an objective reality uncontaminated by the psychologist's point of view. Thus, the results of intelligence tests were believed to reflect an objective reality: those who did better were viewed as naturally superior. The risk of this argument for a country that lacks a traditional system to legitimize social stratification—such as an aristocracy or castes—is clear: those "naturally" superior belonged to a meritocratic class that embodied the aptitudes needed in the construction of a democratic America. The work of Carl Brigham, the creator of the SAT and one of the most influential people in the early development of testing in America, illustrates this point. According to Owen (1985):

> Brigham intended his test to establish a "scale of brightness" on which the "native capacity" of the nation's best and brightest young men could be measured and compared. The SAT was to be the cornerstone of a new American social order-the aristocracy of aptitude, the meritocracy. (p. 189)

Both the belief that psychology could define and measure intelligence and the belief that testing was an objective instrument that only "discovers" people's natural capacities came to education without being seriously questioned. As a matter of fact, the creation and development of special education greatly contributed to the reinforcement of these two beliefs. The success of IQ testing during World War I led individuals to think that intelligence tests could be applied to classify people in other institutions. Schools were some of the first institutions to embrace this new way of sorting students with the implementation of special education programs. A new professional class, psychologists, and a new discipline, educational psychology, emerged as an indispensable part of this project. They were assigned—and are still today—the two basic functions that define special education (Mehan, 1992): labeling and placement. Both of them used intelligence tests as a main instrument.

A parallel can be drawn between how intelligence constructed a particular idea of meritocracy and how labeling and placement worked toward the exclusion of those students who did not belong to this meritocracy. During the past decades, special education has been criticized for the overrepresentation of non-whites and economically deprived students (Tomlinson, 1982; Barton and Tomlinson, 1984; Gibson, 1986; Oakes, 1986; Lipsky and Gartner, 1989; Sapon-Shevin, 1989; Mehan, 1992). Indeed, it seems that those regulations that address specific discrimination, such as the PL 94-142 Act that tried to place students with disabilities in less restrictive environments, succeed more in extending discrimination than in eliminating it (Ferguson, 1989). Despite these criticisms, special education has grown so strong during the twentieth century that it is now considered an indispensable part of the educational structure (Barton and Tomlinson, 1984). This fact invites us to rethink the functions of this program as we critically consider the meaning of this expansion. We must not be blinded by the humanitarian discourse that views the expansion of special education as simply a provision of resources for children with disabilities. Indeed, we need to examine the socio-political interests that this program serves by uncovering the connections between special education and race, class, and gender-related axes of power.

Sleeter (1986) and Sapon-Shevin (1989) expose some of these connections. During the 1970s, some special education categories were redefined and expanded in order to respond to the social pressure for more egalitarian policies in schools. As Sleeter argues, students who during the 1960s had difficulties in reading could be classified as "learning disabled" or as "slow learners." Differences in scores between those categories were minimal, but major consequences followed different placements. In the first category, the cause was assumed to be organic, and the students were expected to improve with the right educational support. In the second, the cause was thought to be environmental and the students were not expected to improve as far as they remained in the same milieu. Accordingly, most white middle-class students with reading difficulties were classified as learning disabled, while low-income children and children of color were disproportionately categorized as slow learners. This situation radically changed when the civil rights movement demanded that schools discard the category of slow learners as highly discriminatory:

> In 1973, the category of mental retardation was redefined, lowering the maximum IQ score from one standard deviation below the mean to two (Grossman, 1973), which dissolved the category of slow learners. The intent of these moves was to pressure schools to teach a wider diversity of students more effectively. Instead, many students who previously were or would have been classified as retarded, slow or culturally deprived were now classified as learning disabled (Sleeter, p. 52).

The reclassification of students with learning difficulties generated an increase in the number of students eligible for special education. Some researchers (Barton and Tomlinson, 1984; Tomlinson, 1985) connect this expansion to the changing labor market's needs for a permanent group of unemployed workers. Interestingly enough, the students accountable for the increasing of special programs were not those with sensory or physical handicaps but those from less-privileged groups and those defined as unable or unwilling to participate in what was considered the normal curriculum. During the 1970s, those students were caught in a school dynamic that tried to balance the push for excellence supposedly demanded by the new technocratic society with the movement toward equality and its request for educational help for students in need. School standards were raised to respond to the first demand; vocational education programs were expanded to respond to the second. As a consequence, the gap between students who succeeded in schools and those who could not follow the regular curriculum widened, and the latter were tracked as learning disabled. Once diagnosed as such, they were directed to special programs that, Barton and Tomlinson argue, prepared them for the unskilled positions of the market and, eventually, put special education at the service of new forms of economic production that required the unemployment of youth from marginalized social groups.[2]

A crucial element in the expansion of special education was the notion of special education needs (Gibson, 1986; Tomlinson, 1982; Tomlinson, 1985). The ever-increasing number of categories of educational handicap—England, for example, went from two to eleven from 1893 to 1945—generated many tensions within schools. On the one hand, forces claimed the need to break down old categories in order to make diagnosis more precise and to recognize new categories of handicap. Autism and dyslexia, respectively, are good examples of the this tendency. On the other hand, every new category forced the administration to provide more specialized resources and, of course, to make a bigger economic investment in this provision. In this context, statutory definitions of handicap were replaced by the notion of special education needs, a more descriptive one. The focus was no longer on the definition of categories but on the needs presented by the students under those categories. Students with different educational handicaps could be diagnosed as having the same needs, and, consequently, they could benefit from the same educational resources and the same special aids programs. In addition, this new notion allowed schools to expand new categories of handicap without questioning the school structure and the inequalities embedded in this expansion. Learning disabilities illustrate this case. Defined in relation to the acquisition of reading, this category serves to diagnosis those students who could not achieve this task within the standard time, regardless of the causes of this difficulty.

Unfortunately, what was described as a move toward equality—considering the students' needs rather that their abilities—very soon proved to be an even more sophisticated instrument for promoting inequality in schools. Non-English speakers, for example, could be sent to speech therapy along with students with mild hearing impairments without considering how some differences among these students could make their needs appear similar. Such a situation came from the failure to acknowledge that needs are "relative, historically, socially, and politically" (Tomlinson, 1982, p. 75). Under the new rationale, there was no recognition that assessment and diagnosis of need takes place under particular historical, cultural, and political conditions. The notion of special education needs, thus, came to legitimize even to a greeter degree the individualization and depoliticization of special education. By not contextualizing the particular notion of needs used and the power relations under which this notion was originated, special education needs appeared as a universal notion removed from its political context.

Not surprisingly, the de-contextualized and universalized definition of special education needs came to legitimize the existence of an unspoken "norm" that benefited those students from privileged social groups. Moreover, it came to legitimize assessment as a process of measuring individual needs in relation to this never-explicit standard. According to this norm, all individuals can—and should—achieve certain abilities in a particular way and at particular stages of their lives. Classrooms are a good illustration. Organized in age-homogeneous groups, all students are expected to develop certain abilities within the length of yearly courses. Those who succeed in this development are considered part of the norm or "intelligent," and those who do not are classified as in need of special education. The case of literacy illustrates this dynamic. Disability is defined to a great degree in relation to what is considered "literate." If the individual shows evidence of linguistic intelligence—the kind of intelligence particularly valued at school—he or she is classified as literate. The absence of this evidence classifies the student as in need of special education. Linguistic intelligence becomes the universal norm upon which every student is measured. Consequently, those students who are not English speakers or who belong to a cultural group that understands literacy differently, like Native Americans or African Americans, are very likely to be placed in special education programs (Poplin and Phillips, 1993).

The notion of special education needs incorporated three important beliefs that had a profound impact in perpetuating two separate tracks—regular and special—within the school system. First, it supported the idea that the assessment of needs is more important than the study of causes. Thus, it made it even more difficult to differentiate between what Tomlinson (1982) calls normative and non-normative categories of disabilities. Normative disabilities are those that, even if the category opened to debate, would bring some normative agreement between professionals and non-professionals. Deafness, blindness, or severe mental disabilities are examples of these categories. Non-normative disabilities are those that are open to interpretation in light of their social, historical, and political circumstances. Feeble-mindedness, maladjustment, and learning disabilities would belong to this group. Normative categories, according to Tomlinson, contain children from all social classes while non-normative categories contain almost exclusively children from the working class. Differentiating between these two categories is extremely important in order to address the causes of educational failure. However, the notion of special education focused on the *individual*'s deficit and, in doing so, did not serve to expose this distinction but rather worked to obscure it even more. Since students with different disabilities could present the same need, the cause of the disability became even less important which, ultimately, left the implicit attribution of educational backwardness to environmental and family deficiencies unquestioned.

Second, special education needs presupposed that the presence of students with normative categories is what makes special education necessary and impossible to dismantle. Because needs are understood in relation to a fixed norm, differences between normative and non-normative categories became merely a question of degree. Both a child with mental disability, for example, and a child that has difficulties communicating in a school setting that is completely unfamiliar and unfriendly to him/her can be diagnosed as having personality disorders and can be sent to the same special education program. Individual programs would be developed for both of them. The only difference would be that while the former will need special aids on a regular basis, the latter would be expected to steadily overcome the difficulties and, thus, to remain in special education only temporarily. Since children with normative categories of disability will always necessitate special aid at school, it is assumed that the same aid can benefit the rest of the students. Without interrogating who is really benefitting from these programs and how, the presence of these students in the school will always serve as a legitimation of the existence of two separate tracks (special and regular). Although I do not mean to negate the differences in the degree of help needed in relation to the severity of the disability, I do believe that not differentiating between the nature of needs can prevent schools from seeing their own role in constructing disability. Indeed, it prevents them from differentiating between disability and handicap, a differentiation that Linton, Mello and O'Neill (1995) find necessary. While the nature of the disability would be the same in most situations, the degree of handicap is relative to the situation. If someone has paraplegia, for example, his/her disability would involve the paralysis or limitation in his/her mobility. His/her handicap, however, would be the condition of being unable to go into all the places that do not accommodate his/her needs for mobility. Schools that do not accommodate to students with different kinds of disabilities are, according to this reasoning, contributing to their handicap.

The third way in which the notion of special education needs presents tracking as necessary is in its reinforcement of the idea that there is one curriculum that fits all students and that the adaptation of students to this curriculum is intrinsically good and guarantees equality. In the same way that there are invisible standards that define intelligence, there is an assumption that these standards should be achieved by following a unified curriculum. Those students who cannot achieve these standards by themselves would be evaluated and diagnosed, and the curriculum would be adapted to their particular needs. Usually conducted through individual programs, the process of adapting "the" curriculum has been viewed as one of the most important changes for equal opportunities for students with disabilities. Taking a more critical perspective, however, we can see how this process weakens rather than strengthens the possibility for equal opportunities. During the last decades, curriculum theorists aligned with theoretical approaches such as postmodernism and feminism (Pinar, 1994; Slattery 1995; Kincheloe, 1993; Aronowitz and Giroux, 1991; Giroux, 1993; Grumet, 1988) have criticized the conception of curriculum as a value-free body of fragmented information and have exposed its political nature. To them, curriculum is not the innocent provider of social opportunities but the embodiment of those discourses that shape the social, historical, and political forces of a particular historical moment. Indeed, they claim that curriculum contains and exercises social relations of power and shapes people's identities according to these relations. From this perspective, the purpose of curriculum adaptation has to be questioned: if curriculum is not a unified body of knowledge but a body of discourses, what are the discourses that have been privileged by adapting all students diagnosed as having special needs to "the" curriculum?

The need for education, particularly for educational psychology, to take this question seriously and to rethink itself in relation to it appears urgent. I believe that, in order for this task to be accomplished successfully, educational psychology needs to take into consideration three particular aspects of the notion of intelligence that the above analysis tried to foreground. First, intelligence is a political construct and, as such, it embeds race, class, and gender relations of power. As Joe Kincheloe and Shirley Steinberg (1993) state "those who were excluded from the community of the intelligent seem to cluster around exclusions based on race (the non-White), class (the poor), and gender (the feminine)" (p. 298). It is necessary, thus, to take intelligence out of the discipline that monopolizes its use, psychology, and to hold this notion responsible for the dynamics of identity involved in its conceptions. Psychology in general and educational psychology in particular can not afford any longer to be removed from the public conversation on the politics of identity.

Second, intelligence is bounded by the historical conditions and systems of meaning that originated the concept. Educational psychology needs to understand that no concept, discipline (including itself), or social structure can escape the historical specificity conveyed in the paradigms, assumptions, and beliefs that shape their conception and development. Particularly, educational psychology needs to understand the possibilities and limitations of the modernist paradigm under which it originated and how this paradigm shaped the discipline. The modernist claim for objectivity, for example, helps us to understand why intelligence remained unquestioned for so long. Modernism assumes that the act of knowing involves a sharp separation between the person who knows (the knower) and the object of knowledge (the known). Thus, it proclaims that the latter is "objective" and not contaminated by the perception of the former and that rationality is the only valid way of knowing. The Piagetian theory of intelligence—the one that basically colonized education for many decades—fell very neatly into this assumption. Piaget assumed that intelligence is a cognitive process that develops with maturation and that reaches its highest state when it comes to the formal operations. At this point, the individual, the knower, is naturally provided with the necessary cognitive structures to make an "objective" interpretation of the world in which she/he lives. Stemming from this assumption, intelligence was understood as a biological condition that, although improved by the dynamics of accommodation and assimilation, led to only one valid way of knowledge: the rational one.

The third characteristic of intelligence that deserves particular attention is its socially constructed nature. Although, as stated earlier, intelligence is very seldom explicitly defined, the understanding of this notion changes in relation to time and field. In the workplace, for example, a Fordist way of production identified as intelligent those workers who had the ability of producing more than the others. In the post-Fordist mode of production,[3] an intelligent worker can adjust to the rapid changes of the market and has the ability to switch roles within the workplace. This point is particularly important since it is here where the possibilities for change reside. It is necessary to create a new notion of intelligence grounded in a more emancipatory system of meaning that can understand individuals as active subjects involved in their own educational process. Post-formal thinking (Kincheloe and Steinberg, 1993) attempts to undertake this project from a theoretical discourse rooted in critical theory, feminism, and postmodernism. From this location, post-formal thinking calls into question the principles of modernist objectivity and criticizes it for making the psychometric definition of intelligence appear natural. Defined as a new way of cognition that understands the production of knowledge as a political act, post-formal thinking conceptualizes cognition as an active process in which individuals actively engage in making meaning, both in rational and nonrational ways, of their lives by combining the information received and their previous experience and understanding. Therefore, it embraces the belief that no process of knowing exists outside the socio-historical conditions that originate it, and it is concerned with how the power relations carried by these conditions shape people's consciousness. Indeed, postformal thinking denounces objectivity as an instrument of the depolitization of social and educational issues by converting social relations of power into individual issues.

Piaget's theory of development, specifically the assumption that formal operations are the highest stage individuals can reach, appears from this perspective as a suspicious translation of the principles of the Enlightenment into a theory of development that legitimizes a particular body of knowledge: the one produced by the Western White Male. By making rationality the only valid way of knowing, his theory privileged reason over emotions, materialism over spirituality, and individualism over community learning. Consequently, social groups such as women, Native Americans, African Americans, Latinos, or any other group that did not produce knowledge in the same way were marginalized by virtue of being classified as less intelligent.

Post-formal thinking criticizes traditional theories of intelligence in an important way: it breaks the individual-society dichotomy that originated them (Henriques, Hollway, Urwin, Venn and Walkerdine, 1984). The notion of the individual as a unitary and non-contradictory entity that lives in a particular environment is substituted in this theoretical approach by the notion of the subject, a notion that refers to the complex dynamics that shapes people's identities in multiple ways in relation to the social, historical, cultural, and political conditions under which they live. Both Piaget's theory of intelligence and theories that originated as a critique of it, like Gardner's theory of multiple intelligence,[4] fail to make this shift. While both of them claim that the individual and environment are related in unknown ways, they are unable to overcome the dichotomic division of these terms and to explain how individuals are, at the same time, part of and shaped by the environment. According to this new conceptualization, educational psychology, for example, would be accountable as part of the discourses that construct subjectivities. By creating social categories, it also creates a certain identity for those labelled under those categories. Learning disability is not only a term that categorizes certain groups of people but also an identifier that, in many aspects, shapes the lives of those who are said to have learning disabilities. Hanson (1993) illustrates this dynamic when writing:

although testing is usually considered to be a means of measuring qualities that are already present in a person, one of my two central theses is that tests to a significant degree produce the personal characteristics they purport to measure. The social person in contemporary society is not so much described or evaluated by tests as constructed by them. (p. 4)

To conclude, I would like to raise a final question: what are the new ways of understanding that post-formal thinking bring to critical educators concerned with social equality? Undoubtedly, the more promising possibility stemming from this way of thinking is the understanding of intelligence not in terms of personal abilities but in terms of social and political identity. It invites us to see intelligence as a part of the politics of identity and to rethink disciplines such as educational psychology and school structures such as special education in relation to it. To this extent, post-formal thinking appears as the theoretical umbrella from which a more emancipatory notion of intelligence can be constructed. Theories of mental functioning that emphasize the social origins of cognition, such as the one developed by Vygotsky, for example, can be taken up more fruitfully when complemented by the study of how the relation of power embedded in social relations shapes people's identities and perceptions. More importantly, post-formal thinking can provide the ethical ground to pursue ways of education to empower people by providing them with the understanding of how they construct their own knowledge as well as how the knowledge that they receive is produced. Maybe then it would be easier to think of the disappearance of special education. Maybe also we can picture heterogenous classes with students of different ages and backgrounds (including students with disabilities) that engage in the critical understanding of their social locations and in which we can fulfill our role as educators. Maybe we can finally find a way of making special education a way of helping students to have more control of their lives rather than a way of tracking them.

Endnotes

1. In "Citizens and Citizenship" (1990), Stuart Hall and David Held argue that the debate about citizenship has to be reframed, particularly by the political Left, in relation to a much more diverse and plural society. Nation-state used to be the entity to which the modern language of citizenship primarily referred. However, there are many factors in the present that erode the sovereignty of this entity. Among these factors, the authors mention, in the case of

England, the presence of different ethnic and cultural groups resulting from the colonial state, the growth of regional nationalism in
Scotland and elsewhere, the prospect for greater European integration, the weakening of the old East-West frontiers under the
Gorbachev offensive, and the growing pace of international interdependence and globalization.

2.   According to Barton and Tomlinson, there is a strong connection
     between the expansion of special education and the increase of pro-
     grams for the "less able" and the unemployment in the young sec-
     tions of population in England. In 1974, 80,000 under-twenty-year-
     old students coming from special education were unemployed; in
     1981, this number rose to 532,000.

3.   Harvey (1991) calls this mode of production *flexible accumulation*
     and defines flexibility as its main characteristic. Opposed to the
     rigidities of Fordism, this new regime brings flexibility with respect
     to labor process, labor markets, products, and patterns of consump-
     tion. He argues that the new enhanced powers of flexibility and
     mobility have allowed employers to exert stronger pressures of
     labor control on a workforce which, ultimately, implied high levels
     of structural unemployment, rapid destruction and reconstruction
     of skills, modest (if any) gains in the real wage, and the roll-back
     of trade unions' power. The labor market structure under the flexi-
     ble accumulation regime contains three different groups of work-
     ers. In the first one—a steadily shrinking group according to
     Harvey—workers are full-time employees with a permanent status
     who enjoy greater job security, good promotion, re-skilling
     prospects, generous pensions, insurance, and other benefits. The
     second group consists of full-time employees with skills that are
     readily available in the labor market, such as clerical, secretarial,
     routine, and lesser-skilled manual works. The third group is com-
     posed of employees with even less job security than any of the oth-
     ers. It includes part-timers, casuals, fixed-term contract staff, tem-
     poraries, etc.

4.   Gardner understands logical-mathematical as just one kind of intel-
     ligence. He argues that there are, at least, six more types of intelli-
     gence: linguistic, musical, spatial, bodily-kinesthetic, interperson-
     al, and intrapersonal. Each child would show evidence of one of

them. Although this theory allows us to consider other areas of knowledge as a source of intelligence, Gardner's theory does not constitute an alternative to Piaget. Like him, Gardner understands intelligence as a group of abilities that the individual is genetically provided with and that the environment can either expand or constrain but not change. To this extent, Gardner's theory is as limited as Piaget's by the dichotomy of individual-society in which the complex interactive nature of their relationship and how this relationship shapes people's identities are completely dismissed.

References

Aronowitz, S. and Giroux, H.A. (1991). *Postmodern education: Politics, culture, and social criticism.* Minneapolis and Oxford: University of Minnesota Press.

Barton, L., and Tomlinson, S. (Eds.) (1984) *Special Education and Social Interests.* London: Croom Helm; New York: Nichols.

Block, N.J. and Dworkin, G. (Eds.) (1976) *The IQ controversy: Critical readings.* New York: Pantheon Books.

Ferguson, D.L. (1989). Severity of Need and Educational Excellence: Public School Reform and Students with Disabilities. In *Schooling and Disability* (pp. 25–56). The National Society for the Study of Education.

Gardner, H. (1983). *Frames of mind: The theory of multiple intelligences.* New York: Basic Books, Inc., Publishers.

Gardner, H. (1991). The tension between education and development. *Journal of Moral Education, 20(2),* 113–125.

Gardner, H. (1995). Reflections on multiple intelligences: Myths and messages. *Phi Delta Kappan, 70(3),* 200–209.

Gibson, R.(1986) *Critical theory and education.* London, Sydney, Auckland, Toronto: Hodder and Stoughton

Gindis, B. (1995). The social/cultural implication of disability: Vygotsky's paradigm for special education. *Educational Psychologist, 30(2),* 77–81.

Giroux, H.A. (1992). *Border crossings. Cultural workers and the politics of education.* New York and London: Routledge.

Giroux, H.A. (1993). *Living dangerously: Multiculturalism and the politics of difference.* New York: Peter Lang.

Grossman, H. (Ed.). *Manual on terminology and classification in mental retardation (rev.ed.).* Washington, DC: American Association of Mental Deficiency.

Grumet, M.R. (1988). *Bitter milk. Women and teaching*. Amherst: The University of Massachusetts Press.

Hahn, H. (1989). The Politics of special education. In D.K. Lipsky and A. Gartner (Eds.) *Beyond separate education: Quality education for all* (pp. 225–241). Baltimore, London, Toronto and Sidney: Paul H. Brookes.

Hall, S. and Held, D. (1990). Citizens and citizenship. In S. Hall and M. Jacques (Eds.) *New times: The changing face of politics in the 1990s*. London: Verso.

Hanson, F.A. (1993). *Testing testing: Social consequences of the examined life*. Berkely, Los Angeles and Boston: University of California Press.

Harvey, D. (1991). *The condition of postmodernity*. (5th ed.) Cambridge, MA and Oxford, UK: Blackwell.

Henriques, J., Hollway, W., Urwin, C., Venn, C., Walkerdine, V. (1984). *Changing the subject*. London and New York: Methuen

Herrnstein, R.J. and Murray, C. (1994). *The Bell Curve: Intelligence and class structure in American life*. New York: Free Press.

hook, b. (1994). *Teaching to transgress: Education as the practice of freedom*. New York and London: Routledge.

Kamin, L.J. (1976). Heredity, intelligence, politics, and psychology: II. In N.J. Block and Gerald Dworkin (Eds.), *The IQ Controversy*. New York: Pantheon Books.

Karier, C. J. (1976). Testing for order and control in the corporate liberal state. In N.J. Block and G. Dworkin (Eds.), *The IQ controversy*. New York: Pantheon Books.

Kincheloe, J.L. (1993). *Towards a critical politics of teacher thinking. Mapping the postmodern*. Westport, CT: Bergin and Garvey.

Kincheloe, J.L. and Steinberg, S.R. (1993). A tentative description of post-formal thinking: The critical confrontation with cognitive theory. *Harvard Educational Review, 63*(3), 296–320.

Kincheloe, J.L. and Steinberg, S.R. (1996). Who said it can't happen here? In J.L. Kincheloe, S.R. Steinberg and A.D. Gresson III (Eds.), *Measured lies. The Bell Curve examined*. New York: St. Martin's Press.

Linton, S. (1994). Reshaping disability in teacher education and beyond. *Teacher Education, 6* (2), 9–20.

Linton, S., Mello, S., O'Neill, J. (1995) Disability studies: Expanding the parameters of diversity. *Radical Teacher, 47*, 4–10

Lipsky, D.K. and Gartner, A. (1989). The current situation. In D.K. Lipsky and A. Gartner (Eds.), *Beyond separate education: Quality education for all.* (pp. 3–23). Baltimore, London, Toronto and Sidney: Paul H. Brookes.

Marks, R. (1976-77) Providing for individual differences: A history of the intelligence testing movement in North America. *Interchange,* 7(3), 3–16.

Mehan, H. (1992). Understanding inequality in schools: The contribution of interpretive studies. *Sociology of Education,* 65(January), 1–20.

Minnich. E.K. (1991). Discussing diversity. *Liberal Education,* 77(1), 2–7.

Newman, D., Griffin, P. and Cole, M. (1989). *The construction zone. Working for cognitive change in school.* Cambridge, MA: Cambridge University Press.

Oakes, J. (1986). Tracking, inequality, and the rhetoric of reform: Why schools do not change. *Journal of Education,* 168(1), 60–80.

Owen, D. (1985). *None of the above: Behind the myth of scholastic aptitude.* Boston: Houghton Mifflin Company.

Penuel, W.R. and Wertsch, J.V. (1995). Vygotsky and identity formation: A sociocultural approach. *Educational Psychologist,* 30(2), 83–92

Pinar, W.F (1995). *Understanding curriculum: An introduction to the study of historical and contemporary discourses.* New York: Peter Lang.

Poplin, M. (1988). The reductionistic fallacy in learning disabilities: Replicating the past by reducing the present. *Journal of Learning Disabilities,* 21(7), 289–400.

Poplin, M. and Phillips, L. (1993). Sociocultural aspects of language and literacy: Issues facing educators of students with learning disabilities. *Learning Disability Quarterly,* 16, 245–255.

Putman, J.W. (1993) *Cooperative learning and strategies for inclusion: Celebrating diversity in the classroom.* Baltimore, London, Toronto, Sydney: Paul H. Brookes Publishing Co.

Rogoff, B. and Morelli, G. (1989). Perspectives on children's development from cultural psychology. *The American Psychological Association,* 44(2), 343–348.

Sampson, E.E. (1993). Identity politics: Challenges to psychology's understanding. *American Psychologist,* 48(12), 1219–1230.

Sapon-Shevin, M. (1989). Mild disabilities: In and out of special education. In *School and Disability*. The National Society for the Study of Education.

Sapon-Shevin, M. (1992). Celebrating diversity, creating community. In S. Stainback and W. Stainback (Eds.), *Curriculum considerations in inclusive classrooms: Facilitating learning for all students*. Baltimore, London, Toronto and Sidney: Paul H. Brookes.

Sleeter, C. E. (1986). Learning disabilities: The social construction of a special education category. *Exceptional Children, 53*(1), 46–54.

Sleeter, C. and Grant, C.A. (1986). Success for all students. *Phi Delta Kappan, 68*(4), 297–299.

Stainback, S. and Stainback, W. (1989). Integration of students with mild and moderate handicaps. In D.K. Lipsky and A. Gartner (Eds.), *Beyond separate education: Quality education for all*. (pp. 41–51). Baltimore, London, Toronto and Sidney: Paul H. Brookes.

Stainback, S. and Stainback, W. (1992) *Curriculum considerations in inclusive classrooms: Facilitating learning for all students*. Baltimore, London, Toronto, Sydney: Paul H. Brookes.

Tomlinson, S. (1982). *A sociology of special education*. London, Boston and Henley: Routledge and Kegan Paul.

Tomlinson, S. (1985). The expansion of special education. *Oxford Review of Education, 11*(2), 157–165.

Tomlinson, S. (1988). Why Johnny can't read: Critical theory and special education. *European Journal of Special Needs Education, 3*(1), 45–58.

Wertsch, J. (1991). *Voices of the mind. A sociocultural approach to mediated action*. Cambridge, MA: Harvard University Press.

CHAPTER EIGHTEEN

The Demise of Disability: A Post-formal Possibility

Audrey M. Denith

Years ago, on the way back from a social event for individuals with mental retardation, the young woman I had sponsored and taken to the event shared her observations of the evening with me. She told me that she knew the other people at the dance were "retarded" like her. When I asked her how she knew, she told me that their skin felt just like hers. Marietta was about 23 years old and had an IQ of about 35. This would place her in a category of "trainable mentally retarded," an individual who could be trained for some repetitious skills and limited self-care but would not be able to think in the abstract, make accurate judgments, or engage in analogous thinking. Yet, she was able to identify characteristics of specific individuals that go beyond what her IQ and its prognosis would indicate to be within her ability. She synthesized new knowledge, transferred it, and applied it to her own understanding of the socially constructed category of mental retardation.

Few would consider Marietta "intelligent"; contemporary society views intelligence as fixed and exclusionary, a characteristic which some individuals possess and others do not. The Latin word *intelligere* means to gather and choose apart. Therefore, the point of intelligence is not to simply retrieve thoughts from memory but to find patterns in the ideas one has collected. Marietta demonstrated a discerning ability to detect a pattern through the sense of touch in her observation of other individuals who were "retarded." Modernists' perceptions of Marietta's intellectual abilities via the use of intelligence testing would not endow her with this capability to recognize patterns within a particular context. The standardized intelligence test administered to Marietta did not evaluate her beyond a few narrow areas and, as a result, her schooling was prescribed on the basis of these perceived limitations to focus exclusively on self-care and basic survival skills.

What can the "disabled" teach us about the nature of intelligence? What new manifestations of intelligence can researchers discover by asking questions that have never been posed before? Marietta provides researchers with an excellent example of how limited notions of intelligence fail to assess the true potential of individuals. Why does our limited view of intelligence remain uncontested and understood as natural phenomena? How can these notions be challenged in a postmodern era? These are some of the questions that post-formal researchers seek to uncover in their quest to expand the understanding of disability and intelligence. Through the use of the post-formal tenets of etymology— the exploration of the forces that produce what a given culture understands to be knowledge—and pattern—the understanding of the relationships that undergird the lived world—this paper will explore the origins of our assumptions about intelligence, the influence of our limited understanding of intelligence on the education of students with disabilities, and the possibility of alternate notions and new possibilities for thinking about disabilities in a postmodern era.

Post-formal Thinking and Research Goals

Post-formalists are postmodern thinkers who recognize that the world we live in today is much different than even that of the most recent past. The Industrial Age has been replaced by an era marked with rapid change, multiple truths, and absolute uncertainty. The world has advanced beyond the Age of Reason, the Scientific Revolution, the Enlightenment, and the Industrial Revolution into a world that is based predominately on the needs of late capitalism. In this era, notions of scientific thinking are being questioned and the boundaries imposed within the scientific regime are being contested. Indeed, many intellectuals in this post-modern era, are questioning previously held "regimes of truth" as they continue to probe and disturb the distributions of absolute knowledge (Foucault, 1980; Greene, 1986; Lather, 1992).

Post-formalism intersects with postmodern theories and is useful as a strategy to bring into question notions of universal knowledge that remain uncontested and understood as natural. Beyond this, post-formalism attempts to explore the political with its analysis of power and subjectivity, allowing us access to the social constructions of truth and the manner in which truth is molded by the mal-distribution of power and resources (Kincheloe and Steinberg, 1993).

Like postmodernists, post-formalists believe that schools are not the contributors of democratic social order that modernists would like us to believe. They are, in fact, oppressive organizations that seek to shape the way individuals think, interact and relate to one another. Schools construct cultural, racial, gender, and socioeconomic forms of domination which serve capitalism and the existing social order. A post-modern analysis of schooling attempts to seek the multiple voices which can not be heard within this notion of universal truth and absolute objectivity. Within this search for multiple voices, post-formalists bring into question notions of intelligence (Leistyna, Woodrum, and Sherblom, 1996; Kincheloe and Steinberg, 1993).

Post-formal thinking expands the boundaries of the nature of intelligence into the unknown. While the modernist paradigm has constructed intelligence tests to determine the absolute potential of individuals through the assessment of a few narrow and culturally privileged skills, post-formal thinking moves beyond the certainty and authority of this by-gone era. Intelligence is not understood as fixed or exclusionary. It is not found in select individuals and is not necessarily hierarchical. Rather, different intelligences are apparent in every person. Intelligence is not cumulative, nor does it end at a stage of formal logic. It is not separate from the environment, and it is not seen in fixed and pre-determined stages (Kincheloe and Steinberg, 1993).

This search for new infinite and previously unrecognized forms of intelligence is the central goal of post-formal thinking. This shift or change in the psychological foundations of educational practice involves the willingness of individuals to see that mainstream cognitive discourse is just one of the many approaches to the analysis of thinking and learning. The hidden assumptions, the false notions, and the social and historical contextualization of mainstream cognitive psychology are no longer ignored. New positions are claimed and new insights are offered to explain the possibilities and to affirm the potential of those yet to be discovered. The foundation of new visions of cognitive theory are conceptualized and new ideas about what constitutes "intelligence" are formulated.

Etymology and Pattern

Post-formal thinking asks us to analyze what we know and why we believe something to be true or not. By adding a critical, historical dimension to this, post-formal thinking assumes that we are never separate from the historical and cultural forces which surround us and create the knowledge we understand to be true in our world. Understanding the formation and origins of our own thinking within the everyday traditions from which we operate requires that we examine the way knowledge has been produced and the forces that contribute to it. By utilizing Foucault's (1984) concept of genealogy, we begin to examine the processes by which social forces shape our understanding of what constitutes knowledge and the manner in which these forces help form our own subjectivities. Thus, by examining the historicity of disability and childhood in the Western world, we can begin to visualize the way "disability" has been shaped by the dynamics of power within the larger political, cultural, and economic spheres and how specific notions of intelligence and disability are embedded with our culture and provide the driving force for current practices.

Throughout Western history, the term "disability" has had different connotations. From antiquity to the modern day, an individual with a disability can evoke pity, fear, disdain, and even, envy. The history of disability in the western world is a colorful one, not unlike the story of other marginalized groups. Safford and Safford (1996), in their detailed history of childhood disability, trace its origins from the time of Aristole through the Enlightenment and to the present time. Aristole proclaimed that "no deformed child should live." Plato decided that the "offspring of the inferior, or the better when they chance to be deformed, will be put away in some mysterious, unknown place, as they should be" (Safford and Safford, 1996, p. 4). Infanticide was common practice although Boswell (1988) states that the "exposure" or abandonment of infants was much more popular as ancient peoples believed that the children would be picked up and cared for by spiritual beings. Much later, in Roman times, people could purchase a dwarf or any individual with a deformity for their own amusement or as a means of entertainment for the powerful and wealthy. As late as 1815, for an admission fee of $.01, people could pile the kids into the carriage and spend the afternoon viewing the inmates at London's Bethlehem Hospital (Bedl'm), a practice that continued in the early hospitals in the United States.

In the Middle Ages, Christianity's influence promulgated new beliefs about the appearance of human deformities or deficiencies. During this time, children with deformities were considered the result of original sin, the sins of the parents, or the workings of Satan. Christianity's reliance on the original sin of Adam and Eve as explanation for phenomena not fully understood would no longer recognize children as the holy innocents but as just punishment for the past indiscretions of their ancestors. The western world began to move from the barbaric practice of infanticide to the more "humane" practice of abandonment. Children were discarded in hospices or left to the pity of passers-by on the streets. Children of affluent parentage were, sometimes, able to take the vows of the convent or the monastery while the children of the poor were left to work as laborers or given over to prostitution.

By the fourteenth century, western cultures had begun a network of foundling homes: havens for the poor, the disabled, and the illegitimate. The numbers of children left at these homes grew substantially after their inception, encouraging the abandonment of more small children to the care of these institutions. Unfortunately, most died in childhood from the incurable and communicable diseases of the day. It was during this time that the first separate homes for individuals with specific disabilities were founded. Blind children were given charitable aid in the hospices set up in Europe, and, later, homes for the deaf became prevalent in many western societies.

While ancient practices seem barbaric to us, we need only make one trip to the supermarket and let a glance at the local tabloids affirm modern society's continued fascination with human aberration. One can still view individuals with deformities at carnivals which employ these people and present them to the public for a small fee. In my hometown of Allentown, PA, the viewing of "freaks" in private tents beside amusements rides and rows of livestock at the annual city fair is a concurrent event. Infanticide, in some forms, is still an option. In1978, as a pre-service special education teacher in college, I viewed a disturbing film which depicted the slow starving death of babies born with Down's Syndrome who were denied life-saving surgery at their parents' request because of their "disability." Abandonment, as well, is an alternative for those who give birth to children with disabilities. Just last year, a woman I know and her spouse relinquished their long-awaited newborn to an adoption agency when it was revealed that the child had irreversible mental retardation.

Beginning in the 1700's, medical doctors became the first group to begin identifying specific disabilities in children. The first book on birth defects written by a French surgeon, Ambroise Paré, was published and depicted thirteen causes of birth defects, all of which were based on superstitious notions regarding expectant maternal behaviors. A Swedish alchemist, Theophrastus von Hohenheim, became interested in the chemical causes of disease and was the first to associate mental retardation with disorders such as cretinism. Antiquity is colored with references to men in the medical fields who were instrumental in laying the foundations for the medical model of disability in the Western world. While philosophers and poets remained concerned about the fate of these children, the diagnosis and treatment of those with disabilities fell to the medical profession, where they would remain until the early twentieth century when child psychiatry was founded.

Perhaps the most famous of all physician-educators was Jean Marc Itard, a young surgeon, born in 1774, who had served in the French Revolution. Itard was assigned the challenging task of treating a young boy about twelve who had been discovered in the forests of Lacaune. "The wild boy of Aveyron" or Victor, as Itard named him, had no language, had been isolated from human contact and appeared to be deaf and dumb. The boy was regarded as an "idiot." As the education of so-called "idiot" children was considered futile in the eighteenth century, Itard's interventions with Victor were revolutionary and many are still practiced today. Itard used a sensory approach to reach Victor and set forth an educational plan complete with learning objectives and methods of prompts, cues, and reinforcement for specific behavior exhibited by stimulus presented, the forerunner for the very foundations of special educational practice in the twentieth century. Additionally, Itard used auditory stimulation, visual training, and stressed imitation and repetition of phonemic and graphemic concepts, all of which are practiced in some form today. Itard's assumption that Victor's "idiocy" was a result of antisocial habits acquired in the wild as well as the physiological changes wrought on by exposure to the elements of nature and not necessarily those of an inferior biological birth ignited the ideologies which form the basis for our modern approach of "corrective" education (Safford and Safford, 1996).

Indeed, our contemporary school programs for children with disabilities operate within this functionalist paradigm with its direct roots in the early practices afforded to these individuals. Bound in a sociology of regulation which studies its practices through explanations that are rational and controlled, contemporary educators identify children's non-typical performances and failure in schooling as pathological. Educational practice continues to rely fundamentally on the fields of biology and other natural sciences, which views the phenomena of measurement and manipulation as effective treatment for students who are defective. Moreover, this approach regards schools as incompetent organizations to be regulated and controlled for greater efficiency (Skrtic, 1995; Burrell and Morgan, 1979; Heshusius, 1989). Skrtic summarizes the work of several authors when he contends that the practicing assumptions within education are:

1. student disability is pathological
2. classification of students and differential diagnosis of ability or disability is an objective and useful practice;
3. programming for students within the field as a rational and organized system benefits diagnosed students;
4. progress in special education is a rational-technical process of step-by-step improvements in diagnostic and instructional techniques. (p. 68-69)

Skrtic maintains that these functionalist theories of human pathology and rationale organization are so engrained within education, they have become social norms rather than isolated and identifiable theories. As a result, theory into practice is not examined and the origins of the field remain buried in our assumptions about the validity and usefulness of the field. Furthermore, Skrtic contends that this functionalist framework and the resulting socio-cultural norms which guide special education actually thwart the democratic ideals some believe operate within the educational arenas. Thus, the manner in which students are determined to be "misfits" and receive an education outside of the mainstream hinders equitable education for all.

While the mainstay of coexistent educational programming is vested in the practices of ancient physicians, small coteries of people did strive to provide humane treatment and benevolent care to individuals with disabilities throughout history. For example, colonies for the mentally ill and the retarded operated in Belguim as early as the seventh century. Families within the colonies sponsored inflicted children or adults, and harsh punishments were strictly forbidden while kindness was encouraged. The late 1800's ushered in a rash of reform movements advocating better treatment of individuals with mental illness and those considered to "idiots." However, most advocates for individuals with disabilities were more concerned with protecting society from these misfits than the well-being of the poor and the unfortunate. In the mid-1800's, one clergyman in charge of large mission for children, referring to the poor and disabled, said, "This dangerous class has not yet begun to show itself as it will in eight or ten years . . . they will poison society" (Wishy, 1968, p. 16-17). Unfortunately, even these reforms were overshadowed by the efforts of the medical field to explain deformities and create treatments to cure folks, especially afflicted individuals from affluent families (Safford and Safford, 1996). Unfortunately, these attitudes are prevalent today. Just recently, a young student teacher under my supervision, explained a similar regard for the poor and less fortunate after her first day in an inner-city school in which 2 of her 5 math classes were geared for "slow" students of Latino backgrounds. "I don't want to teach these kids. . . . I want to teach math and I want to do it in a much better school."

While current practices in education are certainly a reflection of the inception of the medical model, the Industrial Revolution continued the castration of the ideals of democratic education from its beginning. As federal law required factory owners to hire one "idiot" child for every 20 poorhouse inmates, poor children with disabilities became a source of cheap labor in the mines and factories during the nineteenth and early twentieth centuries. Since their destiny was so bleak anyway, industrialists were regarded by some as benefactors of the poor, regardless of the 12-to-15-hour workday for children as young as four years of age, more than half of whom were crippled or died as a result of their labor in these early factories. Finally, their immigrant status and membership among the poorest of the poor permitted draconian measures of physical and emotional abuse. Examples of young children beaten, whipped, and chained in factories were sorely evident, but few paid heed to these atrocities (Safford and Safford, 1996).

Despite the compulsory schooling mandates passed prior to the influx of immigrant children, the education of children from immigrant backgrounds or those who were poor or disabled was not a concern in the early part of the century. Schooling was clearly limited to select groups. Finally, the economic pressures wrought on by the Depression of the 1930's when most adults had difficulty securing employment coerced the enforcement of compulsory schooling. Education in the United States, at least at the elementary level, was forced to deal with a growing heterogeneous school population.

After the Depression, large numbers of children experienced difficulties in the traditional classroom, which proved inept in its efforts to educate diverse children. As a result, the elementary classroom became the "sorting machine" of students (Spring, 1972), the means by which schools served as sites for keeping the poor in their place and ensuring that the privileged were afforded opportunities for maintaining the status quo. Sincere efforts to separate or compartmentalize education became a major priority, and a subsequent division gave birth to two new fields within education. The field of special education was cultivated in the early part of the century as a means to remove and control the most unmanageable students while a second field of school administration sought to rationalize educational practice according to the principles of scientific management and a desire to streamline the operation of schools as if they were industries. Thus, schools became regarded as incompetent organizations, which needed to be regulated and controlled for greater efficiency, while students displayed behaviors which necessitated alteration and counsel in order to maintain the efficiency of the institution (Skrtic, 1995; see also Corbett, 1996).

At roughly the same time in our history, just after World War I when American politics began to tout education as a means to spur the economic growth of the country, intelligence testing became the most popular tool for sorting and categorizing children, ensuring that such growth would not be impeded by mixing the capable with those less able. The early versions created by European and American psychologists determined that intelligence was native and not capable of being enhanced through educational programming. The clandestine purpose of intelligence testing, to regulate society according to a larger political and economic agenda, was evident to only a few scholars in the early part of the century who vehemently opposed the use of these tests (Spring, 1990; Kliebard, 1995). Nearly a century later, the intelligence test is still used as the primary tool for sorting and classifying students according to their native abilities. From the beginning of the schooling process in this country, children are grouped, sorted, and arranged within the classroom for differentiated curricular content and pace of instruction. After elementary school, separated classrooms offer the same differentiated curriculum and pace. In the secondary school, separate classes and, even, separate schools (i.e., vocational, preparatory, etc.) sort, classify, and arrange students. Perhaps, no greater sorting exists than for children identified as having special needs or being disabled. The experience of sorting begins in the preschool years, before formal schooling, in district, county, and federally sponsored early intervention programs and private programs such as Easter Seals and United Cerebral Palsy. In primary and elementary schools, these "special children" often remain in separate classrooms or receive "learning support" outside of the classrooms of their age-appropriate peers. These children are not a homogenous group, and, much like their peers who remain in the "regular classroom," their needs and desires differ accordingly. Yet, the manner of sorting students and determining some to be "disabled" or in need of "special" education is taken for granted as an objective, benevolent practice designed to care for and "treat" students as though they are truly different from the rest (Kirp, 1974).

Sorting and classifying students fits appropriately within the consumer-capitalist model of our society which affords worth to those who produce the most in the least costly fashion. There are numerous tasks to be done, some more difficult than others. Capitalist society can compensate for some of the lag created by those who cannot perform certain tasks; however, the rewards are reserved only for those who are fully competent. Thus, schools, in our culture, heed to a rigid set of institutionalized norms which govern what is permissible and what is not and what is rewarded and what is not.

Some researchers contend that our technological society has become so advanced, there is little use for individuals who can't function on the intellectual level needed for the appropriation of technological advancement. The need to develop techniques to reach those who may not exhibit competencies necessary for modern life is an integral component of educational dogma. Requiring that everyone achieve specific literary skills becomes the goal of education in general, while the goal of special education is still finding alternate methodologies for those who are not able to develop the prescribed competencies as quickly and in the same manner as others (Tomlinson, 1982; 1988).

Still, others entertain the possibility that special education could serve as the appropriated placement for those destined to be the most lowly of all workers—manual workers in a post-industrial culture. Since a large majority of special education students hail from families in the lower socio-economic classes or from minority ethnic and racial groups, it appears as though the field reproduces the lower status of these groups within a dominant culture (Tomlinson, 1988).

The need to expand the conceptual framework about intelligence and disability has come of age. The manners in which powerful sources in society continue to control the destiny of individuals by the use of such testing needs to be examined publicly. Educators and parents seldom ask meaningful questions about the value of IQ tests. Their wide use as a powerful tool in determining educational programming for virtually all school children in the United States remains a major determinate in arranging the classroom experiences of millions of youngsters and, ultimately, in sealing their educational fate. Most practitioners assume that the tests are accurate measures of intelligence and equitable means for determining the school course for youngsters, and their limited scope is seldom questioned by those who determine the special education placement of certain children. The very use of the IQ test makes assumptions that the fault and the cause lie with the student, not the test nor the society in which the test was constructed. As others have noted (Poplin, 1987; Tomlinson, 1988) and as Kincehloe notes again in his introduction to this text, the conclusions of the test are widely accepted and rarely questioned: those who score lower than others are less "smart," less capable, and less worthy while those who score higher are brighter, more capable, and more worthy.

The IQ test, itself, is far from a pure and scientific tool. Since the early part of this century, American and Europeans have established the IQ test as a means of retaining their own superiority over other ethnic and racial groups. People who helped standardize the IQ tests in the early part of the century identified Mexican, Spanish, and African Americans as dull and deficient when measured by IQ tests (Tomlinson, 1988). The use of IQ tests as a means of segregating people according to race, gender, and social class is still evident today. Ultimately, the low scores on IQ test serve to lessen the responsibility of the schools, teachers, and others in striving to uncover the covert and complex elements of intelligence in human beings and debunking the prejudices inherent in our society.

Nearly 100 years after its inception, the IQ test continues to serve as the single most effective means for segregating individuals who do not fall within the scrupulous norms required in a capitalist society. Unfortunately, the mainstream has not considered the possibility that such a segregation removes the likelihood of erudition through contact with those considered "disabled." McDermott and Varenne (1995) in their study of culture and disability state that we are arrogant to believe that we know better than others and we are even more foolish to not appreciate what others know in their own terms. Marietta provides a fine example of this with her explanation of mental retardation. The assumption that there is only one right way to be in a society encourages the misconceptions that those who are divergent are missing something, that it's their fault, and that they deserve to be shut out. In fact, when we explore the patterns that have determined "disability" in our society, we see that it is not the individual who is really "disabled," but it is the culture that disables and is disabled. Consider the example of the people living on Martha's Vineyard. For over 200 years prior to this century, the people of Martha's Vineyard off the coast of Cape Cod, Massachusetts, had a high rate of genetically inherited deafness. One person out of 155 was deaf. Yet the people of Martha's Vineyard hammered out a society in which being deaf was as equal and everyday as being a hearing person. Everyone used sign language regardless of their hearing ability. Most people were unable to distinguish hearing people from non-hearing people except in regard to reading. The deaf were the more adept readers due to a local ordinance that provided mandatory reading instruction for all hearing-impaired individuals. Everyone on Martha's Vineyard had a job to do, and whether one did his job faster than another was not important. These people hammered out a manner of living with each other that benefited their society. Everyone learned that being able to hear or being deaf did not necessarily alter the quality of one's life. In fact, the deaf played an equal and non-distinguishable role in the culture. Their mastery of trades, rate of marriages, and economic successes were unmarked from others on the island. Deafness was something the community worked with in a process which empowered all of the citizens (Linton, Mello and O'Neill, 1994; McDermott and Varenne, 1995).

While in our contemporary society being deaf is highly consequential, the people of Martha's Vineyard decided collectively that a physical difference did not matter and would not contribute to any one person's isolation from the rest of the group. The deaf were considered different but not disabled on Martha's Vineyard. Nor was deafness an individually based characteristic; as McDermott and Varenne point out, "one can not be disabled alone" (1995, p. 33), for it is the culture which disables some and enables others. Disability, then, becomes a reflection of the rigidity and institutionalization of particular norms within a given culture. Thus, we see that it is the culture which is disabled and not the individual.

Unfortunately for the people of Martha's Vineyard, the growth of tourism and the ensuing influence of a much larger culture infiltrated the island and the deaf became disabled. They were pitied, shunned, and feared by the growing number of tourists who visited the island. Some attempted to explain the phenomenon through religious tracts or tried to remedy their plight and, finally, offered theories to extinguish the genetic occurrence. Eventually, the deaf people of Martha's Vineyard disappeared. Thus, we see that the development of criterion against which all members are measured is wholly dependent upon the nature of the culture itself, not the individuals who are so labeled, categorized, and segregated from the rest.

Through this brief historic odyssey, it becomes apparent that our society views disability as "other"—an un-normal, undesirable deficit. Our present-day notion of disability has evolved as a socially constructed phenomena created to ensure the omnipotent power of certain religious groups, socio-economic classes, white ethnicity, the dogma of early capitalism, and the subsequent influence of twentieth-century consumerism. We can also begin to understand the relationship between the power structures which have relegated economic blame onto schools and the role that contemporary education plays in accepting and reinforcing these socially constructed notions as a means of gaining power and fortifying existing power structures. When the existing patterns within special educational practice are examined, we may observe that our cultural assumptions regarding disability are indicative of the flaws within our society rather than those of any individual. In the analysis of cultural pedagogy in this postmodern era, it is imperative that we locate disabilities from within the power plays of dominant groups and as a result of historically construction notions of disability.

Post-formal thinking has provided a tool in the deconstruction and re-conceptualization of the nature of intelligence and the meaning of disability. Through a view that situates modern educational practices within a paradigm that has remained uncontested even through its failures and insignificance for a post-modern society, this paper has explored the patterns that have shaped our consciousness and influenced the pedagogy of modern education. This effort to move beyond simple cause-effect processes and the philosophies that favor pathology as explanation for difference and regard scientific management as mainstays of good practice must continue despite the obstacles that continually thwart the practice of equitable education for all.

References

Boswell, J. (1988). *The kindness of strangers: The abandonment of children in western Europe rom late antiquity to the Renaissance.* New York: Pantheon Books.

Burrell, G. and Morgan, G. (1979). *Sociological paradigms and organizational analysis.* London: Heinemann.

Corbett, J. (1996). *Bad-mouthing: The language of special needs.* London: The Falmer Press.

Foucault, M. (1980). *Power/ knowledge: Selected interviews and other writings, 1972-1977.* (Ed. and Trans. C. Gordon). New York: Pantheon.

Foucault, M. (1984). *The Foucault reader* (Ed. P. Rabinow). New York: Pantheon.

Greene, M. (1986). In search of a critical pedagogy. *Harvard Educational Review, 56*(4), 427–441.

Heshusius, L. (1989). The Newtonian mechanistic paradigm, special education, and contours of alternatives: An overview. *Journal of Learning Disabilities, 22*(7), 403–415.

Kincheloe, J.L. and Steinberg, S.R. (1993). A tentative description of post-formal thinking: The critical confrontation with cognitive theory. *Harvard Educational Review, 63*(3), 296–320.

Kirp, D. L. (1974) . Student classification, public policy and the courts. In T. Hehir, and T. Latus (Eds.), *Special education at the century's end: Evolution of theory and practice since 1970.* Cambridge, MA: Harvard Educational Review.

Kliebard, H. M. (1995). *The struggle for the American curriculum: 1893-1958.* New York: Routledge.

Lather, P. (1992). Critical frames in educational research: Feminist and post-structural perspectives. *Theory into Practice, 3*(2), 87–99.

Leistyna, P. Woodrum, A. and Sherblom, S. A. (1996). (Eds.). Introduction. In *Breaking free: The transformative power of critical pedagogy.* Cambridge, MA: Harvard Educational Review.

Linton, S., Mello, S., and O'Neill, J. (1994). *Disability studies project: Expanding the parameters of diversity: Disability studies in the Hunter College curriculum.* Hunter College, New York, NY.

McDermott, R. and Varenne, H. (1995). Culture as disability. *Anthropology and Education Quarterly, 26,* 324–348.

Poplin, M. S. (1987) . Self-imposed blindness: The scientific methods in education. *Remedial and Special Education, 8*(6), 31–37.

Safford, P. L. and Safford, E. J. (1996). *A history of childhood and disability.* New York: Teachers College Press.

Skrtic, T. (1995). (Ed.). *Disability and democracy: Reconstructing (special) education for postmodernity.* New York: Teachers College Press.

Spring, J. (1972). *Education and the rise of the corporate state.* Boston: Beacon Press.

Spring, J. (1990). *The American school: 1642-1990.* New York: Longman.

Tomlinson, S. (1982). *A sociology of special education.* London: Routledge and Kegan Paul.

Tomlinson, S. (1988). Why Johnny can't read: Critical theory and special education. *European Journal of Special Needs Education, 3*(1), 45–58.

Wishy, B. W. (1968). *The child and the republic: The dawn of modern American child nurture.* Philadelphia: University of Pennsylvania Press.

CHAPTER NINETEEN

Math Education
Target: Number[1]

Peter Appelbaum

1. The Incident

Devin takes five cubes and puts them on his mat. Josh tosses two into the "pot" in the middle and grabs a 10, thinks again, picks up one of his two cubes, and places the 10 in the middle of his mat, the cube on the right with some others. Caresse carefully counts three cubes, puts them on her mat, rearranges them to fit in a nice, neat row with five others already there, and counts how many she has all together: "1, 2, . . . , uh, 3, 4, 5, 6, . . . 7, 8." She continues counting the cubic portions of a 10 rod in the middle of her mat: "9, 10, 11, 12, 13, 14, 15, 16, 17, eighteen."

We're playing "Target Number Up and Down." In this game, before we start, each child picks a "target number" between 50 and 100. Rolling a conventional six-sided die, the child takes the number of base-ten blocks from the "pot" corresponding to the number rolled. Each child does this at the same time with his or her own die. When they get to their "target number," adding on with each die roll, they continue the game, from now on subtracting the number rolled from the cubes on their mat and putting them into the "pot" until they have no more left on their mat. The children are glad to play this game with me on the floor in the hall outside their classroom. Their teacher taught them how to play yesterday. They start right away as soon as I tell them what we're doing. "Oh, O.K., we played that yesterday," they say pleasantly, writing down target numbers on their mats, such as "89," "93," and "97." The atmosphere is one of gentle contentment as the play continues.

The teacher asked me to encourage the children to look for "short-cuts." For example, if they have 17 and roll a 4: instead of taking four cubes, then putting the four with the seven, counting out ten little unit cubes, and trading them for a 10 rod, students might realize that they could take a 10 to begin with, if they put six cubes into the pot (because three of the four new ones, together with the 7 on the mat, would make 10, leaving one more cube for a total of 21). So I observe the five children in the hall with me, ready to pounce on an appropriate moment for suggesting the idea of looking for shortcuts. I quickly notice Tyrone in this very situation: with two 10s and three 1s on his mat, he rolls a 6, which gives him 29. Then he rolls a 6 again. He takes six cubes from the pot, drops them on his mat, adds four from the pile already there, puts the ten cubes back in the pot, takes a new 10, and ends up with three 10s and five 1s, 35. I say, "Tyrone, Ms. Taggen suggested that we should look for shortcuts today. Like, just now, instead of taking the six new cubes, then making a 10 and trading, could you have thought ahead, and, instead of taking the 6 and trading for 10, could you think of taking the 10 and putting some cubes into the pot from your mat?" He instantly understands: "Sure," he says with a smile, "I could just take the 10 and put in 4 of the 9 I had here." How did you figure that out? "It's easy—I added 4 to the 6 I rolled to make the 10 when I traded." "Oh," I say. "See if you can plan that way for a shortcut as you keep going." He nods, rolls a 1, and takes one unit cube from the pot. It's amazing to me how compelling this activity is for the children. They all just keep on rolling, taking cubes, and trading, with no pause or break.

Josh, who had been listening to our conversation even as he kept on rolling, smiles, rolls a 3, puts 7 into the pot, and takes a 10. "Explain what you just did," I ask Josh. "I put in 7 and took a 10." "Why?" "Because I had 48 and 3 more makes 51, so I made the 1 and took a 10 for the 50." "How did you know to leave just one cube on your mat?" "To make fifty-*one*," he says, as if I am pretending to be stupid. Apparently, the cubes are not modeling the operation of addition for Josh; he is just making the cubes match the sum he gets when he adds the numbers in his head.

I glance at Devin. He has about thirty 1s on his mat, and a 10. "Devin, are you trading for 10s?" "Oh," he says, counting out 10 blocks and trading, counting out another 10 and trading, and so on. He has been pleasantly rolling the die, and taking the number rolled from the pot— no trading for 10s, just mindless collection of cubes. He has been perfectly happy to enjoy the activity this way.

Caresse continues to carefully count out a block for each dot on her die and slowly place the cubes in rows on her mat, next to a 10 rod. When the cubes match a 10 rod, she trades for a new ten for her collection on her mat, and continues counting individual cubes. She has four 10s on her mat, three in a cluster and one with seven cubes lined up against it. She rolls a 5. Caresse counts one at a time: 1, 2, 3; stops and trades for a 10; continues to count: 4 . . . 5 . . . I ask, "Caresse, instead of counting until you get ten little cubes here, could you think ahead and find a shortcut, so that you can just take a 10 and put some cubes back into the pot?" "What do you mean?" she asks, annoyed that I have interrupted her well-organized routine. I show her. "Look, this is what you just had before. . . . " Reproducing her mat, I put the die down with a 5 on top. "You rolled a 5. Now instead of counting out 5, and trading for a 10, could you tell me how many cubes will be here after you trade?" Lining up the cubes with 2 sticking out beyond her 10, she says, "two." "So," I suggest, "if you know that, can you save yourself energy and not take all the cubes first?" "I don't know," she falters. "Think about it as you keep playing." "O.K.," she says quickly, anxious to get back to her rolling and taking cubes.

It is hard to keep track of each student, even though I only have five in the group. I haven't said anything yet to Pag—What is she doing? "Pag, tell me what you're thinking about as you play." She has eight 10s and two 1s on her mat. She rolls a 1. She takes a cube, saying, "I rolled a 1 so I take a 1." She rolls a 1 again, saying, "I rolled a 1 again." Now she has 8 tens and 4 ones. She rolls a 6. "So I take 6," she says. She places the 6 cubes on her mat and rolls again. "Pag, could you trade now?" "Yes," she says, "there's 10 there but I like to wait until I have more to trade." "Oh." She rolls a 4. She counts out 6 from her mat, puts them in the pot, and takes a 10. "How did you do that?" "Well, I took 4, I mean, if I *took* 4, I would trade the 10 there already, so I put the 6 in plus the 4 I could take makes the 10." "Great, Pag, Ms. Taggen wanted me to ask you to look for that kind of shortcut today." She smiles and continues to roll.

The children are startlingly on task, it seems. They don't pause, but roll take, roll take, roll, take trade. Soon they are hitting their target numbers. They start subtracting what they roll from their mats. I suggest to the group that they keep looking for shortcuts when they roll.

Josh continues to "miss the point." He subtracts in his head, then makes the cubes match his result. The cubes are a waste of his time, I think. Tyrone continues to "get it completely." With each roll, he thinks about taking or putting cubes, thinks about trading, then figures out a shortcut. Devin continues to move the number of cubes he rolls, usually collecting so many cubes that they are falling off of his mat before he trades them in in bunches of tens. On the way down to zero from his target number, he sometimes puts the cubes into the pot from his mat, sometimes forgets and takes the number of cubes from the pot and puts them on his mat. He enjoys the task, even as he is not engaged in any way with the concepts that the blocks and the activity are intended to model. Pag, on the way down, gets confused about whether she should be taking cubes or putting them into the pot. She soon stops worrying and alternates. Brief queries to Devin and Pag cause them to be more careful on their next roll, but they quickly jump back into their established routines. Caresse, however, has understood what Ms. Taggen wants. She is slower than the others, counting out cubes ever so carefully each time she rolls; but by the end she is using a shortcut each time she can, and accurately.

Is this activity a "success"? It looks like math and sounds like math, and it is "hands-on", so it must be good, right? The searing realization that the activity is lacking in a link between the concepts of place-value and procedural forms of knowledge for at least three of the five children gnaws at me as I drive back to campus. I decide to tell this story of my morning in my N-8 Mathematics Methods course. The students have been espousing an uncritical love of manipulatives and hands-on activities for the last few weeks. Perhaps this will interest them. But I also want my students to note that such an activity helped me very rapidly get to know an enormous amount about the five students I worked with. As a performance assessment task it might have merit. Can they appreciate this?

2. The Lesson

An hour later I am relating my story to my class. I demonstrate Devin randomly collecting cubes with overhead base-ten blocks. I explain Pag sometimes subtracting from her mat, sometimes subtracting from the pot, usually but not always using a reasonable shortcut procedure. I mimic Josh, adding or subtracting in his head and then making the cubes match his calculation. "What do you think?" I ask. My students quickly suggest the activity does not link conceptual and procedural knowledge. They have been primed for this. They note a number of problems with the activity: Since each child is playing by her or him self, there is no interaction among them, no need to communicate ideas or explain their result or process. The activity itself is somewhat meaningless, with little purpose. The target number choice is random and does not matter—it is a false choice. Otherwise, there is no decision-making and no reason to care about accuracy. Indeed, the willingness of the children to continue the activity surprises my students. They want to know why the children did not invent their own game. In fact, they suggest this should be the activity: the *group* should design a better game. Short of this, my students offer attempts to turn the activity into one with some semblance of purpose.

Variations Offered

- Group students in pairs working toward a commonly agreed-upon target number. They take turns. The first person back to zero wins. Here students might care about each others' adding and subtracting.
- Class members predict the number of rolls it might take for a given target number. Each person tries it and the class records the data. For various targets, students are chided into trying to become more accurate in their predictions. Prediction strategies are discussed at length in between repeated data collection.
- Pairs work with a common target. Players take turns rolling the die. On each roll, they may choose to add or subtract the number to or from either their own mat or their competitor's. First person back to zero wins.
- Same as above except players may either take the number of new ones from the pot or give the other player the same number from their own mat. They then discuss how to make the game better.
- Players start so that one person has 100, the other has zero. They take turns rolling the die. On each roll they may add that number to their own or subtract that number from their partner's mat. The goal is to work cooperatively to get each person to 50, and then back to the original start-up situation. They play several times and try to use fewer rolls each time, trying to figure out a reasonable "par" for the game. Students are again asked to improve upon the game.

I am pleased. But I wonder: Will my students think this way when *they* are the teacher? Why don't more teachers think this way?

I ask my students what they know about the five children I talked about. Very little, they say, because the children did not have a chance to explain their reasoning for their actions. I share my own thoughts: that Josh basically doesn't need the cubes to model the operations; that Devin and Caresse have been "taught" that they can do this, and the lesson has provided a model for them, but that I wish they had been given an activity that allowed them to construct this idea on their own in the context of useful borrowing and trading; that Pag has the procedure down pat but needs more opportunities to explain the procedure in terms of the concepts; that Devin understands place-value but needs a meaningful activity that puts adding and subtracting with place-value in a context that has a purpose for him. We talk on a bit, but in the end my students reaffirm their naive worship of hands-on manipulative activities as more crucial than the construction of purposeful projects in the classroom. We talk about ideas that would encourage the students talking to each other, and listening to each others' ideas about place-value and operations. The need for relationships between number facts or their application to the problems of the "real world" does not yet enter this conversation, constructing in Joe Kincheloe's terms "cognitive illness." This makes me think.

3. One Month Later

I have been hired by a suburban school district to run a workshop on "Meaningful Mathematics with Manipulatives." My assignment is to offer teachers an advanced discussion on problems that arise with manipulatives and to suggest inexpensive home-made materials. After an introductory conversation in which the 20 in attendance mainly critique manipulatives as messy and taking too much time, I offer the Target Number Game as something to think about. I ask them to think about two things: (a) the quality of homemade material as a model of place-value (I have distributed around the room graph paper, cardboard, and plastic strips and squares, sticks and nubs); and (b) the potential of the game. They play the game. I ask them what they think. One person says it offers practice in adding and subtracting. Another says it is hands-on. A third says she doesn't like the graph paper strips because her students would eat them. I ask for concerns or criticisms of the activity. No one has any, until after a long pause one teacher suggests that, while this game might be "good" for more affluent districts, her "kids" need to first practice the basics before they can be applied to this sort of activity. I hand out a sheet with my students' concerns and their suggestions. The teachers complain, "If it isn't any good, why did you make us play it?" "Because I want you to think about how *you* might do the same thing with the activities suggested in *your* teachers' manual. They're not always as good as *your* ideas would be." They are bewildered.

4. Pomo Pugnaciousness

In the above constellation of stories, is there a hidden story about race and economic inequality? There must be since neither are raised. Is there another story about the role of mathematics in the school curriculum? There must be because this is not mentioned. Is there a story about power and knowledge? There must be since they were not mentioned. Of course we can critique the encounter, the reporting of the encounter, or my own participation and choices. We can offer alternative curricula which establish "place-value" and "addition of two-digit numbers with regrouping" within thematic units, project-based inquiries, or more efficient skill drill exercises. What strikes me, however, is the disjunction between my own abhorence of the repetitive rolling and adding, rolling and subtracting, and the students' contented embracement of this same experience. I have constructed a dichotomy, a dualism, which I find viscerally frightening, but which my methods students accept and adapt, and which the teachers in my workshop do not judge or notice as relevant to the decisions they make in their practice as teachers.

I see the mindless participation of the second-graders as an enactment of ironic pleasure. In his introduction to this text, Joe Kincheloe refers to Terkel's (1970) description of workers withdrawing emotionally from their labor, and students learning early in their school lives, "moving through the day without affect, staring straight ahead at nothing in particular," that school has no larger purpose. Kincheloe notes how quickly children learn that school has nothing to do with their passions—indeed, he writes, their emotional health is irrelevant. What activities like "Target Number" do is establish *motivation* as a problem of a scientistic pedagogy in search of technical and scripted solutions: how do we motivate children to attend to the regrouping and place-value? These activities turn each of the five children into isolated problems to diagnose, leading to prescriptions: keep Josh off of the base-ten fix; give Tyrone and Caresse an extra dose; retest Pag for the right level of dosage; and Devin, he needs special clinical attention. Kincheloe is on target when he raises the specter of modern positivists chopping up learning into chunks of data to be chewed in decontextualized fragments and stale morsels of chalkdust. More to the point, the dismembered mathematics these children are asked to consume feeds them as much a message of mathematics as politically neutral and aesthetically inert as it lays out a dish of pablum. Absent are attributes of intuition, imagination, surprise, anger, and curiosity. But the reconstruction of mathematics as including these and other attributes is not so clearly established. This is partly due to the role mathematics is often assigned in the common sense construction of formal, rational thought. The legacy makes it severely threatening to challenge such a view of mathematics as ironic or deceitful because, in challenging such pervasive presumptions, one risks the danger of being misunderstood as attacking the accuracy and coherence of someone's rationality rather than the notion of rationality itself.

Brian Rotman (1993) has helped us to see that the threat is even more severe. "No doubt," he writes, "the idealized imaginings of mathematics answer, as a familiar, unproblematic, innocuous part of everyday wishing and thinking, to the desire for order, regularity, repeatability, form, pattern, and harmony." (p. 156) Socially constructed as much as any other cultural artifact, mathematics appears "true" because our construction of "true" is imbricated in Rotman's list of the "everyday wishing and thinking" but also because a tautological definition of consistent and persistent truth and reliability dovetails with a mathematics built upon a tradition of picking those regular, repeatable, formed, patterned, harmonious concepts and procedures that have the properties of regularity, repeatability, form, pattern and harmony! "But," as Rotman writes, "poised behind such desires is an absolute desire, introduced into the meaning of number and so into the imaginings themselves . . . the desire is for no less than that the grandeur and imprimatur of eternity be stamped on the objects of mathematics and the truth one discovers. In this way one can identify with a transcendent being, can move, outside history in His [sic] dominion."

"The fantasy of a transcendental origin, an ultimate guarantor of truth unsituated in time, space, or history, for whom or out of whom the infinity of numbers is/was/will be always there, has proved difficult to resist," continues Rotman. (p. 157) Yet why are we led from a seemingly harmless "game" (although I would have to claim "Target Number" does not conform to a genuine definition of "game" in a mathematical or philosophical sense) to the claim that young children are being forced to live outside of time and history in a meaning-drained fantasy of "truth"? Only in a form of scientistic research that examines the incident under a microscope without its links and web-like connections to innumerable other like incidents and social contexts would allow us to marvel at such a wildly "extreme" claim. It is in the day-to-day repetition of similar "mathematical" encounters that the mathematics is reconstructed perpetually in a way that supports such an absurdist framework. Such practices work to reconstruct the active learner as an example of Piaget's assimilator, thinking outside of reality; the accommodator, immersed in relationships and exchanges among the thinker and a world of objects, is perceived as "slow" in developing appropriate skills and language facility.

Similarly, it is in the racially-charged community, in which African American parents tend to persist in condemning the public school curriculum as not academic enough, lacking in the teaching of basic skills, and deficient in discipline, that the scene takes place. The school is 50% white, 50% black. The white parents tend to persist in demanding ever-more thematic, integrated teaching and non-competitive, cooperative projects. The African American principal tends to persist in calling for more rigor as "preparation for middle school," where the children are combined with students from other schools in the district. The white parents like to say they have a black principal but work around her to accomplish their goals. In *this* context, Tyrone and Caresse *need* the pedagogy offered; the two African American children in the group of five "need" this pedagogy, much like recent "special" programs for "urban youth" (a code for race) provide the "self-esteem" and "culturally-based curricula" that "these" children "need" (Appelbaum, 1994). Josh, a white child, possibly does not "need" this pedagogy; he already adds and subtracts well and would "flourish" in a thematic unit project that challenged him to apply his skills in "meaningful ways." Devin, another white child, does not learn well in such formats; his teacher tells me he thrives on personal, individualized attention away from the group, and she expects him to be "up to grade level" by the end of the year if she continues to set aside time every week for a short conference session. Here we can see a racially coded unfoldment of pedagogy and assessment that might be compared with the conclusions of others that find a pattern of white children being treated as "apprentices" who already have knowledge and of African American children being treated as if they do not have knowledge and experience instruction as "teaching." (Gee, 1987; Ladson-Billings, 1995) There are also hints toward gender-influenced interpretations. Pag, a white girl, can adapt to what the teacher wants, but she and Caresse, who competently demonstrates comprehension of the task but also persists in her own (less "efficient"?) style of performance, are easily compared "unfavorably" with the "male standard" set by Josh and Tyrone. Thus are gendered interactions with mathematics set in motion well before this second grade incident.

5. Teaching as Story-Telling

Curriculum is more than a pipeline through which facts and skills get injected into students. As Keiran Egan has emphasized in many contexts, teaching is a form of story-telling *about* the content, and about what it means to know and learn (Egan, 1988, 1990, 1992). Yet his poignant example for mathematics illustrates well the sort of story that is often told about mathematics and its central purpose in the school curriculum. Egan encourages teachers to compare their curriculum organization with the story-telling qualities of fairy tales, one attribute of which is the dramatization of binary opposites. For mathematics, and for place-value in particular, Egan suggests the magical drama of power versus power-lessness. In a unit coordinated with Colonial American social studies, students are introduced to the theme: they hear about how pioneer families would help each other out when a crow needed to be removed from a barn. Crows are about as good as people at counting—they can recognize around five objects in a cluster. So, if a farmer went into a barn and waited for the crow, the crow would know that one person went in and would not fly in himself until that farmer went out. Again, if two, three, four or five farmers went in, and one or two walked out, in an attempt to fool the crow, the crow would *still know* that a couple of farmers were waiting with shotguns to shoot him dead. Now, if a bunch of farmers help each other out, and a group of seven or eight go into the barn, one farmer can hide out while the rest go back out. The crow will lose count and fly in to find his nest. BLAM: the hiding farmer no longer has to worry about the crow eating his seed stock. Extensions of this story can move children into the study of different animals and their relative ability to count. The story would be consistent with the drama: whales and dolphins, who can count up to 12, can outsmart people and save themselves in various ways; counting is placed in the life cycle in terms of the power or lack of it that the counting ability enables the animals have. Back to arithmetic: The myth of the origin of troops in the military is conveyed and acted out by the children. A general calls his advisors and says, we need a better system for keeping track of our soldiers, or we will never beat our enemy. One advisor after the next fails to come up with a scheme, until one genius suggests having each soldier drop a stone into a vase as they walk past the general: each time a vase is filled with ten stones, that group of soldiers is clustered into a team of ten men; ten vases are grouped into ten tens of men, and so on. The general then is able to plan the movement of his troops with such precision and creativity that the battles are won with great finesse. Thus is the notion of counting and place-value intimately linked with the normalization of counting as a tool of power and the ability to take another living being's life. Even the *Calculus*, often the keystone of school mathematics, is implicated through its etymological origin in the meaning of its name—the word is Greek for the stone or pebble used for counting. Taking the story a step further, Davis and Hersh (1981) string along Archimedes, scribes and astrologers, and the mathematicians of Napoleon, continuing on to the development of operations research techniques during World War II, the marriage of mathematics and physics in the atomic bomb projects, Norbert Weiner's controversial work in prediction and feedback that led to his later work against the "nonhuman use of human beings," the origins of the computer industry in the intensified cold war space race, and the futurist notion that while World War I was the chemist's war, and World War II was the physicist's war, World War III will be the mathematician's war.

Christine Keitel (1989) has written another story of mathematics as power, in terms of its role as a "technology" or tool that people use to accomplish newly possible tasks. Ledger systems of accounting, for example, made it possible for a whole culture of mercantilism and a merchant class to emerge in medieval Europe. As Keitel notes, however, this form of accounting and the use of columns for adding and subtracting numbers of and costs of objects also structured a form of culture that previously did not exist, to which people adapted in the slowly emerging assumptions of trade systems within capitalism. More specifically, Cline-Cohen (1982) writes a history of mathematics education as one of "calculation," pointing out that calculating the population to be governed and the idea of a calculating population (assisting the running of government and the emerging capitalist system) were intimately linked. Students in schools today are smoothly enculturated to this notion of being calculated and studied as objects of pedagogy and administration, and are similarly "prepared" to both calculate and be calculated. Valerie Walkerdine (1988, 1990) continues the story one step beyond by recording and analyzing the ways in which bourgeois democracy was to be upheld, not by a coercive pedagogy but by a "natural" pedagogy of love, in which reason would unfold. "Reason was to become the goal of a technology designed to provide reasoners who could govern, and those who might, at least, be hoped to be reasonable, not pushed to rebellion by repressive and coercive pedagogy." (Walkerdine, 1990, unnumbered)

In Egan's storytelling, the teacher constructs a resolution of the story: mathematics should be learned and practiced for the power it yields. You, too, can count better than stupid animals and uneducated people, so you too can get the jobs such skills promise. Of course, the story might also be resolved in other ways—a less optimistic moral that focuses not on the power promised but the objectification of people through numbers: a libertarian fear of big government; a distrust for the numbers claimed by military and government statistics; a distaste for the anonymity and subsequent loss of community fostered by contemporary studies of "average" people and the loss of attention to particular individuals (Greene, 1973). We might study how the school has turned each of us into objects of study, through calculations of various projective data about our "ability" or "personality," twisting each of us into a particular projective future. We might further examine the role of numbers in mystifying the public rather than communicating information: "termination units" in discussion of new weapons in Pentagon budgets, hard-to-understand units of radiation leakage that spring forth in local debates about the location of a new toxic waste dump or faltering power plant, the manipulation of testing data to satisfy local taxpayers that the schools are accomplishing their stated goals; data used in arguments about "raced ability" (Bachman, 1996; Kincheloe et al., 1996).

In the construction of our curriculum, we should note a common practice of using relatively "small" numbers because, as some psychologists would tell us, children need to learn about numbers that they can construct concretely. Big numbers are hard to see and feel and thus inappropriate for young children. The concept of place-value is introduced within this larger curricular context, in which big numbers are for the powerful big people, little numbers for the constructed powerless little people. The ageism within the curriculum is implicit but important. Walkerdine is relevant in this discussion as well (Walkderdine, 1989; Walkderdine and Lucy, 1989). In studies of girls and mathematics, working-class girls were found to have intimate understandings of large numbers and abstract mathematical reasoning in their home life; middle-class girls' lives were distant from such interactions with mathematics. School mathematics based on presumptions of middle-class lives did not meet the needs of either female population. But the key point here was that we should not presume a certain universal model of development that psychologists could abstract from studies of children; in fact, such universal models are often flawed in terms of class, race, and other categories by which children might be grouped and clustered.

Place-value might not even be a concept to be taught when various family and life experiences are taken into account; like abstract concepts of good/bad, fair/unfair, tasty, fun, etc., place-value might indeed be a concept that many children bring with them to school along with comprehension of large numbers.

By "teaching" place-value, however, we tell a variety of stories about the world and the idea of numbers in that world. For most of us, numbers are a natural truth that we can see and use to understand reality. They are basic skills essential for successful life experiences and jobs. Rotman's recent work on a non-Euclidean arithmetic articulates how hard it really is to imagine that numbers are as socially constructed and context-specific as Euclidean geometry. The idea that there might be a more generalized notion of number and quantification for which linear series of counting is locally "reasonable" but totally absurd for other contexts is almost impossible to fathom. Indeed ethnomathematics has argued for years that "Western" mathematics is not as universal as we wish and has told alternative stories of worlds incommensurable with this so-called universal truth of arithmetic (Pinxten et al., 1983, 1987; Fasheh 1989, 1990). By subjecting children to particular "models" of the concept of place-value without first trying to understand what models they bring with them, we are denying even a range of cultural variants *within* this narrow cultural construct of "Western" mathematics (Lave, 1991; Carraher, 1989; Mellin-Olsen, 1987; Ladson-Billings, 1995). Instead of "teaching mathematics" we are teaching that in school one must understand what the adult tells you to do; a new layer of obfuscation is sometimes added to neutral or negative affects, occasionally positive enrichment, on top of what might be brought tacitly with the child to school.

An understanding of the "popular culture of mathematics" that is indeed brought with the child to school might actually prove useful to both the teacher and the children; at times, however, we might find that popular culture resources for mathematics meaning might buttress regressive notions of mathematics as a disempowering form of alienation, yet for this information we should still be grateful (Appelbaum, 1995). In this respect, the role and nature of dice games in and out of school provides an interesting link to the Target Number activity. Because many children's games use dice, it is tempting to think that the use of dice in *this* context will speak to the problem of motivation as constructed by contemporary educational practice. Because dice are used in casinos for various gambling games, we might want to argue that school is teaching an interest in such games at the same time as preparing children for these adult activities. Because role-playing adventure games use dice yet are marginal in their social acceptance and acknowledgment, student use of fantasy and role-playing adventure games for pleasure might be something to which teachers might want to attend. The particular construction of parallel play in the context of dice games might have interesting ramifications for students' placement of this activity within a perspective on games and competition. For example, the expectation that the interaction of the probability of dice rolling and the learning of something about place-value, might be met with students imagining a way in which place-value has something to do with chance and probability! Yet in all of the above, we must still be aware of the presumption within all dice games, gambling activities, and associated use of dice, that numbers and a linear series of infinite counting numbers constitute a truth constructed by a legacy of acceptance within a culture of military strategy, accounting systems, calculation as a governing practice, and other associated notions of "the way things are." When we "teach" place-value, we are teaching this story about number and counting, and associated truths about these stories as stories of "reality."

Meanwhile, we should also understand that when we teach in this way, we are supporting the perpetuation of a certain notion of what teaching is, should be, and can be. If courses in methods of teaching mathematics critique such activities and then place students in practicum classrooms where the "real" teachers condemn such critique and even are skeptical about the efficacy of the activity discussed in this article, then what we are teaching our future teachers is a lesson in avoiding acceptance of new ideas about teaching and learning. Preservice teachers experience conflict exposing them simultaneously to a range of strategies and examples of teachers not using these strategies to negotiate a terrain of crisis—i.e., the structure of teacher preparation necessitates that teachers learn to disparage "professors' ideas" and embrace a disempowering strategy of non-engagement with curriculum in favor of a technical "neutral" psychologicization of practice. Played out as hostile non-engagement with professional development that reduces contributions to their professional practice to "what works" (Howley and Spatig, 1996), such a pedagogy is an apprenticeship in and mastery of the avoidance of post-formal thinking (Kincheloe, 1993). Teachers "must" learn how to see facts without seeing these facts in any social, cultural or political context. They "must" understand student behavior according to prescribed theories and facts rather than through the filters of a range and variety of metaphors. They "must" learn to think of mathematics as a collection of neutral truths disconnected from particular contexts or purposes. Place-value is then known and prepared as a collection of disassociated techniques and facts removed from meaning, purpose, flexible critique, etc. "Shortcuts" for exchanging cubes are then able to be held as a goal of instruction, within a prepackaged curriculum on place-value devoid of social, cultural, or political purpose, indeed, far removed from any immediate purpose other than to exchange cubes for 10s.

6. New Stories

It is important, however, to recognize that the failure of "Target Number," if indeed it fails in any way, is not due to its relationship to games in any sense. Games can be educational in the best sense of the word. What seems to be key is that participants have to make decisions and live with the consequences of their decisions (Goodman, 1995). When people criticize games as educational environments, they are usually worried that the practice *in a theoretical environment* that is part of the game is not going to help people make theoretical decisions in a "practical" environment. Fred Goodman writes that the issue really comes down to the quality of the metaphors produced by the game as opposed to the validity of the model behind something that intends to "simulate" real-life practical experience. The strength of an educational activity that has something to do with place-value, then, would have to respond to Goodman's theory that the activity not be planned in accordance with how it helps a child practice "in theory" rather than "in reality" (due, in the construction of educational actions, to the nature of school as removing children *from* reality in favor of them practicing in theory . . .), but in terms of how well it helps a child practice theorizing. It is here that possible conflicts arise out of dissonant notions of the purpose of schooling, parallel to the need for prospective teachers to learn an avoidance of theorizing about learning and schooling in support of a "what works" philosophy of practical application: We ask just what it is that the students are doing when they are playing "Target Number Up and Down." Are they practicing something in a theoretical fashion? Are they practicing theorizing about numbers? Are they practicing something that is in fact a practical skill? (Goodman, p. 189)

Indeed they might be doing any of those things. But the overwhelming sense I got by being there with them was that they were, in the best sense of the words, "passing time." For many people, passing time harmlessly, especially if it has some sort of social sanction to it, seems like a perfectly "reasonable" and attractive thing to do. If decision making can be minimized, then consequences can be avoided (or at least responsibility for negative consequences). There is a sense in which playing with dice is playing with the "theory" of probability, and that seems to be comforting to many. In this sense, the children who are not theorizing at the level of imagining short-cuts are, nevertheless, practicing theory. At the same time, they are not, as *I* might be, focusing on getting the "job done," but rather on keeping the time passing, on making time go by in an endless rhythm that *avoids* negative consequences. This is what Fred Goodman has elsewhere called "practicing the theory of existence." That this dovetails rather nicely with passing time in mindless routinized jobs is not all that surprising and supports traditional correspondence theories of social reproduction in overt ways (Bowles and Gintis, 1976). The cultural interpretation of such practice might be that students do not "understand" place-value, but "get used to it." Perhaps this is what is meant in some circles by "mental habits," in others by "mathematical enculturation" (Bishop, 1988).

"Target Number" raises for me a whole new set of questions about "assessment," including how to form a relationship with children versus the need to carry out surveillance. The common reduction of learning to "accommodation" leads to a need to observe and analyze a student's progress in focuing on factual and procedural knowledge. "Critical equilibration," as Kincheloe describes it, would allow a teacher recognize the value of long-term accommodation experiences; the relationship between teacher and student becomes a key feature in the stimulation of searching and research-based student activities that do more than enable a student to describe prescribed concepts in terms of facts and procedures. David Hawkins writing in the 1970's of children developing "mental habits" through a "vast and essential redundancy of . . . practices" reminds me of the ways that "schemata" ("ways of going at a subject matter, strategies") need to be rehearsed, enjoyed, and reflected upon, first using the words and performing things "unreflectively," then slowly over time rehearsing them in activities that point to new aspects of comprehension and reflection (Hawkins, 1980). At first we might decide that this supports the "getting used to it" approach to pedagogy. However, he writes of a "second level" which comes "when the *schemata* or strategies the learner has acquired are transformed, by the learner, into vehicles of a new kind of meaning and interest." (p. 102).

Hawkins raises yet another point about "abstraction" and "schemata." He asks us to think about an issue that often gets confounded with this notion of shifting from concrete particulars to the second level of attending to the schemata by which we deal with the particulars itself: this other issue comes up in the uses of "abstract" to denote formal rationalized schemes of operation in a manner that is "detached . . . [or] . . . looked at apart from all but a careful delimited context." (p. 108) Manipulative materials designed to model concepts for school mathematics are carefully designed to avoid the first kind of abstraction initially, so that students may deal with concrete particulars of a sort that are not mere symbols but concrete examples of the concepts. The materials are highly stylized so that the intended concept is "pretty unsubtly there, if you already know the secret, while all the other inevitable properties of the concrete object are de-emphasized by standardization." "So it turns out," writes Hawkins, "that this material is abstract in both my senses, heavy with conceptual intent *and* cut off from nature's variety and interconnection." Are manipulatives inherently "bad" then? Rather, the pedagogical issue is parallel to a discussion of manipulatives; this pedagogy needs to be unraveled from the manipulatives and discussed on its own terms.

What Hawkins *likes* about manipulatives is that children are playful and "'eolithic' and can find more unintended uses for the concrete materials than they can find for printed tokens, crayons and work books." By this he means that children can easily invent purposes for the materials and use them in ways that then produce "meaning." Think of stories like the one in Parker's (1993) *Mathematical Power*, or Kohl's (1976/86) *On Teaching*: at the beginning of the year students are left to themselves to explore the materials that they will be using, and develop amazing, creative projects. These stories articulate the "eolithic-ness" Hawkins is noting.

> I use the word *eolithic* in memory of our remoter ancestors who had to start life with objects not intended for *any* purpose, but who after picking up the stone, for example, invented uses for it. The first invention was not the object—but the purpose. (p. 108)

"By now," we see his answer.

> When we speak of "abstract thinking" do we mean thinking that is in an insoluble capsule, unrelated to the wealth of experience that can make it come alive? That can be done with Cuisenaire rods and

> geoboards as surely with paper and pencil—or almost as surely. There
> is a time for such thinking, of course, but it should be very late—as
> late as a child's readiness to grasp the partial isomorphisms between
> the concrete reality and formalized systems of signs. Or do we mean
> the cultivation of intuition, of analogy, of the mind's power to order
> and schematize? No time could be too early, I think, for that. (p. 109)

I suppose we need to ask that silly question, 'why do we have schools,
and what should people do in them?' When we observe a typical classroom, we see a bunch of activities designed to train students as assimi-
lators. When we critique what we observe, we suggest a focus on critical equilibration that emphasizes accommodation. When we reflect on
people learning in out-of-school encounters, we begin to note, with Joe
Kincheloe, how people do not make formalistic generalizations but
reshape cognitive structures to account for unique aspects of what is
perceived in particulat contexts. The person learning *in context* thinks in
terms of what she or he *might* encounter in similar situations, what strategies *might* work in such contexts. What might it look like to strive for
such situated knowledge in the public school classroom? Deborah
Loewenberg Ball (1992) raised the same issue in response to a third grade
class' interaction with mathematics with and without manipulatives:

> The context in which any vehicle—concrete or pictorial—is used is as
> important as the material itself. By context, I mean the ways in which
> students work with the material, toward what purposes, with what
> kinds of talk and interaction (p. 18)

"Target Number" encapsulates thinking in a way that requires
surveillance of children's thoughts, as opposed to an activity that would
elicit interest in children's intuitions and analogies. This is a subtle but
important distinction. Assessment in the second case would be an
attempt to consider how one might provide a rich environment for the
child, a way that they might benefit from an idea that the adult has, a
search for materials that enable the adult and the children together to
think *about* something. In the first case it is reduced to tallying skill
attainment. In the second case, assessment would tell the teacher
whether or not he or she had provided an activity for which a *purpose*
could be invented.

Because educational practice is often constructed by our perspective on it to conform to a problem of motivation and surveillance, we
can sometimes misread an event in ways that do not call attention to the

student's effort and related identification of interest and self. Stephen Brown's (1981) work helped me understand this by writing of mathematical problem solving and posing in terms of Dewey's (1913) *Interest and Effort in Education*. Dewey addressed the question about whether teachers should be responsible for getting children "interested" in the (possibly dull?) things they do in school. Another perspective might be that students would be assumed to provide the "effort," regardless or even perhaps because of the "uninterestingness" of the activities in school. Typical for Dewey, it turns out in the end that both of these contrasting points of view create a common basic fallacy—they assume an externality from the self of the object, idea, or end to be mastered. Interest, for Dewey, becomes the "principle of recognized identity of the fact to be learned or the action proposed with the growing self." Assessment would focus not on task-specific objectives with such a concern about "interest," but on "the predominating direction of [the student's] attention . . . feelings . . . [and disposition] while . . . engaged in the task."

> If the task appeals to him [sic] merely as a task, it is as certain psychologically as is the law of action and reaction physically, that the child is simply engaged in acquiring the habit of divided attention; that he is getting the ability to direct eye and ear, lips and mouth to what is present before him so as to impress those things upon his memory, while at the same time he is setting his thoughts free to work upon matters of real importance to him." (Dewey pp. 8,9; Brown, p. 33)

But let's return to preservice education. Here my dilemma is that preservice teachers typically have not experienced manipulative materials as students or teachers and need to be *introduced* to manipulatives before they can think about any critique of them. In fact, my students are suspicious of newfangled techniques and act as if I need to convince them of the efficacy of the manipulatives. Questioning their validity, function, purpose, etc. is often reduced to a "first level" of winning them over to a constructivist model of teaching based on manipulatives and "hands-on" learning despite the fact that labeling these teaching strategies as "newfangled" misrepresents them and obscures their long history or successes. Absent entirely from this discussion are alternative pedagogies of arithmetic and number facts that connect them with social practice, cultural politics, and other branches of mathematics. The fact that reform-oriented literature and methods texts often characterize constructivist approaches that incorporate manipulatives and problem solving approaches as something new actually works against them for students who wish to get a job and keep it ("fit in"), rather than develop a visionary philosophy and transform the nature of education. How can we redesign certification programs so that students are able to contextualize, critique, and challenge current practice and still move beyond this initial critique to a point of subtle distinctions?

Aspiring teachers need experiences rich in critical equilibration followed by periods of anticipatory accommodation. One possibility that meets directly their own expectations for "practical experience" in school classrooms, but simultaneously challenges their presumptions about the purposes of a school, is to *begin* with the student teaching internship. This would prolong the period of critical equilibration. An extension of this certification program that continues to reverse the typical, commonsense professional paradigm would provide a series of less-intensive field-work placements with more careful analysis of these practicum encounters as "case studies" that form the basis for anticipatory accommodation. Final prearation for teaching would culminate in an extensive period away from field work devoted to "applied hermeneutics"—use of meaning-making abilities to anticipate what may happen next and what should be done to prepare for such eventualities. At first glance this organization could be misinterpreted as a reproduction of Piaget's move toward increased assimilation away from real-world immersion; the important features would be careful relationships among preservice teachers and their college-teachers who promote conversations toward the aim of critical equilibration and anticipatory accommodation.

Let's think now about inservice education. A school district recently responded to my request that inservice work be planned to avoid the entertainment of "what works" philosophy in favor of long-term consideration of issues that grow out of the teachers' own experiences with manipulatives in their classrooms. Such work with teachers is consistent with reform efforts to provide support for the adoption of pedagogical practices promoted by the National Council of Teachers of Mathematics *Standards* documents (NCTM, 1989,1991, 1995). In these projects, professors team up with individual teachers for extended periods of time, so that they can discuss the day-to-day nuances and dilemmas that arise in changing one's pedagogical strategies (Ohanian, 1992; Parker, 1993; Romagnano, 1994; Davis, 1996). In the context of this psychologicization of professional development, the professor becomes a clinical therapist as the teacher attempts to renegotiate meaning in everyday practice. For researchers who have spent time trying to figure out how to get teachers to think about and talk about their teaching, the mathematics pedagogy becomes a topic for *both* to take as an object of study. The asymmetry of power created by a pairing of professor and practitioner perpetuates theory-practice dualisms even as the research works to undermine them.

Like my preservice students, teachers I work with (despite acquaintance with manipulatives through workshops and conferences) seem to need a multilayered learning experience parallel to what Hawkins refers to in regard to abstraction. An initial activity with manipulatives or problem solving is met with dismay and dismissal. Subsequent discussion and open-ended activities elicit complaints about a "lack of clear objectives," a "need for more structure," and a challenge to make the workshop or course more relevant to the realities of teaching in "today's schools." If a school has accepted me on faith (or, as I establish a "reputation," on personal knowledge of what I have to offer), the second or third meeting soon turns into a "conversion experience." "I see the light," one participant recently remarked, as he took center stage and began retelling his attempts to think about his classroom in terms of some of the metaphors we had discussed in our previous meeting. In a graduate course, particular problems are often secretly "tried out" in students' classrooms; by the third week, some "converts" speak positively about their experiments with these "new ideas." Like Hawkins, I find there needs to be a "playing around" period with these ideas about teaching and learning, a period of critical equilibration. With adults who come with expectations of a consumer society—that they should get a clear bang for their buck, and early on too—this presents a challenge for the facilitator's serenity and confidence in the approach, because the playing around appears to the participants as a disrespectful lack of attention to their needs and desires. The complication comes with the determination of whether to push past the plateau of playing around with the materials of teaching and learning toward that other layer of abstraction Hawkins refers to, the one where the materials and strategies of teaching and learning can be theorized about and critiqued in a way that produces "meaning," a period that establishes anticipatory accommodation as a legitimate educational encounter. In my graduate courses, we view videotapes of our teaching. In these snapshots of classroom life, there are examples of creative teaching as well as clear evidence of malaise. We point to specific details as examples of how the teachers are already meeting NCTM *Standards* (1989, 1990, 1991, 1992, 1995). I find that some graduate students warm to the indirect "praise": it helps them see that they have skills they can build on even as they still squirm with dissatisfaction. Others become alienated and wonder why we are "wasting time" with these tapes that cause so much anxiety and embarrassment. There is a point in the middle of the semester when people want to critique others' teaching but do not believe they should. This is the critical moment in the course. Subsequent self-videotaping can elicit the same need for critique as the videos brought in by classmates and viewed in class; it is the second and third round of tapes that allows for a post-formal perspective on one's own teaching. Students become desperate for more courses to help them alleviate the tension. In these future courses, we begin to critique the "new" methods; instead of trying them out and dismissing them, we can like them and then challenge them to meet our new "standards" that have to do with social and cultural issues, political ramifications, and new-found crises of self-confidence in our teaching. Have I built a new cult of ME instead of the "transcendental truth" of pedagogy? What I work towards is the formation of a community and a network of professional contacts. The community diffuses this prophet-disciple danger when it is successful.

7. New Projects
I have tried in this analysis to demonstrate the ways that certain research questions and theoretical ground work are understood only through a kind of shifting back and forth between micro and macro perspectives on social and epistemological terrains. It is within the cracks and crannies between and threads of interaction among classroom incidents, teacher education, and professional development that my own work as a mathematics educator can be interpreted as telling its own story; in this story, mathematics, research pronouncements, and pedagogy all become characters subject to interpretations of subjectivity and action, social structure, and cultural change. What I think we "need to do" is ask for careful explications of the ways that a discussion of the epistemology of number, the presentation of pedagogical options in a preservice program, and the processes of lesson planning by practicing teachers inform each other. I also believe we "need" to ask when and how we might be able to inject at any articulation of these characters in the story new forms of linkage that will have effects that we can witness as transformational. With others (Goodman 1995; Joseph and Burnaford, 1994; Brown, 1981) I can suggest the usefulness of metaphors and discussion of metaphors as having this kind of impact. Like Foucault (1980) I have

had small successes as an "intellectual terrorist" by placing metaphors in locations in ways that cause the explosion of conceptual bridges. In the rebuilding of the bridges is a brief moment of hope that the new bridge can be different, that the construction will open up the possibility of an invention of *purpose*. The effect is one of new threads woven in new ways that emphasize "new interactions." Brown would call the purpose "problem generation." The trick is to do this in a way that wins the hearts and minds of those around you, in the style of the French Resistance, rather than to present yourself as the harbinger of chaos and destruction. Extending the metaphor of the French Resistance, must we then, those of us who work in education, resort to the image of restoring a former golden past, and can this be successfully played out? Can we think of recapturing the authority and means to determine who we are? We turn to Sartre, de Beauvior, and their theoretical progeny as we recognize along with Brown that the matters of education pertinent to mathematics educators are much broader than those of understanding mathematics.

We are in this sense searching for ways to *generate questions* rather than researching to provide answers, and it is in this sense that I can begin to interpret for myself and, I hope, for the reader as well what this essay is "all about." Because we are discussing at least three sites of learning and knowing and because we are looking for implications of the articulation, I can benefit from an adaptation of thoughts on the pedagogy of mathematics as a metaphor for the learning and teaching of "education" as a discipline. As I have learned much from Stephen Brown on the art of problem posing for the learning of mathematics, I can apply his thoughts here as well and say that the learning and teaching of *this* research has as its goal the generation of questions to ponder rather than solutions to teaching/learning problems. The kinds of questions we ask and the problems we generate as mathematics educators are to a great extent the ways we are known to others. Efficacious dialogue in the setting of this essay, as in the teacher-student dialogue of a classroom, requires a sorting out of what each participant believes ("regarding the nature of mathematics, the nature of his or her own mind, and the personal significance of shared experiences," writes Brown). As Hawkins, Ball, and Brown agree, the "answer" is not some sort of "open math environment" unless it, like any number of other environmental options, honors dialogue as a genuine interchange which the teacher as well as the student can hope to increase his or her awareness of self and the generation of problems or purpose. What I read them as calling for is nothing other than a revolution in what mathematics education is all about. The pie-in-the-sky quality of such a statement does not detract from the seriousness of its intent or need. Our "target number" for ourselves must become a vision of new "non-Euclidean" mathematics education. Locally, it might look like mathematics education as we know it. Various practices would resemble those we have grown up with and understand in "Euclidean terms." But our comprehension of the purpose and practice of these techniques and metaphors would have undergone so profound a reconstruction that their presence could never have the same meaning for us again.

Endnote
1.   I want to thank Mildred Dougherty and Rochelle Kaplan for their responses to early drafts of this chapter.

References
Appelbaum, P. (August,1994). Is the self-esteem engine losing steam? Mathematics education, the self, and the politics of race. Biennial Meeting of the International Network of Philosophers of Education. Leuven, Belgium.

Appelbaum, P. (1995). *Popular culture, educational discourse, and mathematics*. Albany, NY: SUNY.

Bachman, K. (1996). Education for all students: A case study. *Educational Transitions*, 1 (1): 16–19.

Ball, D. (1992). Magical hopes: Manipulatives and the reform of math education. *American Educator*, Summer, 16(2): 14–18, 46–47.

Bishop, A. (1988). *Mathematical enculturation: A cultural perspective on mathematics education*. Boston: Kluwer Academic Press.

Bowles, S. and Gintis, H. (1976). *Schooling in capitalist America: Educational reform and the contradictions of economic life*. New York: Basic Books.

Brown, S. (1981). Ye shall be known by your generations. *For the Learning of Mathematics*, 1(3): 27–36.

Carraher, T. (1989). Material embodiments of mathematical models in everyday life. In Christine Keitel (Ed.), *Mathematics, education, society*. Paris: UNESCO Document Series No. 35.

Cline-Cohen, P. (1982). *A calculating people: The spread of numeracy in early America*. Berkeley, CA: University of California Press.

Davis, B. (1996). *Teaching mathematics: Toward a sound alternative*. New York: Garland.

Davis, P. and Hersh, R. (1981). *The mathematical experience*. Boston: Houghton Mifflin.

Dewey, J. (1913/1975). *Interest and effort in education*. Carbondale, IL: Southern Illinois University Press.

Egan, K. (1988). *Teaching as storytelling: An alternative approach to teaching and curriculum in the elementary school*. Chicago: University of Chicago Press.

Egan, K. (1990). *Romantic understanding: The development of rationality and imagination, ages 8–15*. New York: Routledge.

Egan, K. (1992). *Imagination in teaching and learning: The middle school years*. Chicago: University of Chicago Press.

Fasheh, M. (1989). Mathematics in a social context: Math within education as praxis versus within education as hegemony. In Christine Keitel (Ed.), *Mathematics, education, society*. Paris: UNESCO Document Series No. 35.

Fasheh, M. (1990). Community education: To reclaim and transform what has been made invisible. *Harvard Educational Review* 60(1): 19–35.

Foucault, M. (1980). *Power/knowledge: Selected interviews and other writings*. Brighton, England: Harvester Press.

Gee, J. (1987). What is literacy? *Teaching and Learning*, 2(1): 3–11.

Goodman, F. (1995). Practice in theory. *Simulation and Gaming*, Silver Anniversary Issue, Part 3 (June): 178–190.

Greene, M. (1973). *Teacher as stranger: Educational philosophy for the modern age*. Belmont, CA: Wadsworth.

Hawkins, D. (1974). *The informed vision: Essays on learning and human nature*. New York: Schocken Books.

Howley, A. and Spatig, L. (1996). The popular culture of teaching. Paper presented at the annual meeting of the American Educational Studies Association, Montreal, Quebec, November 6-10, 1996.

Joseph, P. B. and Burnaford, G. (1994). *Images of schoolteachers in twentieth-century America*. NY: St. Martin's Press.

Keitel, C. (1989). Mathematics education and technology. *For the Learning of Mathematics*, 9(1): 103–120.

Kincheloe, J. (1993). *Toward a critical politics of teacher thinking: Mapping the postmodern*. Westport, CT: Bergin and Garvey.

Kincheloe, J., Steinberg, S., and Gresson, A. (Eds.) (1996). *Measured lies: The Bell Curve examined*. New York: St. Martin's Press.

Kohl, H. (1976/86). *On teaching*. New York: Schocken Books.

Ladson-Billings, G. (1995). Making mathematics meaningful in multicultural contexts. In W. Secada, E. Fennema, and L. B. Adajian (Eds.), *New directions for equity in mathematics education*. Reston, VA: National Council of Teachers of Mathematics/Cambridge University Press.

Lave, J. (1991). *Situated learning: Legitimate peripheral participation*. New York: Cambridge University Press.

Mellin-Olsen, S. (1987). *The politics of mathematics education*. Dordrecht, Holland: D. Reidel.

National Council of Teachers of Mathematics (1989). *Curriculum and evaluation standards*. Reston, VA: NCTM.

National Council of Teachers of Mathematics (1991). *Professional standards for teaching mathematics*. Reston, VA: NCTM.

National Council of Teachers of Mathematics (1995). *Assessment standards for school mathematics*. Reston, VA: NCTM.

Ohanian, S. (1992). *Garbage pizza, patchwork quilts, and math magic: Stories about teachers who love to teach and children who love to learn*. New York: W.H. Freeman.

Parker, R. (1993) *Mathematical power: Lessons from a classroom*. Portsmouth, NH: Heinemann.

Pinxten, R. Van Dooren, I., and Harvey, F. (1983). *Anthropology of space*. Philadelphia: Universtiy of Pennsylvania Press.

Pinxten, R., Van Dooren, I., and Soberon, E. (1987) *Towards a Navajo geometry*. Ghent, Belgium: K.K.I.

Romagnano, L. (1994). *Wrestling with change: The dilemmas of teaching real mathematics*. Portsmouth, NH: Heinemann. ·

Rotman, B. (1993). *Ad infinitum: The Ghost in Turing's machine: Taking the god out of mathematics and putting the body back in*. Stanford, CA: Stanford Universtiy Press.

Terkel, S. (1970). *Hard times: An oral history of the Great Depression*. New York: Pantheon Books.

Walkerdine, V. (1988). *The mastery of reason: Cognitive development and the production of meaning*. New York: Routledge.

Walkderdine, V. (1989). *Counting girls out*. London: Virago.

Walkderdine, V., and Lucy, H. (1989). *Democracy in the kitchen: Regulating mothers and socializing daughters*. London: Virago.

Walkerdine, V. (1990). Subjectivity, discourse and practice in mathematics education. In R. Noss, A. Brown et al. (Eds), *Political dimensions of mathematics education: Action and critique*. London: Dept. of Mathematics, Statistics and Computing, Institute of Education, Universtiy of London.

CHAPTER TWENTY

Science Education
Post-formal Thinking and Science Education: How and Why Do We Understand Concepts and Solve Problems?

David B. Pushkin

Introduction

When asked to write a chapter on the relationship between post-formal thinking and science learning, I must admit that I was at a loss. In science learning, we discuss lower-order thinking, higher-order thinking, and even critical thinking. Contemporary science education research (SER), particularly physics education research (PER), is very dominated by Piagetian theory. Naturally, the peak of Piagetian development is the formal operations stage; reaching this stage is considered quite good in science learning standards.

However, what about beyond? More importantly, what exactly are we looking beyond in the first place? At the formal operations stage, learners are said to be capable of complex tasks that involve logic and deduction. What exactly are those tasks, and how complex can they be? If we consider that formal operations are more abstract than concrete operations, from a science perspective, one might surmise that this could be in the form of word problems as opposed to arithmetic exercises. That being the case, suppose we look at two examples of what high school physical science students might encounter on a quiz or test:

1. How many miles will you travel in 5 hours, maintaining a constant driving speed of 50 miles/hour?
2. A truck, traveling at a constant speed of 30 miles/hour passes a car at rest. At the moment the truck passes the car, the car accelerates

from rest at a rate of 5 miles/hour/hour. When will the car overtake the truck, and how far will the car have traveled?

It is clear that the second example is more complex than the first, and it is also clear that the second example requires a more detailed application of the laws of motion than the first. However, what has this second example taught us? Essentially, all this second example has taught us is that a learner who may be at the formal operations stage is capable of solving multi-step word problems involving a limited scope of algorithms (i.e., equations, or physical laws). This is what we refer to in SER as a higher-order thinking skill; a one-step calculation is considered a lower-order thinking skill. While a learner at the formal operations stage may be a higher-order thinker, and solving the second example is not completely free of challenge, this is hardly an illustration of the deep and critical thinking an adult needs to encounter as a scientifically literate member of society. Thinking should be more than brain teasers and other forms of mental gymnastics.

Why is this so? According to Lewis and Smith (1993), lower-order skills are learned while higher-order skills are reasoned. Although such an assertion gives credence to the parallels with concrete and formal operations, the magnitude of these parallels is amplified by Kincheloe and Steinberg (1993) stating: "Formal thinking à la Piaget implies and acceptance of a Cartesian-Newtonian mechanistic worldview that is caught in a cause-effect, hypothetico-deductive system of reasoning" (p. 297). Looking back to the second example, we develop a new sense of its ambiguous purpose. Although this example may serve the purpose of giving students practice manipulating equations for motion, the example is devoid of any true context and meaning. It represents calisthenics with tools, yet nothing will be crafted. Formal operations, sadly, is the stage at which one has mastered obedience; in science, this is the stage at which one knows the rules and the recipes. It is unfortunate to report, but most introductory physics textbooks offer examples similar to the two provided; higher-order thinking is a "pie-in-the-sky" goal in such courses.

An ongoing debate in the PER community involves the question: Does conceptual understanding preclude problem solving, or does problem solving imply conceptual understanding? This paradox will not be easily be solved, since there is considerable disagreement on what conceptual understanding and problem solving mean. To illustrate the degree to which modernistic thinking has gripped many in the PER establishment, some members of the community consider the discussion pointless until an absolute functional definition of those terms is presented.

In general physics, student learning is often measured by the ability to solve quantitative problems, especially for large lecture courses (McMillan and Swadener, 1991). Although this is not the only aspect of problem solving, a problem will be defined as the kind of task that one usually finds at the ends of the chapters in a textbook (Maloney, 1994). Maloney (1994) identifies three major areas of research on physics problem solving:

1. How individuals solve problems
2. Pedagogical methods for improving students' problem-solving abilities
3. Types of problems, questions of transfer, and what students learn from solving problems. (p. 327)

Forinash (1992) contends "too many students leave the standard two-semester physics course without an appreciation of the broad spectrum of problems currently being addressed by working physicists" (p. 11). A possible reason for this contention is that many end-of-chapter problems are presented as theoretical exercises, such as the two earlier examples, often without any integration of concepts or practical application.

Therefore, it is important to recognize that in the general physics course, "problem solving" must be accompanied by the development of "physical thinking" in the students, and the tests should include questions that allow to measure the degree of "physical comprehension" of the students (Alonso, 1992, p. 778).

Both Forinash (1992) and Alonso (1992) reinforce McMillan and Swadener (1991), who state: "A numerical solution to a problem in any situation is useless without some conceptual and interpretive knowledge of what that answer means" (p. 669). Physics is more than simply arriving at a numerical result; an understanding of the significance of that result is of equal importance.

> What are the limits of human ways of knowing? Where might we go from here? Such questions have both research and pedagogical implications—as do our emancipatory system of meaning and our notion of critical constructivism. Drawing upon our systems of meaning, we cannot help but anticipate ways of knowing and levels of cognition which move beyond Piagetian formalism. Adults do not reach a final cognitive equilibrium beyond which no new levels of thought can

emerge; there have to be modes of thinking which transcend the formal operational ability to formulate abstract conclusions, understand cause-effect relationships, and employ the traditional scientific method to explain reality. We know too much to define formality as the zenith of human cognitive ability. (Kincheloe, 1991, p. 44)

Alonso (1992) offers two intriguing terms, "physical thinking" and "physical comprehension." What do they generally mean? In a critical sense, they essentially mean the same thing, a qualitative understanding of the problem. In order for physics students to successfully solve a problem, they need to have a general sense of the phenomena being presented, the concepts or laws being illustrated, and the methods of problem solving. In short, students need to have the gist of what the problem entails; this is no different from the first clue of a riddle.

However, the essence of problem solving begins, continues, and ends with heuristics. One needs to be thinking throughout a problem: *What's going on? How did things look at the start? What happened then? What happened after that? What will the end result be?* In addition to asking the *how* and *what* questions, one always needs to ask *why*? Science is a wonderfully broad context, with evolving theories, irrefutable laws, and flexible methodologies. It is because of this broad context that problem solvers need to look beyond the regurgitation of facts and mimicking of algorithms. As Rosenshine, Meister, and Chapman (1996) state:

> A cognitive strategy is a heuristic. That is, a cognitive strategy is not a direct procedure or an algorithm to be followed precisely but rather a guide that serves to support learners as they develop internal procedures that enable them to perform higher-level operations. (p. 182)

If learners are to become critical thinkers, we as educators must understand what the foundation of critical thinking in science is, and how we can provide learners with meaningful experiences to develop critical thinking skills.

Cognitive Aspects

There are many studies examining students and classifying them by their problem-solving abilities. Successful problem solving generally requires four types of schema-specific knowledge (Maloney, 1994): (1) declarative knowledge, (2) procedural knowledge, (3) situational knowledge (deJong and Ferguson-Hessler, 1986), and (4) strategic knowledge

(Schoenfeld, 1978). Studies have shown problem solvers tend to be more procedural and situational in their orientation when successful, and more declarative-oriented when not (Chi et al., 1989; Ferguson-Hessler and deJong, 1990). Successful problem solvers are more sensitive to what they do not clearly understand than others. As a result, they tend to be more reflective, more critical, more meta-analytic, and more application-oriented (Alexander and Judy, 1988; Garner and Alexander, 1989; Wandersee, 1988; Wandersee, Mintzes, and Novak, 1994).

Briefly examining each type of knowledge, one can see the direct links between declarative knowledge and concrete operations, as well as procedural knowledge and formal operations. Declarative knowledge is quite fact-oriented and the basic "building block" of science learning. Although a mastery of declarative knowledge is hardly a predictor for successful problem solving (to reconsider the earlier argument on conceptual understanding), the odds are high that a successful problem solver has a strong command of declarative knowledge.

Procedural knowledge, on the other hand, is very algorithmic in science learning. Solving word problems, manipulating algebraic expressions, and calculating results are all manifestations of this type of knowledge. Because word problems in physics could provide learners opportunities for multi-step methods and combined algorithms, it is not too surprising to see considerable emphasis on formal operations in an introductory course. Piaget, after all, according to Driscoll (1994), considered propositional logic (i.e., hierarchy of facts) the "hallmark" of formal operations. Formal operational reasoners are also considered to have the ability to imagine possibilities above and beyond current reality (Driscoll, 1994). However, as stated earlier by Kincheloe (1991), this latter characteristic is not necessarily the case.

Why is this so? Consider the case of a student trying to rationalize the difference between a block sliding up an inclined plane versus the block sliding down the incline. Granted, each case involves Newton's second law of motion (i.e., $\sum F = ma$), and most of the forces are identical in each case. However, not all of the forces are identical in each case; the context has changed due to the direction of motion. As a consequence, the forces interact with each other differently, and the net result will change.

Unfortunately, this particular student did not see any distinction between the two cases; she considered the changes in force directions to essentially negate, and thus calculated the same acceleration for each case (Pushkin, 1996a). Her reasoning was *if I'm pushing the block up the incline, I'm using the same amount of force as what caused the block to slide down.* This is what I refer to as a *pseudoconcept* (Pushkin, 1996b). This student has taken a concept out of context; it is neither absolutely correct nor incorrect.

I allowed this student to hypothetically wheel me down an access ramp in a wheelchair, then allowed her to push me back up the ramp, but only half-way. At this point, I asked her to let go of the wheelchair; she became very nervous, and said "Oh I can't! You'd roll back down and crash into a tree!" When I asked her why, she started to realize that her effort to push me up the ramp was not simply an effort against surface friction but an effort against friction *and gravity*. What she finally started to realize was that she was working against two forces, not one, as she had assumed earlier. Yes, she was using the correct protocol for solving the problem; however, she was not taking the context of the problem into consideration.

This same student also encountered difficulty with forces at angles. In most introductory physics books, a force is commonly defined as a push or a pull. However, does this imply that a push and a pull are the same thing? When one pushes or pulls at angles, this is certainly not the case. For example, if one pulls up on the handle of a piece of luggage to drag it along the floor, it seems lighter in weight. Why? Because when one pulls at an angle, one is pulling *forward and up*. By pulling up, one is taking away from the gravitational pull on the luggage, thus making it seem to weigh less than it really does.

However, when one pushes at an angle, they are pushing *forward and down*. Although the object is still moving forward as the pulled object was, by pushing down on the object, one is adding to the gravitation pull on it; the object now seems heavier. I asked this student to drag a chair across the carpeted area outside my office; then I asked her to push the chair back. In each case, she tried to keep her arms at the same angle relative to the chair and apply the same amount of arm strength. What did she observe? Pushing the chair was more difficult. Why? She encountered more friction on the carpet? Why? Because she was pushing down on the chair, making it seem as if she were pushing both the chair and the floor. The laws of physics were still the same; only the situation changed.

What this learner developed was situated cognition. She had a basic grasp of the declarative and procedural aspects of force problems; her lack of situational and strategic knowledge is what contributed to her difficulties. It is not enough for students to know how to substitute numbers into $\sum F = ma$; students need to see how this law is applied to a variety of examples. Science is a very creative field; critical thinkers are creative learners. A formal operational reasoner does not have the opportunity to be creative, because s/he has learned to master and replicate a process over and over again; how could one imagine beyond reality if reality is inertial?

The critical thinker does have this ability. The critical thinker is able to look at every problem as if it were a novel idea. *What does it look like? What does it remind me of? How are they similar and different?* The critical thinker experiences a rapid spread of activation within his/her information processing network (i.e., schema or conceptual framework). The critical thinker sees the problem very holistically, identifying the fundamental laws of physics that govern the phenomena s/he observes. The critical thinker then searches his/her conceptual hierarchy to develop a specific context for the problem, a context unique to all other problems. With the establishment of this unique context, the critical thinker can develop a problem solving-strategy for that specific situation and *that specific situation only.*

How different is this from preparing specific sauces for specific types of fish? How different is this from the mannerisms one uses around Aunt Bernice as opposed to Grandma Sylvia? All learners have the ability to be critical thinkers. All learners have the ability for situated cognition. All learners have the ability to think on a post-formal level. If all learners have this ability in everyday aspects of life, why are they said to not have it in academic aspects of life? Why are they said not to have it in science courses, especially the physical sciences?

Emancipating the Curriculum

Commissioner of Education for Massachusetts, David Sneeden, led the fight for the efficiency perspective as he advocated the establishment of separate vocational schools to train students in specific job skills. To create an efficient society, Sneeden argued that schools must produce workers who valued tradition and upheld virtues such as obedience, punctuality, and deference to authority. Opposing Sneeden was John Dewey who contended that the vocational education Sneeden proposed viewed student needs as subservient to economic needs defined as the interests of employers. Sneeden's efficiency, Dewey argued, meant adapting students to the existing industrial order. Dewey felt that workers should be masters of their own industrial fate and worker education should develop intelligence in such a

way that workers could envision more democratic work arrangements. On a variety of levels Dewey recognized over eighty years ago
what we have called the fragmentation of modernism. He also recognized the ways that schools contribute to this fragmentation.
(Kincheloe, 1995, pp. 10-11)

Noted political scientist Sheila Tobias often suggests that those successful in the sciences succeed on the basis of their OQ versus their IQ.
By OQ, Tobias refers to an "obedience quotient," a measure of how well
a student learns to follow the rules. To be a formal thinker, one needs to
learn how to master the rules; post-formal (critical) thinking requires
looking beyond the rules.

> A long-existing problem in our schools, particularly in science class-
> es, is the need for correctness. Piagetian conceptual change focuses
> on coming to consensus with the "accepted conception"; alternatives
> are misconceptions (Maloney, 1994). In modernist classrooms, we
> teach students that there is only one scientific method, only one way
> to write a lab report, only one way to formulate a hypothesis, and only
> one way to define scientific terms. If we think of the three stages of
> conceptual change: assimilation, accommodation, and equilibration,
> the message becomes loud and clear: here is the correct way to look
> at it, accept it, and understand that your way is wrong. If your inter-
> pretation is contrary to the book's, you are questioned, if not interro-
> gated. If your interpretation comes from a journal or author that is
> "not mainstream," you are scolded, if not sanctioned. If you are tak-
> ing time to contemplate things that others deem insignificant, then
> you are misguided. (Pushkin, 1995, p. 13)

A phenomenon I sense exists in many university science departments involves the prevalent philosophies of *perpetuation of the species*
and *survival of the fittest*. What do these Darwinist philosophies mean?
Many science departments—be they biology, chemistry, or physics—
appear to believe that the primary purpose for their existence is to produce
majors. University faculty are growing old; replacements will be needed someday. Where will those replacements come from? The majors we
teach! After all, who better to replace us than our academic offspring?
However, there lies the paradox. What will our academic offspring
be like? Quite similar to ourselves, if some had their way. *After all, we
worked hard for years to attain the rank, expertise, and success we
enjoy. We learned from our academic parents, and look how well we
turned out. If it's good enough for us, it's good enough for the next gen-*

eration. If we see things so clearly, why bother with reform? How obvious does it need to be before we realize how dissatisfied we are with our teaching and curricula? As educators, can we really live with ourselves by blaming it on today's students?

Unfortunately, there *are* science departments that subscribe to this first philosophy; they *are* the ideal image of a scientist, and teaching science is no different than being made in our Creator's image. Anything less would seem an affront to science and its hallowed tradition. Science is often looked upon as an apprenticed trade, where process and sequence are the dominant themes.

What of this *survival of the fittest* philosophy? The debate has endured for years as to whether secondary and higher education should be a pump or a filter. Should we be pumping well-rounded learners into a democratic society, or should we be filtering the weaklings from the desired pool of technicians and technocrats? Do introductory science courses (notoriously physics and organic chemistry in some universities) need to be "weed-out" courses? Do we reserve only the best science education for those most suited for a career in science, or do we educate the entire population (Babcock, 1996; Hobson, 1996a,b; Hoogstraten, 1996; Pushkin, 1996c)?

Again, the question screams out: *what is the primary purpose of a university science department*? The answer should be precisely what many middle and secondary schools have realized for years: *to educate all learners in a branch of knowledge for future life*. Nowhere in this statement do I mention education as an exclusionary process, nor do I mention what future life should hold for learners. At the very least, we hope all learners will have a future life of adulthood, responsibility, freedom, and fulfillment. In this day and age, that's a very nice goal to have for learners. But the cold reality remains that all learners deserve an education in science, albeit not to the same degree but enough to make intelligent decisions in the home, with personal health, on issues of policy, and for the well-being of society as a whole. All members of a democratic society deserve to be on a level playing field, where everyone has a common foundation of knowledge; science cannot afford to flame the fires of inequity between the *haves* and *have nots*. Having expertise in science is one thing; having a monopoly on knowledge is another.

However, even more critical for science departments is the issue of epistemology. If science departments do not come to terms with their views of teaching and learning, the species will be perpetuated, only the fittest will survive, inequity will continue, and reform will be a meaningless fad. Why do we teach? What do we teach? How do we teach it? To whom do we teach it to? Many skeptics of critical thinking might wonder if there is a shifted emphasis towards student-centered curricula at the expense of pedagogy. Not necessarily; curricula should always reflected the marriage between cognition and pedagogy. However, for those who consider cognition and pedagogy mutually exclusive, there needs to be an awakening to the concept of curricula that enhance cognition because of supportive pedagogy.

One of my most personal realizations as an educator is the fact that I am not particularly linear (sequential) in either my thinking or teaching. For a scientist, this is quite unusual, since we've been aware for over a decade that science and math people are very abstract and sequential learners; I tend to be more global and random, seeing science as a "big picture" comprised of several subcontexts. As a social constructivist, I am considered neither particularly organized nor efficient in my teaching. When I write lecture notes too far in advance for a class, I often think "gee, I can't believe I wrote such awful stuff" and then ad-lib in the lecture hall. When I write tests and exams, I often write them at the last possible moment, since I do not have a concrete sense of where the class will be content-wise by test time. When I teach the writing of chemical formulas in chapter 2 of an introductory chemistry course, I cannot help but discuss valence electrons and oxidation states of elements, typically chapter 6 material. When I teach electric fields in introductory physics, I cannot help but discuss atomic structure theory. Why am I like this?!

In a word, I want learning for my students to be *purposeful*. I do not want my students to learn writing chemical formulas for the sake of it. I do not want my students to learn about inclined planes as a mental exercise for applying trigonometry. I do not want my students to learn about Dalton's atomic theory as stale words that I paraphrased from their textbooks. And I do not want my students to learn science as if it were a routine void of soul and emotion. I want my students to see why science is a part of me, why it keeps me up at night, and why it makes me smile when I discuss it. I neither encourage my students to become scientists nor like science, but I do want them to sample my academic joy, gain insights as to why it's my joy, and decide for themselves whether and how they might share my joy. I want to give my students the freedom to choose how science might be part of their future; how can one choose without being offered choices?

Since the "truth" claims of science are tied to the methodological imperative, it insists that science must be held immune from the influences of social and historical situations. Science, therefore, is truth and can, for this reason, represent itself by means of its procedures, by which the objects of investigation and apprehended. Hence, the self-criticism of science is conducted within the boundaries of its own normative structures. Further, science insists that only those inducted, by means of training and credentials, into its community are qualified to undertake whatever renovations the scientific project requires. (Aronowitz, 1988, p. viii)

I want to give my students a purposeful learning experience so that they can derive personal value from what they learn. I want to give students like Julia, Keshia, and Monina the opportunity to think for themselves, something they never had in their high schools in Newark, Paterson, Passaic, Elizabeth, or Union City, New Jersey. I want to give older students like James, Mariana, Walter, and David the opportunity to grow comfortable with the quantitative aspects of science after a number of years removed from high school. I want to give students like Lisa, Rey, Barb, and Deb an opportunity to believe in themselves as potential people of science when they doubt whether they belong in the class. I want to give *all* of my students the opportunity to be challenged, to succeed or fail, and to learn something about themselves as thinkers. In essence, I want all of my students to strengthen their individual learning curves, what Vygotsky calls *zones of proximal development* (Driscoll, 1994; Pushkin, 1996d).

But if we desire to give students such opportunities, we must create a nurturing classroom culture, an environment cognitively and affectively conducive to learning. But if we are to create such cultures, we must come to terms with our epistemologies regarding teaching and learning. To adopt curricula and pedagogy that we do not believe in is like being in a loveless marriage; our internalizations are needed to encourage their internalizations.

Unfortunately, many educators of science have an epistemology stuck in tradition. They teach from the same textbooks every year. They teach from the same yellowed lecture notes every year. They write the same exams every year. They are more than stable and consistent; they are inert. To build on this point, please consider two stories:

1. A year ago, I decided after a number of years that I would teach the first semester of introductory physics, Newtonian mechanics, begin-

ning with the concept of energy, rather than the standard concept of kinematics. My reasons for this change were as follows:

1. My students were nontraditional science majors in an interdisciplinary curriculum.
2. Energy is a central concept to all sciences.
3. I had observed many students through the years using the work-energy theorem as the central concept in their equation webs, a study tool I helped them develop in my classes.

When I shared this idea with colleagues in the PER community, everyone was aghast. *How can you do that?! How do you expect them to understand physics?! What were you thinking?!* When I asked for reasons against such an approach, I received the following:

1. You have to begin with chapter 1; that's why textbooks are written this way.
2. You need to begin with kinematics; how will they understand Newton's laws without knowing what acceleration means first?
3. If you don't give them all those word problems at the beginning of the book, how do you expect to weed kids out of the course?!

I chose to ignore my colleagues and their linear logic; I proceeded to teach a course that evolved sideways. Granted, the students were uncomfortable with the approach, which also incorporated social constructivism (Pushkin, 1996d). They rebelled at first but eventually grew to grudgingly accept this unconventional experience. The students' reaction was no surprise; most college students are dualistic, linear thinkers (Kincheloe, 1995), helplessly dependent on their professors to lead them by the nose. However, it was surprising to hear the overwhelming negative reactions by the faculty who found social constructivism so foreign, if not evil, to their way of teaching. While it took roughly six months to educate the students on what their experience meant, it took almost twice as long to educate the faculty.

2. In my current environment, there is an ongoing debate as to the merits of recitations in the general chemistry course. One of our members has been floating the suggestion for some time, but it fails to go further with anyone. There are some genuine reasons for recitations not necessarily being an elixir for learning ills: how to not change course numbers or credit hours; how to justify faculty contact hours; how to

control class sizes with a given number of faculty; and how to efficiently utilize limited classroom space. Unfortunately, for each genuine reason, there appears to be a questionable reason: *Don't take away from our 3-hour lab class. I need that lab time to get to know my students outside of lecture. We do enough problem solving in lecture class. We'd have to be more accountable for assigned homework problems. This could cost extra money. The extra time probably won't make much difference. I like things the way they already are.*

While change for the sake of change is unwise, resistance to change for the sake of resistance is worse. Such resistance traps educators, students, schools, curricula, pedagogy, and learning. Educators need to be open to different ideas, perspectives, and policies. Openness need not be equated with blind acceptance; openness can be a sign of thinking and discourse on a higher cognitive plane. If we are willing to discuss what our views of teaching, learning, and curricula are, then we will be better able to understand what is (and is not) appropriate for our students as well as for the academic community at large.

> The strong historical connection between academic subjects and external examinations is only partly explained by "the need to teach these subjects in such a way and to such a standard as will ensure success in the School Certificate examination." The years after 1917 saw a range of significant development in the professionalisation of teachers. Increasingly, with the establishment of specialised subject training courses, secondary school teachers came to see themselves as part of a "subject community." The associated growth of subject associations both derived from and confirmed this trend. This increasing identification of secondary teachers with subject communities tended to separate them from each other, and as schools became larger, departmental forms of organization arose which reinforced the separation. (Goodson, 1993, p. 30)

It is unfortunate when science teachers at the introductory level lose sight of their purpose as educators. Too many middle and high school general science teachers think their purpose is to prepare kids for the biology course. Too many biology teachers think their purpose is to prepare kids for chemistry. Too many chemistry teachers think their purpose is to prepare kids for physics. Too many think their purpose is to prepare kids for college.

What of the introductory chemistry, physics, and biology professors at the college level? Too many think their purpose is to prepare undergraduates for graduate study or medical school. Few realize that many students would simply prefer to have a reasonably-paying job upon graduation.

Why is this "assembly line" mentality so prevalent among those who teach science in our schools? Is it necessary for middle schools, high schools, and colleges to dispense knowledge to learners as if they were adding components to an automobile? If science, and the learning of it, is relatively nonsequential, why must it be taught sequentially? Why must initial missteps become livelong academic curses for a learner?

Even worse is the notion that science has so many sacred cows, that curricula remain essentially constrained by traditional topics. All-too-often, we hear of physics professors who teach algebra-based and non-math-based physics to students as watered-down calculus-based physics. We hear of chemistry professors who teach general chemistry as "baby P-Chem." We hear of science professors who teach courses for nonscience majors no differently than for science majors; only the grading curve varies. People chose career paths for many individual reasons; their curricula should reflect that. Would one teach a plumber how to be a carpenter? Would one teach a nurse how to be pharmacist? Why teach a future historian how to be an engineer or geneticist?!

Does this mean I have less faith in the abilities of nonscience majors compared to aspiring scientists? Absolutely not; many who do not aspire careers in science actually have more ability than those who do (Pushkin, 1991; Tobias, 1992). However, I do need to take their interests into account. As one student recently shared with me "you are the first science professor I've actually wanted to learn from; you make chemistry seem useful for my career as a nutritionist." Any caring educator should be able to make such an impression on students. This is why educators need to be more conscious of Pedagogical Content Knowledge (PCK, Shulman, 1986); teaching should be something more than what we do to earn a paycheck.

Until those teaching science come to terms with their learning goals for all people, we will never truly see curricula or pedagogy that serve learners' best interests, regardless of ability, regardless of interests, regardless of major, and regardless of career aspirations.

Analysis

Being a novice learner in science is difficult enough; learning in a culture that promotes meaningless exercises makes science a very unpleasant experience. Why is it that many college faculty argue how supportive they are towards promoting critical thinking by students, yet teach 3 hours of "chalk and talk" each week, assign only end-of-chapter problems (versus conceptual questions), and give tests that are dominated by word problems?

Consider a student in my elements of chemistry course for food/nutrition majors. This young man apparently took AP Chemistry in high school and had a marginally satisfactory score on the standardized exam. The young man inquired if he could "place out of the course, because this is all review to me (we had just finished the first chapter in the course)." When he took his inquiry to the department chair, reservations were expressed, since his score would indicate that he did not necessarily understand everything from his prior class. Our advice was for him to stay in the course and strengthen his background for future chemistry courses.

When the class received its second test of the semester, this same young man said upon handing in his paper "I can't wait till you start giving calculation problems; I hate these conceptual questions." My response? *"Now you see why we wanted you to stay in this course!"* What this student (and many more perhaps) considered appropriate for a science course was what we disdainfully refer to as "plug-and-chug." To him and others, the physical sciences are supposed to teach you *how to put numbers in for letters*. Science is not a field of study; it is an endurance test of algorithms.

And yet, where does this image come from? When colleges of engineering pressure high school, college, and university science departments to emphasize problem solving in their introductory courses, introductory science courses emphasize multiple-choice testing, and introductory science courses require a successful score on a *math* placement test, it is not difficult for a young learner to develop such a mental image of academic science. When university science professors wonder "is there a contradiction between research and teaching?" (Saperstein, 1996, p. 16), one cannot help but ask *what took you so long to realize this?*!

Science departments teach students that science is a process; they do not necessarily understand what declarative and procedural knowledge mean, but they certainly understand how to use them. Science becomes a hegemonic tradition in academia, an infliction that transcends generations. To foster higher-order thinking, science departments twist students' arms to the point of submission; students become helplessly dependent on the authority of their department and profession.

Unfortunately, those who promote critical thinking also have the potential to twist arms of faculty and students alike. As much as critical thinking intends for students to develop self-sufficiency in preparation for a democratic society (Siegel, 1988), these same proponents of critical thinking also believe that it is important to initiate students into the "rational tradition" of their field. In other words, critical thinking is considered the ability to view "through the lens of specialty," learning to think like the expert. In the modernist view of education, there is no contradiction; the critical thinker is the apprentice who has mastered. This is *not* critical thinking. Where is the emancipation? Where is the contextualization? Where is the individuality?

As we struggle with the contrast between modernism (i.e., the paradigm of being led by others) and postmodernism (i.e., the paradigm of leading oneself), we must ask: *Why does the expert view things in this manner? Whom does the expert depend on for his/her view?* The likelihood is that the expert is quite emancipated, quite contextualized, and quite individual. Is it necessary to teach students how to be emancipated, contextualized individuals, or should we respect students for already being such? Do we teach students how not to fail, or do we give them educational opportunities to learn how some ideas fail while others succeed?

Post-formal (critical) thinking is supposed to be the ability to see beyond boundaries, ask difficult questions, and seek elusive answers. Post-formal thinking is an individual phenomenon; we all reach this stage at different rates. Post-formal thinking is a level of understanding based on context. Post-formal thinking is a viewpoint based on freedom and choice. To promote post-formal thinking is to provide a curriculum of opportunity. To promote post-formal thinking is to provide a curriculum of respectful expectations. To promote post-formal thinking is to use authentic assessment. To promote post-formal thinking is to share the value of content, pedagogy, and cognition.

From the science education perspective, to be a post-formal thinker is to be a life-long learner and educator; all of us are learners and educators regardless of which side of the classroom we occupy. We should want opportunities to explore ideas as well as share ideas. We should not look at science as a process, apprenticeship, or initiation; there is no "holy grail" in knowledge, as knowledge is constantly evolving. Science should be a fascinating context within the broader context of knowledge, a challenging context composed of concepts, applications, variations, and speculations. Science should be a perspective of the world, not greater or lesser than any other. Learning science should be purposeful; teaching science should reflect this. Science learning and teaching should reflect the same fascination scientists have asking questions and seeking answers, but the experience should reflect the same independence and creativity scientists enjoy, not the hegemonic control of modernist science.

Acknowledgments

I would like to thank all of my colleagues who have offered insights regarding critical thinking and science education, especially Pamela Delaney, Dennis Stachura, and Jose Figueroa, who have spent considerable time debating worthwhile issues with me here at MSU. As always, I thank my mentor and friend, Joe Kincheloe, for egging me on once more and encouraging me to expand my perspective as a science educator.

References

Alexander, P.A., and Judy, J. (1988). The interaction of domain-specific and strategic knowledge in academic performance. *Review of Educational Research, 58*, 375–404.

Alonso, M. (1992). Problem solving and conceptual understanding. *American Journal of Physics, 60*, 777–778.

Aronowitz, S. (1988). *Science as power*. Minneapolis, MN: University of Minnesota Press.

Babcock, G.T. (1996). More on education. *Chemical and Engineering News, 74(40)*, 7.

Chi, M.T.H., Bassok, M., Lewis, M.W., Reimann, P., and Glaser, R. (1989). Self-explanations: How students study and use examples in learning to solve problems. *Cognitive Science, 13*, 145–182.

Chi, M.T.H., Feltovich, P.J., and Glaser, R. (1981). Categorization and representation of physics: Problems by experts and novices. *Cognitive Science, 5*, 121–152.

deJong, T., and Ferguson-Hessler, M.G.M. (1986). Cognitive structures of good and poor novice problem solvers in physics. *Journal of Educational Psychology, 78*, 279–288.

Driscoll, M.P. (1994). *Psychology of learning for instruction*. Boston: Allyn and Bacon.

Ferguson-Hessler, M.G.M., and deJong, T. (1990). Studying physics texts: Differences in study processes between good and poor performers. *Cognition and Instruction, 7*, 41–54.

Forinash, K. (1992). What are we trying to do in our introductory course? *American Journal of Physics, 60*, 11–12.

Garner, R., and Alexander, P. (1989). Metacognition: Answered and unanswered questions. *Educational Psychologist, 24,* 143–158.

Goodson, I. (1993). *School subjects and curriculum change.* London: Falmer Press.

Hobson, A. (1996a). Incorporating scientific methodology into introductory science courses. *Journal of College Science Teaching, 25,* 313–317.

Hobson, A. (1996b). Teaching quantum theory in the introductory course. *Physics Teacher, 34,* 202–210.

Hoogstraten, C. (1996). Educating nonspecialists. *Chemical and Engineering News, 74*(33), 66.

Kincheloe, J.L. (1995). *Toil and trouble.* New York: Peter Lang.

Kincheloe, J.L. (1991). *Teachers as researchers: Qualitative inquiry as a path to empowerment.* London: Falmer Press.

Kincheloe, J.L., and Steinberg, S.R. (1993). A tentative description of post-formal thinking: The critical confrontation with cognitive theory. *Harvard Educational Review 63*(3), 296–320.

Lewis, A., and Smith, D. (1993). Defining higher order thinking. *Theory into Practice 32*(3), 131–137.

Maloney, D.P. (1994). Research on problem solving: Physics. In D.L. Gabel (Ed.), *Handbook of research on science teaching and learning* (pp. 327–354). New York: MacMillan.

McMillan, C., and Swadener, M. (1991). Novice use of qualitative versus quantitative problem solving in electrostatics. *Journal of Research in Science Teaching 28,* 661–670.

Pushkin, D.B. (1996a). New insights on novice learners: Phenomena unique to the introductory level. *Journal of Research in Science Teaching,* submitted for publication.

Pushkin, D.B. (1996b). A comment on the need to use scientific terminology appropriately in conception studies. *Journal of Research in Science Teaching, 33,* 223–224.

Pushkin, D.B. (1996c). More on education. *Chemical and Engineering News, 74*(40), 7.

Pushkin, D.B. (1996d). Where do ideas for students come from?: Applying constructivism and textbook problems to the laboratory experience. *Journal of College Science Teaching,* in press.

Pushkin, D.B. (1995). The Influence of a computer-interfaced calorimetry demonstration on general physics students' conceptual views of entropy and their metaphoric explanations of the second law of thermodymanics. Unpublished doctoral dissertation, Pennsylvania State University.

Pushkin, D.B. (1991). Does Fear of the "Nerd" Label Dissuade Young Females from Pursuing Science? *Journal of College Science Teaching, 21*, 71.

Rosenshine, B., Meister, C., and Chapman, S. (1996). Teaching students to generate questions: A review of the intervention studies. *Review of Educational Research, 66*, 181–221.

Saperstein, A.M. (1996). Research versus teaching? *Physics and Society, 25*(4), 15–16.

Schoenfeld, A.H. (1978). Can heuristics be taught? In J. Lochhead and J.J. Clement (Eds.), *Cognitive process instruction* (pp. 315–338). Philadelphia: Franklin Institute Press.

Siegel, H. (1988). *Educating reason.* New York: Routledge.

Shulman, L.S. (1986). Those who understand: Knowledge growth in teaching. *Educational Researcher, 15*, 4–14.

Tobias, S. (1992). *Revitalizing undergraduate science: Why some things work and most don't.* Tucson, AZ: Research Corporation.

Wandersee, J. H. (1988). The terminology problem in biology education: A reconnaissance. *American Biology Teacher, 50*(2).

Wandersee, J.H., Mintzes, J.J., and Novak, J.D. (1994). Research on alternative conceptions in science. In D.L. Gabel (Ed.), *Handbook of research on science teaching and learning* (pp. 177–210). New York: MacMillan.

About the Editors and Contributors

Patricia H. Hinchey is an Associate Professor of Education at Penn State University and author of *Finding Freedom in the Classroom: A Practical Introduction to Critical Theory*, Peter Lang, 1998.

Shirley R. Steinberg teaches at Adelphi University and is the general editor of *Taboo: The Journal of Culture and Education*.

Joe L. Kincheloe teaches Pennsylvania State University. He is the author of many books and articles.

Peter Applebaum is an Associate Professor of Mathematics Education at William Patterson University.

Kathleen Berry is a Professor of Education at University of New Brunswick, Fredricton.

Vicki K. Carter is completing her doctorate at Penn State University in Adult education.

Audrey M. Denith is an Assistant Professor of Education at University of Nevada, Las Vegas.

Raymond A. Horn, Jr. teaches in the Pennsylvania Public Schools.

Sharon L. Howell is completing her doctorate at Penn State University in Adult Education.

Aostre N. Johnson is a Professor of Education at St. Michael's College in Vermont.

Marianne Exum Lopez is the author of *When Discourses Collide* Peter Lang Publishing, 1999.

Marcia Middlesworth Magill teaches in the Pennsylvania Public Schools.

David P. Pierson is completing a doctorate in communications at Penn State University.

David B. Pushkin is an Assistant Professor of Education at Montclair State University.

Encarna Rodriguez is a Doctoral Student in Curriculum and Instruction at Penn State University.

Lourdes Diaz Soto is a Professor of Bilingual Education at Penn State University.

Leila Villaverde is a lecturer at Penn State University and adjunct professor at Adelphi University.

Danny Weil is an educational consultant and lawyer with the Critical Thinking Institute in Guadalupe, California.

Elise L. Youth teaches in the Philadelphia Public Schools.

Index